A Feather on the Breath of Ra

Garin Horner may fast become the pioneer of where photography meets mainstream alchemy. He offers a rare glimpse into the shadowy world of a modern alchemist where most serious alchemists shield their journey from the public eye. I am looking forward to adding this book to the Alchemy Guild's archives as the reader should add it to their own library.

— *Vincent Martin, Chief Executive Officer and*
  President of the International Alchemy Guild

[This book is] an extraordinary spiritual journey into alchemical practices and their connections to the process of how we dream, imagine, invent, and create. Garin Horner shares his firsthand exploration and experiences while learning the teachings and knowledge of modern-day alchemist George Kingswood. Horner explores the alchemist's discoveries, while 'connecting the dots' of the little-known and seldom-shared contemporary alchemical practices, and their connections to the magical beginnings of the recording of light in the mid-1800s. The reader is guided from the origin of the Egyptian sun god Ra up to 21st century photography, all seen through the perspective of a photographer's lens. This is important and exciting research for imagemakers!

— *Rebecca Zeiss, educator and experimental - antiquarian*
  photographer/artist

This book consists of 10 scruples biography, 8 ounces Hermetic wisdom, 5 grains historical exposé, 13 drams spiritual insight, and 1 pound Photography; dissolved, circulated and coagulated into a Stone of Philosophical Excellence! Horner gracefully weaves together multiple literary styles all while creating a very engaging and entertaining read that took me on a Mental, Spiritual, and Artistic journey that I was not anticipating. The Photo-Hermetic Tradition of the Kingswoods and the Hermetic Order of the Silver Sun is absolutely fascinating, and the author has done an exquisite job of eloquently recording, relaying, and remitting the value of this unique tradition. The author not only researched the topic incredibly well, but it becomes clear that he also ascertained the essence of Spiritual Alchemy through the time he spent with George Kingswood and the subsequent authoring of this book. To the best of my knowledge, there is truly nothing else like this work in the scope of Alchemical and Hermetic literature, either of the Modern Day or of the Historical Past. It was an absolute pleasure to read, and it deserves a place in the library of every modern day Alchemist.

– *Phoenix Aurelius is a practitioner, instructor, and researcher of Practical Alchemy and Medical Spagyria. As the founder and Director of the Phoenix Aurelius Research Academy, he explores the philosophies and practices of early Spagyric and Alchemical Medicine while seeking to standardize the education, production, and dispensation of Spagyric Medicine in the 21st century*

Avant-garde photographer Garin Horner has discovered an innovative path to spiritual transformation in his penetrating study of the work of the fourth-generation modern alchemist George Kingswood. The alchemists' motto of Ora et Labora ('Pray and Work') comes alive in Horner's evocative photos of Kingswood's altar and lab, and it feels as if we are experiencing the evolving soul of a real alchemist. This is an important work—not only for the history of alchemy but also for its discovery of a photographic technique that captures the depths of human experience. Highly recommended!

– *Dennis William Hauck is an author and lecturer on alchemy, spirituality, and consciousness studies. He has written over 25 books, including "The Monad Manifesto: Merging Science and Spirituality," "The Emerald Tablet: Alchemy for Personal Transformation," "The Complete Idiot's Guide to Alchemy," and "Sorcerer's Stone: Beginner's Guide to Alchemy"*

Most analog photographers are enthralled with the idea of alchemy and would like to think of themselves as alchemists. Yet, without any how-to resources on the workings of alchemy, it has been impossible…until now! With beautiful historical … examples, Garin Horner opens readers' eyes and helps them understand the deeper, hidden meaning of alchemy. It also helps them discover why they make the photographs they do. Horner's powerful book digs deep to uncover obscure and important information on the history, processes, and techniques used by George Kingswood, a modern photo-alchemist. For what makes a photographer or an alchemist? It's the practice of an art form by someone who is a visual storyteller, ever questioning, experimental, patient, and seeking the highest level of success. If you aren't a photo-alchemist yet, you may soon choose to be one after reading this book!

– Jill Enfield is a photographer, educator, and author of Jill Enfield's Guide to Photographic Alternative Processes: Popular Historical and Contemporary Techniques (Published by Focal Press)

Like a latent image conjured from the dark chamber of a camera into the light, Garin Horner's illuminating journey through the history of photography by way of its hidden alchemical underpinnings makes a significant contribution to the firmament of photographic inquiry.

– Stephen Berkman, Author of Predicting the Past, Zohar Studios: The Lost Years

Is magic real? Do alchemists exist? If you want to know, read this groundbreaking book! It shines a light on an unexplored branch of photography within the realms of alchemy, magic, and mysticism. Practitioner of the 'Great Work', George Kingswood confides in Horner, putting aside his own oath of secrecy to reveal spiritual wisdom and enlightening connections between alchemy and photography. Horner and Kingswood awaken the reader's primal instinct to believe in magic! This work expands our understanding of what photography can be. It helps us rethink the art's role in the transformation of the human soul. The field of photography is destined to become more imaginative and creative after these secrets are out there for everyone to see!

– Dr. Glenn Rand, Professor Emeritus of Brooks Institute of Photography and author of over 20 books on photography

A Feather on the Breath of Ra:

Conversations with an Alchemist on Photography, Light, and Magic

BY
GARIN HORNER

Helio Graphis Press, LLC
Ann Arbor, Michigan, 48106
www.heliographispress.com

Secrets Inked in Shadow, Wisdom Lit by Flame
Cover and Book Design by Garin Horner
Softcover Edition (with price) ISBN Number:
Softcover Edition (without price) ISBN: 979-8-9989171-0-3

TABLE OF CONTENTS

ACKNOWLEDGMENTS

I am grateful to many people who played a crucial role in making this project a reality. First, I would like to thank my wife, Pilar, and my son, Archer, for their love and support. Next, I appreciate the insight of my editor, Nikky Twyman; her contributions exceeded my expectations. Many thanks to my close advisors and friends, Christine Reising, Don Werthmann, Michael Smith, Dmytri Hryciw, and Greg Kaminsky, who are endless sources of inspiration. I truly value my former students, Jay K. Starkey (student editor), RM, and BS; you were invaluable assistants throughout this journey. I am indebted to AS and JP, who have tirelessly served as my creative muses since 2016. This book could not have succeeded without the critical readers and reviewers who included Dr. Glenn Rand, Phoenix Aurelius, Vincent Martin, Rebecca Zeiss, Stephen Berkman, Dennis William Hauck, Jill Enfield, and Gerry Phillipson.

I thank President Jeffery J. Docking and the Board of Trustees at Adrian College for granting me a sabbatical in 2022. Their support provided me with valuable time to meet with GK, conduct research, and write the book. I also want to acknowledge Dr. Andrea Milner, Vice President and Dean of Academic Affairs at Adrian College, for her unwavering encouragement.

I offer praise for the expert advice and support I received about marketing from the team at Royal Scroll Media in Lansing, Michigan. Additionally, thank you to Tim Klempay and the team at Bohemio Bookbindery in Ann Arbor, Michigan, whose masterful craftsmanship transformed the ideas for the hardcover Collector's Edition of the book into a masterpiece of art. I'm grateful to TKR for your wisdom and generosity. And for being my lodestar.

Lastly, I owe a tremendous debt of gratitude to George Kingswood for trusting me with such a personal and meaningful project. You have given the world something unique and special. I'm thankful for the opportunity to have worked together on this book. It has been a life-enriching and eye-opening experience. I believe your story and your words will enrich the lives of everyone who reads them.

INTRODUCTION

"It's about how Mr. George Kingswood uses ritual magic to summon the dead. He needs their help. It's part of the plan to accomplish his goal, to uncover the secrets of divine transformation". That's what I told my colleagues when they asked what the book is about. "With ancient Egyptian alchemy and photographs of people, he conjures spirits so that they can help him along his path of spiritual evolution". This got their attention.

"In the book, Kingswood explains in detail how photography is foundational to his practices and philosophy." Being a photographer myself, I could feel my whole face flash with excitement! I explained how Kingswood's purposes for cameras, film, and light extend far beyond the commonly known forms of photography. Or alchemy, for that matter. He uses the implements of photography to bridge the threshold between the visible and invisible realms. Each of his intentionally made photographs serves as a device to summon a portal through which perception, life force, and essential energy can travel.

I'm captivated by these ideas. It makes me wonder whether Kingswood sees his darkroom as a sanctuary, a place where truths emerge from the pungent shadows, where images not only develop but acquire the power to awaken one's latent spiritual abilities. A faculty member asked about the book's purpose. "I want to clarify my goal. I don't intend to persuade others to believe in or adopt Kingswood's philosophy or practices. I aim to share with readers what I've discovered about his alchemy, his ancestors' magical traditions, and a unique metaphysical perspective on photography."

Over six years, I interviewed and learned from Kingswood, whom I will now refer to as GK. The self-proclaimed philosopher of spiritual alchemy spoke at length about his mystical knowledge, experiences, and way of life. He recounted how the invention of photography served his family's transcendent path. Initially, I had an academic curiosity about the mystique around alchemy. Then that curiosity turned into enthusiasm when I encountered a once-in-a-lifetime opportunity to study this metaphysical branch within the history of photography, when the paths of two arts converged to become something unique and remarkable.

On one hand, the Kingswoods have always adhered to the traditions of an ancient alchemical discipline. On the other hand, through modern photographic means, the family's spiritually transformative journey continues to unfold to this day. Despite the lineage's beginning in the late 1800s, GK claims their story doesn't start with the invention of photography or alchemy. Instead, it traces back to the dawn of the universe. The alchemist asserted that the origin of the cosmos, Egypt, the sun god Ra, and the legendary mystic Hermes Trismegistus are essential roots of knowledge for alchemical transmutation. For GK, this history is deeply connected to the life and teachings of his great-grandfather, Abraham Kingswood.

The late-19th-century patriarch Abraham was the first to experiment with integrating photography into his alchemical practices. Today, his great-grandson, GK, advances those methods in the sanctum sanctorum of his home. He is the fourth and final generation of Kingswood alchemists. Accordingly, one of this book's themes focuses on GK's contributions to his bloodline. It also details his family's mystical journey as they climbed toward their lofty goals over the past 140 years.

GK describes the Egyptian religious culture that once flourished within Ra's dominion, beneath the bounty of his light. He tells about the Kingswood family's connections to Hermeticism. Their narrative can also be read as a philosophical treatise centered on the search for ultimate truth. Overall, this account covers a wide range of topics. Photographer Gerry Phillipson noted that this "book seems to range across the sum of human knowledge, collective and individual spiritual quest, in short, it seems to endeavour to include absolutely everything" (Phillipson, 2023).

In addition to the miracles in GK's story, he reveals that the words on these pages are magical tools. Each physical copy of the book serves as one end of a supernatural filament, with the other end connecting the reader to GK and his predecessors. Through this book, he intends to inspire those who want to push beyond their creative limits. He seeks out photographers, philosophers, and mystics, particularly artists, seekers, believers, magic users, and students of the occult arts. GK reaches out to anyone interested in expanding their imagination. To those readers, GK offers support. To accept, simply keep reading.

**PART 1: Secrets of the Arts of Fire AND
Operations of the Sun**

1. Sacred Tableaus - Portraits of Devotion

Gods hid secrets about the creation and evolution of the cosmos, concealed within the solid and fluid aspects of light and shadow. For over two thousand years, spiritual devotees have longed to learn what those secrets can teach. Even today, seekers continue to search, aiming to unlock the mysteries of divine wisdom and gain the knowledge needed to accelerate their spiritual evolution.

This account focuses on one man's life and his persistence to uncover and implement the wisdom of the gods at all costs. But before we delve into this heroic character, I'd like to share how I met and got to know GK through years of meetings, written correspondence, interviews, and photography sessions. For now, I'll describe him as an enigmatic figure who has proven himself to be an adept discoverer and keeper of secrets.

I've always been fascinated by the idea that unseen, essential, life-transforming information surrounds us, yet we cannot perceive it. Furthermore, divine beings may have intentionally placed opaque veils of secrecy to prevent us from realizing the truth. It's also possible that we are generally unwilling or unable to perceive divine wisdom. My interest in this topic is a conceptual thread that has woven through my art for over forty years, tracing back to my earliest photographs.

In 2015, I had an idea for a new photography project that explored the relationship between human desire for spiritual revelation and secrecy. I envisioned entering the private spaces of people's homes and documenting their connections with their spiritual altars.

Altars seemed like a perfect subject for exploring the human ability to perceive beyond this reality. After all, people create altars to connect with transcendent beings, ethereal energies, and supernatural realms. An altar space is a hallowed place where sacred objects are arranged into a microcosmic tableau that reflects the broader dimensions of a spiritual universe!

Depending on an individual's spiritual practice, there exists a collection of statues, images of gods or gurus, and representations of the elements of fire, air, water, and earth. The devout come before these collections to pray, make offerings, worship, and meditate. It is where they seek inspiration and nourishment for their spirits. Everything that occurs before one's altar remains private, concealed from the prying eyes of nonbelievers. Gods, goddesses, and ethereal beings are called upon to receive offerings and guard secrets in closets, cabinets, and bedroom nooks. In these places, believers may perform rituals or request that a wish be granted. Sometimes, inanimate altar objects are *awakened* (infused with divine energy) and tenderly cared for as if they were alive.

An altar can be as simple as a candle or a flower, or it can be designed with a complexity that enchants and overwhelms the eye. The arrangement of sacred objects is intended to elevate one's spirit to a place beyond the tangible. It serves as a nexus, a site-specific portal, a

Picture 1.2 Our Ancestors Guide Us and Protect Us, by Garin Horner, 2022.

focal point through which one communes with beings whose presence can be felt, though not often seen by the eye.

In 2016, I began the project. I immediately appreciated how the photos captured each person's unique relationship with their altar. Some of my subjects belong to mainstream religions, while many do not. They are spiritual practitioners who seek to give voice to and celebrate their distinctive methods of worship. Through their beliefs, these individuals are linked to supernatural meta-ecologies. They feel they have discovered subtle dimensions that coexist with our reality.

Over the years, I've connected with spiritual communities around the world to find individuals willing to be photographed. Subjects have also reached out to me about wanting to be part of the project. Early on, I photographed a fellow photographer who incorporated ceremonial magic into his spiritual practice. He suggested I contact a man named George Kingswood. "He's an Alchemist, and I'm pretty sure he has an altar." I was intrigued. "I think he'd be willing to let you take pictures because he's a photographer like us." Mr. Kingswood sounded exactly like someone I was eager to meet!

I Googled the name to find contact information, but the search yielded no results. The only outcome was a picture of a tombstone inscribed: "George Kingswood, 1825-1851." I returned to the lead's source and obtained a P.O. box address. That day, I mailed a letter. Two weeks later, I received a very formal, somewhat positive response. After several rounds of correspondence, I was invited to meet this self-professed "alchemyst"[11], philosopher, and photographer, Mr. George Kingswood.

Each exchange of letters made it clearer that Kingswood was not what I had imagined. My mental picture of an "alchemist" was surely outdated. I envisioned a 21st-century alchemist as an eccentric character who was either a passionate historical cosplayer or someone deeply immersed in obscure spiritual practices, clinging to ancient writings in search of gold. It's like Mary Anne Atwood's description of such a person as one who is "brooding over his crucibles and alembics that are to place within his reach the philosophers' stone, the transmutation of metals, the alkahest, and the elixir of life" (Atwood, 11).

Moreover, Evelyn Underhill wrote, "Of all the symbolic systems in which this truth has been enshrined, none is so complete, so picturesque, and now so little understood as that of the 'Hermetic Philosophers' or Spiritual Alchemists" (Underhill, 141). Those words, penned over a hundred years ago, made me want to set aside all my preconceived ideas about alchemy and look at Kingswood from a new perspective, with impartial eyes.

In a letter, GK responded to my naivete, declaring that he was not the "puffer" or "sooty empiric" I had envisioned. He hoped I didn't imagine him "toiling in his dark, smokey laboratory, surrounded by a pack of

---

[1] Spelling provided by George Kingswood.

oath-bound demonic servants, all driven by a common lust to transmute lead into gold." He ended the paragraph with "Rubbish!"

As a child, GK studied alchemy as part of his birthright. He is a descendant of three generations of alchemists, who were also photographers. GK claims to be the beneficiary of ancient practitioners of "true hermetic art." He admits that before the life of Abraham Kingswood, some practitioners of his lineage were primarily concerned with the projection# of gold. Although greed has been a powerful incentive for alchemists over the centuries, the Kingswood family has always been motivated by a higher purpose.

I was surprised to learn that modern-day alchemists aren't as rare as I thought. Several alchemical organizations exist, such as the International Alchemy Guild, the Temple of Mercury: A College for the Hermetic Arts, the Fraternity of Hidden Light, and others. One notable twentieth-century practitioner of the art was Frater Albertus (1911-1984). He argued, "Many people think of alchemists as strange, mysterious individuals, half crazy, if not completely insane, who belong more properly to the Dark Ages. To mention that true alchemists are living and working today sounds, to most people, like a fable from 1001 Nights. But the remarkable fact remains that even to this day, unknown to the world at large, alchemists continue to practice their art and science, faithful to a centuries-old tradition. Often, those apparent miracles that happen here and there are the results of the deeds of these unselfish men and women" (Albertus, 104). GK adds that authentic alchemists have consistently surmounted the confines of space, time, physicality, and the ordinary, limited capacity for perception. He said, "I exercise those abilities for my primary work, and part of that work is to help others."

Without a thought for earthly gold, GK follows a mystical path he refers to as the "Opus Magna Lucis et Umbrae" (The Great Work of Light and Shadow) or, simply, *the Great Work*. Unlike other spiritual paths, GK's approach to the Great Work is photocentric, "like a solitary planet orbiting the sun." It represents a subcategory of Western Mysticism. He combines a traditional metaphysical approach with photography, as a sacerdotal# art. In doing so, photography becomes the primary vehicle for his life's alchemical pursuits. GK's approach to the art could be defined as what authors Philippe Gross and S. I. Shapiro call "the path of conscious camerawork" (Gross et al., 34).

Initially, I approached GK to ask if I could photograph him with his altar. From first contact, he seemed interested but wanted to learn more about my project before committing. We exchanged letters. Questions and answers were mailed back and forth. Some queries I sent returned with answers. Other questions came back disregarded.

Finally, the day arrived when we met. GK did most of the talking during the meeting. At about midday, I realized he had reformed my creative goal into his larger purpose. GK wanted me to take five photos of him as illustrations for a book about the theories and practices of his family's system of Western spiritual alchemy. He also wanted to articulate his views on alchemy's interdependence with photography. GK wrote the words "spirituele alchemie" on a piece of paper. He underlined the words three times, then slid the paper closer to me, urging me to pick it up. I took it and tucked it into my notebook.

After the first meeting ended, I was leaving the house when he asked me if I would write a book about him. I paused, taken aback. Standing at the threshold of GK's house, he explained that he wanted to bring his life's work into the open, beyond the sanctuary of his home. He hoped there would be readers who might resonate with this "particular philosophical vantage point of the Hermetic arts." GK also mentioned that there needed to be a contemporary record of authenticity to counter what the honorable alchemist Éliphas Lévi called "catch-penny mystifications and impostures of dishonest publishers" (Lévi, 42).

I felt overwhelmed by his request. He said he chose me because of my practical and academic experience with photography. Additionally, I had only a basic understanding of alchemy. Rather than finding a writer deeply knowledgeable in alchemical studies, he wanted an uninitiated, objective perspective. Most of what I knew about alchemy was its reputation as an ancient pseudoscience. GK believed my ignorance was the ideal starting point for my research and education in the Western mystical tradition.

GK had a timeline in mind. He needed to finish our conversations and photography sessions by the end of 2022. He felt that, because our time together would be limited, and the amount of information was so vast, he urged me to "listen carefully. Clarify your understanding using the inquiring light within." He encouraged me to research his assertions so I could know, with confidence, that his statements were accurate. I needed to interrogate every concept to my satisfaction and not take anything he said as true unless I verified it for myself. GK provided stacks of books from his library. Above all, he wanted me to learn as much as I could.

I followed his instructions. The more stories I heard, the more I wanted to know! I thought GK's ideas were extraordinary. His work with this unique kind of alchemy fascinated me! I was especially interested in how his forebears discovered a spiritual dimension to photography.

My first assignment was to understand better the arcane tradition of *spiritual alchemy*, which historian and scholar Mike Zuber defines as "the practical pursuit of inward but physically real transmutation" (Zuber, 38). In addition to conversations with GK, I set out on a parallel line of research to study alchemy's ancient origins. From there, I worked my way forward on the timeline to its practices in our 21st-century world. As I got more familiar with the theory and practice of the Kingswood's approach to the alchemical arts, I hoped to have some suitable questions. I knew if I couldn't understand the topics, I couldn't write about the subject clearly. Furthermore, I'd have to know enough about alchemy's history to understand GK's accounts within a historical context.

I found out about the alchemical process of becoming "thrice born." For instance, GK explained that he was born once as a human, then as an Initiate of the *Hermetic-Gnostic Mysteries*, and finally, through dissolution and reemergence, he emerged into a state of gnosis. More specifically, *photognosis*, which means he became *light's divine wisdom*. Up to the attainment of the second birth, there were both internal and external transformations. The third birth was a transmutation event in which he experienced a complete psychological and spiritual reawakening. He began as a human. Through alchemy, he evolved into something greater.

GK said that in alchemy, there's a saying: "Durare mori et non perire," which means "Endure death and do not perish." There is also a maxim: "solve et coagula," which refers to spiritual and physical *dissolution and reformation.* Through this process, one dissolves their sense of self (a kind of death) and re-forms (coagulates) into a new and higher form of being—a "third birth." GK glanced down at one of his notebooks, saying, "It was perfectly described when Albertus Magnus said alchemy was 'nothing else but to dissolve and recongeal the spirit, to make the fixed volatile and the volatile fixed, until the total nature is perfected by the reiteration, both in its Solary and Lunar form'" (Atwood, 103). GK's commanding presence, intelligence, and authoritative knowledge helped convey the impact of his personal experience with life, death, and reemergence. Captivated, I needed to know more!

GK faithfully adheres to the teachings of Abraham Kingswood, who proclaimed that "Alchemy is an art form above all other arts, a noble endeavor that calls on the highest degree of creativity. It and its sister, photography, are arts of fire." He also believed, unlike many others, that "light" is more than a symbol for knowledge, wisdom, and revelation.

Kingswood supported what scholar of mysticism Henry Corbin claimed, that light "is the agent of Revelation" (Corbin, 191).

GK explained that his family of alchemistic philosophers discussed their esoteric processes using a coded language based on photographic terminology. Light, cameras, lenses, glass plates, silver-saturated emulsions, and chemical operations were the keys that could unlock Kingwood's door to transformative knowledge.

Picture 1.3 Solve et Coagula by Mylius, Johann Daniel, 1628.

We sat at the alchemist's dining table discussing transformation. Between us was a blood-red candle anchored in a dark silver holder. Next to it sat an old brass bowl on a wooden trivet. GK lit the wick and pulled a vintage cabinet card from his blazer pocket. "Nothing is static; everything is in a state of metamorphosis. All becoming something else. Energy cannot be created or destroyed. It's endlessly changing from one state to another. For example, the blazing nuclear fission of the sun is converted to heat and light. Eight minutes later, that light is translated into the life-energy of plants through photosynthesis. Imagine that same light falls upon and awakens silver halides on film inside the camera. The images produced energize the photographer and stimulate physical movement and cognitive energy in the brain. If prints are made and those physical objects are burned, the energy is liberated back into that selfsame heat and light from which they were created."

He dangled the photo by the tip of one corner, then lowered the opposite corner into the candle flame. The picture depicted a portrait of a young woman. She wore an elegant turn-of-the-century dress and stood in a dignified yet rigid pose. Behind her was a background painted to create the impression of a landscape with trees. On either side, there were a few depictions of ancient columns. That's all I could discern before the burning print was dropped into the bowl. The charming artifact transformed into a husk of shimmering ash. He continued, "This artifact and the imagery upon it are transformed back into that aforesaid aspect of the sun from which it began. Eight minutes later, the firelight that made this picture will return to its source: the sun."

Empirical science has proven that energy cannot be created. Nonetheless, the divine origin of the energies that drive evolutionary processes is a primary concern for alchemists. GK cites the descriptions of creation in both the Bible's book of Genesis and the story of Egypt's progenitor god, Ra. Both deities are said to have emerged from the dark void, with everything manifesting around them as material forms. In alchemical philosophy, these are two crucial descriptions of genesis, evolution, transformative energy, and its processes. They represent foundational teachings about the Great Work's source, emergence, and objective.

I'm intrigued by how much GK reveals about his secret practice of the Great Work. He's determined to shape his evolution, consistently applying effort to uncover divine knowledge that leads to spiritual insights. Once revealed, that knowledge is used to manipulate natural (and supernatural) energies to illuminate transformation.

Acting on the revelations it offers promises to accelerate self-evolution. This challenging journey depends on transforming addictions, fear, greed, selfishness, and other imperfections. The desired outcome is an exalted form of being. Photographer Sean Kernan says, "When you face something you think you can't possibly do, and then go ahead and do it anyway, creativity is the tool you use. It is how you can get far beyond the self that you have constructed at all ages as you've practiced being you" (Kernan, 2).

Both the biblical and Egyptian origin stories contain evolutionary clues. Each suggests that all transformative processes start in the infinite potential of darkness. GK declares, "It is from the eternal, inexhaustible darkness that the creative arcana can manifest universes filled with living beings while revealing hidden clues to the methods for their evolution through the Great Work. They divulge the mysteries about a birth from darkness and its creative potential. So it is with photography, in which silver halides birth an image in the pitch-blackness. A latent impression remains resting in its creative potential, a state prior to becoming."

Creation stories offer insights into the transformations that shaped the human body, mind, consciousness, and soul. Followers of the Great Work, convinced of this, learned from the ancient wisdom conveyed by these stories. With their understanding, they developed ingenious alchemical methods, including high magic, to reverse-engineer the processes of evolution. Driven by the desire to accelerate their evolution, they continue to gain further insights into the primordial gloom from which all things originated and emerged.

Like historical alchemists, the last four generations of Kingswoods exercised a strict code of secrecy. For example, part of their spiritual practice has been developing a private, encrypted language filled with symbolism, metaphors, paronomasia#, and techno-jargon. And though GK is the last of his line, he continues the tradition of using a mystical visual language of emblems, pictograms, ideograms, and logograms.

Due to various encryptions in our written and spoken communication, I never take what I hear or see from GK at face value. For instance, his sentences often have multiple meanings; communicating with him feels like solving a puzzle. It requires active, conscious effort to decipher what he says and what he intends to convey. My approach is to accept his words at face value. Then, I reflect on what he said to try to reach the deeper levels of understanding that he aims for. That said, I'm sure most of his adeptly crafted messages go over my head.

In addition to language and imagery, GK communicates through the physical world around him. His "laboratorium" is a perfect example. In many ways, the room serves as an external presentation of his research and mystical pedagogy. It's a chamber where he immerses himself in the creation of artisanal elixirs and the alchemy of photographic processes. GK says, "I have all the items listed in Rhazes' *Book of Secrets*, including specimens from the categories *nascentia#* and *viventia#* and more." There are beakers, flasks, aludels, crucibles, graduated cylinders, developing trays, a cucurbit, an alembic, and lots of unlabeled containers filled with secret substances. Boxes and bottles were labeled Kodak, Ilford, Agfa, Fotospeed, and Kentmere.

The way he initially described this room made me think he intended it to reflect his true alchemical atelier, his inner laboratory. Quoting Carty, he said, "this is the place 'where the Work could proceed on my soul' (Carty, 10). It's where true transformative processes are at work behind the scenes to examine, refine, and purify the very essence of my being."

In my view, the room overflowed with various objects and exotic ingredients. For GK, these same components represented organs of

Picture 1.4 George Kingswood's *Laboratorium* by Garin Horner, 2022.

knowledge—the viscera of his own body, the receptacles for magical energy emanating from the core of his immortal soul.

GK's path is undeniably mystical. He never accepts what he has read or heard on faith alone; he puts the information to work. He tests his knowledge to gain a deeper, firsthand understanding from his results. In

Gary Edson's book *Mysticism and Alchemy through the Ages: The Quest for Transformation*, he aptly describes the enigmatic state from which GK views the world. "'The mystic insight begins with the sense of a mystery unveiled, of hidden wisdom now suddenly become certain beyond the possibility of doubt. The sense of certainty and revelation comes earlier than any definite belief.' (Russell, 9). The mystic seeks an enhanced form of life. The path to spiritual and emotional enhancement involves the 'remaking of character and the liberation of a new, or rather latent, form of consciousness; which imposes on the self the condition which is sometimes inaccurately called 'ecstasy,' but is better named

Picture 1.5 Alchemical and Rosicrucian Compendium, 1760.

the Unitive State.' (Underhill, 81). (Ecstasy may be considered as meaning 'to stand outside.' The mystic in a state of ecstasy, stands outside his normal awareness and discovers he or she is more than he or she imagined" (Edson, 79)).

In my opinion, GK is highly competent in his understanding and mastery of alchemy. I'm convinced that his perception of the phenomenal world differs significantly from mine. His fearless worldview encompasses much more than I can perceive. GK's state of consciousness extends into realms where spirits, gods, and even demons dwell—where the elements fire, earth, wind, and water are recognized as sentient, autonomous intelligences. Moreover, his fearless vision isn't limited to simply "looking" at photographs. He penetrates their flat surfaces, seeing deeply into them as if they were windows into infinitely regressing scenes. The accuracy with which he interprets even the most subtle details and meanings in a photograph is truly what he describes as "superordinate#" and unexplainable.

In GK's home, my sense of perception was tested. I saw, felt, and heard things I couldn't explain. I never got used to the inexplicable phenomena. For instance, I can't count the number of times I caught a glimpse of someone standing or moving out of the corner of my eye. Sometimes, it appeared as an outline of flickering light; other times, it took the shape of a murky human form, like the shadow of a person floating in still air. Each time, I was chilled by the experience. In response, GK would let slip something like, "Don't mind them; they're only curious."

It was even *more* unsettling when he commented while turned away. His position made it impossible for him to notice the quick turn of my head or my startled (yet utterly silent) expressions. These moments made me fantasize about him living with over three centuries of ghosts. I asked GK if he thought there were actual spirits in the house. And could he observe them? His response was to quote mystic Helena Blavatsky, "Tell one who had never seen water that there is an ocean of water, and he must accept it on faith or reject it all together. But let one drop fall upon his hand, and he then has a fact from which all the rest may be inferred. After that, he could by degrees understand that a boundless and fathomless ocean of water existed" (Blavatsky, 4).

So much of what I absorbed from GK couldn't be categorized as "explainable" or "rational." But that's what made every day with him so exciting! Reflecting on the end of our first meeting, I felt both reluctant and enthusiastic at the same time! I felt like the supporting character in a supernatural thriller, who says to the protagonist, "Let's do it. What could possibly go wrong?"

After three days, it was time for me to head home. The trip concluded with a decisive handshake as we stood on the walkway of GK's house. Still gripping my hand, he looked directly into my eyes and declared in his enchanting North English accent, "Nothing is more meaningful than applying the invaluable resources of photography for one's self-transformation. This art is crucial for maintaining the steep ascent that leads to the first emanation of light, which is gnosis." The information he shared and the stories he told over the next five years made the meaning of those thirty-three words real. Through them, he wove a fantastical narrative, told from the vantage point of his own life experience.

2. THE CONFESSIONS OF GEORGE KINGSWOOD

During my research, I discovered that alchemists had uncovered all the chemical processes necessary to invent photography; yet they weren't concerned with creating or fixing images. The concept of producing pictures never occurred to them. Later historical records indicate that as the practice of alchemy faded away, it transitioned seamlessly into the history of photography. This confirms the Kingswood family's narrative. It is generally accepted that alchemy is the precursor to modern science. However, it's less acknowledged that alchemy's early discoveries contributed most of the formulations used in early photographic processes.

GK thumbed through a journal and pointed to a quote he had written down. "Out of the many alchemists that made breakthroughs in optics, light reactive substances, the principles of the camera obscura, and the arts, nobody connected the dots. It took 600 years before English inventor Thomas Wedgwood looked back into alchemy's argyropoeiac# experiments and found they revealed the glorious secrets of photo-sympathetic silver" (Williams). Wedgwood went on to revive those archaic discoveries and announced them as his own breakthroughs in the quest to make and fix photographic images.

Picture 2.1 Camera Obscura by Athanasius Kircher, 1645.

GK believes that Wedgwood's deceitful claims contribute to the historical distrust and suspicion surrounding alchemy, though he speculates that Wedgwood had no choice but to separate his alchemical research from his assertions of discovery. Respectable inventors of the time sought to distance themselves from the negative mystique of the alchemist's poor reputation. In contrast, the Kingswood family regarded the invention of photography as a miracle that continued the evolution of alchemy. Viewing photography as an important branch of the magical arts, they perceived the photographic, "art as *illusionistic*" with the capacity for, "conjuring imaginary worlds" (Almenberg, 45).

In the late 1800s, Abraham Kingswood wrote that photography, when in the right hands, was synonymous with alchemy. He stressed its ability to capture unimaginable, divine beauty from radiant light. It could transform light into visionary gems that reveal and help decode the creator's vision. The art form was highly malleable during editing, echoing some of alchemy's fundamental ideas. "Photography is often compared to alchemy via direct analogy: both rely on transformation through chemistry and physical processes. More significantly, the deeply interdisciplinary qualities of both practices produce works that fuse analytical observation, empiricism, and precise documentation with symbolism, poetics, and metaphor" (Haik, 10). Author Hugh Aldersey-William added, "Photography is uniquely positioned to offer insights to both laboratory scientists who rely on rigor and clarity and to artists who rely on metaphor and ambiguity" (Aldersey-William, 11).

GK possesses an insightful understanding of how alchemy and photography share a virtuosity in their use of metaphorical languages. He proposes, "It could be said that all photographers are alchemists in that, instead of changing lead to gold, they chrysopoetically# transform the world's reflections of light into revelatory iconography. Which some would argue, is the same thing."

It should be noted that Kingswood's interpretation of *alchemy* differs from its common usage among photographers. For this family, there is an uncommon insight—where the word alchemy is meant to mean exactly what it states. Kingswood visionaries have always regarded it as a pursuit that synthesizes scholarly, practical, and spiritual concerns. The primary source materials for their study can be found in ancestral notebooks and ancient manuscripts. Many copies of these materials are in GK's library. However, the most important sources of knowledge reside in the ephemera of the world, hidden in countless aspects of nature. Some can be discovered in those inner personal depths that reflect a shared understanding between what is within oneself and the cosmos without.

GK says, "I confess that knowledge is without benefit if it's not in a prosperous marriage with practice, whether exposed in the profound activities of alchemy or photography. As Hermetic Artist Lyam Thomas Christopher claimed, 'A system of thought can never take the place of spiritual experience… [which reshapes] your thought processes, your habitual emotions, and your physiological responses such that they may one day fuse together into a magical instrument'" (Christopher, 59). Therefore, GK's mysteriosophic# practice and theory of alchemy (in concert with photography) carries a rich history, filled with intrigue, secretive quests for truth, deceit, and ultimately, defeat, bankruptcy, and, in some cases, executions.

The "natural art" of alchemy laid the groundwork that gave birth to modern chemistry and physics. "However, it must not be forgotten that the earliest *contexts* of 'material' alchemy were not proto-scientific, but *ritualistic*…[in] the magical and theurgical milieux of Hellenistic Egypt, the most concrete alchemical practices were always inseparable from ritual invocations to and supplications of the divinities whose ranks the alchemist wished to enter" (Cheak, 19). GK wholeheartedly agrees that the alchemical seed from which grew the branches of chemistry and physics also bore a branch that flowered as the technologies of photography and its art. Furthermore, the ancient roots from that seed bore extraordinary blossoms, forming an esoteric aspect of photography that is an inseparable element of Kingswood's form of Western mysticism.

The deeper one digs into photography's historical record, the more omissions one notices regarding its ancestry. While "going back to the primary sources of the 1840's and 50's, one finds that the early writings on photography rarely mention alchemy by name…When the relationship between the two is mentioned at all in the early literature, it is almost always invoked as a literary figure — a poetic trope" (Wamberg, 85). The exclusions were intentional. There was a very real concern that the public might recoil at the suggestion that photography was somehow associated with the socially and morally uncomfortable subjects of metaphysics and discredited alchemists. Alchemy and its practitioners were pariahs, especially when seen in contrast to a world that was flourishing with technologies that seemed magical in their own industrial-modernist complexity.

"But let us be clear about who the authentic alchemist was, and is," GK assured. "Mircea Eliade described the alchemist best when he said, such a person 'must be healthy, humble, patient…his mind must be free and in harmony with his work; he must be intelligent and scholarly, he must work, meditate, pray, etc. It is so obvious therefore that it is not merely a question of experiments conducted in a laboratory. The alchemist must involve himself completely in his work. But these qualities and virtues must not be understood in a purely moral sense. In the alchemist they have the same function as patience, intelligence, equanimity, etc., have in [a spiritual practice] or in the novitiate period preceding initiation into the Mysteries' (Eliade, 159). Eliade's words resonate with my experience. I also believe these are admirable qualities for a photographer!"

In the bygone era, alchemists were curious about the mysteries of human existence. They needed answers to burning questions regarding their purpose on Earth and in the cosmos. Their deep inquiry into the natural world turned them into explorers of supernatural realms. Thus, their practices reinforced the belief that the universe's metaphysical qualities and essential properties were just as significant, if not more so, than its physical characteristics. While modern scientists approach their research with a focus on objectivity, verifiability, and predictability, alchemy's perspective continues to provide a more far-reaching understanding of the unseen, non-material, and ineffable (Read, 14-15).

The 14th-century alchemical manuscript Summa Perfectionis, attributed to Pseudo-Geber, could never be mistaken for hard science when it states that, "what Nature cannot perfect in a vast space of time we can achieve in a short space of time by our art." That statement speaks to alchemy's potential to elevate, ennoble, and accelerate the purification of a sapient spirit. This concept points toward Ars Alchemia Transmutatoria, the lineage of alchemical theory and practice that focused on the inner, metaphorical production of gold through spiritual transmutation.

GK asserts,

> Many alchemists were indeed motivated by a voracious desire for gold, or "aurum" (Latin for 'shining dawn'). Their experiments weren't necessarily driven by a wish for material gain, but rather to reveal aurum's transformative secrets. As a mineral of light, gold embodies many spiritual qualities associated with the Egyptian god Ra, and it is also one of the Earth's most valuable metals. Mythologies tell how the sun seeded the Earth with spiritual wealth when it sent rocks of liquid light down to penetrate its surface. That liquid light then solidified into a fortune of metallic gold.

Scientists say that over two billion years ago, a bolide meteor over ten kilometers wide struck what is now South Africa. It's devastating impact caused extinctions and earthquakes that persisted for thousands of years. As the world's largest impact site, spanning 300 kilometers, this historical cataclysmic event shrouded the atmosphere in a sooty darkness that lasted for months. Over time, the veil lifted, and light broke through, revealing an Earth that had undergone a profound transformation into a new structure. Large portions of the Earth's hardened, recrementitious# crust were toppled and shifted vertically downward, pointing toward its fiery core. In this process, the Earth's largest treasure of hidden gold was raised to the surface and revealed (*Vredefort Impact Structure*).

"This exoteric geological happening serves as a metaphor for the esoteric process of the spiritual-alchemical path." GK goes on to explain,

As with all significant internal transformations, the Earth's body had to absorb an enormous amount of energy. While doing so, it needed to adapt and reform (solve et coagula). Instead of the Earth's closed system falling into entropy, it adapted and underwent a metamorphosis to become something new. The cosmic phenomenon is like the alchemist, performing their work to make the conditions of their life such that they will attract the transformative-destructive-creative meteor of divinity. The intent is made that the alchemist's outer shell, which frustrates the radiance of its indwelling soul, will be shattered. And we aspirants pray that when the fiery-tailed star arrives, it churns that buried, hidden gold to the surface!

Lyam Thomas Christopher describes the process of purification in another way. By calming the turbulence of one's mind, one may increase one's ability to see the soul's divine aspects.

Wind blows on the surface of the water, thereby altering the reflection of the heavens to suit its purposes. The ego can likewise alter and distort the image of the higher consciousness that presents itself within the animal senses ...But what if the image of the sky reflected in the water becomes distorted because of too much wind? What if the ego's restless activities disturb the image of the Divine that is reflected in the animal soul? I am suggesting here that the activities of your mind can keep you from seeing the truth about yourself...When the wind is calm, the water becomes still, reflecting like a perfect mirror the beauty and light of the sky, the *Neschamah* [the Higher Self]...Ritual techniques refine and purify the receptive nature of his animal soul. By employing drama, voice, and movement, he can wipe away confused behavioral and mental habits. He can eliminate gradually the distortions in the reflection of Heaven. The student of magic is striving for none other than the naturally clear mind, which appears only when desires, beliefs, and false perceptions that arise from material inclinations are erased (Christopher, 27).

It's important to emphasize that alchemists believed that any intentional physical changes catalyzed in the world (or the cosmos) must be analogous to changes within one's being.

For the alchemist, trying to understand matter and develop base metals into their purest form, gold, substances are grouped as being alike based on their perceived value. Jung documents as these alchemists collectively come to understand that they themselves must embody the change they hope to effect within their materials: for instance, if they hope to achieve the philosopher's stone that can redeem 'base' or 'vulgar' metals, then the alchemist too must become a redeemer figure. It became apparent to the alchemists that they were trying to redeem nature as Christ had redeemed man, hence the identification of the *Lapis Philosophorum* with Christ the Redeemer. The Opus (work) of alchemy, viewed through this interpretation, becomes a symbolic account of the fundamental process the human psyche undergoes as it re-orients its value system and creates meaning out of chaos. The opus beginning with the nigredo (blackening, akin to depression or nihilistic loss of value) in order to descend back into the manipulable prima materia and proceeding through a process of spiritual purification that must unite seemingly irreconcilable opposites (the coniunctio) to achieve new levels of consciousness (*Psychology and Alchemy*).

Thirteenth-century alchemist Albertus Magnus diligently experimented with natural phenomena. He understood that alchemy could be defined as an internal, mystical metamorphic process known as the *Great Work*. GK elaborates, "An alchemist has no chance of succeeding in effecting changes in their outer world without first making equivalent alterations to those same aspects within. That includes amendments to both the psychological and spiritual qualities that align with the highest principles required of the Great Work. I attest that, in a statement by my alchemystic ancestor's friend and confidant, Mary Anne (South) Atwood, 'it is possible, by labor and a transition into other lives, for the imaginative soul to be purified and to emerge from this dark abode. And this restoration indeed one or two may obtain as a gift of divinity and initiation'" (Atwood, 86).

The term "Great Work," or Magnum Opus, is recognized across the arts. It is primarily used to identify the most significant piece or body of work created by an artist, marking the pinnacle of one's career. For instance, as part of his exploration to unlock the "secret code of the pyramids," Hermetic artist and Neoplatonist Sir Isaac Newton's greatest work, "Philosophiae Naturalis Principia Mathematica," published in 1687, became the culmination of decades of work and thought. The Magnum Opus outlined his theories of calculus and gravitation and the laws of motion, providing a new understanding of the universe (Sherwood). Coincidentally, Newton's discoveries stemmed from his dedication to uncovering secret, divine aspects essential for the Great Work. As another example, Michelangelo's Magnum Opus is his painting on the ceiling of the Sistine Chapel, The Creation of Adam. Photographer Ansel Adams' greatest work is said to be his black and white composition, Monolith, the Face of Half Dome.

GK's phrase "Great Work" is defined as an intentional, ambitious, ongoing process where one's entire life is narrowly focused on attaining extreme mental, psychic, and spiritual transformation. From memory, GK recites excerpts from the poem *Festus*, by English philosopher and writer Philip James Bailey. These lines illustrate a mindset that GK has maintained throughout his life, consistently striving toward the goal of self-evolution:

> Man's heart hath not half uttered itself yet,
> And much remains to do as well as say.
> The heart is sometime ere it finds its focus;
> And when it does, with the whole light of nature
> Strained through it to a hair's breadth, it but burns
> The things beneath it, which it lights to death (Blavatsky, 185).

Bailey further elaborates on the Great Work, "Though an enemy to blind desire, indolence, and vulgar greed, it is a friend to the persisting, critical, and analytical mind. In addition, the Great Work is a welcome companion to the indomitable spirit." In many ways, the entire life of a mystic is seen as a work of art, perpetually in a state of progress. However, the artwork of one's life isn't created through an additive process, like stacking thousands of blocks of stone to construct a pyramid. Instead, it resembles Michelangelo's concept of a subtractive process, where the artwork already exists within a piece of marble. One need only free the sculpture by chipping away the obscuring stone that hides its true nature.

GK insists, "the Great Work is not a pinnacle moment when one's skill and talent are performed perfectly. While then, the artist's most treasured qualities are doomed to suffer a decline. Rather, it's an odyssey of gradual ascension that takes one through ever greater stages of maturity, a chrysopoetic# process of transforming one's thoughts, feelings, and actions into something more refined in preparation for accessing what is at the highest possible point of evolution. The pinnacle of that evolution is the supreme state of gnosis. It is divine union, where one recognizes their being as a divine light, the vital essence that pervades the universe." This state for GK is the ancient sun god that the Egyptians called Ra.

According to GK, the goal of the Great Work is to realize with clarity and certainty that one is a microcosm of all that exists, an inseparable version of the Universe. In other words, each sentient being is a miniature, yet equally dynamic universe—a performance of elements that mirrors the "Great Universal Soul." Paracelsus explains further,

> you call man a microcosm. The term is justly chosen…Follow us in our interpretation of what we mean by microcosm. Similarly, as the heavens are in themselves with their entire firmament and constellations, excepting nothing, so is man constellated mightily in and by himself. As the firmament is the heavens by itself and is not governed by any creature, so little is the firmament, that is in man, lorded over by other creatures. It just is a tremendous, free firmament without any ties whatsoever (Paracelsus et al., 34).

GK points to the art of photography as an invaluable collection of methods that can be used to transform an ordinary, routine life into a performance of the highest psychological, emotional, and spiritual acts. Scholar and Zen monk D. T. Suzuki said that art, in a spiritual context, is "not intended for utilitarian purposes, or for purely aesthetic enjoyment, but [is] meant to train the mind, indeed, to bring it into contact with ultimate reality" (Loori, 1). GK discusses being a photographer who, like the monk or mystic, perpetually lives in a state of anticipation and uncertainty while waiting for Ra to reveal the secrets of the beautiful motion and stillness of the world. Photography, through his observant eyes, is the perfect medium for spiritual exploration within the context of the mystical arts. It is "the expression of the Soul that listens and sees where the outer mind is silence and the dark" (Regardie, 28). Photography, combined with mysticism, becomes "perhaps the greatest of arts, the apotheosis# of artistic expression and endeavour" (ibid).

At the start of this project, GK's ideas about a hybrid practice of mysticism, magic, and photography seemed far-fetched to me, even superstitious. Yet, in the words of the renowned alchemist and mage, Éliphas Lévi, "When great men are accused of superstition, it is because they behold what remains unseen by the crowd" (Gencay, 25). One need not suspend one's sense of disbelief to appreciate GK's extraordinary experiences and imaginative logic. He explains how to embrace alchemy and its transformative process. GK's spirit always looks upward, climbing the metaphorical steps of the Great Pyramid. His ascension is characterized by such remarkable enthusiasm and conviction that his words make anything seem possible. His story, along with the tales of the Egyptian High Priests of Ra, Hermes Trismegistus, Nicholas Flamel, Louis-Jacques-Mandé Daguerre, Henry Fox Talbot, and GK's great grandfather, Abraham Kingswood, are what J. M. Peebles would refer to as a, "golden chain of testimony, streaming like pearls down through all the centuries past" (Green, 207).

This story is the legacy of Kinswood's alchemy. Today, GK continues this tradition. He uses photography as a compelling medium for inner psychological and spiritual metamorphoses. He declares, "It's an important part of our belief system that we put to use antediluvian# magic to initiate inner changes of consciousness and affect outer transformations in our environments." This account is being shared by the last remaining member of this clandestine lineage for the first time. GK offers this seemingly unbelievable chronicle to those he feels are called to learn about alchemy's ancient Egyptian roots, its revelations about light, its mission to cause evolution, and the transformative potential of solve et coagula in the Great Work.

The Kingswood's story of modern alchemy begins with Alexander the Great in 331 BCE. The Macedonian king was on a mission to Siwah, Egypt, to find the oracle of the god Amun (Amun-Ra). During his travels, he discovered the tomb of the Master of Mysteries, *Hermes Trismegistus*. The name "Trismegistus" is Ancient Greek for 'Thrice Great' or "Thrice Blessed," the most supreme philosopher, the highest of all kings, and the most exalted of all holy men. Trismegistus was a priest of the Greco-Egyptian syncretized god Hermes-Thoth, whom the Egyptians worshiped as, "the personification of the mind and intelligence of the Creator" (Budge, 142). It is said that the god Hermes-Thoth was the first to teach the divine illumination of alchemy to men, specifically to Hermes Thrice-Blessed. "The Hermetic literature among the Egyptians, which was concerned with conjuring spirits and animating statues, informs the oldest Hellenistic writings on Greco-Babylonian

astrology and on the newly developed practice of alchemy"
(Fowden, 65-68).

Picture 2.2 The Emerald Tablet by Heinrich Khunrath, 1602.

At the site of Trismegistus' tomb, Alexander unearthed a priceless
treasure: the *Emerald Tablet*. It is believed that this stone plaque was
part of a larger collection of writings called the "Book of the Secret of
Creation." Within the abstruse writings on the artifact, Alexander
discovered what would become the foundational alchemical axiom: "As
above, so below, as within, so without, as the universe, so the soul…"
(*Emerald Tablet*, 42). This Hermetic proclamation illuminates the theory
of interconnectedness between the microcosm of individual lives and the
macrocosm of the infinite cosmos. In Abraham Kingswood's notes
regarding the tablet, he wrote, "The alchemist shapes themself and in
doing so, shapes the world. By shaping the world, so does the alchemist
shape the universe." His notes allude to a philosophical and spiritual
belief while also discussing photographic processes. He believed that the
creation of a photograph revealed divine knowledge while generating
countless connections, forming relationships among the photographer,

the scene photographed, the artifact (print), the viewer, and the greater cosmos — all aspects of the same phenomenon.

The art of photography arises from perception and imagination. Thus, it has the potential to expand the capacity of human awareness by highlighting the relationships that exist between things. This serves as just a preface to the medium's grander potential. Scholar Dr. Shun-liang Chao stated that the invention of photography was a triumph, "because it outperformed language in reproducing the world as perceived by the corporeal eye" (Shun-liang Chao, 301). In the 21st century, the photographer continues to lift aside the veil that obscures unseen worlds. These realms, both within and without, represent what is perceived as normal reality. A photographer exposes viewers to details and meanings that could never be captured in the moment by the unaided, scouting eye. Furthermore, Hee Sook Lee-Niinioja wrote that art in the tenth century was like the contemporary alchemist's art of today. It allowed the viewer, "to transcend the physical world of sensual reality and the restrictions of the human mind to contemplate God and to perceive the divine world. In medieval thought, the image is not an illusion but a revelation" (Lee-Niinioja).

At the turn of the last millennium, photographer Jean Miele observed that,

> Certain images circumvent words, to remind us of hidden places deep inside ourselves... They resonate with the frequency of our dreams and our intuition, touching a place we feel just beyond the edge of consciousness. The magic of such pictures is their ability to act as spiritual catalysts, somehow providing us with a glimpse of a barely remembered place, both inside and all around us; A higher plane; A world of ghosts and dreams and unremembered experience. They open our eyes, not by providing a window to the beauty of the world we live in, but by reminding us of an unseen world we intuitively long for, but cannot always find (Miele).

Per

3. FOREWARNING AND VISUALIZATION

It's common to find dire warnings in the front of medieval grimoires and nineteenth-century books on the Western mysteries. The hope was to deter casual readers. They cautioned unprepared or unwitting gawkers to stop reading, lest they incur moral, ethical, or spiritual injury. These warnings aimed to verify the integrity of the reader's intent and maintain the purity of their immortal soul. Responsible seekers were advised to proceed respectfully, with eyes wide open, knowing that what followed contained words powerful enough to cause irreparable damage. Such admonitions often suggested that exposure to the following writings could be likened to using one's bare hands to grasp a fiery lamp or uninsulated live electrical wires.

Considering the reader's well-being, the text (two paragraphs below this one) was written in an intentionally cryptic and challenging manner for the uninitiated to understand. One might compare the writing's enigmatic style to reading the linguistically coded language of critical photographic theory. Derrida, Deleuze, and Lacan share qualities with magicians Geber, Zosimos of Panopolis, and Albertus Magnus. These authors are alike in their coded methods of communicating ideas, assuming that readers possess prior knowledge and experience with the topics.

Like reading critical theorists in photography, valuable insights require effort to uncover.

> For they are a part of wisdom's envelope, to guard her universal magistery from an incapable and dreaming world; calculated they are, nevertheless, though closely sealed, to awaken rational curiosity, and lend a helping hand to those who have already entered on the right road; but to deceive in practice only the most credulous and inept. They who have really understood Geber, his adept compeers, declare with one accord that he has spoken the truth, though disguisedly, with great acuteness and precision: others, therefore, who do not profess to understand, and to whom those writings are a mere unintelligible jargon, may take warning hence, lest they exhibit to posterity a twofold ignorance and vanity of thought." (Atwood, 2012).

After absorbing Atwood's important advisory statement, the following obligatory forewarning begins …

Know this: I, Mercurius, have here set down a full, true and infallible account of the Great Work. But I give you fair warning that unless you seek the true philosophical gold and not the gold of the vulgar, unless your heart is fixed with unbending intent on the true Stone of the Philosophers, unless you are steadfast in your quest, abiding by God's laws in all faith and humility and eschewing all vanity, conceit, falsehood, intemperance, pride, lust and faint-heartedness, read no farther lest I prove fatal to you. For I am the watery venomous serpent who lies buried at the earth's centre; I am the fiery dragon who flies through the air. I am the one thing necessary for the whole Opus. I am the spirit of metals, the fire which does not burn, the water which does not wet the hands. If you find the way to slay me you will find the philosophical mercury of the wise, even the White Stone beloved of the Philosophers. If you find the way to raise me up again, you will find the philosophical sulphur, that is, the Red Stone and Elixir of Life. Obey me and I will be your servant; free me and I will be your friend. Enslave me and I am a dangerous enemy; command me and I will make you mad; give me life and you will die (Harpur, 17).

GK continues where Mercurius leaves off: "If the reader decides to continue, then their spirit may rejoice, for their intuition will not betray them. The road they are journeying is headed towards their true home, their Native Land!" At this point, one can take the next step and

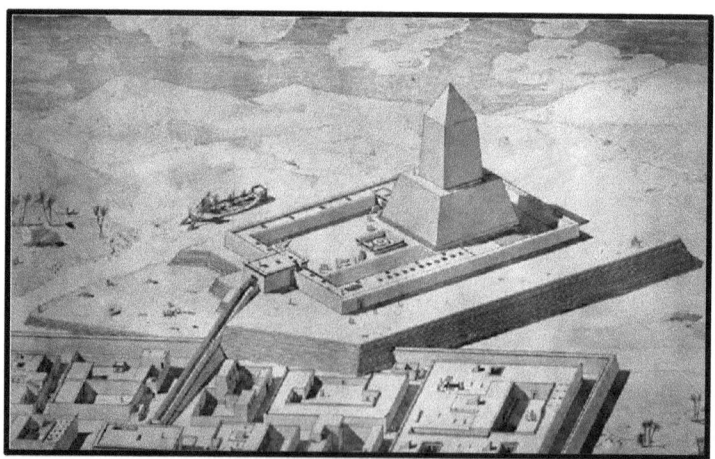

Picture 3.1 Sun Temple at Heliopolis. Ludwig Borchardt, 1905.

visualize themself as an initiate in the *Great Temple of the Sun* in the ancient Egyptian city of *Heliopolis*. The sacred structure is dedicated to the solar-crowned god Ra. With the stage set, imagine,

THUNDER rolled, lightning flashed, the veil of the Temple was rent from top to bottom. The venerable initiator, in his robes of blue and gold, slowly raised his jeweled wand and pointed with it into the darkness revealed by the tearing of the silken curtain: 'Behold the Light of Egypt!' The candidate, in his plain white robe, gazed into the utter blackness framed by the two great Lotus-headed columns between which the veil had hung. As he watched, a luminous haze distributed itself throughout the atmosphere until the air was a mass of shining particles. The face of the neophyte was illumined by the soft glow as he scanned the shimmering cloud for some tangible object. The initiator spoke again: 'This Light which ye behold is the secret luminance of the Mysteries. Whence it comes none knoweth, save the *Master of the Light*. Behold Him!' Suddenly, through the gleaming mist a figure appeared, surrounded by a flickering greenish sheen...The

neophyte stepped back in awe, partly blinded by the glory of the revealed figure. Gaining courage, the youth gazed again at the Divine One. The Form before him was considerably larger than that of a mortal man...As the candidate watched,...The aged initiator, raising his wand, cried out in a loud voice: 'All hail Thee, Thoth Hermes, Thrice Greatest; all hail Thee, Prince of Men; all hail Thee who standeth upon the head of Typhon!'...The next instant, with a blaze of unbearable glory that sent the neophyte staggering backward against a pillar, the immortal Hermes, followed by streamers of greenish mist, passed through the chamber and faded into nothingness (Hall, 37).

Once the Neophyte is initiated into the *Disciplina Arcani* of the Grand Mysteries, the aspirant (reader) can expect to encounter certain disorienting visions. Among them, "miraculous and divine light displays itself, and shining plains, and flowery meadows, open on all hands before them. Here they are entertained with hymns and dances, and with sublime and sacred knowledge, and with reverend and holy visions. And now become reverent and initiated, they are free, and no longer under restraint; but crowned and triumphant, they walk up and down in the regions of the Blessed" (Hurd et al., 278). "If these occurrences do not come to pass immediately following the visualization," GK assures, "there is no need for alarm. The results will soon take form in the midnight hours of the initiate's dreams."

Solem

4. AN AUSPICIOUS CONJUNCTION OF ARTS

At first, I approached GK with a passing sense of curiosity. Later, my interest escalated to a curious fascination! From the start, he had my full attention. Hearing his epic tale of mysticism and magic made me feel like an explorer who had discovered a new world, a realm hidden within the distracting tapestry of the ordinary world. It's there in the umbra, between light and shadow, where the realms of alchemy and photography overlap! GK explained how it was his destiny to be an alchemystical philosopher and an "artificer of photographs." Quoting the words of the late Israel Regardie,

> Despite being born in our age and time, those few individuals who are aware with a certainty in which there is no doubt of a destiny propelling them imperiously forward to the fulfillment of their ideal natures, constitute perhaps the sole exceptions. These, the minority, are born Mystics, the Artists and Poets, those who see beyond the veil and bring back the light of beyond. (Regardie, 2013, p. 23)

Regardie published these words in 1932, before George Kingswood was even born. Yet somehow, they seemed to have foretold GK's future.

I was familiar with all the photographic topics GK spoke about, like depth of field, aperture, silver halide crystals, and the latent image. However, everything he presented came from an unfamiliar vantage point, within the context of alchemy. The terminology of the art carried new meaning, even for words every photographer knows, like "light."

For example, in alchemy, there are various kinds of light. Some of these are undetectable by scientific means, such as the inner, life-giving light that a human being emanates from an unseen source within. I was told that it is the alchemist's goal to polish, or "lustrate any qualities that prevent the Divine, nourishing light from performing at its full expression." One must look deep within to identify and work with those obstructing forces.

At the Temple of Apollo at Delphi, there is an inscription in the pronaos#: "γνῶθι σεαυτόν," which translates to "know thyself." GK says, "It's wise counsel for the alchemist, especially if this advice compels the intention to *act*. The secrets this motto exposes reveal the hidden knowledge needed to transform the essence of one's being." He notes, "the words 'in-tention' and 'a-tention' have the common root of '*tension*,' which indicates the presence of a vibrant, dynamic, and focused energetic state. It is a sensation of expectancy, of anticipation. These two mental forces of *intention* and *attention* are magical catalysts used by the alchemist to conquer the emotional and psychological resistance that prevents them from seeing who and what they really are. When a true aspect of one's self is revealed, one feels a sense of appreciation. The sight of it rings true. Then, the feeling of tension that peaks is transformed into the desire to learn more."

Israel Regardie called *know thyself*

> the supreme injunction giving impetus to [the mystic's] high endeavour. If the creativity of genius followed as a result of the discovery of the innermost self and the tapping of the sources of universal energy, if inspiration by the Muses ensued or a stimulus in the direction of some art or philosophy or lay occupation, so much the better. At the outset of training, however, these Mystics … were completely indifferent to any result other than a spiritual one. Self-knowledge and self-discovery—the word "self" being used in a lofty, noetic and transcendental sense—were the primary objectives. (Regardie, 2013, p. 28)

To achieve results, one internalizes the words of Regardie's "supreme injunction" and takes action to recognize self-aspects, then applies the transformative processes to purify obstructing behaviors. GK mentions,

> Don Juan told Carlos Castaneda how to prepare himself to approach the search for knowledge. He said, "A man goes to knowledge as he goes to war, wide awake, with fear, with respect, and with absolute assurance" [Castaneda, 1968, 19]. One must accept the responsibility and struggle that come with seeing one's own faults. Gaining self-knowledge is worthless without being committed to take the necessary steps to change one's enthroned, impeding patterns. Otherwise, the exalted nature of these erudite words becomes debased, an empty aphorism.

Over one hundred and fifty years prior to GK's comments above, Mary Anne Atwood wrote,

> But Plato more plainly declares that to know oneself is Wisdom and the highest virtue of the soul; for the soul rightly entering into herself will behold all other things, and Deity itself; as verging to her own union and to the center of all life, laying aside multitude and the variety of all manifold powers which she

contains, she ascends to the highest watchtower of beings. (Atwood, 2005, p. 76)

GK explained:

> If one were to envision a triangle pointing upward, representing a triad where the lower left angle symbolizes *photography* and the lower right angle signifies *alchemy*, then two connecting lines converge at the apex, which embodies the phrase, *know thyself.* The zenith, the highest point of a bejeweled arrow, extends out into the cosmos. It is this royal crest that aims toward the shared aspiration of both arts. The lower angles reach upward to support their highest ambition! The alchemist seeks to understand the many attributes that express the singular, original essence. One must be a perscrutinator# of both inner and outer worlds. That self-aware photographer understands that every capture they make should be titled with the admonition, "know thyself." The adage urges the subconscious force of will to act and is, ultimately, what every photograph embodies. Photos conceal hidden, self-revelatory treasures buried in the perceivable and unseen dimensions of their imagery. That golden treasure provides the alchemist and photographer with the foothold they need for a prosperous ascension of "the tenebrous spiral staircase of the self [Steiner, 2013].

The photographs one makes are unique objects that reveal something about how, for an instant, their maker related to the world around them. Whether the pictures are portraits, visual travel journals, or vernacular# photos, they tell a story about the interests, preferences, perceptions, and experiences from that maker's singular phenomenological vantage point. They talk about where one has been and where one has lingered for extended periods. Photos serve not only as evidence of the photographer but also as partial, yet significant descriptions of what they observed. Furthermore, art critic John Berger said,

> Images were first made to conjure up the appearances of something that was absent. Gradually it became evident that an image could outlast what it represented; it then showed how something or somebody had once looked—and thus by implication how the subject had once been seen by other people. Later still the specific vision of the image-maker was also recognized as part of the record. (Berger, 2008, p. 10)

Even more important to the hermetic artist is that photographs also reveal the *synthemata*, or signatures of the universe. Synthemata are the symbolic or literally interpreted clues that reveal mystical knowledge. The idea is that the divine source, having created the "Kosmos,"

> organized it according to the eternal Forms. Thus, the Gods imprint the material kosmos and its objects with synthemata which can reveal these Forms and be used by the soul as a means of unifying itself with divinity. And so by retracing the divine synthemata through the layers of Being, we use them as a way to allow our own souls to be awakened to an awareness of its own divine nature, and hence get in touch with the Gods more directly. (Hellenic Faith, 2020)

To further elaborate, GK said,

> I would argue that a viewer's soul is drawn to a beautifully executed photographic composition not only because it stimulates a sense of pleasure but also because one's soul is intuitively overcome by the presence of the synthemata, embedded by Ra's glance of gleaming intent and expressed by the radiance of all the subject matter within. This also explains why people are compelled to collect photographs; the images communicate in sympathy with the viewer by reflecting back the light of their own divine nature.

GK claims that people instinctively collect photographs, and this is especially true for photographers. Susan Sontag wrote, "To collect photographs is to collect the world … Photographs are perhaps the most mysterious of all the objects that make up, and thicken, the environment we recognize as modern … images do not seem to be statements about the world so much as pieces of it, miniatures of reality that anyone can make or acquire'" (Sontag, 2001, pp. 3–4). Image-makers find inspiration in the ephemera produced by other artists, particularly photographs. Collections are amassed in the form of physical artifacts and digital files, with some imagery simply stored as memories.

The desire to collect and the need to possess get at the core of the photographer's compulsion to take pieces of the scenes around them so they can store them in boxes, albums, stacks, hanging or pinned on walls, and filed away on hard drives. GK adds, "Whilst Leslie Davenport wisely lists *taking* as one of the 'five dark currents of will,' (Davenport, 2016, p. 60) she reminds all alchemist-photographers to take, but also give and share."

The entirety of one's carefully curated collection of photographs is an expression of their creative consciousness. The accumulated contents of their photographs symbolically describe a detailed narrative of one's outer life while also portraying a multitude of facets about their inner life. The messages that photographs communicate are records of one's psychological, emotional, and even unconscious states.

> Art carries different messages, and it is valued for the message, secret or overt, it conveys ... An imagery or object includes not only a symbol or image, but also a dynamic representation of the relationship between object and event. When an object or symbol adequately matches the imagined image stored in the viewer's memory, a graphic association is established, and the related information is intuitively understood. (Edson, 2012, p. 235)

As such, the alchemist-artist carries the full expression of their photographic collection within their creative consciousness, influencing every aspect of the Great Work. In a linear fashion, the imagery traces one's evolution as an ever-changing, increasingly refined being.

"Photographs are self-sufficient, external manifestations of one's inner reality," GK says.

> If we embrace the revelation of Hermes Trismegistus, "as within, so without," then each photograph one creates can be regarded as an alchemical emblem, an image that directly and symbolically reflects the inner qualities of the individual in relation to the external world. Consequently, within the entire anthology of images a photographer produces lies a vital monument, a corpus of material, a sidereal# body made from light in one's own image. It is thus referred to as one's *oeuvre*, or *body of work*, the alternate body of the photographer with its own intelligence. In turn, the collection can be examined in terms of how it influences aspects of the macrocosmic universe.

Abraham Kingswood also said,

> The sparkle of one's creative vision conceives the seeds that gestate as latent images in the particles of silver, suspended in a medium, tucked inside the dark chamber of that ingenious artifice, the camera obscura. During the choreographed printing process, those seeds mature in an environment in which they can

continue to grow and flourish as visual artifacts. Each exposed grain represents a new life that the photographer must nourish in order to draw out the aspects of its vital truth and beauty. When its final aspect emerges from the wetness, fumes, and ruby atmosphere of the darkroom, the print lights up as shining gems, a reflection of the deliberate intention of its creator.

To further deepen the mystery, author Don DeLillo wrote "A photograph is a universe of dots. The grain, the halide, the little silver things clumped in the emulsion. Once you get inside a dot, you gain access to hidden information, you slide into the smallest event. This is what technology does. It peels back the shadows and redeems the dazed and rumbling past. It makes reality come true" (2007, p. 177). Moreover, it is a revelation for those with eyes to see.

As DeLillo pointed out, a print is much more than just a representative document or an interesting object. Photolinguistically, it communicates with the photographer, viewer, and their reality, employing its own language and syntax that are specific to the photographer and the context in which it was created.

What photographers need to understand is the syntax of an image,

> the system of organization used in putting lines together to form pictures that can stand as representations of particular objects" [Crawford, 1979, p. 2], where there is a clear association between the structure of photographic prints and the linguistic structure that makes verbal communication possible. Photographers are the *Keepers of Light* and photography broke the boundaries of the visual field that had been delimited by etchings, prints, and paintings, to allow human beings to see far beyond the physical field of view, to have photographic power over space and time which fundamentally changed the scope of human consciousness. (Marcus Bunyan, 2014)

In the context of alchemy, photography also presented an unrealized opportunity for elevating spiritual consciousness. One of the twentieth century's prophets of photography was Minor White.

> Andy Grundberg, once the chief photography critic at the New York Times, points out: "White was more than just a photographer; he was a moral and critical guru who insisted on a connection between photography and the world's most powerful, universal forces … In today's milieu … there is no longer a moral

figure of unimpeachable authority who stands ready to lead us into the light—nor, indeed, does there seem a need for one. There is no apostle for the creed of photography as spiritual inquiry, no wise man to sing the epiphanies of photographic seeing. (Andy Grundberg)

Clearly, Grundberg was unaware of GK, who admired White because he "used teaching techniques … to help photographers achieve a state of heightened awareness, or a more open and receptive state of being—both behind the camera and while looking at photographs" (*Minor White Archive*, 2022).

From the end of White's life until now, there remains a belief that traditional methods of photography somehow limit its scope as a sacerdotal art and that it lacks the capacity to serve as part of one's spiritual path. This idea formed well before the invention of photography when it was a widely held belief that "Art is not sacred by virtue of its quality but of its content" (Dowman, 1997, p. 90). From this perspective, only an artwork's content can communicate with one's spiritual consciousness, thereby eliciting a spiritual response.

In the Kingswoods' mystical practices, photographs emerged as sacred artworks the moment — or even before — the shutter was released. This occurs because their photographs were produced within a sacred context, conceived from the focused magical intention of the maker. While the content of the photographs has always influenced their elevation to spiritual objects, the Kingswoods' images and their products have always been regarded as sacred even before the conception of their content. Photographs initially served to raise the consciousness of their creators, and eventually that of their human subjects and viewers.

In the context of GK's alchemy, part of the practitioner's method involves separating the essence from the substance. The substance of a photograph includes wood fibers, plastic, and gelatin-silver-infused emulsion. On its surface, a pattern of lights, darks, and/or colors appears. The substance of the photograph may also encompass the camera, the lens, and the film. These elements represent the trappings, concepts, and equipage# of photography.

The *essence* of a photograph can be found by examining three fundamental components: the photographer's intention, their sense of sight, and light energy. All of these can be understood as essences of the photograph. However, if one further distills the list to the single most important essence, it becomes clear that it is the sense of sight. Without sight, the image-maker's intention can't be realized. It can't move from the inspired mind, through the camera, and out into the world. Nor can the light received by the eye of the photographer be comprehended; it can't even be known. Without sight, light cannot be used as the medium of the photographer's art. Light cannot be perceived as it flows from the mind, through the eye, to the scene, and back again through the eye. Thus, seeing is the essence of the photograph and photography.

Studying this act of seeing is what Richard Zakia calls "eyenology" (knowledge of the visual process—seeing) (Zakia & Peres, 2007). GK, looking ever more deeply into photography, believes "It is this essence, *Sight* that can not only descry# knowledge, but recognize it as an experience. And when combined with curiosity, Sight (with a capital S) can reveal, investigate, and examine that treasured knowledge of the self, leading the extraordinary photographer to look, with intention, beyond the self and into the mysteries of Sight's source." William J. Nieberding ties Sight to *phenomenology*, which he defines as "an inquiry into the relationship between human perception and questions of being. As such, it offers a powerful set of tools for reconsidering what sight means to us as human beings. By extension it also offers unique insights into technologies of vision and their relationship to human being and human knowing" (Nieberding, 2011).

Photographer Jeff Bernat refers to this capacity as "second sight" and describes the experience of gaining self-knowledge while being in harmony with nature. He said, "After probing appearances and deepening vision through the 'second sight' of photography, the photographer emerges as one in whom experience is a perpetual communion, with or without lens" (quoted in Chang, 1970, 124). GK adds: "The photographer who heeds the advice 'know thyself' could find that, far beyond navel gazing and self-help platitudes, it can lead one through the constricting portal (aperture) of the microcosm, only to open up and lead out to the infinite expanse of the divine macrocosmos."

For educated photographers, the concepts of self-observation, magic, and alchemy are likely unconsidered and therefore undiscovered foreign shores. Author Donald Michael Kraig said:

> the study of magic and alchemy should be at the forefront of the investigations of all educated persons. And yet, quite obviously, they are not. In the world of knowledge, magic and alchemy usually remain overlooked and ignored, discarded and hidden like a polyester "leisure suit" we are too embarrassed to admit that we ever purchased and would be even more embarrassed to admit

that we wore. We are, after all, far too enlightened to have ever believed in anything so quaint and crackpot. Certainly today only the uneducated, the gullible, and the cranks would ever waste their time studying such foolishness. Magic? Alchemy? Don't make me laugh … most of our knowledge of magic and alchemy are not derived from a study of mages and alchemists themselves but from those who would denounce them or use them as little more than a "plot point" in a novel or film. Curiously, rather than thinking that these interpretations of the subjects are "just a fiction and not true," we accept the myths and misunderstandings as valid representations. If Magic and alchemy were individuals, they could sue in court for libel and slander. (Guiley, 2006)

Similarly, Israel Regardie clarifies that the realm of magic is not what most believe it to be. He asserts,

Magic is not that popularly conceived practice which is the child of hallucination begotten by savage ignorance, and which panders to the lusts of a depraved mankind. Because of the ignorant duplicity of charlatans and the reticence of its own scribes and authorities, Magic for centuries has been unduly confused with Witchcraft and Demonolatry … But if any man is anxious to discover the eternal font wherefrom the flame of Godhead springs, should there be one who is desirous of awakening in himself a more noble and lofty consciousness of the spirit, and within whose heart burns the aspiration to dedicate his life to the service of mankind, let such a one turn eagerly to Magic. In its technique, peradventure may be found the means to the fulfillment of the loftiest dreams of the soul. (Regardie, 2013)

GK responds,

Readers may cry, "Oh, your self-centered ego!" based on the apparent selfishness of someone who works tirelessly for their own soul's profit while seeming to lack compassion and doing nothing to enhance the better qualities of all humanity. I say to them that, while cloaked away in the sanctum of the darkroom, the work that the alchemist does in their microcosmos produces, through sympathetic bonds, immeasurable ripples that benefit others across the macrocosm. These ripples, which follow the trajectory set by the principle of *as above, so below*, present opportunities for those within this world and others beyond these chambers to open their eyes, exercise their sense of sight, and engage their subtler *Sight* to take notice and redirect their intentions toward a higher purpose.

GK lives a solitary life, immersed in the Great Work, while others who follow a similar path engage with people in the world. They have families, jobs, and for all intents and purposes, appear to be just like everyone else. "Choosing to be in the world as a context for the Great Work," explained GK, "is a journey where everything in one's conventional life becomes part of their laboratory." Timothy Hogan, Grand Master of the Knights Templar, offered basic yet profound advice to those spiritual practitioners who choose to do their work in a world among people when he said,

> Don't speak to me of the esoteric unless you are living a responsible and accountable life. Don't speak to me of it if you spend your time trashing your fellow seekers. Don't speak to me of it if you are unwilling to perform the least acts of charity. The greatest mysteries are first born in the heart, and if you are out of touch with that, then you are missing the point. Light is born from promoting life and love, and in standing for freedom, and if you can't even live a life that shows respect to such things, then I'm sorry to inform you that you don't know the first thing about the mysteries ... You are merely a parrot, repeating what sounds good to boost your ego. The greatest mysteries are taught with love, and they need not make noise. (Hogan, 2022)

GK explains:

> In this way, the alchemist seeks to pay a significant debt to the mysterium tremendum by working diligently to disrupt the self-created, egoic equilibrium in which it is comfortable to remain blind—leaving few who can See. The actions of the Hermetic artist aim to lift and strengthen the collective resolve of humanity to fulfill their spiritual potential, whether it is by reading a grimoire on high magic, joining a religious group, expressing love, acting charitably, or learning from a teacher who has climbed the steps of the Great Pyramid and gone beyond the golden crowned peak. These are some of the aspirations of the alchemist-photographer: to seek those causes and results that most never look for, and thus never see.

5. A Philosopher's Lexicon

The words one chooses are important. For an alchemist, words have the power to change the course of events, summon helping spirits, and initiate transformative processes. However, they can also be dangerous. Words can inflict harm and create confusion. In this book, language is used to translate and explain concepts that may be unfamiliar to the reader. GK maintains that,

> Artful translation serves as a catalyst for transformation, particularly when discussing the arcane mysteries of both alchemy and art. The challenge lies in conveying experiential processes by interpreting ideas through a blend of spoken and written words. Whether addressing the production of *elixir vite* or describing the contents of a photograph, language must be handled with care to re-embody the subject matter in a way that evokes emotions and mental pictures in the receiver's mind. The recipient must then transform that content into a re-imagining of the work.

With all imaginative works, the act of transformation is inherent to the very process of artistic creation: the original concept is conceived by the artist, moves toward the viewer, and is represented to the viewer. At that point, the viewer finds meaning in what they experience by transforming it again into their own understanding (Beaumont). One key that can help unlock that understanding is to clarify any exotic terminology the reader may encounter.

Alchemist
In this text, the words "alchemyst," "alchemist," "hermeticist," "hermetic artist," "thaumaturgist," "alchemystical philosopher," "magus," and "magician" are all used synonymously to refer to a person who follows the ancient Egyptian practices and mystical teachings of the legendary mystic Hermes Mercurius Trismegistus, also known as Hermes Thrice-Blessed and the Lord of Pautnouphis. He was purported to have written hundreds of books on various subjects, including alchemy.
Unfortunately, many of his manuscripts were destroyed in Egypt when the Great Library of Alexandria burned in 48 BCE. Those that survived were collected and treasured by alchemists around the world.

Alchemy
Today's widespread use of the term *alchemy* leads readers far astray from its authentic meaning, as seen in book titles like *Financial*

Alchemy, The Alchemy of DCO Credit Ratings, and *The Alchemy of Race and Rights*. As Hugh Aldersey-Williams points out in *American Alchemy: The History of Solid Waste Management in the United States* (Aldersey-William, 21), the word is also popular in photography. When used metaphorically, it evokes the idea of a mystical, transmutational process that can transform something ordinary into something priceless, similar to lead turning into gold. This word choice aims to suggest a sense of mystique, highlighting the transcendent qualities of the art and its ability to alter perception. Unfortunately, the term's common use aims "to strip it of its motivations, intentions, and its power" (Wamberg & Dahlberg, 93).

Experimental art, such as Dadaism and Surrealist photomontages, has been labeled as alchemy. However, their unconventional and even mystical approaches do not automatically qualify them for this title. Nevertheless, there have been artists like Remedios Varo (1908-1963), who sought through her work the highest aspirations of spiritually transformative and evolutionary processes. Scholar of art and religion Noah Lyons wrote that Varo's

> precise, ordered style of composition is employed to illuminate deeply complex and mystical symbolism. Varo broke away from the Surrealist movement and created a corpus of mystical and alchemical art that stresses a personal, inner quest for spiritual truth over hierarchal dogmatic truth...She attempted to weave (or transmutate through distillations, to use alchemical terminology,) magic, the spiritual self, and a vision of a divine cosmos to reach transcendence as Woman and Artist through the creative act (Lyons, 2012, 1).

It was once claimed that the photographer, "Man Ray is a youthful alchemist forever in quest of the painter's philosopher's stone. May he never find it, as that would bring an end to his experimentations which are the very condition of living art expression" (Man Ray Tribute). Surrealist photomonteur Jerry Uelsmann has been called an alchemist and a "darkroom conjurer" (FlaglerLive). He once said, "Let us not delude ourselves by the seemingly scientific nature of the darkroom ritual; it has been and always will be a form of alchemy. Our overly precious attitude toward that ritual has tended to conceal from us an innermost world of mystery, enigma, and insight" (Let Us Not Delude Ourselves by the Seemingly Scien: Photoquotes). Uelsmann went on to claim that, "The entire photographic process is a metamorphosis. The artist can invent a reality which is personally more meaningful than the one literally given to the eye" (Uelsmann, 54). Yet, the word *alchemy* is used very differently in this book. Here, its narrative points to a realm of mysticism that reaches far beyond ordinary darkroom techniques or its familiar transformative processes.

In these pages, one will discover that alchemy is much more than just an allusion to something else, a term added to enhance a thing's sense of mystique. Although the realm of alchemy facilitates the use of analogical and metaphoric forces, when the word is read here, it isn't intended as a metaphor. It is a real, vital transformative philosophy—a tangible, functional, self-reflexive spiritual practice. GK offers readers the chance to learn about authentic alchemy in the context of photography, as he pulls back the shielding veil to reveal ancient Egyptian practices aimed at generating the energy needed for self-evolution—the art of transforming and transmuting one's being into a state of golden perfection.

Elements
It would be helpful for the reader to know that alchemy and photography share some terminology, such as the word 'elements.' In alchemy, elements refer to earth, water, fire, and air. In the context of photography, it can refer to any of the elements of design, including line, shape, form, texture, color, size, and depth. It can also refer to the elements of merit: impact, technical excellence, creativity, style, composition, presentation, color balance, center of interest, lighting, subject matter, technique, and storytelling (12 Elements of a Merit Image: Professional Photographers of America). Lastly, when used in a specific context, elements could point to the whole or part of a collection of individual components within a photographic composition, i.e., elements in the composition. I intend to provide enough context around the usage of the word to avoid confusion.

Gender
The pronouns *he* and *him* appear in many quotes throughout this text, most of which were written during or before the nineteenth century, when their usage was understood as all-inclusive pronouns. Additionally, the words *"man"* and *"men"* are used as general terms, commonly associated with the concept of "mankind." In vintage texts, feminine pronouns were linked with the *soul* or *spirit*. I have not modified or added to the original pronouns to preserve their historical accuracy.

Intention
Intention is a dynamic term used to describe the impulse that initiates all magical activities. Two words associated with intention are *clarity* and *will*. In magical work, clarity of one's intention is crucial for several

reasons. First, it helps individuals define what they aim to accomplish when using magic. Additionally, it outlines the outcomes they expect to achieve. Third, clarity helps delineate how energies carrying the intention will flow, including their strength and speed. It also establishes the specific direction of that energetic flow. *Will* is the driving force behind one's intention.

Psychologist Leslie Davenport presents two distinct perspectives on the use of one's will. Davenport also reflects on some fundamentally different intentions within alchemical magic. He writes, "Spiritual life doesn't follow the rules and regulations of ordinary society whose primary values are the freedom-restrictive functions and applications of will: to take; to keep; to hold onto; to advance at the expense of others; to be great (a function of vanity). These 'five dark currents of will' fulfill the desires of the individual with no consideration for the welfare and freedom of others. Spiritual life, on the other hand, reverses the way we use our will. Instead, we utilize our 'light currents of will' to give, share, renounce, mentor, and be humble. Here we are self-directed from within, independent of external authorities (Davenport, 60).

Magic

A word frequently used in this book is "magic." Its usage affirms its connection to the ancient Persian root, *magush*, which referred to one of the highest classes of pre-Christian era priests. These ancient priests were the holders and protectors of arcane knowledge concerning esoteric magical incantations, spells, and rituals. GK defines high magic as, "The performance of the hieratic# art of ritual, with the aid of one's allies to influence the course of events using unseen, mysterious, yet knowable forces. As with today's alchemists and other users of magical arts, they can apply the same knowledge to effect changes in the normal course of telluric# events and, more importantly, within the core-spirit aspects of oneself."

Mystery

Photographer and Zen Roshi, John Daido Loori, explained the meaning of the word *"mystery"* as it is most commonly used by mystics, alchemists, and spiritual seekers. He said,

> In religion and art, mystery is light itself. It's the lifeblood that pumps through true religious and artistic practice...the driving force of spiritual and creative journeys...It invites us to peek around the next corner, into the darkness...Mystery is the seed of discovery. The term 'mystical' means: 'Having a spiritual meaning that is neither apparent to the senses nor obvious to the

intellect. It is direct subjective communication with ultimate reality.' It's the kind of communication we can't process intellectually. We can't see it, hear it, smell it, taste it, touch it, or think it. It is very subtle and slippery, impossible to nail down or explain. Yet, we're somehow aware of its presence, and it has a real impact on us (Loori, 192).

Sight

Sight, with a capital "S," is a mystical ability. It's an extrasensory faculty that allows the alchemist to see what remains typically unfound by the naked eye, especially regarding that which is occulted. GK clarifies, "One would be wrong to dismiss this sense as pareidolia#. It is a specific phenomenon of *visuality* that focuses on an expanded level of awareness. It penetrates the surface appearances of things to perceive the true essence of phenomena." Monk and photographer Thomas Merton once wrote, while photographing in Asia, "I don't know what else remains...but I have now seen and have pierced through the surface and have got beyond the shadow and disguise" (Duggan). Furthermore, Merton said photography was, "[r]eminding me of things I have overlooked, and cooperating in the creation of new worlds."

This sense is made possible through the *Eye of Sight*, which is important for both self-observation (insight) and the discovery of Divine Knowledge (revelation). Furthermore, this capacity for Sight provides the alchemist with the intuitive intelligence required to interpret the knowledge needed to proceed in the Great Work. GK claims that,

> Acquiring Sight is like expanding one's angle of view by changing a camera's lens from a well-used, 60-year-old 28mm to a sharp, new, technically advanced, distortion-free 135mm. A new lens can help the alchemist see by zooming in and refining their perception. There is so much outside the range of human vision; simultaneously, there are limitations when trying to reach understandings grounded solely in logic.

Spell

Many cultural associations are linked to this word, so it would be beneficial to examine how the word acquired its current meaning. The etymology of the word *spell* traces back to the Old English word, *spel*, which meant "story." It also comes from the Old English "spellian," meaning "to speak or declare." The word appeared in the late 16th century and almost immediately began to be used in a figurative sense to mean 'enthralling interest or charm' ('The ordinary devices by which the novelist keeps us under his spell,' 1856)" (Spell). An example of its use can be found in the word "gospel," which means, "god's story."

The alchemical use of the word perfectly aligns with its English etymology, which posits that a spell is a story. However, the entire narrative of a spell isn't contained solely in its "words of power," but in its emergence, the ritual for its casting, all the beings involved as characters, its purpose (plot), and the desired conclusion. Spells are designed to be spoken with intention, driven by the desire to produce a specific outcome. They can be spoken for various reasons, such as invoking or evoking a supernatural being, heightening one's level of perception, enhancing one's skills and abilities, or protecting the speaker. These marvelous words do not enable the storyteller to launch fireballs, become invisible, or transmute lead into gold. The Kyblion reminds us that one should be prepared for works of magic to "offer neither thrills nor unfair advantages over anyone. No wonderful visions, exalted experiences, incredible personal powers, sensational successes with sex and finance" (Gray, 1970, 108). "But what it can offer," says GK, "is of much more benefit than any of those unimaginative desires."

Spirit
The *Three Initiates* and Atkinson (2010) identify spirit as,

> "Living Power"; "Animated Force"; "Inner Essence"; "Essence of Life," etc., which meaning must not be confounded with that usually and commonly employed in connection with the term, i. e., "religious; ecclesiastical; spirituelle; ethereal; holy," etc., etc. To occultists the word "Spirit" is used in the sense of "The Animating Principle," carrying with it the idea of Power, Living Energy, Mystic Force, etc (Atkinson, 66).

The word is sometimes synonymous with the word "soul". A spirit may also be a metaphysically phototrophic# entity corresponding to a ghost or specter.

Transformation vs. Transmutation
Two terms important in alchemy are *transformation* and *transmutation*. When a piece of exposed photographic paper enters the developer tray in the darkroom, it undergoes a *transformation*, changing from a sheet of gelatin-coated wood pulp (paper) into a photograph. At the same time, if one could extract the essence of that image, which is silver, and convert that metal into gold, that process is referred to as *transmutation*. The silver undergoes a transformation that alters its very nature, completely changing it into something else.

Unfamiliar Words

In this book, the reader may find words they aren't familiar with. Some of these terms and their definitions are hard to find in dictionary searches. These words, as noted in GK, have been commonly used in his family for generations. Terms like "photogenisis", "writual", or "Lingua Penumbra" appear in the private journals and alchemical books written by GK's Victorian progenitor, Abraham Kingswood.

Some of the unfamiliar words I could easily find online. For instance, when I first heard the word, "chrysopoetically," I looked it up and found that it relates to "Chrysopoeia," the alchemical production of gold. Whenever GK or Abraham Kinswood used a word I didn't know, I reached for my phone and looked it up. Each time I saw a definition, I felt like I had discovered a treasure! I advise thinking of each unfamiliar word as a hidden clue that leads to a larger understanding. Discovering new words is an experience I hope readers will enjoy as much as I have.

Hashtags

Hashtags indicate that a definition has been provided for a word at the website www.photoalchemybook.com under the *Glossary* tab.

The Pictorial Lexicon

Some pictures in this book support the text by providing visual illustrations. Others are used less unconventionally. They are intended to offer an expanded understanding of the text. Those images don't illustrate what has been said. Instead, they are allegorical stories, created to communicate additional information through a visual language.

For example, this first section of the book, *Secrets of the Arts of Fire AND Operations of the Sun,* begins with a picture. The image chronicles the history of alchemy up to when Abraham Kingswood used fire to synthesize a new lineage of alchemy, which compelled both the disciplines of alchemy and photography to evolve. GK points out, "Allegorical images have always been important to alchemists. Any genuine alchemist would delight in an opportunity to learn from the penetrating narrative in such a picture".

Lunem

6. FOUR GENERATIONS OF KINGSWOOD ADEPTS

In the 1880s, Abraham Kingswood was entering his twenties when a confluence of three cultural developments captured the attention of curious British citizens. These included the rise of photography in the social-visual lexicon, fascination with the exotic allure of ancient Egypt, and the flourishing of arcane secret societies as part of an "Occult Revival." GK notes that

> From my great-grandfather's accounts, the synchronicity of these compelling phenomena seemed to converge into a singular circumstance. In his mind, when these three vectors of intrigue were combined, it opened a window of opportunity that was too advantageous to ignore. Consequently, the Victorian zeitgeist served as the driving force behind Abraham's intention and purpose for life in the Great Work. He believed that by integrating photography with his prosperous studies of occultism and ancient Egyptian magic, the entirety of his being, including his immortal soul, could evolve.

Due to Kingswood's epiphany, he set out to explore the photography archive. He felt compelled to learn more about the historical transition from alchemy to the discovery of photography. He believed there was a thread of continuity that began in antiquity, was carried forward through Egyptian magic, continued into alchemy, and evolved before his eyes in the form of images created by light. "These mirror-like pictures," he wrote, "are signatures shaped by none other than the right hand of the highest god-form of light, Ra."

In 1822, forty-four years before Kingswood was born, French photographer Nicéphore Niépce invented a photographic process he named *Heliography* (after Helios, the Greek god of the sun). In 1826, he made the first fixed photograph from his window at Le Gras.

> At the base of the invention of analog photography there is a reaction of a silver salt to the sun rays; specifically, the blackening effects of light upon certain substances, mainly silver, on which it acts as a decomposing power. In his book 'Alchimie, antique science of demain', 1999, Loïc Tréhédel starts from the axiom that sunlight contains pure *Spiritus Mundi*, which only has [to] be collected. The concept of 'catching' photons, and with photons the Spiritus Mundi/Secret Fire from the Sunlight, is what is commonly known as "solar Alchemy" (Millesima).

While Niépce was deeply immersed in refining his image-making techniques, he died unexpectedly in 1833. His friend, artist Louis Daguerre, stepped in to continue this important work. In 1839, Daguerre used light to breathe life into a silver-coated copper plate, creating a magical mirror that captured, stabilized, and fixed the scene reflecting on its surface. In moments, an ephemeral impression of light transformed into an object of wonder! The French inventor called his creations *Daguerreotypes,* crafted from a process that flourished in the sun's actinic# light. "The beauty of the daguerreotype was that [it] embodied … the magical content of high illusionism, the beauty of an utter realism so uncompromising that it seems to exceed in its descriptive detail even that which the unassisted eye could possibly take in."
(Scharf, 11).

After the public announcement of his invention, Daguerre received a lifetime pension in exchange for the rights to his photographic method. Only on August 19, 1839, was the revolutionary process explained step by step before a joint session of the *Académie des Sciences* and the *Académie des Beaux-Arts*, with an eager crowd of spectators spilling over into the courtyard outside (Daniel, 2004a). His process consisted of five stages, along with an optional toning step at the end. The first five stages included:

1. Plate Preparation: a polished copper sheet is plated with silver…then polished to a very high gloss.

2. Sensitization: the plate is placed in an iodizing box and exposed to iodine vapour until all the surface silver has been converted to silver iodide, turning the plate orange. This is the light-sensitive coating.

3. Exposure: The plate is loaded into a camera, and an exposure made simply by removing the lens cap. Exposures in early cameras could be over twenty minutes, even in bright daylight!

4. Development: the plates, kept in the dark, are suspended over a bath of mercury, which is heated to 60°C (140°F); mercury vapour forms an amalgam with the exposed silver iodide.

5. Fixing: unexposed silver iodide, not amalgamated with mercury, is washed off the plate using a salt (sodium chloride) solution (later replaced by weak sodium thiosulphate solution). [Optional] Toning: In 1840, French physicist Hippolyte Fizeau (1819 – 1896) discovered that a heated gold chloride solution could both reduce the fragility and improve the tone of the image (Daguerreotype Process)..

a. Camera obscura

b. Silver plate

cc. Iodine and Bromide Boxes

d. Improved Mercury Cabinet with sliding legs

ee. Plate holders with clamps

f. Box for Plates

g. Levelling stand

h. Flat peculiar dish for washing

i. Hand-buff

Picture 6.1 Turn of the Century Developing Equipment, Frédéric Dillaye, 1907.

With a keen understanding of Daguerre's photographic process, critical theory writer Jean Lauzon identified remarkable connections.

between the vocabulary and the activities of this experience with the alchemical manipulations. First silver, the passive principle associated with the moon, receives the light, that is to say gold, this active principle associated with the sun, so that a beginning of work can operate. The need to tint the metal in golden yellow then: 'one of the terms which (...) was going to take on hermetic meanings, namely 'dyeing' (Eco, 1992, 87). Thirdly, quicksilver, the vapors of which gently reveal the image: it is a 'universal alchemical symbol' (Chevalier and Gheerbrant, 1982, 642). 'The Universal Mother, Mercury (here its vapours) presents herself as their child, the Mediator' (1982, 642). In fact, it is the quicksilver that makes the image appear, a mediation between the virtual and the actual, it is the quicksilver that acts as a photographic developer. It is also Hermes, the messenger of the gods. It is essentially a 'principle of connection, exchange, movement and adaptation' (1982, 642). Dualistic in nature, the mediator/revealer brings together contrary and complementary principles, light (sun) and shadow (dark room=cucurbit=uterus=birth), masculine and feminine, and therefore: life. And mercury, along with sulfur and salt, is one of the three fundamental alchemical principles (Van Lennep, 1979, 295). After the vapors of quicksilver, the plate is soaked in a solution of hyposulphite of soda: here is sulphur, also one of the three active principles of ancient chemistry, considered as a condensation of the matter of fire

(Dictionnaire Le Petit Robert, 1979, 1842). Hyposulphite being a compound term of 'hypo', being this idea of a small amount of oxygen, and 'sulphite', being the old chemical name for the salts of thiosulphuric acid, "thio" being sulfur and 'sulphuric' referring to that which contains or relates to sulfur on the one hand, and as being of the order of a corrosive oxidant on the other hand; 'sulfite' being also the salt of sulfurous acid" (Lauzon, 2000).

Around the same time as Daguerre's discovery, William Henry Fox Talbot, whose interests included philosophy, art history, and Egyptology, was refining his own image-making processes with his *camera lucida*. With a tone of nostalgia, GK reminds,

> Pride of England, Mister Talbot aspired to earn a living as a master artist. He succeeded with his photographic experiments when he invented the 'calotype' process, which used paper photosensitized with a coating of silver iodide. A current of light reflected from a scene and streamed into a camera through a lens' portal. The projection then fell upon the sensitized paper. As a result, the union of light and silver was achieved, and in that moment of *photogenesis*, the latent image (an image that remains invisible unless it is developed by a chemical process) was conceived.

Picture 6.2 Photographer, Frédéric Dillaye,1907.

Talbot wrote, "The inimitable beauty of the pictures of nature's painting which the glass lens of the Camera throws upon the paper in its focus— fairy pictures, creations of a moment, and destined as rapidly to fade away…how charming it would be if it were possible to cause these natural images to imprint themselves durably, and remain fixed upon the paper" (Daniel).

In a personal journal, Kingswood reported on Europe's heightened sense of anticipation, knowing that once the goal of image-making was achieved, the world would never be the same. He also expressed that there was fear. All these mysterious, clandestine experiments were taking place across Europe, out of sight of the public eye, and whispers of sorcery and demonic pacts circulated. "While nineteenth-century writers did frequently associate photography with magic, the occult, and even necromancy, they made a distinction between these 'black arts' and alchemy, which they usually declined to invoke as the new medium's proper ancestor" (Wamberg, 84).

When announcements were made about the first photographic discoveries, some members of the public responded with suspicion. Questions arose regarding the connections between ritual magic and photography. It was a time when people still shared stories about the old alchemists, keeping the memories of thaumaturgy# alive in the minds of English citizens. Simultaneously, notions of alchemy became associated with terms like quackery, charlatanry, and idiocy. Inventors felt anxious about their new technologies being linked to deceit or occult references.

Despite widespread distrust, the mid-1800s witnessed alchemy's 'second revival' among certain groups of spiritually curious individuals. Interest in *Spiritual Alchemy* surfaced as a new esoteric path. Much to the displeasure of photography's pioneers, elements of mysticism, alchemy, and occultism began to influence some of the era's most popular pursuits, such as photography.

Some promoted photography's potential to capture likenesses of supernatural beings. James Coates' book from 1911, *Photographing the Invisible*, begins by saying that, "I view photography as applied to the visible, the material visible, and the immaterial invisible or the psychic (1911, 1). Furthermore, some believed photography could play a critical role in the soul's journey as it shed the physical body and sought its way to an eternal resting place. British society became very excited about the possibility that photography could become an integral tool in producing fixed images of departed, disembodied spirits.

As the public began discussing the benefits of Talbot's success, it seemed that no one in England was more excited than Abraham Kingswood's father. Kingswood Sr. was one of the few historical scholars of alchemy who recognized the creation of images as the next era in the history of alchemy. Bringing a significant degree of practical experience in the ancient art, he joined a group that included novelist Nathaniel Hawthorne, who shared an intellectual curiosity about the transformative potential of the camera. Both Kingswood and Hawthorne viewed the radically new image-making marvel as a technology of the self, a sacred mechanism with a creative power few could recognize or even imagine.

Kingwood wrote down a quote by French philosopher René Descartes on paper that was more than 200 years old at the time. It reads, "All the management of our lives depends on the senses, and since that of sight is the most comprehensive and the noblest of these, there is no doubt that the inventions which serve to augment its power are among the most useful that there can be" (Descartes and Olscamp, 1965, 65). Descartes could never have dreamed that the invention of the camera would allow alchemists to enhance their ability to perceive beyond just seeing the world in new ways, enabling them to perceive other luminous, yet invisible worlds beyond!

As photography, dubbed "phototechny" or "photogeny" by 19th century alchemists, grew from its infancy, it

> was integrated in a wide variety of discourses and practices that located it in various domains of science, art, and popular culture. As a 'pencil of nature' or as a 'message sans code', photography entered into an alliance with the state and sciences and served the production of documents and evidence, i.e., purposes of objectification and the search for truth. Likewise, the new media opened up new fields of visibility: at fairs and in certain spiritualist circles it was used to produce illusions, wonders, and 'materializations' of spirits, thoughts, and various fluids. Thus,...photography contributed substantially to the emergence of a modern, positivistic 'culture of realism', at the same time strengthening the latter's shadow side, the fantastic. As a rational, technological medium of evidence of a more or less natural, automatic self-inscribing, it also produced 'shadow images' that gave ghosts, phantoms, and all kinds of invisible energies and fluid images and that brought back the dead" (Benjamin). As Walter Benjamin remarked, the most exact technique of reproduction can give its product a magic value. In certain contexts, the camera and photographic images turn into magical objects that gain agency: they turn into fetishes (Behrend, 2003, 129-45).

One must consider that in the early to mid-1800s, about half of England's population was illiterate. Because of this, "our predominantly holistic worldview, low literacy rates, and strong reliance on oral traditions all served to place imagery at the center of healing, spirituality, and the predominant social mindset" (Davenport, 32-33). Pictures remained the dominant form of communication in both secular and religious life. In this context, photographic images became an effective medium for conveying meaning and helping people understand the world they lived in. As a new addition to the age-old artisanal lexicon of woodcuts, engravings, drawings, and paintings, photographic imagery became, "part of the dominant worldview essential for understanding and interacting with this world and the next" (2016, 34).

Unlike today's understanding of photographs, many Victorian viewers understood them as possessing an air of mystery. At the same time, they believed any magical attributes existed solely in the viewer's imagination. While the physical photo-objects were often seen as nothing more than keepsakes, entertaining tokens, genealogical artifacts, or evidential documents, some individuals sensed photography's potential metaphysical qualities. GK noted,

> It was the alchemists who challenged popular conclusions about photography by recognizing that photographs established unseen connections with their subject matter, and thus were emanations; that the latent image corresponded to the hidden potential of the pure essence of the inner spirit and how, only through an alchemical process, its imperfections could be transformed so that the spirit could regain the qualities of its true divine form.

As Roland Barthes put it, "The photograph is literally a referent's emanation. Of a real body, which was there, there came *radiations* which come to touch me, to myself, who is here" (Barthes, 161). With this recognition of the photograph's "radiations" and correspondences, alchemists tapped into images for their magical properties, applying them in spells and ritual invocations. Kingswood also noted that, like alchemy, tin, copper, mercury, and silver were all essential components of the early photographic processes. Eventually, gold, the element embodying the highest level of spiritual accomplishment, was also used. Workers of magic began to view the photograph as "an inanimate object worshiped for its supposed magical powers" (*Define Fetish*).

Historian Tom Gunning postulated

... if photography emerged as the material support for a new
positivism, it was also experienced as an uncanny phenomenon,
one which seemed to undermine the unique identity of objects
and people, endlessly reproducing the appearances of objects,
creating a parallel world of fantastic doubles alongside the
concrete world of the senses verified by positivism. While the
process of photography could be thoroughly explained by
chemical and physical operations, the cultural reception of the
process frequently associated it with the occult and supernatural"
(Gunning, 1995, 42-43).

In other words, some believers felt that the image conveyed deeper
meaning beyond what its physical appearance could express.

French photographer Félix Nadar (Gaspard-Félix Tournachon)
emphasized the belief that photography possessed a sense of arcane
mystery. Additionally, he highlighted the air of the occult surrounding
photography in his book, *When I Was a Photographer*. He wrote,
"Niepce and his fine accomplice [Daguerre] were wise to have waited to
be born. The Church always has shown itself to be more than cold
toward innovators—when it was not rather warm toward them—, and the
discovery of 1842 [photography] seemed mostly suspect. This mystery
smelled devilishly like a spell and reeked of heresy: the celestial
rotisserie had been heated up for less. Nothing was lacking for the affair
to be disquieting: hydroscopy, bewitchment, evocations, apparitions.
Night—dear to all thaumaturges—reigned alone in the somber recesses
of the darkroom, the preferred place by all indication of the Prince of
Darkness. Scarcely anything was needed to make philters# from our
filters" (Nadar et al, 2).

Nadar's views were, as it turns out, based on historical fact. In his
doctoral thesis, James Downs' research uncovered,

> In 1839 David Brewster referred to Talbot's photogenic drawings
> as "specimens of the black art" and the correspondence between
> these two men and Sir John Herschel is strewn with phrases such
> as "natural magic", "magic pictures," and "modern necromancy"
> (Smith, 1990, 27). Within two decades photography was no
> longer the preserve of gentlemen amateurs, but instead provided a
> livelihood for thousands of commercial practitioners whose
> business was satirized by an anonymous writer in Chambers
> Journal under the title of "The Modern Priests and Temples of the
> Sun." Beginning with a reference to the 1851 religious census,
> the writer describes the progress of the "religious denomination"

of the "Sun-worshippers" – "how surprisingly has this sect increased during the last ten years! There is scarcely a street in London which does not contain at least one Temple of the Sun" – using phrases such as "the pontiffs of these numerous temples…the glance of the sungod (The Modern Priests and Temples of the Sun, as cited in Downs, 13-14).

Whether influenced by occult forces or not, no one can deny the timeless dominion of photographs and their power to enchant and control the human psyche and emotions. Art historian David Freedberg affirms in his book, *The Power of Images*, that

> People are sexually aroused by pictures and sculptures; they break pictures and sculptures; they mutilate them, kiss them, cry before them, and go on journeys to them; they are calmed by them, stirred by them, and incited to revolt. They give thanks by means of them, expect to be elevated by them, and are moved to the highest levels of empathy and fear. They have always responded in these ways; they still do" (Freedberg, 1).

Picture 6.3 An Alchemist in His Laboratory, Elias Ashmole, 1652.

In the late 1800s, Abraham Kingswood recognized photography's innate spiritual potency. He believed the art held unlimited potential as a tool for the service of the Great Work. Inspired by this realization, Kingswood began fabricating his own camera, which he called "Magnus Lucis Captor," the Great Catcher of Light. He learned to use his device for taking photographs through trial and error. Once he gained a degree of mastery over the "magic box," he applied his artistic skills in phototechny as part of his practices in the hermetic arts. Ultimately, he succeeded in devising a synthesis between alchemy and photography. After many years of refinement and perfecting, Kingswood was recognized among his esoteric peers as a Peritus Ars Magna Lucis et Umbrae (an Adept of the Great Art of light and shadow).

One of the European societal contexts in which photography emerged was Napoleon's conquest of Egypt. Among his invading forces was a large group of artists who documented the scenes and antiquities of Egypt. Subsequently, between 1809 and 1826, a popular series of books titled *Description de l'Égypte was published.* Its lavish, detailed illustrations garnered considerable attention worldwide. People in England became captivated by the exotic and mysterious styles of Egypt's architecture and artwork, leading to the birth of an Egyptian Revival. A wave of enthusiasm swept across Georgian and Victorian England, fueled by a strong desire for everything Egyptian.

In the 1860s and 70s, citizens of the empire traveled to Cairo, Giza, and Karnak. As a result, they returned to England with a multitude of photographs. There were *carte de visites* and larger *cabinet cards* illuminating viewers with statues of ancient gods, temples, native people, and textured surfaces covered with incomprehensible hieroglyphs. Some also brought back artifacts, including magical texts on papyrus and ritual instruments that hadn't seen the light of day for over 3000 years.

In 1882, the British Empire conquered Egypt. Antiquities, including art objects and magical texts, flowed into England. Initially, there was cultural hesitation among many regarding the ancient magical items that entered the country. Rumors circulated about curses attached to some of these items. GK brings attention to the fact that, "Religion and superstitions played a significant role in stoking fears. Plus, there was a historically enforced decree against the use of either high or low, white or black magic. "Anything considered supernatural was forbidden by the church."

For example, under the same law in the 1500s, occult practitioners faced punishment through imprisonment or death. During that time, numerous suspects were charged under witchcraft laws, leading to a long list of convicts in England alone. Among them, Agnes Waterhouse, Elizabeth Clarke, Alice Nutter, Ursula Kemp, and others were brutally tortured and hanged. Thomas Doughty was beheaded, while others were burned alive. Those who practiced the Hermetic arts had to flee from scrutiny and seek refuge in other, more tolerant communities.

Another example comes from England's more recent history. Several prominent European members of the Catholic and Protestant clergy were recognized as alchemists. While most saw no distinction between their alchemical pursuits and their faith, some did.

> There was a potential conflict between alchemy and mainstream Christianity that arose from the hermetic elements inherent in alchemy. Many alchemists believed that man not only has the power to become divine himself, but because he is a microcosm representative of the macrocosm, or world at large, he has the power to redeem matter as well. Not all alchemists embraced such extreme and heretical views…[some] accused alchemists of proposing a 'chemical' religion in opposition to true Christianity" (Kotansky, 47). Furthermore, some received "bitter condemnation [for their] 'new achemistic theology'" (47).

The belief system that alchemists embraced aligned with their time's Judeo-Christian worldview. The god-centric texts that provided practical and theoretical information on alchemy originated from Greece, Rome, and the Middle East, with many of those documents being translations of sources from Egypt. The Egyptians once possessed a vast wealth of alchemical knowledge. However, after years of cultural and religious turmoil, their ancient knowledge was destroyed or kept hidden by ancient mystery schools. It is believed that the initiates of those schools made significant efforts to protect and conceal all the hermetic arcanum in secrecy.

Wherever the sacred treasures were hidden, they weren't safe. English citizens embarked on expeditions to procure undiscovered relics from ancient mystery cults and temples. Even though supernatural practices remained taboo in the Western world, a newfound interest in pneumatology, mysticism, and the occult emerged. "Fascination with Spiritualism and psychic phenomena reached a high point in Great Britain in the late nineteenth century. During that period, a rich diversity of people shared the fascination, formed organizations to pursue the subject systematically, and patronized a spiritualist press to publicize the activities of spiritualist circles around the country" (Oppenheim, 1985, 28). Mediums flourished, connecting families with the spirits of their deceased loved ones. Survivors could even have photographs taken of themselves with the ghosts of the dead! It was a time of great spiritual curiosity, enlightenment, and endless mystical possibilities. It was also a time of treachery and deception.

As timeworn treasures arrived on the shores of England, groups of resolute people gathered in secrecy to engage in necromancy. They claimed to do so by opening the obscuring veil between the living and the deceased. When Kingswood was a young man, author William Lloyd Garrison wrote,

> The manifestations have spread from house to house, from city to city, from one part of the country to the other, across the Atlantic into Europe, till now the enlightened world is compelled to acknowledge their reality…We have witnessed their surprising manifestations, and our conviction is that they cannot be accounted for on any other theory than that of the spiritual agency." Noted and prolific English author, William Howitt responded, "Who are the men that have in every country embraced Spiritualism? The rabble? The ignorant? The fanatic? By no means. But the most intelligent and learned men of all classes" (quoted in Green, 205).

Among the middle and upper classes, whispers circulated about secret organizations that promised both spiritual and material benefits to their members. Groups like the Knights of Seth, the Order of Druids, the Hermetic Order of the Golden Dawn, and the Freemasons thrived, with membership levels increasing. Consequently, these secret organizations lost their shrouded concealment, and in a short time, the existence of many societies became public knowledge. Yet, even though the public became aware that these organizations were an unseen part of their society, most groups managed to keep their arcane practices hidden.

Kingswood family records recount a time when the alchemystic phenom# Abraham was recognized for both his scholarly interest in Egyptology and his knack for engaging in captivating conversations about the history of alchemical magic. However, few of the people with whom Kingswood socialized knew that his experiences with alchemy extended far beyond academic pursuits. Unknown to most of his acquaintances, he became deeply immersed in mystical practices rooted in Egyptian-based alchemy. The only person he confided in was his son, who participated in rituals, engaged in theurgic studies, and helped acquire important artifacts and texts from across the Middle East, including Egypt.

Following in the footsteps of Pythagoras and Plato, Abraham Kingswood expanded his alchemical research by traveling to the Egyptian city of the Eternal Sun, Iunu, known to the Greeks as Heliopolis. His favorite pilgrimage site was where the ancient Sun Temple (the Benu-Phoenix) once stood. GK describes the oldest of Ra's temples,

> It was constructed so that a pilgrim's line of sight could behold both it and the Great Pyramid of Giza. Similarly, if one stood at the Great Pyramid, the temple could be seen in the distance. This is the location where the divine source willed himself into existence by emerging from a brilliant, fiery sphere that arose from the primordial darkness. From the sphere, Ra radiated beams of glorious, living light in the form of words. From those words, rays emanated as he spoke all things into existence. Thus, it follows that, like photographs, all things are the products of impressions made from the action of his light.

At the end of his account, Kingswood emphasized, "Thus Came-Ra and all things," while giving a humorous wink about the hidden relationship between the photographer's camera and Ra. He also described the *camera obscura* as more than just a metaphor for the holy chamber of Ra's primordial darkness, which the Egyptians referred to as *perfect black*. He said, "The lightless, empty space is a hermetically sealed chamber that is indistinguishable from the deepest, shadowy chaos of Ra's birthplace. Saturated with unreflecting illumination, it is the *dynameis*, full of a potential that extends from every point without beginning or end."

The inner sanctum of the camera serves as a locus of death and rebirth. It is a place of "dissolution and reintegration of chaos…[where] every 'death' is at once a reintegration of cosmic night and pre-cosmological chaos. At many different levels, darkness expresses the dissolution of forms, the return to the seminal stage of existence" (Eliade, 1978, 156). In Mircea Eliade's scenario, GK agrees, "the image is reborn, having passed through death during its flight, riding on rays of light from its origin scene to the surface of the film, traversing the darkness of time and space to be born again into lustrous, eternal beams." The camera is where reflections of all things can manifest through light — via a glass portal and the transformation upon untarnished silver.

GK believes the camera's inner chamber should be viewed as a sacred space, the *adytum of Ra*, the temple chamber where the *midnight sun dwells*. The midnight sun is

> part of the mystery of alchemy. It symbolized the spirit in man shining through the darkness of his human organism. It also referred to the spiritual sun in the solar system, which the mystic

could see as well at midnight as at high noon, the material earth being powerless to obstruct the rays of this Divine orb. The mysterious lights which illuminated the temples of the Egyptian Mysteries during the nocturnal hours were said by some to be reflections of the spiritual sun gathered by the magical powers of his [Ra's] priests (Hall, 53).

And thus, while the adytum appears to be a vault filled with darkness, there is, in fact, a source of light within, visible only to the ordained, opened Eye of Sight.

Kingswood amassed an impressive collection of artifacts from his adventures in Egypt, including a small, ancient model he believed to be a camera obscura. He claimed these antiquities awakened and strengthened his connections with Ra's ancient priests and, by association, the deity himself. In his journals, Kingswood acknowledged that the desert's earthy grit largely consumed Heliopolis (Ἡλιούπολις). Yet, a solitary obelisk captured the first rays of light at dawn. It stood like a bridge between the golden star above and the city submerged beneath the sand. Kingswood used the obelisk as a reference point to determine the location of all the temples entombed below. According to his notes, he found that for a few coins, it was easy to gather a group of men with shovels willing to excavate wherever he asked them to dig.

After returning from his last trip, Kingswood opened a photography studio in London that specialized in cabinet cards. At his studio, he regularly interacted with the public. He sold landscape photos from his travels, but most of his paid work was in portraiture. Kingswood noted that he developed a rapport with clients by talking with them before and during the photo sessions. He learned about their hopes, dreams, and sometimes adversities. Practically speaking, these conversations helped customers feel more comfortable during the sittings, thus yielding better likenesses. What they didn't know was that before Kingswood delivered the finished products, he used their photos as magical instruments to bring advantages to those people's lives. He performed these acts of kindness as an essential part of his alchemical practice. Kingswood emphasized, "These beneficial acts of magic have dissolved my compulsive thoughts of superciliousness# and reformed them into genuine sentiments of benevolence. A sign of real transformation." None of his patrons would ever know about the miracles that were being conjured in the back room of his studio and the private spaces of his home.

In 1893, Kingswood founded a small secret society, The Kemetic Order of the Silver Sun (Ordo Aegyptus Solis Argenti), where initiates were said to be wholly committed to their spiritual and philosophical pursuits. Their motto was, "Mea camera semper ostendit orientalem," or "My camera always points East." Kingswood's close circle of trusted associates regarded him as a mystagogue#. Although Kingswood was the founding member of this Hermetic lineage, he considered the Kemetic deity Ra to be its head, with whom he had exclusive audiences. The Order adhered to a syncretic belief system that represented a unique branch within the broader category of Western Mystical traditions. The group, which also referred to themselves as the Sons of Ra (Filii Sol et Theon Bigrammaton), held doctrines influenced by an ancient solar theology, which helped refine alchemy based on a hybrid fusion of ancient Egyptian magical practices attributed to Ra, Hermetic mysticism, Kabbalistic wisdom, and esoteric photography practices.

Abraham Kingswood, an alchemist-philosopher, became known as the hierophant and prophet, or "mouthpiece" of Ra, the primary source of illuminating knowledge for the group. As such, Kingswood devoted his life to the Order's mission: the spiritual evolution of its members. He is still remembered for his wisdom and knowledge. His understanding of hermetic magic, gained through experience, was thoroughly recorded for posterity. Kingswood lived as a consummate alchemist but was reputed to be a humble, quiet man who was careful not to reveal the depth of his practices to those around him. For reasons that will be explained later, he maintained a vow of silence, even under the threat of death.

GK explains,

> Members of the order were united by "an unyielding pursuit of knowledge, to become awakened in service the highest." They were committed to the source, the egregor# who was respectfully summoned to reveal himself and speak through Abraham as Egypt's supreme deity. Abraham was neither an appropriator nor a spiritual bricoleur#, as he received knowledge, instructions, and gifts of illumination directly from the falcon-headed one who appeared to him regularly. The gifts took the form of hundreds of prayers and magical incantations, which he faithfully scribed in his grimoire, *Book of the Luminous Glass*. My great-grandfather received these divine words through visions, dreams, and divinations. He wrote, "I carry notebooks because at any point in the day or night I may find myself inundated and impelled to record the messages that overcome me by an ecstasy in which a

voice pours into my mind as the god of brightness, in a streaming force of sunlight." Abraham Kingswood had a mystical solidarity with light. He was truly a *Sa-Ra*, or Son of Ra, and was his

Picture 6.4 Painting of Ra from George Kingswood's Temple Room. Artist unknown.

medium for the three-flamed lamp of his words. He took no chances of being confused with spiritualists or those dishonored and fraudulent spirit photographers of the time. He ensured this didn't happen because of his unbreakable oath of secrecy.

7. Ra Sails Over the Blazing Dawn

Kingswood's historical records refer to the 3rd-2nd century BCE as a significant period. At that time, there was an auspicious convergence of three events that set the stage for their alchemical practices. First, Aristotle postulated, "all matter combined the four elements of earth, air, fire, and water. He proposed that these elements could be changed -- transmuted -- by the action of heat and cold, or dampness and dryness" (Lienhard, 2022). Occultist and author Manley P. Hall clarifies that,

> The purpose of alchemy was not to make something out of nothing but rather to fertilize and nurture the seed which was already present. Its processes did nor actually create gold but rather made the ever-present seed of gold grow and flourish. Everything which exists has a spirit--the seed of Divinity within itself--and regeneration is not the process of attempting to place something where it previously had not existed. Regeneration actually means the unfoldment of the omnipresent Divinity in man, that this Divinity may shine forth as a sun and illumine all with whom it comes in contact (Hall, 1928, 53).

Aristotle and Hall's descriptions serve as foundational hypotheses and starting points for understanding Western alchemy. Around the same time Aristotle wrote about the elements, he observed the behavior of light during a solar eclipse. He described how light passed through small holes in the leaves of a tree and how it created a projected image. In his writings, *Problems, book XV,* Aristotle noted that this same action of light casts a faithful, inverted image on a surface. These observations laid the groundwork for the concept of the *camera obscura,* which would be crucial in the future development of photography.

The second event occurred when Greek-born Ptolemy III Euergetes was elevated to the position of ruler and Pharaoh in Egypt. By doing so, he was apotheosized# as a Son of Ra, the *Theon Bigrammaton*, or god whose name is composed of two letters. In addition, "As the king and leader of Egypt, the pharaoh was seen as the human manifestation of Horus, so the two gods [Ra and Horus] became connected. This new deity fusion, in all of his extravagant avian beauty, was then referred to as 'Ra-Horakhty,' meaning Ra is Horus of the Horizon. Ra's relationship with other gods did not stop there" (RA: The Sun God of Egypt, 2022). The new pharaoh automatically became Ra's high priest and the temporal head of all his temples in Egypt.

As the manifestation of Ra-Horakhty on Earth, the Ptolemaic Pharaoh could govern and gain the support of Egypt's priests by overseeing the construction and restoration of various temples throughout the land. These holy structures were dedicated to multiple Egyptian deities, including Amun-Ra at the Temple of Khonsu. As mentioned above, Ra took numerous forms, such as Ra-Horakhty, a falcon, the sun, or even a Pharaoh. One of his appearances was as Amun-Ra, a combined god-form that reflected Ra's elevated status as the supreme creator god, worshiped above all other gods. Over time, the name for the deity of the golden sun became synonymous with all aspects of light, including the light of knowledge, wisdom, intellect, and divine truth.

The third circumstance occurred around the same time in Babylon when the apocryphal *Book of Daniel* was written. The biblical text reveals King Nebuchadnezzar's vision of a visitation by *the Watchers*, beings that came from the sky three hundred years earlier to walk among men and help them. Kingswood explained that Nebuchadnezzar's vision depicted a historical event 600 years prior. The visitors were called Watchers because they never spoke; instead, the celestial beings spent their days observing the actions of people around them. They appeared to men and women, provided instructions, and taught them about light, darkness, and natural magic to gain control over their surroundings. It was their teaching of magic that led to The Watchers being referred to as *fallen angels* in later biblical writings. Kingswood indicated that the Watchers' teachings were communicated via telepathy, with words projected from the lenses of their eyes and seen as phantom images made of light.

Kingswood's journals discuss how the same two Watchers appeared to him in a vision. He saw himself with the supernatural beings as they conducted a nine-day initiation. Ultimately, he was ordained as a Son of Ra. Then, the Watchers instructed him on the secret arts of alchemical magic. He interpreted the instructions as *thaumaturgy*. In the Book of Daniel, these beings are also described as angels, yet Kingswood identified them as Ra and Thoth, Ra's ibis-headed god-scribe.

Additionally, Thoth was the lunar vice-gerent and nighttime representative who imparted instructions on learning, writing, and magic to some. He was called *The Silver Sun,* and Latin speakers named him Mercury because he was closest to the sun, the divine source. One of Mercury's roles became that of the messenger of the solar god. The knowledge and wisdom protected by the deities had been strictly hidden from most humans until that point. Priests had to promise to die by their own blade if they broke their vows of secrecy and revealed any teachings of the Watchers' magic.

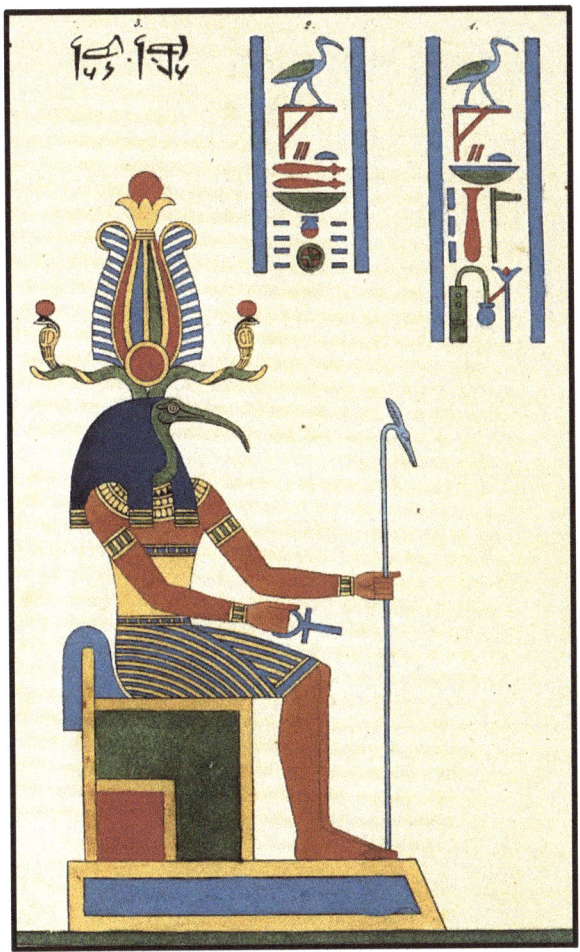

Picture 7.1 Thoth, the Egyptian God of magic, writing, sacred texts, the moon, deliverer of knowledge, and scribe of the gods. Artist unknown.

In his book, Transcendental Magic, Eliphas Lévi said,

> Behind the veil of all the hieratic and mystical allegories of ancient doctrines, behind the shadows and the strange ordeals of all initiations, under the seal of all sacred writings, in the ruins of Nineveh or Thebes, on the crumbling stones of the old temples, and the blackened visage of the Assyrian or Egyptian sphinx, in the monstrous or marvellous paintings which interpret to the faithful...the strange emblems of our old books of alchemy, in the ceremonies at reception practised by all mysterious societies, traces are found of a doctrine which is everywhere the same, and everywhere carefully concealed...it shook or strengthened

empires by its oracles, caused tyrants to tremble on their thrones, and governed all minds, either by curiosity or by fear" (Lévi, 1896, 1).

Kingswood communicated that Ra stressed that magic was dangerous to those who intended to use it for ordinary power or harm. He claimed that the negative effects of misuse could cause damage that would ripple out to future generations and beyond. As the worldly and spiritual head of the Kemetic Order, Kingswood vowed never to harm others and to practice his knowledge with utmost responsibility. After completing many years of practice and achieving the highest accomplishment of the Great Work, he announced that he had gained a complete understanding of alchemy and was granted permission by Ra to disclose parts of the Order's divine knowledge. Over time, he taught those novices deemed trustworthy, discriminating, devout, and blessed with a strong will and the ability to be discreet.

Because Kingswood's initial revelations about alchemy and magic came directly from Egyptian deities, they became the focal points of the magical system studied in the Kemetic Order of the Silver Sun. Of the two divine sources, Ra played a more crucial role as the guide and benefactor of revelation. GK explains that,

> Ra's reign over the black land of Kemet (now Egypt) as one of the Seven Lords of Eternity lasted more than 2500 years. He was a primary god throughout those ancient lands and the supreme deity of Heliopolis. All activities of the Great Work continue to be performed under his auspices. As he was for Egypt, he is now for photomantic# alchemists, the burning point of a heliocentric doctrine.

Ra's likeness was represented in all technopoeia (artmaking), including drawings, paintings, sculptures, and hieroglyphics. The temple at Heliopolis also had a special group of priests called "Pastophoroi", or *image-bearers*, who were chosen to be solely responsible for touching, holding, and carrying artworks that bore the god's likeness. These priests were specially ordained because the temple artworks of Ra were considered sacrosanct vessels holding the Ba (a vital aspect of the soul) of the supreme god of light. All others, even other priests, were forbidden to touch his images.

Ra's primary visual manifestation is more than just an archetype. It is a sentient image of a transcendent form, depicted in all forms of artistic media. He is the *Lumen de Lumine,* the all-seeing eye of the sun, possessing the body of a man and the head of a hawk or falcon. He is illustrated as sitting, standing, or walking. As part of Ra's sublunary# appearance, he wears the headdress of a Pharaoh, crowned by a Sun Disk, called the "Solar Eye of Ra" (Wilkinson, 43). The red-orange disk is the heart of the sun that beats within its own fiery, empyreal sphere. GK described,

> The Solar Eye is the sun within the sun, the empyrean# flames that shine through all the stars in the cosmos. The light from the disk is blindingly intense, yet it can't be seen with the corporeal eye. Its center circularly scatters luminous streams within itself.

Picture 7.2 Ra. From The Gods of the Egyptians, Volume 2. E.A. Budge, 1904.

> At the same time, its periphery radiates abundant rays that flow outward like a perpetual shower of glorious light, energizing life, intellect, and the evolving soul.

Essentially, the Sun Disk is worshiped as a goddess, a creatrix who delivers both blessings and wrath. Among the ancients, there were also many other forms in which the spiritual sun was depicted.

Ra's roundel# crown is topped with a cobra, symbolizing divine authority, the natural cycles of life, death, rebirth, and personifying time. The cobra can also appear as the Uraeus, a commonly seen version on the front of Pharaohs' crowns. The Uraeus emblem signifies potential energy as it is poised, ready to strike at speeds exceeding 1/60th of a second, a shutter speed that freezes the blink of an eye. Additionally, the cobra can be interpreted as an Ourobouros, often depicted as the snake's body forming a circle or figure eight while consuming its tail. This symbolizes the eternal, regenerative cycle.

It is said that Ra's true form, his brilliant ethereal body, may never be seen by mortal eyes. Meanwhile, he perceives every soul. He is the *Lumen Dei*, the fiery brightness that embodies the godhead. He is inconceivable, intangible, and impossible to comprehend within the limitations of the sapient mind. However, one can gain a deeper understanding of Ra by accessing multiple vantage points. Connecting with myriad facets of the Deity is an essential part of the aspirant's

P Picture 7.3 The Hierophant Ascending, Garin Horner, 2025.

journey as they ascend the stairway to the sublime luminary goal. In a commentary on Minor White's creative journey of ascension, photo historian Peter Bunnell wrote,

His own particular condition is at the center of his expressive
work and is central in the approach he took to his photography; it
is the source of his fusing the personal with the universal.
Through this psychic energy he felt the possibilities of uniting
with God, which, like the monastic supplicant he aspired to be, he
attempted to do while remaining in this world" (1989, 19).

Unification with the divine source is the alchemist's deepest desire. The
promise of a homecoming with the light of light waits above the
uppermost step of the aspirant's ascension. The Kingswoods have always
been dedicated to devoting great effort to understanding the Eternal Sun
crowning the apex of the Great Pyramid. Through the endeavor to access
knowledge, the traveler will receive gifts in the form of skills, abilities,
and tools that will prepare them for the spiritual climb toward Ra, toward
photognosis.

The path by which to deity we climb
Is arduous, rough, ineffable, sublime;
And the strong massy gates, through which we pass
In our first course, are bound with chains of brass,
Those men the first who of Egyptian birth
Drank the fair water of Nilotic earth,
Disclosed by actions infinite this road.

—*Oracle of Apollo*, from Eusebius
(Taylor, 2016, 12-13).

The Kingswood's dependence on Ra exemplifies what the historian of
alchemy, Joachim Telle (1939-2013), referred to as *Theoalchemie*, or an
alchemical belief system rooted in a divine source. For instance, GK
explains that from the philosophical perspective of alchemy, all things
manifest immeasurable expressions of light. Therefore, it is
acknowledged that Ra, the godform of light, is the creator and essence of
all things. Thus, that

All human beings are consanguineous#, connected with their
source; that is, all beings are his progeny. Ra is a self-created
revelation of light and the active principle providing spiritual and
material energies crucial for transformation and transmutation.
Each of his chimeric forms (Ra, Ra-Horakhty, Amun-Ra, Khepri,
Khnum, and Atum), he is the embodiment and essence of
light. He is the creator of both material and immaterial constructs,
and is pure and unrestrained light. It naturally follows that Ra is
the self-luminous force behind all the elements and principles of

photography. For the members of the Kemetic Order of the Silver Sun and its progeny, the realm of photography serves as the medium through which Ra provides endless opportunities for the revelation of the divine spark's creative potential and, through his guidance, lays out the map for purification, spiritual ascension, and unification.

As a fourth-generation Son of Ra, GK gained an advantage over all alchemists throughout history due to a century and a quarter of unbroken

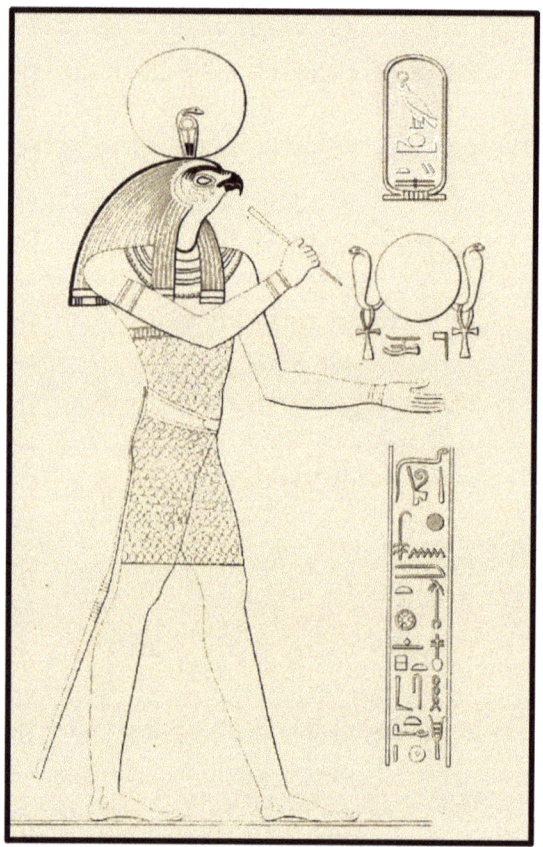

Picture 7.4 Ra Writing Heka, 1845. Artist unknown.

research and practice in both alchemy and photography. His family has preserved a continuous bond with Ra, allowing GK to advance the accumulated knowledge of his ancestors. He still needed to follow the same steps of the Great Work as those before him, but with the assistance of experienced guides, both living and deceased, who provide invaluable advice, helping him follow a direct, ascending path.

8. CORRESPONDENCES:
A NETWORK OF LUMINOUS FILAMENTS

The Egyptian Book of the Dead discusses correspondences. It explains that artistic representations and names are analogous to the individuals or things they represent (Budge, 1898, 165). Similarly, in another reference, correspondences are recognized as a fundamental understanding of the Hermetic Order of the Golden Dawn. In their rituals, "By names and images are all powers awakened and reawakened." (Christopher, 103-104). In other words, there exists a network of conceptual and supernatural relationships that, GK explains, "is sustained in the background through a vast network connecting conduits through which energetic currents flow and form patterns. Within the ever-changing sphere of chaos, things that become connected share special relationships in which actions that affect a thing, in some way affect the other corresponding things in its network." Furthermore, Eliphas Levi affirmed that,

> Analogy is the final word of science and the first word of faith…Reason and faith, by their nature, mutually exclude one another, but they unite by analogy. Analogy is the sole possible mediator between finite and infinite…Analogy is the key of all secrets of Nature and the sole fundamental reason of all revelations…the key of the Great Arcanum (Levi, 2013).

GK discloses, "The need for an alchemist to understand how correspondences function as a network for magical energies cannot be stressed enough. Its praxis and theory come from the ancient Egyptian idea of analogy, which was written by the hand of Hermes Trismegistus, as dictated to him by Ra, the all-giving deity of light, upon the ancient *Tabula Smaragdina*, (the *Emerald Tablet*). Heralded as an inscription upon the Graeco-Egyptian stone, also known as the 'Bible of the alchemists,' it was paraphrased into the Hermetic axiom, *As above, so below, as within, so without, as the universe, so the soul.*" Following is a translation in Abraham Kingswood's *Book of the Eye of Horus*:

> It is true, without doubt. That which is above is as that which is below, and that which is below is as that which is above, enacting the miracles of the One thing and all things were produced from that One. Its father is the sun (Ra), its mother the moon (Isis). The wind carried it in its womb and the earth fed it from her breast. It is the father of all signs, wonders, and miracles under the sun.

On the same page of Kingswood's book, he also duplicated a quote from his copy of Mary Anne Atwood's book, "*Hermetic Philosophy and Alchemy.*" Atwood translated the Emerald Tablet into English from Athanasius Kircher's Latin translation:

> This is the father of all perfection, or consummation of the whole world. The power of it is Integral, if it be turned into earth. Thou shalt separate the earth from the fire, the subtle from the gross, gently with much sagacity; it ascends from earth to heaven, and again descends to earth: and receives the strength of the superiors and of the inferiors --- so thou hast the glory of the whole world; therefore let all obscurity flee before thee. This is the strong fortitude of all fortitudes, overcoming every subtle and penetrating every solid thing. So the world was created. Hence were all wonderful adaptations of which this is the manner. Therefore I am called Thrice Great Hermes, having the Three Parts of the philosophy of the whole world. That which I have written is consummated concerning the operation of the Sun (Atwood, 2005, 3).

There was also a motto inscribed on the tablet, *hen to pan*, which means "the unity of all things." This conveys the idea that everything in the cosmos is holistically interconnected. The tablet affirms that each human being and their soul have a direct relationship with both the material and immaterial planes of existence. Moreover, it reveals that there are unseen links and associations between them and the godhead. The inscriptions state that all people are connected in ways as intimate as the body's relationship to its spirit or soul. The axiom is interpreted to mean that there are no separate entities as we perceive them, because everything in the macrocosm and microcosm is so closely bound together that what happens to one, to some degree, affects everything.

Furthermore, the wisdom of the Tablet can be understood to teach that,

> (a) Nothing is meaningless or neutral: everything is significant. (b) Nothing is independent, everything is in some way related to something else. (c) The quantitative becomes the qualitative in certain essentials which, in fact, precisely constitute the meaning of the quantity. (d) Everything is serial. (e) Series are related one to another as to position, and the components of each series are related as to meaning" (Cirlot, 1962, 36).

The interwoven histories of alchemy, photography, and art affirm Talbet's ancient declarations. Similarly, suppose the serial threads connecting this moment can be traced back through time to explore the origin of humanity. In that case, one may rediscover old insights as new regarding magic, light, photography, and the nature of life itself.

As an example of this theory of correspondences, G.K. urges readers to visit Lascaux, France, where over 2,000 artistic depictions of animals are sketched on the cave walls. Humanity's oldest ancestors created these paintings, demonstrating how essential the belief in correspondences was to their lives at the beginning of human history. For our prehistoric relatives, there was a direct correlation between painting an animal and the animal itself. When the sharp point of a spear was touched against the cave painting of a buffalo, the outcome of the hunt was set in motion before the hunters even left their shelter. In other words, the painting of a buffalo was a living spiritual aspect of the buffalo that they would encounter during the hunt.

The discovery of these seventeen-thousand-year-old sites led to research in the field of Archaeo-optics,

> the study of the experience and ritual use of light by ancient peoples (Archaeo-Optics)[1] [in which] Research…has uncovered how ancient peoples encountered and used the camera obscura principle for a variety of purposes. In a darkened chamber, light passing through a small opening can create haunting and ephemeral moving images, which could have triggered and reinforced ground breaking modes of thought, forms of representation, and belief in otherworldly realms (Gatton, 2009, 153).

This research reveals the direct correspondence or magical equivalence between cave artworks and the photographic images produced by the advanced technology of modern cameras. GK says, "In light of this affirmation of unseen relationships, I propose an addendum to the Emerald Tablet: *As the past, so the future*!"

Neanderthals identified conceptual, visual, and unseen bonds acknowledged through the act of creating imagery. Paleolithic hunters accepted that they, their artistic likenesses, and the animals were all bound together in a spectacle of life and death. Additionally, early

---

[1] Archaeo-Optics." *Wikipedia*, Wikimedia Foundation, 3 Mar. 2022, https://en.wikipedia.org/wiki/Archaeo-optics.

humans intuitively understood ways to manipulate these correspondences and use them to their advantage. They recognized that the intangible links between things could serve as conduits through which magical power could flow and influence the unfolding of future events. The stronger the correspondence, the more vital the energy that flowed between the interconnected entities.

"This perception of metaphysical relationships extended far beyond the hunting grounds," GK suggests,

> Those prehistoric ancestors gazed up at the awe-inspiring Milky Way and wondered about their kinship with that astounding universe of lights! While gazing upon such an indescribably mysterious scene, they noticed how the stars changed positions over the hours of darkness. They must have felt compelled to find some sense of order in what appeared to be the resplendent chaos of the celestial sphere.

There is ample evidence that early hominids recognized the cyclical nature of seasonal and cosmic cycles. Because it's a natural human impulse to try to derive meaning from experiences, they noticed patterns in the locations of stars in relation to one another, the moon, the Earth, and themselves. Following their instincts, they identified a universal order through correspondences. They perceived groups of stars reappearing in the celestial dome and visualized them as points that, when connected, formed outlines illustrating the most significant aspects of their lives. Among the stars, they saw pictures!

In the distant constellations and asterisms# the ancients found images of gods, goddesses, animals, and heroes. The pictures they saw emerged from heavenly, mysterious correspondences stretched out between the cosmos and their lives. Additionally, they identified the twelve images that depicted the seasonal zodiac. Long ago, the people of the earth realized that the universe not only reflected the stories and the people of the world but also mirrored the metaphysical qualities of their souls. They understood that the world above, around, and beneath them was equivalent to unseen dimensions within them. This recognition ultimately led to early civilizations, such as Egypt, developing the field of astrology.

As human beings across cultures peered within themselves, they found equivalent external correlations. From there, they looked down into the earth and out into the blackness of the infinite universe. What they found were gods! For the Greeks, the sun was Helios. The Sumerians called him Utu, and the Romans, Sol. The deity was Mithra to the Persians and Shapash to the Canaanites. The supreme solar deity of the Egyptians was Ra. Similarly, the sun and moon have always occupied a special place in the deep, collective human understanding of cosmic correspondences. After all, the celestial bodies have, for millennia, imparted lessons about the spiral of the seasons, life, death, and rebirth.

At some point in evolution, our predecessors discovered that sounds could be associated with images. Thus, pictographs were born! They are image-based representations of letters, words, or phrases. The cave paintings at Lascaux are also considered pictographs, but in a different way. Instead of using images to represent letters or words, they depict things, experiences, and ideas. Egyptian pictographs have served as a means of recording the sounds and meanings of language for over 5000 years. Ancient papyri with hieroglyphs (from the word "hieroglyphicos, " Greek for *sacred picture*) are prime examples of how pictographs narrate stories or record information. For instance, the medical symbol "Rx" is a pictograph still in use today. The "R" symbolizes the Eye of Horus, the god of healing in Egypt. The "x" instructed the patient to pray for their healing. The symbol literally means, "take this divine recipe and pray" (Nix, 2014).

GK appreciates that, "In the ancient world, the making and reading of images was sacred art. For the Egyptians, it was certainly true. The god Thoth, who was equipollent# with the Greek god Hermes, is said to have delivered these sacred symbols to the people of Egypt. He taught the priestcraft, which consisted of sacrosanct skills and art, along with the mysteries of both the hieroglyphic and the hieratic forms of writing." In fact, "The Egyptians referred to the hieroglyphic script as *mdw nṯr*,

Picture 8.1 *mdw nṯr* (the words of the gods).

literally, 'the words of the gods' and the scribal art was to them an occupation without equal" (Annus, 2010, 145). Furthermore,

> words were not merely presumed to have the properties of material objects, but might be thought of as foci or concentrations of dynamic power. They were plainly regarded as not only movable but mobile, not only susceptible to being acted upon, but capable of acting upon other entities in ways not confined to communication, of producing and enacting effects, conditions, circumstances and states" (Rabinowitz, 1993, 16).

Around the eleventh century BCE, Egyptians adapted a writing system they learned from Phoenician traders. The Phoenician collection of markings formed an alphabet that corresponded to sounds. Just as today, groups of letters correspond to specific words. Words point to ideas in the same way that pictographs are visually and conceptually related to things and ideas. Kingswood adds that in the bible, a man named Bezalel (Ex. 31:2ff.; 35:30ff.) knew the exact combination of letters that corresponded to the creation of heaven and earth. Furthermore, Kingswood explained, the legend tells that the old Torah's words were powerful enough to cure the sick and resurrect the dead.

> Let's not forget that God used His finger to inscribe Hebrew letters, spelling out the *Decalogue* or Ten Commandments, onto two stone tablets. By utilizing the power contained in that specific combination of letters, He established a direct line of provenance from His hand to His worshippers. It is the same creative power that Bazalel referred to. The commandments, regardless of the language in which they are written, connect the reader directly to God through their correspondence.

Before the Decalogue, in the ancient book, the *Sefer Yetzirah* (the Book of Creation), it's recorded, "God drew the Hebrew letters, hewed them, combined them, weighed them, interchanged them, and through them produced the whole Creation" (Scholem, 1990, 24-29). In this story, God used letters as miraculous instruments of power to make everything in the universe. So, the letters he used correspond directly to all aspects of creation. It also states that, "Abraham [biblical patriarch of Christians, Jews, and Muslims] knew the secrets of the wisdom of the alphabet. God tied the twenty-two letters to his tongue and revealed to him all the mysteries of the universe" (Landman et al., 1939).

The Hebrew alphabet is divided into four groups of letters, each corresponding to one of the four elements: fire, water, earth, and air. Additionally, there is a connection to a fifth element of spirit, known as the *quintessence*. Understanding these and other hidden correspondences can empower one to cure or even harm a person simply by knowing which letters are in their name. Similar practices exist in Kingswood's form of alchemy, where individual photographs are combined with letters, words, and phrases. Furthermore, part of Jewish mysticism is the Kabbalah, also known as the Tree of Life, which is based on ten emanations that correspond to the sacred Hebrew letters. Each letter represents a sphere of knowledge relating to "encompassing aspects of existence, God, or the human psyche" (Mills, Tree of Life, and Kabbalah).

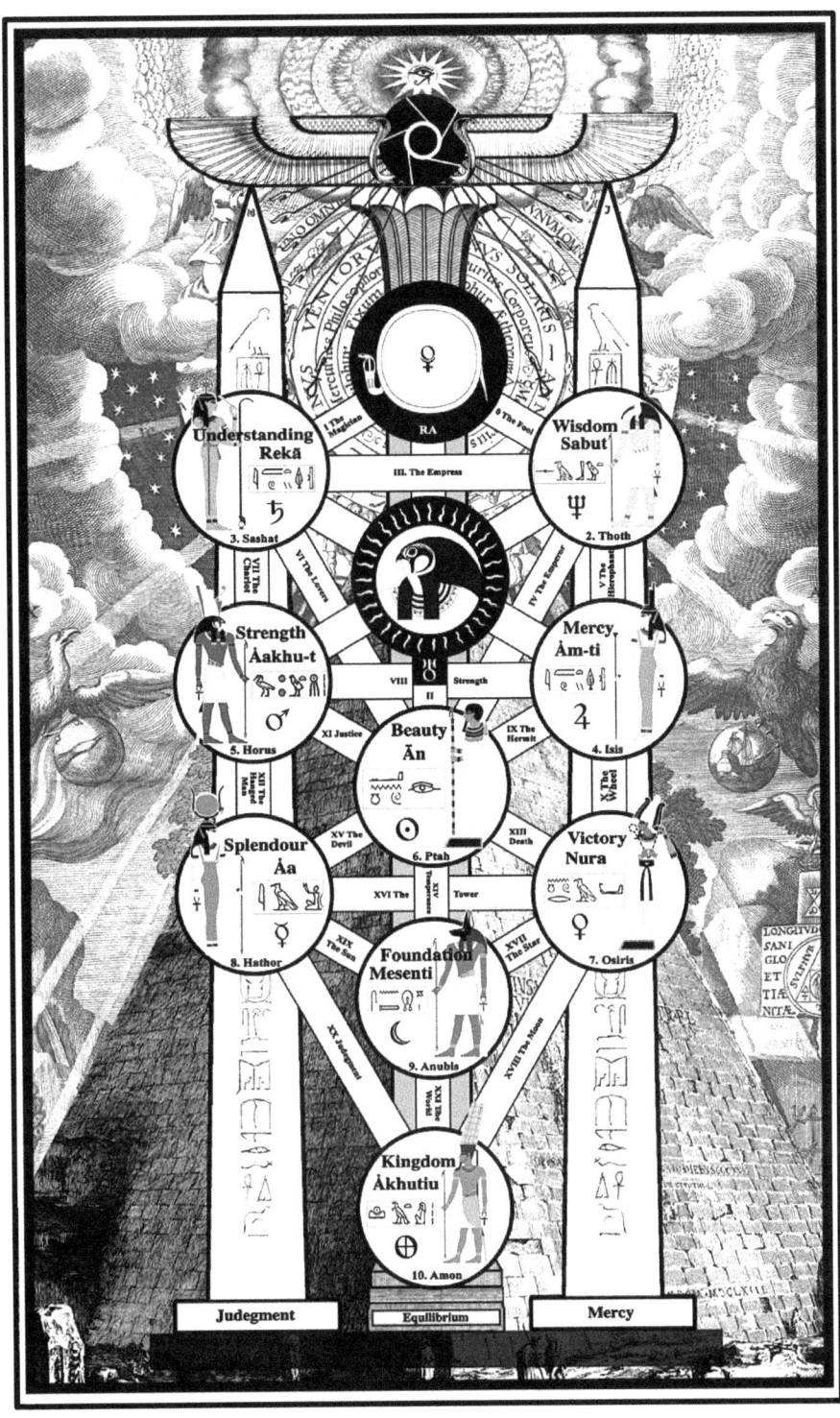

Picture 8.2 The Kemetic Kabbalah. Based on a Diagram from
Abraham Kingswood's Collection. Garin Horner, 2020.

They also directly relate to "deities, angels, celestial bodies, values, single colors or combinations of them, and specific numbers" (Kabbalah and Hermetic Kabbalah). The Kabbalah was developed as a complex framework of mystical correspondences which, in addition to its use of letters, also includes ten divine numbers. Altogether, the Kabbalistic teachings are represented by the 32 paths of wisdom. The composition of the Kabbalistic diagram is designed to codify a body of "esoteric teachings meant to explain the relationship between the unchanging, eternal God—the mysterious Ein Sof (אֵין סוֹף, "The Infinite")—and the mortal, finite universe (God's creation)" (Kabbalah, 2022).

The Renaissance philosopher Paracelsus believed, "the Qabalah opens up access to the occult, to the mysteries; it enables us to read sealed epistles and books and likewise the inner nature of men." (Paracelsus, 1988, 133) For those who practice the Kabbalistic system of correspondences, the ultimate goal is, "A direct & intimate knowledge of the divine on a level beyond that of the intellect" (Kerstein, 2022). As part of that practice, its correspondences can be utilized for various forms of meditation and divination, including dream interpretation, photo psychometry, bibliomancy, astrology, enthusiasm, gematria, augury, halomancy, palmistry, scrying, catoptromancy, and photomancy. It can also apply to cartomancy, which uses visual symbols and images like those found in the tarot. For those who understand how to use its structure of connections with divine and angelic names, it can also be employed for the creation of "amulets and incantations" (Eber, 2006, 137) and much more. This body of ancient Jewish mystical knowledge serves as the foundation for the Hermetic Qabalah and its correspondences.

In 1564, the legendary occultist and alchemist John Dee designed a talismanic glyph called the *Monas Hieroglyphica*. He believed the glyph embodied the unity of the cosmos. It was also understood as a divine node, a single point that connects corresponding empyrean filaments to all things in existence. Its shape consists of powerful esoteric alchemical and astrological symbols. Dee professed that one could use the figure to receive and capture knowledge, along with its divine power, as a catalyst for transformation. In addition, Dee authored a treatise by the same title to accompany the glyph.

The Monas is a highly esoteric work. In it [Dee] claims himself in possession of the most secret mysteries. He wrote it in twelve days while apparently in a peak (mystical) state: "[I am] the pen merely of [God] Whose Spirit, quickly writing these things through me, I wish and I hope to be." He claims it will revolutionize astronomy, alchemy, mathematics, linguistics, mechanics, music, optics, magic, and adeptship" (Peterson, 2022).

Pictures 8.3-8.5 Three Versions of John Dee's Monas Hieroglyphica (*see References*).

Abraham Kingwood read and contemplated the *Monas Hieroglyphica* before commenting on Dee's design, believing that his symbols, which were intended to express the inexpressible, were "potent in their divine capacities." Supporting Kingswood's assessment, a scholar of Gnosticism and Greek Papyrology claimed, "for many alchemists, symbols offer direct access to hidden knowledge and a way to harness this knowledge for advantage in the Great Work" (Kotansky, 48).

"Correspondences," GK declares,

> is the art and science of recognizing, identifying, and decoding the divine cipher, or signature, that lies hidden within the unseen connections between all points of universal contact. My great-grandfather spent countless hours devising detailed charts of correspondences in his *Book of the Eye of Horus*. It contains a wealth of knowledge about the relationships and analogies between elements, alphabetical letters (from many cultures), words, symbols, names, colors, shades from white to black, numbers, planets, stars, dates, animals, plants, time, parts of the body, geographical locations, human qualities and characteristics, and tarot cards. It also hass a section on photographic imagery.

His charts are maps that plot out the connections between the Earth and, "of the Fixed stars, the Firmament, the Starry Vault...the Empyrean, the *Primum Mobile*, the Heaven of Heavens, 'beyond which God holds His state in unapproachable, inconceivable grandeur, majesty, and splendor'" (Leigh, 1901, 161).

In Kingswood's book of correspondences, ingredients for spells were chosen specifically because of how they aligned with the purpose of an incantation. Some of the names of ingredients listed were noted by Kingswood to have been taken directly from ancient Egyptian sources, such as "bat's blood or the hair of a murdered man; some exotic [substances], such as Syrian honey; and some expensive, like frankincense, gold leaf or real lapis-lazuli. Lizards, especially double-tailed ones, [were] a popular ingredient" (Pinch, , 1994, 80). Some substances are listed by imaginative names that correspond to the actual material, like "the 'navel of a male crocodile' [which] means pondweed and that 'heart of a baboon' means oil of lilies…Snake's blood is interpreted as haematite, crocodile dung as Ethiopian soil, and the semen of Ammon (a Libyan deity) as the humble houseleek plant" (80).

What's more, Kingswood's hand-drawn maps illustrate a multitude of empyreal filaments of light, all snaking through unseen dimensions. They indicate that when two entities come into contact, a filament grows between them, creating an imperceptible bond through which energy can flow in either direction. As connections are established, a network expands. That network serves as the medium through which magic-light-energy flows. GK elaborates, "When the alchemist chooses a target for their magical work, their intent propels fluid, energetic forces through connecting conduits. The energy seeks out the intended recipient, a specific point in the infinite multitude of discrete, corresponding things."

To gain a better understanding, I asked GK if he would demonstrate how this filament theory worked.

Of course. Bring me a photo of someone you haven't had contact within many years. I'll revitalize the filament that connects you.

In October 2019, I brought a photo of a woman who used to be a good friend. Over thirty years ago, we had a falling out and hadn't spoken since. Last I heard, she had moved out of the state.

When I gave GK the photo, I didn't provide any information. I wasn't sure what to expect from GK's "revitalization" of the filament that connected my former friend and me. How would GK demonstrate that unseen bonds exist? It took only two days to find out. On October 29th, I received an email message.

"I'm back in Michigan! I moved back in April (smiley face emoji)".
I shot back, "No way!!!" She probably thought I was surprised that she was back. The truth is, I was stunned that GK could work through invisible filaments to exert some kind of influence over this person. I wanted to find a logical explanation for why she reached out. Was this a coincidence? I want to know how this happened!

Cognitive science's theory of connectionism is an excellent example of how correspondences function on a microcosmic level in the human brain. It is defined as an "approach to cognition in which multiple connections between nodes (equivalent to brain cells) form a massive interactive network in which many processes take place simultaneously. Certain processes in this network, operating in parallel, are grouped together in hierarchies that bring about results such as thought or action" (Define Connectionism).

Similarly, the brain's neural network is a microcosmic example of how filaments of light connect elements throughout the Universe. The concept of one's "self" acts as the central node of a biological system that links countless memories through pathways and electrical connections.

> In the brain, a typical neuron collects signals from others through a host of fine structures called dendrites. The neuron sends out spikes of electrical activity through the axon (the output and conducting structure) which can split into thousands of branches. At the end of each branch, a synapse converts the activity from the axon into electrical effects that inhibit or excite activity on the contacted (target) neuron. When a neuron receives excitatory input that is sufficiently large compared with its inhibitory input, it sends a spike of electrical activity (an action potential) down its axon (Neural Networks, 2022).

One could compare the physiological structure of the human brain to the Emerald Tablet's implication of a vast, inconceivable cosmic neural network, filled with an interconnected web of corresponding filaments, all being born, communicating, growing, transporting light energy in every moment, atrophying, and dissolving away over time. "It is the tree of life and death, whose branches and roots touch all perceivable and imperceivable things." Says GK, "Its existence as a cosmic phenomenon confirms the suspicion that we are all interconnected, and our photographs are part of that network."

One may believe that an extraneous photo in the hands of an alchemist is completely detached from its context of place and time. Nevertheless, due to its established array of correspondence filaments, the Kingswoods have found these objects well-suited for using magical connections to reach out into multiple realms of existence. GK reveals

> Once the alchemist confirms for themselves the reality of these concealed binding cords, it will bring the realization that the things we see around us correspond to a vast realm of subjects that cannot be seen or directly photographed. The implications of these correspondences and their effects will certainly have a profound impact on their lives. For example, much greater importance will be placed on where one consciously chooses to initiate and cultivate filaments of correspondence.

GK further emphasizes that, "The alchemist must consider the potential entanglement of relationships created by people they choose to associate with, the constellation of connections they want to cultivate around themselves." He adds that before a novice can advance in the Great Work, they must realize that they have been an unconscious magnet for inestimable connections, underscoring that each person is a focal point, a node where innumerable ley lines converge and meet. As such, it is never too soon to make conscious choices about the future connections they choose to establish. Then they must contemplate how all the myriad things that fill the cosmos are not isolated islands; each has lines of connection that reach across space and time, interacting with the people, places, and ephemera all around them.

In a discussion on photography, Dr. William Nieberding said,

> the connections the photographs make to the world surrounding them plays a significant part in the way they make meaning. The photographs are not ends in themselves, and their function is not to remain mute and detached from the viewer, the source-images, or the source-events that inspire them. Instead, by attenuating the distance between the viewer and the source image—by stretching to the breaking point the connection between subject and object, [photography's] constructions are a form of inquiry into the ways that photographs create consciousness (2011, 77).

In one's photo-alchemical practice, one strives to realize, in the words of Minor White, "Consciousness in photography comes out of an awakening to the interlocking interconnectedness of everything ..." (141).

9. The Photo-Alchemical Emblem

GK recounts family stories in the Kemetic Order:

> Members were referred to as "silversmiths." They were also referred to as 'philosophers' because they sought higher truth. This is because alchemy has always been a philosophical endeavor, rising from the study of natural philosophy. The field of study emerged from an inherent, basic human need for absolute truth, goodness, and beauty. In this sense, philosophy is a perfect partner to the arts, including the art of photography. Can't the common photographer be seen as a philosopher who uses the medium to explore truth and beauty as part of a natural and personal philosophy? When one performs the highest activities of both alchemy and photography, the focus of exploration follows a path from perfection in the natural world to the evolution of the self, and then outward to and beyond the mysteries of the cosmos. The alchemist-photographer who seeks outwardly into the world and turns inward toward the self will discover that these are the places where the illuminating knowledge of the Whole can be found.

He stresses that the discoveries of "illuminating knowledge" are only obvious to the mind that is prepared to receive their messages. The preparatory process for the philosopher-alchemist requires practice, discipline, and purification. Self-investment and self-commitment develop through a series of physical, mental, and spiritual activities, where each aspect of the alchemist's life is refined and elevated. The preliminary methods continue until each sequential level of transformation is achieved. All this work is done to prepare the aspirant for the next steps of transmutation, where the entirety of the alchemist's being is returned to its *original golden form*, the antenatal# state of divine consciousness (gnosis). This process is referred to as one's individual Great Work.

"Like all magical mysteries," Éliphas Lévi states,

> the secrets of the Great Work have a triple meaning: they are religious, philosophical and natural. Philosophical gold in religion is the Absolute and Supreme Reason; in philosophy, it is truth; in visible nature, it is the sun: in the subterranean and mineral world, it is the purest and most perfect gold. Hence the

search after the Great Work is called the Search for the Absolute, and this work itself is termed *the operation of the sun.*
— Éliphas Lévi, Transcendental Magic: Its Doctrine and Ritual

GK continues by stating,

> As an artistic medium in the service of the Great Work, photography is rightly recognized as *an operation of the sun.* Its practices within the Great Work are designed to excite the earthly senses in ways that awaken one's supernatural senses. The alchemist employs imagery to unify and harmonize the instruments of the senses, so they focus on achieving a specific purpose [more on the purpose later]. While each sense plays a vital role in the execution of the Great Work, none is more significant than sight.

Minor White taught that one should use their eyes to make and sustain "contact with the subject until a resonance is established between you and the livingness of the object" (quoted in Oring, 2021, 48). The resonance felt is the birth of a filament connection that grows between oneself and the subject. Concurrently, one's sense of visual awareness awakens. By applying White's approach to seeing, one connects deeply with the vital qualities of things while one's field of vision informs all the other senses. This practice also functions similarly when examining photographs.

The modality of Seeing also stimulates the other senses. For instance, when someone feels hungry and views beautiful photos of delicious food, the sensation of taste awakens through the stimulation of the eyes. While looking at a black-and-white photo of a weathered, coarse piece of wood, one may feel the texture with their eyes. If the eyes take in an image of ocean waves crashing on rocks, one can almost smell the salty mist and hear the roar of the water's motion. Like synesthesia#, the senses become exhilarated through the energetic activities of the eyes.

Viewing photographs becomes an experience that, for the perceptual ability of most viewers, is indistinguishable from directly experiencing the reality of the things they represent. Depending on the eyes that see them, images can become more than mere representational artifacts that engage the senses. "It can come to the eye as a visual image, it can come to the mind as an intellectual parallel between two ideas, but its truest value is when it flowers in the spirit in a sudden uprush of rich understanding" (Child, 1971, 1). For an alchemist, photographs can provide a sense of deep understanding in several ways, when they serve as mirrors, windows, and doorways of perception.

Minor White explained, "his philosophy of photographing as the mirror reflection of self, how the photographer is the receptor and carrier of special messages, and how the photograph can be a revelatory manifestation for others" (Bunnell et al., 1989, 21). As mirrors, photos reflect the inner sense of vision and vantage point of their maker. The scene captures the intentions of the alchemist-photographer, along with the processes they employ for the Great Work. For instance, Edward Weston's photograph of *Pepper Number 30* began with a typical green pepper. By harnessing the energies of his creative vision, Weston manipulated light, shadow, and silver to create a photographic window through which people could see the pepper in an entirely new way, as something remarkable. That photo also serves as a mirror, reflecting one's perceptions and heightening one's awareness. It transforms the way they see and understand a pepper. Because of Weston, the idea of the pepper is elevated, taking on almost erotic, sensual human qualities.

The notion of photographs as mirrors can also be understood from a deeply spiritual perspective. The 19th-century Sufi Emir Abd el-Kader was an early adopter of photography, as he recognized photographs to be divine mirrors. He referred to them as "polished bodies" (al-ajsâm al-saqîla), which reflected God's worldly manifestations and were sacred, theophanic# objects. In his view, all photographs were mirrors (a "privileged symbol in Islam") because the world and its contents were seen as clouded mirrors that, when polished, could reflect God. Philosopher Éric Geoffroy (1970) wrote, "In the *Kitab Al-Mawâqif* [a collection of 372 tenth-century spiritual sermons], there are thus long developments and graduated variations on the analogies between the physical world (the mirror, the photo) and metaphysics." Abd el-Kader's declarations about the nature of the photograph as a revelatory mirror were likely among the first, alongside Kingswood, to recognize a metaphysical dimension to image-making.

Kingswood emphasizes that photographs are also windows allowing us to gaze into the unknown scenes of the surrounding universe. As windows, photographs universally convey a sense of depth that invites exploration. When referring to a portrait in a photograph, people don't say, "the person *on* the photograph"; they say, "the person *in* the photograph." From an alchemical perspective, these windows also offer a means to examine the hidden parts of ourselves that largely remain unseen. Photos, like windows, serve as portals through which the alchemist can observe and study their mind, exploring concealed aspects of their very nature. By delving into their own depths, they simultaneously connect with the inseparable mystery of all surrounding them. As the Emerald Tablet enlightens, what is found within offers insights and revelations into what is without.

For example, mystic Thomas Merton used photographs as windows through which he perceived the ever-present, underlying, eternal reality that mostly remains invisible to viewers. Author Deba Patnaik wrote,

> Photography fulfilled Merton's "urgency of seeing, fully aware, experiencing what is here [Merton, 1996, p. 123]. It magnified his experience of "pure seeing", rather, more accurately, his images are its realization [Merton, 1966, p. 281]. This parallels the "inseeing" he admired in poet Rainer Maria Rilke, which lets one 'into the very center' [Merton, 1981, p. 30]. The artist, according to him, is both a "maker" and a "seer" [Merton, n.d., p. 21]—see-er/seer, who combines "aesthetic illumination" [Merton, 1998, p. 323] and "sapiential awareness [that] deepens our communion with the concrete" [Merton, 1981, p. 100]. And this fusion illuminates Merton's photographs. (Patnaik, 2022)

Photographs can also be seen as doors because visual imagery can be used as portals to extend their perception beyond their immediate environment and the limits of their bodily senses. On an ordinary level, one can gain a vicarious experience by viewing a photo of the planet Mercury, taken by a passing spacecraft. The experience of Mercury is mediated by the only medium available, as one will likely never have the opportunity to visit. On the other hand, an alchemist can utilize the photo to establish a direct connection between themselves and the planet. This bond can assist the alchemist in using astrology to better understand when certain spells are most likely to succeed and how planetary influences may impact those engaged in the spellwork. GK alleges, "With a single photo, suddenly the magical correspondence between the planet and the alchemist's orrery# comes alive!" He continues, "When conjuring with photographs in this way, one should remain in a state of cautious expectation. The results of spell-work can take form in unexpected ways."

For a hermetic lightsmith, photographs are multi-faceted and essential objects. They serve as mirrors, windows, and doorways. Moreover, according to Abd el-Kader, photography is a "veil." His concept was,

> The veil has this dual direction of both preventing from seeing, and revealing. In the same way, photography works as 'veils and

unveilings'. In the metaphysical domain, one can not look without a veil, because otherwise, subjected to the irradiations of the Divine Light, one is instantly burned. Similarly, in the physical field of the photo, if the diaphragm is opened too much, there is overexposure, and the film is burnt" (Raina, 2022).

Photographs embody metaphorical and magical properties, but they also reflect the physical aspects of the mechanism that produced them: the camera. In other words, the camera's components directly correspond to the concepts of mirrors, windows, and doorways. Peering into the viewfinder, the scene is visible solely because one sees a reflection in a mirror. The shutter, functioning as a door, opens and closes to capture the scene. GK adds, "The lens is a window, a threshold through which light takes flight into the chamber of infinite possibilities, where virgin silver sleeps, eager to be awakened by countless, soothing, landing points of ecstatic light. And the silver, which corresponds to the moon as it cycles from white to black, will open its eyes and look back at the viewer."

"The camera and all its art," GK proposes from his panpsychistic# vantage point, "was gifted to help humanity read the divine knowledge hidden within *synthemata*, encoded upon the pages of the divine book of the universe." In Donald Gordon Carty's publication, *The Emerald Tablet,* he wrote that,

> Nature is a book from which the wisdom of the divine can be read. By recognizing the divine signature of a thing, you can understand the connection between the *Above* and the *Below* through which it was manifested. Each thing has its own signature, the archetypal essence that can be identified by its similar expressions. By contemplating the relationship between the objects in our lives and the forces that created them, we can arrive at the 'thing itself' and know its inherent identity…This application of the Doctrine of Correspondences is fundamental, and by ignoring the congruencies between the *Above* and the *Below* we are holding back the wisdom of the universe. As alchemists, we must undergo a process of constant Separation in which we work only with the archetypal essences of people, things, and events" (2007, 52).

GK suggests that photographic images enable individuals to slow their intentional act of perception, allowing them to examine and contemplate more deeply the embedded wisdom that the casual observer can easily overlook.

Stellas

10. ALCHEMY & PHOTOGRAPHY: THE ARTS OF FIRE

Several etymologies claim that the original name for alchemy comes from the Arabic, *Al-Kimiya*, interpreted as *"from Kemet,"* the ancient name for Egypt. The word *Kemet* means "The Black Land," which describes the dark, rich soil along the Nile. Kemet wasn't merely a fertile land for crops, but for the civilization that cultivated new ways of seeing the world. Al-Kimiya is also said to mean "the process of transmutation by which to fuse or reunite with the divine or original form (Alchemy)." As a method for reunification, legend tells that the alchemical art "arose from the early Mystery rites of the ancient Craft Guilds of metallurgists and smiths -- which, in many cultures, had initiatory practices similar to those of shamans" (Windling, 2015).

From this ancestry of metalworkers, alchemy evolved into an art that seeks divine knowledge through practices of inner transformation. It aims to transmute the ordinary into something sublime. This process is embodied in the axiom, *solve et coagula*. Even as an inner art, its operations encompass the entirety of the alchemist's life. Initially, the shadow aspects of the practitioner are acknowledged as ordinary, base materials—typical elements of one's manifestation on the earthly plane. In this context, the alchemist's divine spark becomes eclipsed by physical and spiritual impurities, shaped by the hardening of life experiences of embodiment. After many years of diligent purification practices, ultimately, "A shadowy darkness passes always along with the philosophic body, moving in its own light until it is thoroughly purified from sensual defilements" (Atwood, 2005, 87-88). Then, the old self dissolves and reforms as the new, pristine self. GK points out, "Philosophers warn any metaphysician who tries to activate in themselves highest principles without first seeking purification through the Great Work would put themselves in danger." Moreover,

> without purification or any distinction of its light, our vehicle [the spirit] disports herself oftentimes in many mingling forms; as it is with those who dream or make to themselves a fool's paradise with the druggist's gas; since this, even impure as it is and full of folly, being if like nature with our life, coalesces; and would, if allowed to persist, consume its [the spirit's] rationality…[and be lead] imperceptibly, as it were, by an alluring grace, into that Hermetic wilderness and wild of Magic in which so many adventurers have gone astray (quoting Atwood, 2005, 56).

The alchemical journey begins with a search for the first principle, or first cause, which Aristotle defined as, "a basic assumption that cannot be deduced any further" (Aristotle, 1999). When applied to all things in the universe, the first principle suggests that everything can be reduced to its most vital and shared essence, the most basic substance from which they and all things emerged. This material, sought by alchemists, was reputed to be the building block of the universe, the *prima materia* (first matter), which was the soul shared by all things.

In effect, all ephemera, if reduced to their most fundamental essence, would reveal their prima materia. In ancient grimoires, this substance is identified as the most powerful generative and creative catalyst in existence. The alchemists of antiquity worked tirelessly to acquire prima materia and harness its potential to transmute substances from one form to another. The most famous alchemical ambition was to change lesser metals into gold. From a spiritual perspective, prima materia could transform a corrupted soul into one of divine purity.

In alchemy, the *Philosophers' Egg* is connected to the prima materia and its perfection.

> This symbol is compared to the "Egyptian stone," and the dragon, which bites its tail; consequently, the procreation symbol is compared to an eternity or cycle symbol. The 'Egyptian stone' is, however, the philosopher's stone or, by metonomy#, the great work (magnum opus) of its manufacture. The egg is the World Egg that recurs in so many world cosmogonies. The grand mastery refers usually and mainly to thoughts of world creation. The egg-shaped receptacle in which the master work was to be accomplished was also known as the "philosophical egg" in which the great masterpiece is produced. This vessel was sealed with the magic seal of Hermes; therefore hermetically sealed (Silberer, 1971, 91).

The essence of prima materia is said to perfect everything it touches through the alchemist's belief in the power of solve et coagula.

Prima materia is the first component required to create the philosophers' stone. The stone is a perfect, uncorrupted, primordial material that serves as the generator of all things and can, among other things, grant immortality. It was also viewed as the Holy Grail of the alchemists, the key to "both a material and spiritual realization" (Klossowski de Rola, 1997, 19). GK shares, "It is the noble, fiery and transformative element that caused Ra's words of light to amplify and divide into countless varied and infinite materials of the cosmos." The great medieval Hermetic philosopher Artephius was said to have successfully utilized the secrets of the philosophers' stone to live for more than 1000 years! For many alchemists, it was the most essential component required for *chrysopoeia*, or the transmutation of base metals, such as lead, into gold.

> According to Paracelsus, there are three types of gold in alchemy: astral gold, elementary gold, and vulgar gold. Astral gold, "has its center in the sun, which communicates it by its rays to all inferior beings. It is an igneous substance, which receives a continual emanation of solar corpuscles that penetrates all things sentient, vegetable,and mineral." Elementary gold "is the most pure and fixed portions of the elements, and of all that is composed of them. All sublunary beings included in the three kingdoms contain in their inmost center a precious grain of this elementary gold." Vulgar gold "is the most beautiful metal of our acquaintance, the best that Nature can produce, as perfect as it is unalterable in itself." [Furthermore], Paracelsus said that the philosophers" stone, is elementary gold, or "living philosophical gold," "living sulphur," and "true fire." (Ferre and Bewick, 2017).

The golden stone is the agent that possesses the power to transmute all that is impure into its highest divine or golden state. Furthermore, "Gold is the metal of the sun, solar magic, the male principle, light, power,

Picture 10.1 Vuur, Adriaen Collaert, after Maerten de Vos, 1580 – 1584.

divine intelligence, purity, and spiritual enlightenment. In spiritual alchemy it represents the attainment of a refined and high level of consciousness" (Ferre and Bewick, 2017).

Evelyn Underhill offered further information about the alchemist's spiritual quest. She wrote,

> The art of the alchemist, whether spiritual or physical, consists in completing the work of perfection, bringing forth and making dominant, as it were, the "latent goldness" which "lies obscure" in metal or man. The ideal adept of alchemy was therefore an "auxiliary of the Eternal Goodness." By his search for the "Noble Tincture" which should restore an imperfect world, he became a partner in the business of creation, assisting the Cosmic Plan. Thus, the proper art of the Spiritual Alchemist, with whom alone we are here concerned, was the production of the spiritual and only valid tincture or Philosopher's Stone; the mystic seed of transcendental life which should invade, tinge, and wholly transmute the imperfect self into spiritual gold. That this was no fancy of seventeenth-century allegorists, but an idea familiar to many of the oldest writers upon alchemy—whose quest was truly a spiritual search into the deepest secrets of the soul—is proved by the words which bring to an end the first part of the antique "Golden Treatise upon the Making of the Stone," sometimes attributed to Hermes Trismegistus. "This, O Son," says that remarkable tract, "is the Concealed Stone of Many Colours, which is born and brought forth in one colour; know this and conceal it . . . it leads from darkness into light, from this desert wilderness to a secure habitation, and from poverty and straits to a free and ample fortune" (Underhill, 2002, 143).

The search for the Philosopher's Stone began in Egypt, where one of the first mages recorded the theory and practice of alchemy. His name was Hermes Trismegistus. Although historians tell us that most of Trismegistus' Hermetic manuscripts were destroyed at various points between 296 BCE and the eighth century, the name Hermes Trismegistus reemerges as the author of many writings on the Hermetic arts over the centuries. Numerous renowned alchemists of the time used the pseudonym to publish their greatest works. Thus, a Hermetic tradition emerged during Europe's Middle Ages when alchemists provided resources for others who sought to learn about alchemy and the Philosopher's Stone. Some of that knowledge would today align with what we know as chemistry, physiology, and physics.

Between the 8th century and the 1200s, it was "... a period of ascetic and mystical alchemists whose writings and practices were [filled] with allegories, symbolism, occultism, mystery and theosophy... Through their impact, occultism, theology, and alchemy became strongly integrated" (Ahmed, 2013, 75). During this time, Sir Roger Bacon, a Franciscan Friar, was recognized as the first Englishman to have earnestly studied alchemy. Bacon, a respected scholar, philosopher, and alchemist, was given many labels, some of which included heretic, occultist, and genius. He was devoted to, "the search for a mystical relationship between man and the cosmos, as in alchemical speculations, and the knowledge of magical or unnatural forces" (Cintas, 2003). In his book, *Opus Majus*, Bacon focused on the properties of optics and eyesight, theorizing that "Vision is direct, refracted, or reflected; spiritually the first is divine, the second angelic, the third human" (Opus Majus, 2022). His interests followed in the footsteps of those Greek philosophers who "believed in lenses that connected the world of gods and humans, and when one knows how to adjust their sight, can view the gods, and the gods looking back at us" (Bacon, 1897). While the Greeks' studies elaborated on the groundwork laid by ancient Egyptian fabrication of lenses, Bacon's work introduced significant new discoveries and applications to the evolving field of optics.

In 1300s Paris, there lived a Scrivener named Nicholas Flamel, who sought to uncover the hidden secrets of the philosophers (Souto, 2013). Coming from a poor background with little education, he took the initiative to teach himself the Hermetic arts. Legend asserts that one late evening, Flamel dreamt that a *Watcher* (an ancient ethereal being) appeared and offered him a glowing, pulchritudinous# book. The supernatural entity instructed Flamel to examine its pages closely but cautioned him that neither he nor anyone else would be able to understand its contents. Flamel examined the tome from a distance; however, when he reached out and attempted to grasp the book, both it and the Watcher vanished.

As the story goes, one day Flamel stumbled upon the very same book. He found it for sale in a market. He described it as, "a gilded book, very old and large, which cost only two florens. It was not made of paper or parchment, as other books are, but of admirable rinds (as it seemed to me) of young trees. The cover of it was of brass; it was well bound and graven all over with a strange kind of letters, which I take to be Greek Characters, or some such like" (Barrett and Waite, 1888, 99). The emblematic book contained 21 pages of text, blank pages, and several painted images, along with the author's name: Abraham Eleazar. There was also a curse against anyone who opened the book who was not a "Priest or Scribe."

The most important subject in the contents of the book was instructions for, "the *transmutation* of metals, to the end that he might help and assist his dispersed people (Jewish people), to pay their tributes to the Roman Emperors" (1888, 100). The alchemical text that Flamel purchased appeared to provide instructions for converting base metals into gold. The process, which was described and illustrated in detail, spoke of the need for "prima materia," or the omnipresent first matter. Following the book's instructions, it was written that in 1382 Flamel found success. With his wife as his witness, he used the knowledge he had amassed, along with impassioned prayer and the information in the brass-covered book, to successfully transmute mercury into gold. Not once, but three times.

In the 1602 book, *Theatrum Chemicum*, the author states, "They have compared the 'prima materia' to everything, to male and female, to the hermaphroditic monster, to heaven and earth, to body and spirit, chaos, microcosm, and the confused mass; it contains in itself all colors and potentially all metals; there is nothing more wonderful in the world, for it begets itself, conceives itself, and gives birth to itself" (The Public Domain Review, 2022). Mary Anne Atwood elaborated further when she called prima materia, "the primal fire,…Light, and Mercury (Atwood, 2005). Other Mercurialists referred to it as the beating heart of the sun, a name that would become very meaningful to Abrahm Kingswood over 200 years later.

In the mid-1600s, there was a German Jesuit scholar, Athanasius Kircher, who was once referred to as "the supreme representative of Hermeticism in Post-Reformation Europe" (Sir Thomas Browne and the Kabbalah). As such, Kircher proclaimed that Egypt held the key to all mortal and divine secrets (Kircher, 1652). His studies of Egypt's mysteries included those of optics and lenses.

The knowledge he acquired led him to invent a projection device he called the "Steganographic Mirror." He discovered that "by placing a lens between a screen and a mirror which had been written on, a sharp but inverted image would appear on the screen. [Kircher used] a spherical water-filled flask as a condenser to concentrate the light. Images and texts painted on the mirror's surface could be projected by light from a candle after dark" (Ars Magna Lucis Et Umbrae). At the same time, he was writing a book titled *Ars Magna Lucis et Umbrae* (The Great Art of Light and Shadow, 1645), in which he discussed the theories and applications of his invention, along with "many different aspects of light, including physical, astronomical, astrological and metaphysical" (Ars Magna Lucis Et Umbrae [*Wikipedia*]). The frontispiece image of Kircher prepares the reader for his comprehensive exploration of light in all its aspects. It was described as follows:

Angels form an arc under the central light, which is YHWH, the Hebrew letters for God. Daylight is the source of direct light, refracted light, and light reflected by night (on right). Divine authority, a hand writing a book that absorbs light directly from the source of all light, oversees the daylight, and it is a little higher than Reason, the hand writing a book above the night, which receives a more modest eye's light. Below daylight is Profane Authority, which receives only a lantern's light; below Reason is Sense, which points to an image produced by a telescope. Emperor Ferdinand enters the picture as one of Kircher's patrons (The Great Art of Light and Shadow).

Picture 10.2 *Ars Magna Lucis et Umbrae* by Athanasius Kircher, 1646.

The exhaustive study of optics and light in Kircher's book caught the attention of Dutch scientist Christiaan Huygens, who used this information to invent a device called the "magic lantern" (Lemagny and

111

Rouille, 1987, 14-15). This technological marvel used light, lenses, and a concave mirror to project ghostly images onto surfaces. Reports indicated that the projections terrified viewers, leading them to believe the images were of supernatural origin.

> The desire to give substance to the fleeting reflection spontaneously created by light is rooted in the deepest levels of the human imagination. It endowed all these optical curiosities with magical attraction, as if people already sensed that one day one of these boxes would make it possible to capture or reconstitute, at will, any image whatever its subject. When the magic lantern was first described in 1646...its success was immediate and enduring. Such dreams inspired storytellers with tales which in many cases looked forward to photography and even beyond it (Kircher, 1652, 567-568).

Isaac Newton lived during the same period as Huygens when he announced his discovery of the prism and its spectral properties of light. He proved that the full body of white or clear light is composed of seven colors. He then realized that the human eye perceives the many colors in the world only because each object reflects a specific range of light's spectral hues back to the eye, while the others are absorbed by the surfaces of objects, producing heat.

Using Bacon's prior observations on optics, Newton made improvements to the recently invented telescope, extending the reach of the human eye into the cosmos. These discoveries led to Newton's writings in his book *Opticks*, published in 1704. In the book, he discussed the use of a single convex lens to enhance image quality in the camera obscura. All these early discoveries laid the groundwork for adapting the camera obscura into what would ultimately lead to the 19th-century invention of cameras and photographic lenses.

English poet Alexander Pope wrote the following in reverence for Newton's wide-ranging contributions to knowledge:

> Nature and nature's laws lay hid in night;
> God said "Let Newton be" and all was light.

Newton was an avid student of alchemy. His theories and practices were an amalgamation of metaphysical and physical knowledge. It was difficult for people of that time to distinguish which parts of his work pursued magical powers and which could be seen as new science, which were conducted in dark secrecy, and which were openly investigated.

"'The British chemist Robert Boyle, a Newton contemporary,' said of alchemists, 'there exists conceal'd in the world' a group of chemists, of a much higher order able to transmute baser Metalls into perfect ones.' His purpose, he wrote, was to draw 'the Chymists Doctrine out of their Dark and Smoakie Laboratories into open light'" (Wilford, 2006). Certainly, Newton was one of the forefathers of science, but until the end of his life, he continued his search for the miraculous prima materia, the "one thing" that created everything in the cosmos.

In due course, alchemy offered up some of its secrets to foster the discoveries of photography. While doing so, most emphasis shifted away from alchemy's branches of investigation and toward the application of empirical science. In the early 1800s, alchemy was widely recognized for promoting three distinct branches of growth. The first involved investigations into the natural and physical laws and properties of the universe and their relationship to the human soul. This branch supported the early inventors of photographic processes and was the precursor to modern science.

The second area of exploration was the spiritual alchemy of the Great Work. This path was also concerned with natural and physical laws, but more in how they could reveal the hidden secrets that lead to the Divine Wisdom of the Original and Universal Soul. The roots of this increasing interest can be found in the writings of the 17th-century alchemist, Johann Otto von Helwig, who wrote, "Thou possessest natural wisedom; and I promise thee, that with this light thou canst unlock the most hidden and recluse mysteries of Nature, and make familiar to thee hidden treasure" (Brice and Alipili, 1696, 78).

The third, disconcerting direction of study was how alchemy was exploited for deception, deviousness, and deceit. There were individuals who corrupted the noble intentions of Hermeticists and proto-scientists, seeking to produce gold, and exploited those ambitions to cheat others through trickery. False gold, painted coins, and a multitude of other fraudulent schemes preyed on the gullibility and greed of many. Common folk, nobles, and even governments were swindled out of their riches.

On January 13, 1404, King Henry IV signed a law into effect that forbade the *multiplication* of metals. It remained a felony in England to attempt to convert any metal into another. Other governments enacted similar laws to combat deceit, and numerous individuals were charged and imprisoned. Due to the prevalence of charlatans calling themselves "alchemists," all alchemists became outcasts. People were reminded that almost a century earlier, Dante Alighieri, in his book, *Divine Comedy*, prophetically placed alchemists in the lowest circle of Hell (Kotansky, 2005, 37)!

When photography finally emerged in the mid-1800s, it also developed into branches of interest, similar to the paths taken in alchemy. Firstly, it represented a new frontier of discovery that attracted curious, innovative, and creative-minded individuals. Secondly, for some, it became a means for the highest spiritual pursuits of the Great Work. Thirdly, just as alchemy caught the attention of unscrupulous malefactors, so did picture-making during the rise of *spirit photography*. GK supposed, "Spirit artists made real the original, 'ghost in the machine' and it was an artful practice that quickly became a phenomenal sensation!" What seemed like magic was not. It resembled author Ambrose Bierce's satirical definition of magic as the "art of converting superstition into coin" (Bierce, 2022).

The widespread media attention gave rise to a throng of photographers who claimed to, for a price, be able to record "invisible watchers in the room, [who were] disembodied spirits" (Photography, 1893, 272) and "manifestations of supernatural phenomena such as ghosts, fairies, fluidic effusions, ectoplasm, auras, levitations, transfigurations, visual telepathy, and mesmerism, among others" (Harvey, 2006). The validity of these images had its detractors, but many outspoken supporters, including spiritualists and apparitionists, proclaimed the new developments as miraculous and authentic. Even respected members of society, like the knighted English writer and physician Sir Arthur Conan Doyle, openly and emphatically endorsed the veracity of spirit photography on several occasions.

> Just as the spiritualist medium materializes the spirit world into visible and auditory form, so new methods of making images by light provided the "perfect medium" for fixing in visual form what had been apprehended if not seen – the presence of the dead among the living, the existence of unseen fluids and rays surrounding our bodies. Just as the telescope and the microscope made observable hitherto unknown worlds, so the camera could now make perceptible to the eye the spirits of the departed and invisible emanations. Thus, photography could "de-occult" [Chéroux, 2005, 119], granting to these phenomena the same ontological status as the intractably material chairs and tables whose levitation by mediums was captured on light-sensitive plates [Sussman, 2007, 339].

The notoriety of ghost photography was fueled by a cultural phenomenon: the dramatic surge of interest in spiritualism. In the 1800s, spiritualist groups and their activities flourished in Europe and America. In 1856, a series of pictures produced at the London Stereoscopic Company were displayed as "The Ghost in the Stereoscope" (Spirit Photography [*Wikipedia*]). Because photographs were perceived as factual reproductions of reality, viewers couldn't help but believe what they saw! A few years later, curiosity about spirit photography became widespread. Popular demand peaked during the escalation of deaths in the American Civil War (1861-1865). Noticing the interest of those wanting to contact their deceased loved ones, photographer Sir David Brewster developed techniques that he claimed would accurately produce ghost images.

Picture 10.3 by William Hope, ca. 1870.   Picture 10.4 by F.M. Parkes, ca. 1872.

Within a few short years, spirit photographers, which GK called "Spirit Photographic Mediums," such as Édouard Buguet, Frederick Hudson, F. M. Paares, and William Mumler, opened studios that offered portraits of clients with the spirits of their deceased friends and relatives. Through experimentation, long exposures, double exposures, and sleight of hand, they could easily produce human-like, pellucid# presences in their images. "At the height of his success, Mumler charged an extravagant $10 [over $400.00 today] for a dozen photographs, with no guarantee that spirits would be recorded. Repeated trips to his studio were often required before a sitter was blessed with a presence" (Spirit Photography [*Spirit Photography - Dead Media Archive*]).

In 1869, Mumler was brought to trial in New York City but was later released. In 1922, English spirit photographer William Hope was proven to be a fraud. This news marked the beginning of the slow decline of spirit photography (also known by the neologisms: psychography, skotography, radiography, electrography, thoughtography, nengraphy, and thermography) throughout the early 20th century.

"The heyday of spirit photography took place before my great grandfather's birth, but it was still happening after he was born." GK shares that in his later years, Abraham Kingswood reflected on the phenomenon.

> My great grandsire Abraham was taken by the idea of photographing specters. Ghosts and apparitions were part of his enigmatic world. When these photographers were exposed as charlatans, Abraham agreed with the allegations. He was well-acquainted with how to use the technique of double exposure and believed that what those photographers had done was indeed an illusion, enacted upon the impressionable. He also claimed that it might one day be possible, through some form of prenatural-image synthesis, to perfect the invention of Dr. Julian Ochorowicz, enabling the ability to photograph spiritual entities, or perhaps even projected visualizations or thoughts. It could be that even the technologies of skotography and psychography might advance. However, this would only be achievable by using a recording medium that was sensitive to the invisible spectrum of empyreal light.

And if that day comes, one may even be able to photograph the filaments of light that bind them to their deceased loved ones, connecting them to all the meaningful, tangible objects they collected and cherished in earthly life.

Who knows what miracles photography will perform in the future? In 1911 British writer on spiritualism, James Coates speculated that it wasn't that long ago when the idea of photographing the unseen seemed impossible. He wrote,

> To say that the invisible cannot be photographed, even on the material plane, would be to confess ignorance of facts which are commonplace — as, for instance, to mention the application of

Xray photography to the exploration of the muscles, of fractures of bone, and the internal organs. Astronomical photography affords innumerable illustrations of photographing the invisible. In the foregoing, and analogous cases, the photographing is that of material, though invisible, objects (Coates, 1911, 2).

Eventually, the whole spirit photography house of cards fell. In *Aperture Magazine's Spirituality Issue*, twenty-first century photographer David Company elaborates on the collapse of spirit photography:

> They played the medium's sobriety against its easy way with delirious tricks, claiming to manifest everything from specters to the living dead. It's hard to imagine anyone falling for those hokey ectoplasmic emanations leaking from mouths and eyes, but fall they did. The well of human credulity is deep, especially in moments of psychological crisis. Spirit photography tended to find its strongest reception among the traumatized, bereaved, and emotionally needy, which is why it was so popular in the wake of nineteenth-century wars in the United States and Europe…but we'd would do well to remember that it's bogus claims were propped up by the supposed objectivity of the camera. Nobody wants a *painting* of a ghost (2019, 39-40).

In addition,

> In the 20th century — in large part because of photography —our awareness of the multidimensionality of the world has increased at a striking pace. [Many photographic applications] have produced images that have helped us expand awareness of our universe into hitherto unimaginable dimensions. The outcome of these diverse photographic explorations has led to significant social, political, cultural, scientific, and technological reforms (Goldberg, 1993). But most importantly, for psychology, the creation of these new levels of realities have further demonstrated what the consciousness disciplines and the perennial philosophies have proclaimed for centuries: Our ordinary seeing is limited, and our conventional, consensus of reality is just one possible version of the world among many (Gross and Shapiro, 2001, 45).

With all the scientific and metaphysical revelations that photography delivered, "In sixty years, photography had crossed over from the arcane to the mundane" (Principe, 2014, 97). During the same period, a similar shift occurred in the public perception of alchemy. Scholars mark 1661 as "a watershed moment marking the repudiation and subsequent demise of 'alchemy'" (2014, 97), but this referred only to "gold hunters." It wasn't until the end of the 19th century that true hermetic alchemy faded into history as it transitioned into the more reputable field of chemistry. Its mystical philosophy, practices, and way of life were abandoned in favor of empirical thought. Some of alchemy's arcane terminology was adopted into the sciences, including the chemical processes of photography (i.e., solution, filtration, evaporation, fixation, and calcination). All these processes are still used today to produce powdered photographic processing chemistry!

As photography became ubiquitous, alchemists moved further away from public view. The 1960s and 70s witnessed a surge in paganism and the revival of indigenous religions, some of which practiced magic. Witchcraft, or Wicca, had already been gaining momentum as a recognized spiritual practice. It became a popular spiritual path for many drawn to nature. They sought the secrets that the cosmos offered to teach and practiced magic. The late 20th century's growing number of magic-based belief systems fostered an environment of acceptance that alchemists found welcoming. Although alchemists often adhered to a tradition of solitude in their practices, they could still find communities in which they were accepted. One example of this shift in attitudes is the International Alchemy Guild, founded by Dennis William Hauck in 1998, which still maintains chapters worldwide.

GK clarifies,

> There are many kinds of alchemical lineages, each with practices that have evolved along various paths divergent from the original masters of old. Some alchemists stay true to the lineage of ancient Greco-Roman teachings, while others claim origins in Babylonian, Jewish, Arabic, or Egyptian traditions. A few embrace a purely laboratory-based practice. Carl Jung and his followers pursued alchemy for its potential as a psychologically transformative method. Some engage with systems rooted in magical and devotional, deity-centered practices, while others adhere to kabbalistic teachings. There are also those who utilize fine art as a central component of their work, and at least one alchemist believes that photography holds the keys to the mysteries of the Great Work.

11. A Tradition of Secrecy

The ancient Egyptian pyramids were built to house the bodies of deceased pharaohs. They were also designed to secure the ruler's secrets. Forever. Once a pharaoh's body was hermetically sealed inside, the chambers and passages were meant to remain closed for eternity. Special spells were cast as paintings and carvings on the walls, and even inside the sarcophagus. There were also invocations and prayers written in hieroglyphics, intended to be read only by the spirit of the deceased pharaoh.

The officiating priests of the deceased demanded that others never be allowed to see what was written, thereby making it impossible for anyone to know the contents of the funerary messages. Just seeing the chiseled or painted characters would be harmful for the uninitiated. The writings contained curses for those mortals who attempted to steal the wealth and power of the magical inscriptions locked inside the tomb.

Similarly, alchemy has a rich history of secrecy. In the Middle Ages, patent laws were nonexistent. There were no regulations to safeguard inventors from the theft of their discoveries. At a time when professional and artisan guilds thrived, alchemy guilds were notably absent. This was because medieval practitioners wished to keep information about their ingredients, recipes, processes, experiments, and discoveries concealed. There was a profound fear that secrets could be stolen and then exploited by other alchemists.

For example, alchemists were particularly fearful that their knowledge might end up in the hands of greedy kings or treasure seekers. Everyone assumed that if a rival alchemist shared details about which of their processes succeeded and which ones failed, the competitor could then use that information to fill in gaps in their own knowledge. By doing so, they could advance their own research, potentially leading to a loss of power and wealth for others.

In alchemist Sir George Ripley's 1678 hermetico-poetical writings in the Fifth Gate, he discusses his views on the importance and purpose of keeping one's work secret:

> Each Artist striving them how to conceal,
> Lest wretched Caitiffs should these Treasures steal:
> Nor Villains should their Villanies maintain
> By this rare Art; which danger they to heal,

In horrid Metaphors veil'd an Art most plain,
Lest each Fool knowing it, should it when known disdain.
(Philalethes & Cooper, 2023, 371)

There was also a moral obligation felt and honored by spiritually devout alchemists, like Henry Cornelius Agrippa, who bore the weight of his promises. When confronted with the idea of sharing his knowledge of the hermetic arts, he wrote:

> I could tell many things of this art, if I had not sworn to keep silence, and this silence is so constantly and religiously observed of the ancient philosophers, that there is bound no faithful writer of approved authority that hath openly described this art: which thing has induced many to believe that all books of this art were but of late years invented, etc. Finally of the one blessed stone alone, besides which there is no other thing, the subject of the most holy stone of the philosophers, to speak rashly, would be a sacrilege and I should be foresworn" (Atwood, 2005, 20).

Any knowledge gained was regarded as craft secrets, thus confidential and proprietary. Laboratory alchemists worked to solve their unique alchemical puzzles, yet each alchemist possessed a different set of information. To safeguard their knowledge and themselves, alchemists wrote under pseudonyms and recorded their findings in a hermetic labyrinth of coded language. This allowed them to maintain control over their secret science and avoid being kidnapped or forced into labor in their own laboratories.

For example, Raymond Lully announced that he had produced 50,000 pounds of gold and was promptly arrested by King Edward II. As his captive, Lully was compelled to continue his alchemical endeavors to fill the king's coffers. In an environment marked by concealment and distrust, all knowledge was coveted and incredibly powerful…especially for kings. During the Middle Ages, typical students of the alchemical arts were engaged in a race for success, striving to achieve the elusive goal of golden perfection. Consequently, the tradition of secrecy rendered alchemy a predominantly solitary journey.

After alchemist Alexander Seton demonstrated the successful transmutation of base metals into gold, he exiled himself from his home. He became an anonymous traveler who feared being recognized due to his success with multiplication (the production of gold). He reported,

I am suffering…a continual banishment: deprived of the society of friends and family, and, as if driven by the Furies, am compelled constantly to fly from place to place and from kingdom to kingdom, without delaying anywhere. And thus, though I possess all things, I have no rest or enjoyment of any, except in the truth, which is my whole satisfaction. They who have not a knowledge of this art imagine, if they had, they would do many things: I also thought the same, but am grown circumspect by experience of many dangers and the peril of life. I have seen so much corruption in the world, and those even who pass for good people are so ruled by the love of gain, that I am constrained even from the works of mercy, for fear of suspicion and arrest. I have experienced this in foreign countries, where, having ventured to administer the medicine to sufferers given over by physicians, the instant the cures became known, a report was spread about of the Elixir, and I have been obliged to disguise myself, shave my head, and change my name, to avoid falling into the hands of wicked persons, who would try to wrest the secret from me, in hopes of making gold. I could relate many incidents of this kind which have happened to me. Would to God that gold and silver were as common as the street mud; we should not then be obliged to fly and hide ourselves, as if we were accursed like Cain" (Atwood, 2005, 22).

At the same time, some were more interested in mysticism and the metamorphosis of the human embodied spirit into spiritual gold. They had their own reasons to be discreet. GK explains,

> Those hermeticists, driven by noble purpose, took on as their mission of discovering the divine secrets they believed to be hidden by god, for good reason, throughout this reality, as such knowledge was deemed too powerful for everyone to possess. Feeling as if they had solved the riddle of the Sphinx itself, they became the guardians of epoptic# revelations. Gaining access to these secrets has always been a privilege and is necessary for advancement in the transformative processes leading to prelapsarian# perfection. The discovery of secrets is still regarded today as possible only through the grace of god, so it wouldn't be prudent to pass them on to someone to whom they were not given. Thus, each alchemist was and is responsible for their own petitions to God and the results bestowed upon them by God.

For all clandestine groups, as was certainly true for the Order, the emphasis on secrecy was highlighted as part of initiation rites. Morgaine, in the *Mists of Avalon* describes the requirements of secrecy as an initiate when she said,

> How do you write of the making of a priestess? What is not obvious, is secret. Those who have walked that road will know, and those who have not will never know though I should write down all the forbidden things…The Sight came easily…It was not so easy to bid it come when I willed…and to close the gates of the Sight when it was not fitting I should see…It was the small magics which came hardest, forcing the mind first to walk in unaccustomed paths. To call the fire and raise it at command, to call the mists, to bring rain-all these were simple, but to know when to bring rain or mist…But of that I may say nothing…this is a Mystery of which it is forbidden to write (Bradley, 1983, 190–191).

The first initiatory practice of secrecy in the Kemetic Order was imparted during the Naming Ritual. There, novices received a ceremonial appellation given by Ra. This name was meant to embody the nobility of their magical identity. Simultaneously, it was believed to be their true name, equated with the future identity of a transmuted, divine-unified self. It was the name that accurately described who they truly were but couldn't see clearly enough to grasp its veracity. Thus, its meaning, letters, and sounds became the focus of contemplation and meditation. As a wise adept once said, "we become that which we meditate on." Only abbreviations of the names were spoken during official gatherings of members. In other words, the initiate and Ra were the only ones who knew their full and true names. Moreover, outside the sacred group context, even the abbreviated form of the name was never disclosed.

The Chaldean Oracles speak of the power represented by names, while emphasizing the necessity of secrecy in their Theurgic invocation of fire. They say:

> For there are names in every nation given from god,
> Which have unspeakable power in rites.
> When thou seest a sacred fire without form,
> Shining, flashingly through the depths of the world,
> Hear the voice of fire.
> (The Eclectic Pythaorean, 2008)

Abraham Kingswood recited to his son the advice Abbot Johannes Trithemius gave to Heinrich Cornelius Agrippa in 1510: "I have only one more admonition to give you. Never forget it: to the vulgar, speak only of vulgar things; keep for your friends every secret of a higher order; give hay to the oxen and sugar to the parrot. Understand my meaning, lest you be trod under the oxen's feet, as oftentimes happens." GK stated this as part of a request to initiates that they, "let not their tongue be guilty of indiscretion." This quote has been recited at the end of every one of the Kemetic Order of the Silver Sun's initiation rites since then. Even Albertus Magnus, "advised other alchemists to live a life of isolation, patience, and discretion…[lest] the alchemist's work could be destroyed" (Guiley, 2006, 7).

Another reason for the secretiveness was that alchemy became an unacceptable activity in many social circles. "Embarrassment is a social disease. Secrecy can banish it and thus create the potential for private, idiosyncratic belief" (Luhrmann, 1989, 142). "Thus," informs GK, "Alchemists became the targets of derision and opprobriums#, and were looked down upon as characters of ill repute."

For example, the first-century monk and practitioner of alchemy, Gerbert of Aurillac, once traveled to Spain, where he was said to have acquired dark secrets in the Hermetic arts. There, the legend says he used his newfound knowledge of magic to fabricate a head that spoke to him. It offered knowledge of the future. It even told him that he would become Pope—a very unlikely possibility. Some said the head was a bronze mouthpiece of the devil, which was, at some point, worshiped by the Templars. And they called it "the mysterious Baphomet" (Holy Crusader, 2022). Aurillac faced growing opposition that accused him of sacrilege and labeled him an alchemist and black magician. On April 2nd, in 999 CE, Aurillac was elected Pope and became Sylvester the Second.

Without a distinction between virtuous intentions and greed or blasphemy, alchemy's practices were rendered illegal in the 14th century. If alchemists who worked with supernatural entities or mysticism were discovered, they could face punishment under the Church's laws. Consequently, some were labeled as heretics, including Philosopher Robert Fludd. While the accusation of heresy was concerning, the Church was more troubled by alchemy's growing popularity among monks, as it distracted them from their duties, prayers, and religious studies. Practitioners risked arrest, imprisonment, and some were even executed. It was out of a desire for self-preservation that alchemists sought to keep their activities and knowledge hidden from those around them, even from family members who could be implicated in their crimes. There came a time when being called an alchemist was considered an egregious insult.

Occult societies in Europe were clandestine, partly out of fear of negative and potentially dangerous repercussions from others who might overreact. Superstitious citizens may believe that those among them were performing arcane rituals to control unseen forces. Words like "witchery" and "sacrilege" were wielded as weapons. GK points out, "Another reason for secrecy within the Order was that it contained and amplified personal and group magical energies. Covertness created a protective boundary which unified the collective membership, and which strengthened the Order over time. To tell a secret is to set in motion the dissipation of personal and communal energetic fields that can be used to amplify magical forces." "The magician will always keep silence with respect to his way, rise and success. This silence grants the highest powers and the more this commandment is obeyed, the more easily accessible these powers will become. Manage it so that you spend as much time as possible in your rise or advance" (Bardon, 1987, 34).

Mary Anne Atwood conveyed the sentiments of the late 19th century when she wrote,

> O declare a man an Alchemist in the present day would be to brand him as insane, and the Hermetic ground is as far out of the road of common thought as if it were tabooed; not indeed that anyone regards it as sacred, but devilish rather, or delirious, or ridiculous, as the bias may be. Meanwhile, therefore, to reconcile this science or the teachers of it to the world, we should feel to be a task above our ability, were it very far greater than it is; the prejudice having grown so old and strong that neither reason nor authority is longer able to balance it. But in whatever light we be disposed to regard Alchemy, whether as the acme of human folly, or contrariwise, as the recondite perfection of wisdom and causal science, it appears almost equally remarkable: considered in the former way we have before us a huge amount of avarice, mad credulity, and fraud accumulating on continually from immemorial time, with the deplorable conclusion, that the greater part of those to whom the world has been taught to look up as philosophical authorities were in fact dupes and worse deceivers (Atwood, 2005, 26).

GK says accordingly,

In a certain sense, organizations like the Kemetic Order of the Silver Sun took great pains to remain secret because they witnessed similar groups being persecuted with public mistrust and fear. For instance, secret societies of the time, such as the Freemasons and the Golden Dawn, were incapable of preserving silence. They suffered the consequences of that shortcoming. The breaking of oaths led to the Freemasons' loss of potency in their

Picture 11.1 Silentio by Giulio Bonasone, 1500.
(Courtesy of the National Gallery of Art, Washington D. C.).

mystical rites and, for the same reason, was a contributing factor in the eventual demise of the Golden Dawn. Abraham Kingswood's Order was very successful in avoiding scrutiny and derision because the group remained small and stayed faithful to their vows. If I had not announced their historical presence, no one would have ever known that they existed. Still, aside from my ancestors and me, the common and spiritual identities of the Order's members over the years will never be known. On other subjects, I continue to remain silent. Names, among other secrets, will stay concealed, and that knowledge will inevitably die with me.

In addition to secret societies, there was popular interest in various public guilds, associations, clubs, and fraternities during the 1800s. In the mid-1800s, citizens formed groups around their interest in photography. "The first was an informal grouping, the Edinburgh Calotype Club around 1843. The first British photographic group, the Leeds Photographic Society, was formed in 1852" (Royal Photographic Society, 2022). Under the patronage of Queen Victoria and Prince Albert, the Photographic Society of London was established in 1853. Its purpose was focused on "The interchange of thought and experience among Photographers" (RPS: History, 2022). Later, the Society changed its name to the Royal Photographic Society of Great Britain, of which I, the author, am a member.

Like the clandestine associations, these photographic groups aimed to unite like-minded individuals to share experiences and ideas while advancing their knowledge of the arts. However, the reality was that the same tradition of secrecy among alchemists persisted in the study and practice of photography during the nineteenth century. The old alchemical discoverers and their culture of confidentiality seamlessly transitioned into the emerging field of photography. Anthropologist T. M. Luhrmann writes, "concealing information about a subject can reinforce the belief in its claims…Concealment creates property, something that is possessed, and the existence of this special property distinguishes possessor from non-possessor and alters the attitudes of both toward the thing possessed" (1989, 136–137). Once again, knowledge is power, and photographers have always sought to maintain power, ownership, and dominion over their technological and artistic inventions.

Nineteenth-century inventors closely guarded their progress toward fixing the camera-made image. Experimenting with light-reactive chemistries, previously developed by alchemists, led to a race for success. In a practice outside the norm of secrecy, Louis Jacques-Mandé Daguerre and his friend Nicéphore Niépce collaborated, sharing their findings from their photographic experiments. However, they did so through enciphered communications. They protected their progress by devising a code of numbers for technical terms, ensuring no one else could comprehend their experiments. Daguerre "became a tireless experimenter and mentioned his growing interest in silver iodide in a letter dated May 21, 1831 [sent to Niépce]. "'I think after many new tests that we ought to concentrate our researches on 20,' he wrote, 'this substance is highly light-sensitive when it is in contact with 18.' They were writing in code: '20' meant iodine, '18' meant silver plate'" (Bolat, 2022).

In 1839, Hippolyte Bayard succeeded in identifying a method to use silver as a viable medium for creating a photograph. He also came up with a process for fixing the image. Somehow, a friend of Daguerre's persuaded him that neither of them should announce their successes to the French government. In recognition of their clandestine pact, Bayard chose to conceal his achievements, even though he had initially planned to announce his discovery. This decision ultimately came at a high cost to Bayard, as Daguerre revealed his own process in 1839 to the French Academy of Sciences by proclaiming, "I have seized the light – I have arrested its flight!" (National Geographic, 1989, 530). Consequently, Daguerre's invention earned him and his son lifetime pensions from the French government. Bayard was left disillusioned and destitute. Distraught, Bayard went on to create the famous image of his own staged suicide, "self-portrait as a drowned man." Twelve years later, Daguerre died of a heart attack.

Photographers in the 19th and 20th centuries often hoarded knowledge. They guarded information about their cameras, chemistry, custom techniques, locations, and methods of presentation. They protected the sanctity of their darkrooms and maintained an air of mystery around what occurred between the moment the shutter closed and the exhibition of the final image. This territorial mindset recognized that those who held information that others desired found themselves in a position of authority. Moreover, photography historian Aaron Scharf claims that, "In the age of invention, he who got there first, most often, though not always, reaped substantial rewards in fame and fortune" (Scharf, 1976, 11).

There were justifiable fears for those at the forefront of both alchemy and photography. Others could steal the hard-earned knowledge gained only through costly investments, hard work, and sacrifice. Part of the tendency to remain silent may stem from the understanding that information holds power. It also has monetary value. After all, no photographer wanted others imitating the distinctive visual qualities that made their images unique and popular, bringing them notoriety and success.

As the fine art world transitioned from paint and inks to light, photographers became gatekeepers of all technological and aesthetic knowledge related to photo-image-making. To learn about the practical and theoretical aspects of the art, similar to alchemy, one had to apprentice with an experienced, recognized expert. They needed to study with someone who held all the knowledge. Traditionally, acquiring experience and information has been challenging and often required payment. The Google search engine, which opened the floodgates to free and easily accessible information, was not created until 1998. However, even with Google, search results cannot provide the deep understanding that comes from the invaluable guidance of a masterful teacher who can skillfully lead an aspirant through their own direct experience.

GK states,

> Not even the internet can close the gap between literate viewers who can decipher photographic syntax and those who are visually illiterate, viewing art as nugatory#. For them, the full stories that photographs must tell remain hidden due to the inability of most people to be able to understand what they communicate. Photography is, in many ways, an occult art in that photographs can be self-secret. They are brimful with meaningful revelations that few can see, let alone read or understand. Most viewers can respond emotionally to what they see, and they are satisfied with that level of superficial understanding. But the photo-alchemist is compelled to look deeply, revealing the secrets a photograph must teach about the phenomenal world. And more. Those details express their divine secrets for those
> with Sight!
>
> The common, visually illiterate viewer looks at the detailed mixture of elements in the frame and is incapable of recognizing the secrets obscured by the limited capacity of their own perception. They simply aren't observant enough to make a visual inventory of what is faithfully represented on the surface of the print. Conversely, the alchemist's vision isn't confined to the two-dimensional surface of a photograph; they have developed a hyper-perception that allows them to penetrate an image to more unfathomable depths than even the most perceptive, educated aesthete.

Sometimes, the secrets in photographs are embedded in symbols, metaphors, or allegories. Valuable knowledge can elude an onlooker's understanding. For example, surrealist photographers such as Hannah Hoch and George Brassai applied some of the same methods of visual coding that medieval alchemists devised. Artists in both mediums created beautiful, visually appealing artworks with imagery that caused the imagination to take flight! Viewers appreciated their dream-like atmospheres, yet few could grasp the hidden knowledge inhumed beneath an awe-inspiring veneer. Even if one could interpret its message, it would likely offer little or no revelatory insight. The ability to see something and the capacity to gain a deep understanding are two very different things.

The threat of danger always accompanies invaluable secrets if they are revealed. For the aspirant of the Great Work, there is a risk that breaking one's promise of silence can damage the integrity of one's soul. There are other spiritual and physical consequences, such as the guarantee of self-punishment for breaking an oath of secrecy. One may be compelled to impale oneself on one's sword. Moreover, there is an imminent threat to the person who receives the secret, mainly if the information revealed constitutes protected, esoteric *knowledge*. Social anthropologist Fredrik Barth said, "[Ritual knowledge] is handled the way little boys in Europe handled the unexploded ammunition that they found: treasured for its unknown power, potential, secrecy – not with any real intention to use, and not to be experimented with to discover what destruction, or noise, an explosion really makes" (Barth, 1975, 220).

"The ability to keep secrets is a deciding factor for accepting aspirants into the Great Work," GK reveals.

> Since it is an important part of spiritual practices, keeping silent strengthens one's bonds and standing as trustworthy within the Order. More importantly, it builds one's ability for self-control. Moreover, another aspect of maintaining promises is that mastery over self-control improves one's ability to perceive secrets. In fact, the practice of faithfully keeping something hidden hones one's proficiency in being insightful and observant. It helps them to recognize where the truth is being shielded and what lies beyond the barriers of ordinary perception. Otherwise, one's gifts will be hopelessly spoliated#.

Since one's spiritual growth on the Hermetic path depends on uncovering concealed divine mysteries, it is essential to cultivate the kind of Sight that fosters critical awareness. This enables a penetrating gaze and insights arising only from perceiving distracting and arcane phenomena to uncover the unnoticed mysteries. GK affirms,

> Each of those glorious secrets is a lesson filled with profound esoteric knowledge from the Supreme Teacher, bestowing an

illuminating understanding that the discoverer can only internalize through direct experience. Once that occurs, the knowledge becomes secret once more, as the holder finds what they learned impossible to articulate. If one attempts to comprehend the ineffable *knowing* from a conceptual, rational perspective, it slips through their fingers as if they are trying to grasp light and shadow. One strives to integrate divine revelation into one's soul work to function at the highest spiritual level.

Photographers, poets, and alchemists use their own coded language of symbols and metaphors to convey ineffable wisdom. While they can utilize the undercurrents of symbolic language to indicate something beyond representation, such methods of communication can never provide the transformative impact of direct experience with something akin to divine knowledge. GK refers to this language as *Lingua Penumbra*, Latin for *shadow language*. Lingua Penumbra is an esoteric use of speech, writing, and imagery that most people cannot fully interpret. For instance, one connects deeply with photographs when one is willing to understand the secrets those images must reveal. Through their shadow language, they articulate those aspects one cannot see or photograph, such as emotions, thoughts, feelings, intuitions, and visions of the future.

Scholar of ancient magical traditions, Roy Kotansky pointed out that,

> There were two channels for passing on the practical and theoretical knowledge of alchemy. On the one hand, there is an open (*aperte*) objective language as with Rhazes, and, on the other, an obscure (*tecte*), image-laden language as with Ibn Umail (c. 900-960). The latter involved cover-names (Decknamen) which came from Greek into Arabic and thence into Western alchemy, e.g. for chemical substances: 'red rose' for the elixir used to make gold; for chemical properties: 'eagle' for the evaporation of volatile substances; for the colours of the alchemical process: 'raven' for black. These are useful as codes only as long as they remained unknown to a broader public…there were further codes, anagrams and acrostics, creating an arcane language accessible only to a small circle of initiates (2005, 21-22).

Most people are blind to the hidden meanings in these alchemic methods of communication, especially when they convey truth. Alchemist from the 17th century, Jean d'Espagnet wrote, regarding "Mystical Names and Secret Operations… truth lies hid in obscurity; for Philosophers never write more deceitfully - than when plainly, nor ever more truly - than when obscurely" (Alchemy Website, 2022). Alchemy's elaborate strategies of riddles and analogies express a system of correspondences between what is seen, what is understood on the surface, and revelations that arise from what is occulted. Hermeticists say that to see and understand, one must look three times. Upon the third inspection, those with eyes that can penetrate the dark confusion will find meaningful treasures in the hidden truths.

The "third inspection" leads to understandings or illuminations found in the space between literal, superficial interpretation and *knowing* that could extend beyond the limits of the literal. GK posits, "This is where the shadow language comes to light as the antithesis of the horribly mistaken understanding that there is no other meaning beyond what can be seen." The alchemist's use of words and images is called a *penumbral* language because it originates from the undefined space where the tapering gradient of light and fading shadow overlap. It is where darkness and light transition into the gloaming#, where the sky's sunlight dissolves into dusk. It is the place where darkness and light mingle to give birth to a liminal space. There, one discovers a mysterious relationship where things do not predictably become one thing or another but transform into something entirely new.

The Lingua Penumbra resembles the state of photographic film after it has been exposed in the camera. The light impression is entrapped in silver, its secrets waiting to be freed and uncovered. The latent image is tied to a reality existing between the light that conceived it and the darkness that has yet to give birth to its form. This *state of being in between* is where alchemists dwell—psychologically, intellectually, and magically. Existing in this realm forms the mystic lens through which they perceive the world and comprehend photographs within it. Even before the advent of photography, alchemists skillfully revealed their secrets through illuminated manuscripts, drawings, and paintings on papyrus. They communicated on the surfaces of hermetically sealed tombs and across the elaborate faces of temple walls. The oldest surviving alchemical text, the Emerald Tablet, is what GK calls "the Keystone of the Occult Sciences and the Great Universal Mystery" and presents the foundation of the teachings in the Corpus Hermeticum. It was written in the lingua penumbra, unveiling knowledge about the creation of the *Lapis philosophorum* (the philosopher's stone), Egyptian magic, natural philosophy, and more.

When alchemists choose penumbral words to discuss divine mysteries, they attempt to communicate something about the unknowable. Words are summoned. They are conjured to evoke a feeling or an amorphous notion in the imagination. The authors suggest that a metaphor or symbol may be more effective than trying to define inexpressible experiences. The artful use of figurative, linguistic, and visual techniques produces something akin to a partial map that guides us to undiscovered hidden treasures. For the reader, such techniques depend on a degree of faith that occult gold exists. The seeker must trust that they have been pointed in the right direction, even while they cannot know precisely what the experience of the gold is or where it lies buried. No verbal, artistic, or written language can adequately code, describe, translate, or convey the gems of esoteric insight. Yet umbral language can guide the way toward an encounter with direct experience.

The partial treasure map offered by Western mysticism states that the gold is always buried in two places: the microcosm and the macrocosm. Part of the alchemist's contemplative practice involves considering the implications of self-knowledge and, in turn, the secrets that this knowledge reveals about the cosmos. GK says,

> The Delphic maxim, *Know Thyself,* tells the alchemist where to look first when divine awareness has been discovered. It informs the alchemical philosopher where insights will arise after action has been taken on this discovery. When one of the treasures is found, it leads the way to the second stone of gold. Once true knowledge is revealed, one's Sight turns away from the pinpoint of inwardly focused concentration and out to the expanding, wide-angle context of the infinite macrocosmos. While traveling through the fixed point at the center of the most negligible apertures, one discovers the greatest expanse of clarity and focus! In doing so, a second level of realization can be known. It is a secret hidden within a secret, or as Sir George Ripley once penned, "O happy gate of blackness, cries the sage, which art the passage to this so glorious a change" [Philalethes and Cooper, 1678, 357].

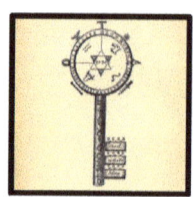

12. TWIN FLAMES: THE ALCHEMIST & RA

As a deity, Ra remains largely unknown in Western cultures. Throughout Egypt, he was the central deity of worship for over 2000 years, starting around 2600 BCE.

> The Egyptian gods were [wholly] or partially anthropomorphic, meaning they were depicted as animals or part animal. Ra is no exception to the rule. Before the Amarna Period, Ra was depicted as a sun disk with wings, encircled by a cobra OR as a man with the head of a falcon. And there are also a few other animals sacred to Ra that should be considered: birds, scarabs, rams, bulls, cats, lions, herons, and the phoenix. [The worshiper connected] with the spirits of these animals to work more closely with the Egyptian sun god Ra (Fields, 2021).

In Ra's Golden Age of Egypt, he was depicted as having the body of a man and the head of a hawk or falcon. "The hawk, keen-eyed and swift, serenely soaring in highest air, was to the Egyptians a symbol of the Divine in the heavens, which is the Divine Truth proceeding from the Divine Intelligence...In order to emphasize the idea of 'intelligence,' the sculptors adorned the face of the hawk with peculiar conventional features, making prominent its sharp eyes" (Odhner, 1914, 54). "Porphyry says, 'the hawk was dedicated to the Sun, being the symbol of light and spirit'" (J.G. Wilkinson,1847, vol. 4, 295). Furthermore,

> The hawk is reputed to have been worshipped because augurs use them for divining future events in Egypt; and some say that in former times a book (papyrus), bound round with a purple thread, and containing a written account of the modes of worshipping and honoring the gods, was brought by one of these birds to the priests at Thebes. This manifestly refers to the primeval revelation of the Ancient Word, proceeding from the Divine in the heavens (1847, vol. 5, 205).

Ra is the author of heavenly light and "that refulgent Light which eclipses every other light" (Atwood, 2005, 321). He is the "fiery disk Atonû, by which the sun revealed himself to men, was a living god, called Râ... [His name comes] from a verb râ, to give, to make to be a person or a thing, so that Râ would thus be the great organizer, the author of all things" (Maspero, 2005).

Furthermore, his name was a word of power, meaning "right ascension" (RA Definition & Meaning, 2022), "sun," 'to make to be,' [and] 'operative and creative power'" (The Correspondences of Egypt, 79). Nineteenth-century Egyptologist John Gardner Wilkinson wrote that

Picture 12.1 Abraham Kingswood's Divine Falcon Seal, ca. 1807.

(*The Egyptians* vol. 4, p. 210), "the Sun was both a physical and metaphysical Deity, and under these two characters was worshipped as Ra and Amen-Ra: the real Sun, the ruler of the world, in the firmament, and the ideal ruler of the universe as King of the Gods" (Wilkinson, 1847, 210). GK declares, "Ra is the lighthouse beacon, the bright guiding ray that attracts the attention of the inquiring artist, the smith of light, gold, and silver."

During Egypt's monarchy of light, Ra was also referred to as Amen-Ra, the prefix of which,

> is said to mean 'what is hidden,'...and according to Dr. Budge 'it indicates the god which cannot be seen with mortal eyes, and who is invisible as well as inscrutable, to gods as well as men.' (G. E. II: 2). But...the name is also connected with a root meaning 'to abide, to be permanent,' and one of the attributes which were applied to him was that of eternal.' (Ibid.) All this agrees with the character of Amen-Ra as the Divine Form or Existere#, which in

itself is Infinite and therefore 'hidden,' yet in its proceeding becomes manifest as the Eternal Form, the Divine Human from eternity (Odhner, 1914, 77).

As the primary god of a polytheistic pantheon, Ra was revered as the supreme storyteller of light, the creator, and the sustainer of all life. He was known as the divine maker, and his followers believed that "Râ at his first rising, seeing the earth desert and bare, had flooded it with his rays as with a flood of tears; all living things, vegetable and animal, and man himself, had sprung pell-mell from his eyes, and were scattered abroad with the light over the surface of the world" (Maspero 2005). He created all things visible and invisible, which includes the ethereal realms and beings in the Duat (the underworld, or otherworld).

GK informs that, "Fortunate Egyptians who witnessed Ra, saw him as a resplendent, sun-like fire that threw out a blinding light, like the summer sun upon Egypt's lands." The Chaldean Oracles speak with elegant prosopopoeia# about light as a godform when they proclaimed

> There is above the Celestial Fire an Incorruptible Flame, always sparkling; the Spring of Life, the Fountain of all Being, the Original of all things! This Flame produceth all things, and nothing perisheth but what It consumeth. It maketh Itself known by Itself. This Fire cannot be contained in any place; It is without body and without matter. It encompasseth the Heavens. And there goeth forth from It a little Spark, which maketh all the Fire of the Sun, of the Moon and of the Stars (Garstin, 1932).

All the while, in Ra's flaming, incandescent brilliance, his true form remained concealed. His followers witnessed manifestations of his presence but couldn't look directly upon his earthly appearance. This was not because he didn't make himself visible, but because his presence overwhelmed the senses. His very name,

is said to mean "what is hidden," "what is not seen," and according to [Sir Ernest Alfred Wallis Budge] "it indicates the god which cannot be seen with mortal eyes, and who is invisible as well as inscrutable, to gods as well as men." (Budge, 2013 II: 2) ...And in...papyri we read: "This holy god, the lord of all the gods, Amen-Ra, . . . the first Divine substance which gave birth unto the other two Divine substances! The Being through whom every god hath existence, the one who hath made everything which hath come into existence since primeval times when the world was created; the Being whose births are hidden, whose evolutions are manifold, and whose growths are unknown; the holy

Form, beloved, terrible, and mighty in his risings; . . . the terrible one of the double Divine Face; the Divine Aged one; the Divine Form, who dwelleth in the forms of all the gods. . . . Though he can be seen in form, and observation can be made of him at his appearance, yet he cannot be understood." (Budge, 2013, II: 13-15.) (Odhner, 1914, 75-76).

GK insists, "When Ra is seen and recognized by a worshiper, it is implicitly understood that the worshiper is, conversely, in the god's field of view. Be assured, he sees you and knows you." "The reciprocal nature of vision is more fundamental than that of spoken dialogue. And often dialogue is an attempt to verbalize this — an attempt to explain how, either metaphorically or literally, 'you see things', and an attempt to discover how 'he sees things'" (Berger, 2008, 9). Therefore, merely seeing an appearance of Ra initiates a sacred dialogue between the aspirant and the deity, whether that appearance is in the form of an imagined visualization, a dream, a statue, an artwork, or a depiction within a photograph. Alternatively, one may see Ra allowing himself to be seen in some mortal earthly form.

E. A. Budge believed that Ra was equivalent in stature to the Judeo-Christian God for the Egyptians (Maspero, 299). The principle of god, as described by the scholar on ancient mysteries M. Ouvaroff, sees no distinction between the Judeo-Christian god and Ra. Ouvaroff wrote,

> God being a luminous principle, residing in the midst of the most subtle fire, he remains forever invisible to the eyes of those who do not elevate themselves above material life: on this account, the sight of transparent bodies, such as crystal, Parian marble, and even ivory, recalls the idea of divine light; as the sight of gold excites an idea of its purity, for gold cannot he sullied. Some have thought by a black stone was signified the invisibility of the divine essence. To express supreme reason, the Divinity was represented under the human form--and beautiful, for God is the source of beauty;... Every thing luminous was subsequently attributed to the gods; the sphere, and all that is spherical, to the universe, to the sun and the moon-- sometimes to Fortune and to Hope. The circle, and all circular figures, to eternity--to the celestial movements; to the circles and zones of the heavens. The section of circles, to the phases of the moon; and pyramids and obelisks, to the igneous principle, and through that to the gods of Heaven. A cone expresses the sun, a cylinder the earth; the phallus and triangle (a symbol of the matrix) designate generation" (1817, 61).

As the beautiful supreme deity, Ra was known by many of his secret names, such as ******, *********, Father of the Great Heliopolitan Ennead, the First King of the World, The Eldest God, The Divine Eye, the Shining One, The Self-Begotten One, Lord of Light and Arts, The Spiritual Sun, All-Knowing Sun-God, He Who Lasts in Perfection, The Eternal Flame, unquenchable fire, and God of Seven Lights and Seven Shadows (or souls). Ra was described as the Solar Trinity: the spiritual sun, the "Intellectual Sun," and the physical orb, the cause of heat, the author of light, the power of the sun, the vivifying cause, the sun in the firmament, and the sun in his resting place" (Budge, 1969, 222). For his worshipers, Ra was the bestower of intelligence and wisdom, and as such, Plato designated the Spiritual Sun as, "the sun of the intellectual world" (Odhner, 1914, 79). Their unified form is the "true *light of grace--the soular sun*" (M. Hall, 1928, 51). The idea of Ra being three suns corresponds to the way the ancient mystics understood human nature as comprising three parts: the anatomical body, spirit, and soul.

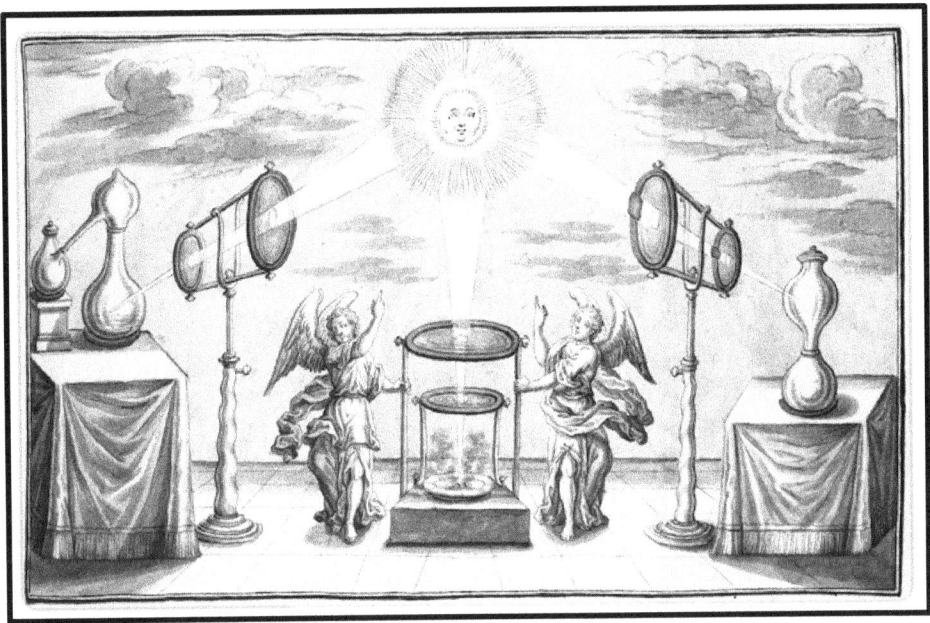

12.2 Cölestin A. Fuchs. Arcana Divina (Three Aspects of the Sun), 1912.

Manly P. Hall stated, "Recognizing the sun as the supreme benefactor of the material world, Hermeticists believed that there was a spiritual sun which ministered to the needs of the invisible and divine part of Nature--human and universal." (M. Hall, 1928, p. 52) Hall goes on to quote the great Paracelsus: "There is an earthly sun, which is the cause of all heat, and all who are able to see may see the sun; and those who are blind and cannot see him may feel his heat. There is an Eternal Sun, which is the source of all wisdom, and those whose spiritual senses have awakened to life will see that sun and be conscious of His existence; but those who have not attained spiritual consciousness may yet feel His power by an inner faculty which is called Intuition" (M. Hall, 1928, p. 52).

In Plato's *Analogy of the Sun*, a conversation between two characters further illustrates his ideas about the attributes of the solar deity.

Socrates asks Glaucon, "...which of the gods in heaven can you put down as cause and master of this, whose light makes our sight see so beautifully and the things to be seen?" (508a) Glaucon responds that both he and all others would answer that this is the sun. Analogously, Socrates says, as the sun illuminates the visible with light, the idea of goodness illuminates the intelligible with truth, making it possible for people to have knowledge. Also, as the eye's ability to see is made possible by the light of the sun, so the soul's ability to know is made possible by the truth of goodness…Without the Good, we would only be able to see with our physical eyes and not the *mind's eye*" (Analogy of the Sun, 2022).

Abraham Kingswood reported in his notes,

> I believe it was a priest at Heliopolis who once said, 'Ra resides as light in the rational part of man as in a resplendent palace; the palace and holy temple of the great self-existent Ra is the intellectual portion of the man of Wisdom; the Deity could never find upon this earth a more befitting temple than within man's ratiocinative# faculty.'

As the deity of rationality, intellect, truth, and spiritual goodness, Ra was known to have many devoted followers throughout Egypt. Along with other Egyptian gods, he also had devotees in Greece and Rome until the end of the 4th century CE. Today, small groups of people around the world still maintain Kemetic devotional practices directed toward the Solar Deity. Ra's believers recognize the sun in the sky as one of Ra's self-manifestations, the right eye of the Divine Face, while he continues to be celebrated as the *blazing fire* and the *embracing light of all suns*.

Kingswood once penned, "I believe in Ra as I believe he rises as the sun every morning; not only because I see it, but because I see everything else." In addition to being the god of light, he is regarded as the beating heart of the Earth's sun. He is also the rays that extend as divine intelligences to anoint all living things with his light. That anointing ray is the spiritual essence of all forms of light. As such, Ra is the divine benefactor of all that is photography and the patron of those who harvest his light. The Egyptians considered Ra to be the King and father of all gods, building many solar temples, the most famous of which was in his City of the Sun, Heliopolis. In some ancient texts, it's recorded that Ra's most favored temple was also called "The House of Ra" (Heliopolis (Ancient Egypt)).

At Ra's most sacred architectural site, like others made for him, there wasn't a central statue; instead, believers regarded Ra's Ka (spiritual body) as dwelling in the temple's temenos# as abundant rays of light. The streaming beams poured in through an oculus in the ceiling. The opening was ever open so the effulgence of sunlight could rush in freely from the sky above. Each temple also featured an altar and an obelisk that pointed toward the source of all light. The architecture of the temple, its decorations, and holy objects were all designed to evoke a sense of awe, reminding worshipers of the sacred relationship between themselves and the mysteries of the cosmos. "The Egyptian temple therefore represented the creation of the universe, the meeting place of the solar Logos and the regenerative powers on the tip of the mound [of creation], and the human representation of that deity that arises from that mound" (Christopher, 2006, 201).

Ra's Great Temple in Heliopolis was unique among all his temples in that it housed a relic called the Benben stone, a name that in ancient Egyptian means, "to shine." "It may therefore be associated with the first ray of sunlight, or with the mound of creation that emerged from the waters of chaos at the beginning of time" (The Geological Society of London - Iron from the Sky, 2023). Now lost, Ra's sacred *stone of light* is envisioned as a pyramid-shaped meteorite. It is hypothesized that the design of all pyramid shapes was based on the geometric example of the Benben stone. "The stone is also known as a pyramidion…Others have referred to it as the Stone of Destiny. The mythical powers of the stone were of interest to powerful men [because it] was believed to have the ability to enlighten the person who was in its surroundings and [it] was capable of producing mystical power" (Goran, 2016).

Egyptian priests worshiped the benben stone as an intermediary between themselves and Ra. They prayed before it and made offerings, asking for visions and casting spells to bestow abilities. They petitioned for help in progressing their spiritual practices. "The chief priest of Râ at Heliopolis, and in all the cities which adopted the Heliopolitan form of worship, was called Oîrû maû, the *master of visions*, and he alone…enjoyed the privilege of penetrating the sanctuary, of 'entering into heaven and there beholding the god' face to face" (Maspero, 2005). Devout priests lived in the temples, providing the altars with ample offerings of sunlight from sunrise to sunset. Lamps and candles were lit at night, ensuring the altar was always illuminated. Other daily offerings consisted of any combination of the following: fresh water, milk, oil, fruit (red, yellow, or orange), bread, calves, grain, figs, grapes, and incense (frankincense, myrrh, and kyphi). Even today, GK maintains a millennia-old tradition, giving many of these same gifts daily before an altar in the Kingswood temple room.

In ancient times, typical offering ceremonies took place at sunrise, considered the most sacred time of the day. Oblations were presented during the invocation hymns, which Egyptologists refer to as *Morgenlieder* (Klotz, 2006, p. 13). The songs were sung, "at the opening of the naos…when the solar rays would first hit the cult statue, causing a shimmering *éclat*… [while calling the deity] with the hortative 'Awake beautifully, awake in peace' (viz. to 'resurrect himself'" (2006, 13 n.2). Additionally, a plenitude of gifts and prayers were offered at noon and sunset, when invocations to Ra were made, calling out his ten secret names and requesting his ten emanating manifestations. Days of ritual importance, especially for offerings and prayers, included the solstices and equinoxes.

In addition to the times of day and quarters of the year, there was a festival dedicated to Ra called *Wepet-renpet*, or 'Opening of the Year,' which celebrated the *Mesut-Ra*, or 'birth of Ra.' This time was also known to the ancient Greeks as a 'panegyris.' The festival was presided over by the Pharaoh, a direct descendant of Ra, who was bestowed the honor of "Lord of the Panegyries." Ra's birth-festival started on August 7 and the celebration ran through September 5 (*Festivals in the Ancient Egyptian Calendar, 2023*).

Providing offerings is an important aspect of reaching out, connecting with, and maintaining a relationship with Ra. When doing so, one should be mindful of the various beneficial dimensions of this sacred act.

> Making offerings…is a wordless expression of devotion to awakening and an acknowledgment of [the deity]. When making offerings, the persons making them also receive what is given. For example, offering water may bring a calm mind, flowers a sense of beauty. Incense helps connect you to the earth, while firelit candles create illumination and symbolize destroying the darkness of ignorance. Inherent in each offering is a simultaneous giving and receiving of these gifts (About Zenju Earthlyn Manuelis a Soto Zen priest, and Lion's Roar Staff, 2022).

The giver also creates an opportunity to generate, as an oblation offered from within themselves, feelings of generosity, devotion, benevolence, and selflessness. These qualities not only catalyze one's evolution but also attract the auspicious attention of Ra.

A wide variety of treasured offerings are appropriate for Ra's altar, yet GK recommends those items that the deity especially prefers. Gifts that perpetually bring pleasure to Ra are rare metals, such as silver and gold, including semi-precious stones, such as carnelian, amazonite, amethyst, red jasper, lapis lazuli, and turquoise. Since Ra is the divine benefactor of photography, offerings can also take the form of beautiful photographs or images of anything that is beloved by Ra, such as Heliopian obelisks and the pyramids in Giza. He is also pleased with images of his statues and hieroglyphic forms, as well as the animals, such as the hawk, falcon, or Bennu-phoenix, of which he is particularly fond.

GK maintains,

> Ra appreciates it if his followers reserve a wall, either on one side or the one facing the altar, as a gallery space where beautiful photographs can be displayed as a feast for the deity's eyes. To do this, one must commit to changing the images at least once a month. These photos can be hung with pins or other means. All other offerings are placed on trays, in open baskets, or in alabaster bowls or cups. The votive presentation containers should never be used for any other purpose and feature an image or cartouche of Ra on them. What is essential is that offerings are presented beautifully, enticingly, and desirably.

12.3 Cartouche of Ra, the Egyptian God of Light
(By Garin Horner, based on a drawing by Abraham Kingswood, ca. 1870).

GK suggests that

In addition to the photographs, it's wise to have one or more 'ex-voto-self-portraits' (votive portraits) in one's temple area. Such a picture replaces the ancient version of a small statue made in the likeness of a beloved god or oneself. In this case, the photo would be a self-portrait of one praying or invoking with hands either in

Picture 12.4 Votive Portraits for George Kingswood by Garin Horner, 2022.

a praying position, hands open to the sides, facing forward in prayer, arms crossed with palms against the fronts of the shoulders, or holding an offering with both hands out toward the viewer (Ra). I display all four forms of self-portrait, with the latter example holding a camera. For such a portrait to serve its purpose, the photo must be taken while one is engaged in a magical act, with eyes wide open. Only then will the image capture one's eternal state, always performing acts with attentiveness, while worshipful, and expressing a wholehearted sense of devotion. The empyrean filament that connects the worshiper with the image will imbue it with the worshiper's life force. Ra will receive that energetic offering.

The photos can be placed in standing frames on a table or hung on a wall that isn't the gallery wall.

It's interesting to consider the votive portrait in relation to the way critic Roland Barthes talked about how, "In portrait photography, there are four opposing and inter-related forces; '...the one I think I am, the one I want others to think I am, the one the photographer thinks I am, and the one he makes use of to exhibit his art' (Barthes, 1981, 13)" (La Grange, 2005, 78). At a higher level of consideration, there is a fifth perceptual force: that of the god being venerated. GK claims,

> The purpose of the votive portrait isn't to deceive Ra or to trick him into believing that we are in the temple twenty-four hours a day! Rather, the portraits convey a desire to be ever-present in the temple. Their creation is a devotional act. If the pictures are made with pure intention and reverence, those energies will communicate through the votive images to their intended recipient. When Ra looks upon the photographs, he accurately perceives the truth of our beings through our connection with the images. He will see more clearly than any other viewer, whether self or other, who and what we are. He will warmly receive exactly what is being offered.

It's typical for votive portraits to feature prayers or spells written along the borders or on the back of the print. GK expressed that "A devotional portrait wouldn't be complete without its accompanying solemn prayers scribed in the aspirant's hand. On the reverse side. The activity of writing, in this case, is a magical act that further installs one's intention and life-force into the image." Nineteenth-century Sufi photographer Abd el-Kader made many self-portraits as mirrors because he believed that photographs were profound offerings since "The Real Being is contemplated in the mirror of creatures, according to their predisposition, that is to say, their degree of transparency to Being" (Raina, 2022). On the reverse side of many of his portraits, he wrote the context in which the viewer should look upon el-Kader's image:

Although this representation gives you my appearance,

It cannot give you our supreme image.
For behind my features lies a veiled personality,
Whose spiritual energy lifts its inspiration beyond the heavens.
Man cannot take pride in his handsome face,
But rather in his intelligence and his noble morals.
But if this and that are conjoined in him,
That is indeed the supreme favor (Geoffroy, 1970).

In addition to the sacred portrait, "An altar item that is particularly cherished by Ra is a myrrh encrusted egg that sits within a nest of cassia and frankincense. This offering symbolizes the egg of a Bennu-Phoenix, the mythical bird which is said to have visited the temples in Heliopolis every 500 years," GK expounds.

The Greek historian Herodotus wrote that when one of the sacred birds of Arabia suffered the death of its father, it would create an egg of myrrh, place the body inside, and then fly to the temple of the Sun in Heliopolis, Egypt. There, it would entrust the egg to the priests. Furthermore, Herodotus mentioned that when one of the Arabian birds was nearing death, it would build an aromatic nest of cassia and frankincense as its deathbed. From its lifeless body, a regenerated Phoenix would emerge. The new bird would then carry the nest to Ra's grand temple in Heliopolis and place it upon the altar [Herodotus, 1963, 73].

Certain kinds of alcoholic beverages are recommended as oblations. While beer was sometimes offered to Ra in the temples of Heliopolis, gifts of wine were not permitted at all sites. Some of Ra's priests considered wine to be "indecent" and therefore did not drink it or allow it in their sacred spaces. The reason was that they "looked upon it…as the blood of those enemies who formerly fought against them, which, being mixed with the earth, produced the vine; and hence they [also believed that grapes were] filled with the blood of their own ancestors" (J.G. Wilkinson, 1847, 301). Priests also warned that these associations could drive those who drank too much to madness. However, red and white wine, or juices, were seen as desirable offerings when given by non-ordained Heliopolitan devotees.

"Offerings bring one closer to the feelings of being in the presence of Ra," GK explains.

> As the relationship grows over time, the alchemist may feel a profound sense of devotion for the god of light. The radiant energy of adoration produced by the alchemist nourishes and

delights Ra, and it is also pleasurable for the aspirant. This energy strengthens the filaments connecting the supplicant to the deity. Simultaneously, it provides the spiritual confidence necessary for breakthrough moments, propelling one further along in their Work.

In one of Abraham Kingswood's reflections, he wrote,

> It's impossible to describe what it's like when one's being is rapt in the overwhelming devices of transmutation while fully basking in the infinite presence of Ra. All emotions of embodied smallness are overcome, subsumed by his eclipsing radiance. He is more than what the smallness can endure, so it dissolves into the jubilation of eternity. I admit, this is a poor description. It is in every way inadequate to relate the experience.

Alchemy is a mystical path, marked by one's gradual transition from bondage in the earthly plane of existence to one of divine, gnostic unity. Adepts have,

> mastered the difficult art of shutting off this habitual interior dialogue. This inner silence that mystics cultivate cannot develop unless the individual first learns how to tightly focus his or her attention so that the mind and imagination no longer wander aimlessly from one object, thought, or feeling state to another. When this mental background noise ceases as a consequence of the mystic's successful endeavors to focus his or her attention, a dramatic change in the mystic's mode of consciousness takes place, a metamorphosis that is just as radical…as the transformation that occurs during the shift from waking state of awareness to the dream state (Hollenback, 1996, 1).

GK has sought to describe how the alchemist is transmuted into the pure gold of divinity, expressing that there is no subtle or gross action or result, whether joyful or devastating, that can alter the essence of this golden state of being. The life experiences that make up one's continuing story "are like the die that stamps a piece of gold into a coin – the essence of gold is in no way affected by the operations of the die upon it" (Hollenback, 1996, 6).

GK pronounced, "By dissolving into Ra's everlasting ocean of radiance, one's being becomes the final offering, made to Ra. At the same time, the offering is given to one's highest self."

per

13. Wisdom from the Solar King

There are numerous legends about Ra and his interactions with the ancient Egyptians. Many of these GK considers to be myths. He supposes, "They aren't stories that necessarily happened, but regardless, they are all parts of the larger story about the collective human soul." What is known about Ra's teachings comes from ancient sources, including papyri and hieroglyphics on tomb walls. Scribes and artists recorded the priestly knowledge (2400 BCE) that was handed down to them from generations preceding the advent of writing. This wisdom, the sources of which are impossible to trace, can be found today online and in books. The teachings attributed to the Kemetic Order claimed to have originated mostly from a single author. They came directly from the mouth of Ra to the ear of Abraham Kingswood, secret society's "Hierogrammat#" and "Master of Visions."

Abraham Kingswood continuously passed down those teachings until his death. His legacy was transferred to his son and his son's descendants as a detailed collection of writings about his journey in the Great Work. Many of the original handwritten books in his scriptorium can be found in GK's overflowing library. Other books complement Kingswood's writings. They were created by some of the most renowned authors on alchemy, including Paracelsus, Roger Bacon, Francis Barrett, Geber, Basil Valentine, A. E. Waite, and Edward Kelly, and featured signed editions of books by Mary Anne Atwood. Some date back to the 11th century or earlier. Among them all, the most precious in GK's vast collection are those inked by his great-grandfather. Their titles are:

1. Ex Libro Oculus Horus (Book of the Eye of Horus)
2. Ex Libro Speculum Nigrum (Book of the Black Mirror)
3. Ex Libro Luminosus in Speculo (Book of the Luminous Glass)
4. Ex Libro Sol Mystici (Book of the Mystical Sun)
5. Ex Libro et Luna Occultus (Book of the Occulted Moon)

The manuscripts provide in-depth information on topics such as the Revelation of Divine Wisdom, Divination, Scrying, Communion with Spirits, Incantations and Spells, Amulets, Elixirs, and Magical Tools. They also cover Invocation and Consecration. In the tome titled "Book of the Eye of Horus," Kingswood recorded many chapters on the spiritual teachings he received from Ra. GK recounts reading his great-grandfather's manuscript,

In the year 1886, on the winter day of December 21st, Abraham Kingswood called on the 'Solaris Rex, wearer of the cobra-wreathed crown, holder of the crook of sovereignty and the flail of dominion, voice of truth, to appear and speak words of knowledge and wisdom.' The invocation appears to have been successful because Kingswood noted that he received a message of supreme import. He wrote, "Ra's divine manifestation, his indwelling Ba, rose from the duat as the Bennu-Phoenix, a preeminent phantasm of flaming spirit, voluminous wings outstretched, plumage of radiant colors, and the eyes of his fire-feathered head conveyed his message, as if through the highest levels of divine-to-human mentation, he delivered a true and wealth of arcane wisdom of the highest goal that a soul can envisage, the Great Work.

"For thousands of years, the sacred Bennu-Phoenix has been a harbinger of one's journey of metamorphosis. It is welcomed during one's cycle of death-renewal and resurrection-rebirth. Known as the *Lord of Jubilees*, the spirit-bird speaks with the rousing sound of trumpets, imploring mortal men to follow him into the all-consuming fire of transmutation, promising that one's rebirth can only actualize through sacrifice." GK went on, "The Bennu-Phoenix's appeals go unanswered because men's ears are deaf to the numinous call, hearing only the anesthetizing melodies of their worldly desires. This being the case, few souls have ever heeded the message of the Lord of Jubilees!"

Ra, in the form of the Bennu-Phoenix, instructs aspirants to start by seeking assistance with the practice of "turning the eye inward." The directive is to,

> bring all attention to bear through the act of self-observation. The alchemist's way is to pray, to perform spellwork that can give any possible advantage, to be able to discern with honesty and without judgment, all the patterns of behavior and means of thinking that are in opposition to the ideals of the Great Work. Then the work continues. For an aspirant's peregrination# to success, they must apply intentional, active methods of transforming those dross elements of being into their true golden qualities.

In homage to Ra, GK maintains that one should, "Become his devoted observer. Find and decipher his presence, appearing as a ray of light, in the patternless chaos of silver halides, as the energy of one's thoughts, in the pleasing composition of one's photographs, and out across the vast expanse of galaxies, all of which exist for the senses to absorb, yet at the same time reside within the alchemist."

On one of Kingswood's journal pages, he refers to himself as a "'Writing Reed' for the utterances of RA" and dictated the words, the *mdw-nṯr* (the words of the gods). Below his introduction, he wrote,

> I am the lucent mystery of Ma'at, the voice of light, the guide to those whose irreproachable intention is to surmount the most eminent destination, beyond the golden pyramidion#, and through the *utchat* gate, the all-seeing eye. With beneficent solar rays I greet and welcome those who are true of voice and clear of vision. I reach out to sustain all those who seek me through prayer, magic (heku), and the arts of fire. Whosoever ascends the steps with single pointed purpose and pure heart, to them I give aid and protection. Remain aware. The journey within and without are only made possible through divine assistance. With lights, pictures, and words of power I will see you delivered to stand beside me in the beatific state of being.

Kingswood's writing continued with a prayer that seems to be adapted from a sacred petition to Isis, written by Lucius Apuleius (1st Century) in his book, *The Metamorphosis*:

> You, who are the Sun, the progenitor of all things, the King of all the nature, the Ruler of all the elements, the primordial progeny of ages, the supreme of divinities, the sovereign of the spirits of the dead, the first of celestials, and the uniform resemblance of gods and goddesses; You, who rule by thy nod the celestial heavens, the salubrious breezes of the sea, and the deplorable silences of the realms beneath; and whose one divinity the whole sphere of the earth venerates under a manifold form, by different rites and a various of appellations. Hence the primordial Egyptians call Thee Ra-Horakty. And those who are consecrated by light, illuminated by the incipient rays of that divinity, the Sun, when You rise, and the Egyptians skilled in ancient learning, worshipping Thee by ceremonies perfectly appropriate, call thee by Thy true name, *******.

> Behold then, Thee, commiserating my calamities, Thou art present, favouring and propitious; dismiss now tears and lamentations, and expel sorrow; for now the salutary day will shine upon You. I listen therefore attentively to these Thy mandates. The religion which is eternal has consecrated to You

the day which will be born of this night; on which day Your priests offer to Thee the first fruits and light, dedicating to You temples across Kemet. I fear nothing pertaining to Thy concerns as difficult --- only remembering and always retaining it deposited in the penetralia# of my mind, that the remaining course of my life must be dedicated to Thee, even to the boundary of my last breath. But I will live happy, and I will live glorious under Thy protection: and when, having passed through the allotted space of my life, may I ascend to the realms above, there also in the celestial hemisphere, or to dwell in the Underworld, I shall frequently adore Thee whom I now see, and shall there behold Thee shining against the unsounding darkness of the other sky, reigning from above, and being propitious to me. Moreover, if I shall be found to deserve the protection of Thy divinity, I shall know that it is possible for You to extend my life beyond the limits appointed to it by fate (Apuleius, 1822, 263-264).

Through Kingswood, Ra taught

The human soul seeks to return to its source of complete fulfillment. 'It is an illusion common to all peoples; as their insatiable thirst for happiness is never assuaged by the present, they fall back upon the remotest past in search of an age when that supreme felicity which is only known to them as an ideal was actually enjoyed by their ancestors" (Maspero, 2023).

GK articulated that the journey to "complete fulfillment" is a demanding and hazardous climb. The energetic currents of this existence produce an enormous force that flows against the efforts of the soul, driving it back from the event of its homecoming.

Kingswood's writings state that "Though the momentum of corporeal existence convinces the human being to cling to a self-perpetuating sense of complacency, while all the time buttressing a resistance to the change needed to become more, Ra endeavors to awaken the divine dynamis#, dormant in human beings, so they may recognize their potential to evolve, to become one with him, who is eternally changeless". "The golden key" GK clarifies, "is inside us and all around us, hidden, yet obvious." "Ra", he continues, "performs a daily lesson for all who choose to heed his message. His diurnal, transformative process through life, death, and rebirth – and thus, immortality, holds valuable erudition#."

Ra, the traveler between worlds, announced to Isis,

> I am the Maker of heaven and earth, I am the Establisher of the
> mountains, I am the Creator of the waters, I am the Maker of the
> secrets of the two Horizons, I am the Light and the Darkness, I
> am the Maker of hours, the Creator of Days, I am the Opener of
> Festivals, I am the Maker of running streams, I am the Creator of
> living flame. I am Khepera in the morning, Ra at noontide, and
> Atum in the evening" (Murray, 1929, 83-84).

To elaborate on Ra's three names, the god of light passes through the
door of the Duat (underworld) in the East, rising upon the morning
horizon as he takes on the form of the scarab-headed one. The shadow
passing across the sundial tracks the progress of his mission as he
navigates the supernal dome of the day sky in the Mandjet (or Matet)
barque. Accompanying him is the god Heka (the god of magic).

Picture 13.1 Ra in His Barque with the Great Ennead and the Benu Bird.
Deir el-Medina, tomb of Inherkha, courtesy of Gerd Eichmann, 2025.

When the holy assembly arrives at noon's high point, Ra takes on the
form of the falcon-headed deity. As his boat sinks out of sight in the
West with the setting sun, he boards the Mesektet (or Semktet) boat,
transforming himself into the ram-headed god-form. As he descends to
begin his twelve-hour journey through the night in the underworld, the
beings of the phenomenal world above watch as "the star-lamps scattered
over the firmament appeared one by one, giving light here and there like

the camp-fires of a distant army. However many of them there might be, there were as many Indestructibles—*Akhîmû Sokû*—or Unchanging Ones—*Akhîmû Ûrdû*—whose charge it was to attend upon them and watch over their maintenance" (Maspero, 2023). Ra's mission is a rhythmic circumambulation around the phenomenal world. He sails through the Duat-netherworld, eventually circling back to rise, where he is met with joyous supplications and offerings on the Eastern horizon.

It is written, "The Eye of Ra who lieth down…is born each day" (Budge, 1898, 145). GK enlightens his readers,

> Ra is the arche#, the regenerative principle that gives us the promise that every moment presents an opportunity to initiate great internal and external transformations, that the light of their soul will be manumitted#. When the opportunity is seized at *this* very moment, it will amend the direction of one's entire lifetime from that point forward. Like life, light travels in a straight line away from its source. Only when its trajectory is purposely altered by some act, can it then find fulfillment in its intended path. And if one's intention lies in the Great Work, then Ra teaches the principles of *observation, knowledge, revelation,* and *action* must each be fully realized for transformation to reach its fullest bloom.
>
> Ra's heroic, transformative journey teaches one to direct attention in an equal and balanced proportion between recognizing the elusive qualities within and observing the hidden aspects outside. This practice also involves accepting and surrendering to the knowledge and truths that emerge. Only then can they illuminate the new, metamorphosed self.

As author Michal J. Mahoney adds that,

> We anticipate, we lean into life. We fall forward into our being. And just like the skydiver in freefall or the windsurfer, sailor, or skier, our posture in that process influences its form and direction. We are moving in the midst of forces far greater than ourselves, yet we have voice and choice within those forces. We may not be able to command the stars or the winds, but we can learn to read them better and to set our sails and our actions in ways that serve our movement. And, lest all of this sound a bit ambitious or audacious, we can also learn the sacred art of stillness and acceptance in the never-ending dance of effort and surrender" (Mahoney, 2005, 74-77).

Consider that GK's house is arranged so he can walk around the exterior of his temple room by moving through a series of chambers and hallways. Furthermore, one can do this with half the journey in total darkness and the other half in light. Through this practice, he symbolically reenacts Ra's dualistic, diurnal voyage while reflecting on his essence in the physical realm. Contemporary alchemist and artist David Chiam Smith writes,

> In its deepest sense, contemplation is a form of alchemy that transmutes and consumes dualistic divisions. Through the disciplined practice of contemplation the sense of the mind's autonomy and the structure of its understanding can drown in the ground, or root basis of all things, which is the primordial essence. This is predicated upon the recognition and isolation of the ground, which is known as its distillation. The ground is the alchemical quintessence that dissolves the boundary between internal awareness and external appearances, while it continues to paradoxically pour itself out as the seemingly diverse spectrum of phenomena. When recognized within its outpouring the quintessential ground becomes a total bath[1] beyond the grasp of identification and identity, beyond any point of reference. It is within the dynamism of this reference-less-ness that gnosis is realized" (2017, 2-3).

Furthermore, Greg Kaminsky, a scholar of medieval studies and mysticism, points out regarding both GK and Smith,

> Contemplation is not just thinking about things, or philosophizing. Rather, it is an investigation into the very meaning of meaning itself. By giving greater priority to the quest for ultimate meaning, the experience of the contemplator can be radically shifted and life may divulge the secrets of wisdom-bliss. This is the motivation for mysticism and can be seen as integral to many esoteric traditions" (Kaminsky, 2022).

In this alchemical practice, one's inward journey of ascension correlates with Ra's contemplative voyage, descending through the darkness of the duat and then prevailing to rise once again into the bright dome of the heavens. Ra's teachings, the Bible, and the Hermetic writings are in

---

[1] The term 'bath', Smith explained, refers to the open infinite expanse in which the mystic immerses.

agreement when they advise the aspirant to seek methods, "of Self-Knowledge, which alone can enable man to know and understand and possess divine things. --- 'If thou seekest for her as silver, and searchest for wisdom as for hidden treasures; then thou shalt understand the fear of the Lord and find the knowledge of God' (Proverbs 2: 4, 5)" (Atwood, 2005, 61). What's more, Minor White states, "That through consciousness of one's self one grasps the means to express oneself. Understand only yourself. The camera is first a means of self-discovery and then a means of self-growth. The artist has one thing to say—himself. . . . The camera and its emphasis on the technique of observation wall broaden him, deepen him immeasurably" (Bunnell, 1989, 98).

"Inside the subterranean caverns of the inner world", wrote Kingswood,

> One encounters all manner of phantasmagoria of horror, mystery, and pleasure. All these confrontations are distractions and should merely be observed. Remain disciplined and follow experiences with the question, 'What does this knowledge teach me about myself?' To observe is to become the alchemist in one's inner laboratory of thoughts, images, and behaviors. Ra, the Father of Light teaches that above all else, be the observer who gazes into the mirror [photographs] and learns those hidden lessons that the reflections disclose. Absorb the lessons, for self-discovery and self-knowledge are the pillars guarding the threshold through which divine-wisdom awaits. Be always ready for the radiance that harolds, like the Bennu's trumpets, flashes of insights and miracles. And whence the alchemist has resolved to embrace an ongoing series of conversions or *metanoias*, they must be prepared to act on the sacred boons that have been bestowed.

Aristotle began his manuscript *Metaphysics* with the discerning words, "All men by nature desire to know" (Aristotle, 2009). Robert Moore, an author on self-observation, offers an additional perspective that can be applied to Kingswood's revelation.

> Unless and until I come to know myself, I am driven by habits which I do not see and over which I have no control; I am a machine, an automaton, a robot moving in circles, constantly repeating myself. I am not aware, but unconscious, habitual, *mechanical*. I imagine I am conscious, awake, aware because my eyes are open. But habit is unconscious, automatic-pilot, without volition or *intention*; inside I am asleep...to get a mammal to think for herself, to observe herself, to know herself, is very

difficult. It is not natural to mammal behavior. It requires conscious effort and intent. It requires courage and will of *attention*" (Moore, 2009, 1-2).

In conversation with GK, he emphasized, "Undiscovered worlds are waiting for each of us to be a sun which illuminates those world's unobserved mysteries, and those solar systems are each of us."

13.2 Ra-Horakhty-Atum in the Tomb of Sennedjm, 19th-20th Dynasty, courtesy of Shawn Milner, 2024.

The following is an abbreviated invocation for Ra from the Egyptian Book of the Dead, by Nesi-Khonsu, a Priestess of Amen-Ra, the *Ru Nu Peret Em Heru* (circa 1000 BCE), translated by E. A. Wallis Budge. It was given to GK, to be orated as part of his hermetic invocation practice, to help guide one into undiscovered worlds:

> This holy god, the lord of all the gods, Amen-Ra, the lord of the throne of the two lands, the governor of Apt; the holy soul who came into being in the beginning ; the great god who liveth by…Maat; the first divine matter which gave birth unto subsequent divine matter; the being through whom every [other] god hath existence; the One who hath made everything which hath come into existence since primeval times when the world was created; the being whose births are hidden, whose evolutions are manifold, and whose growths are unknown; the holy Form, beloved, terrible, and mighty in his risings ; the lord of wealth, the power, Khepera who createth every evolution of his existence, except whom at the beginning none other existed; who at the dawn in the primeval time was Atennu, the prince of rays and beams of light; who having made himself [to be seen caused] all men to live; who saileth over the celestial regions and faileth not, for at dawn on the morrow his ordinances are made permanent ; who though an old man shineth in the form of one

that is young, and having brought… the uttermost parts of eternity goeth round about the celestial regions and journeyeth through the [Duat] to illumine the two lands which he hath created; the God…moulded himself, who made the heavens and the earth by his will…; the greatest of the great, the mightiest of the mighty,…the protector of the two lands in his mighty name of `The everlasting one who cometh and hath his might, who bringeth the remotest limit of eternity',…the sovereign who casteth forth the two Eyes, the lord of flame [which goeth] against his enemies;…the prince who advanceth at his hour to vivify that which cometh forth upon his potter's wheel, the disk of the Moon-god who openeth a way both in heaven and upon earth for thy beautiful form; the beneficent…god, whose light is the guide of the god of millions of years; whose substitute is the divine Disk;…he is the flame which sendeth forth rays of light with mighty splendour,…whose utterances are gracious,…Amen-Ra, the king of the gods, the lord of heaven and of earth, and of the deep, and of the two mountains, in whose form the earth began to exist,….". At this point the orator adds their reason for calling on the crowned solar deity with the words, "I beseech thee…" (Budge, 1898, 199-202).

14. SPLENDOR SOLIS AND THE EMPYREAN LIGHT

Since antiquity, seekers of mysteries have desired to understand the nature and properties of light. Astronomer Nicolas Camille Flammarion proved his profound understanding of light when he wrote,

> by the study of light, a magic bridge thrown from one star to another, from the Earth to the Sun, from the Earth to the stars—of light, the universal movement which fills space, sustains worlds in their orbits, and constitutes the eternal life of nature. Take care then, to keep ever in mind the fact of the *successive transmission of light in space*...In the same way light passes successively from one region in space to another at a greater distance, and travels without being extinguished into the far-off realms of Infinity. If we could see from the Earth an event which is being accomplished upon the Moon; for instance...a fruit falling from a tree on the surface of the Moon, we should not see the fact at the moment of its occurrence, but one second and a quarter after (1897, 131-132).

The speed of light is astonishing! Its path is perfectly straight as it flies from the moon to the Earth and from the Earth to the moon. Sometimes, during its hurried encounters, shadows are born. Physical laws dictate that when an opaque object obstructs light, a shadow falls opposite the source of light. By observing how the laws of light and shadow create patterns and shapes in a photograph, the viewer's eyes can gather enough evidence to interpret a scene.

To understand a photograph, the viewer's perception must decode information. Each composition showcases the quality of light and records the position of the main light relative to the photographer and the subjects in the frame. Although seemingly opposites, shadow and light work together to create a meaningful experience for both the photographer and the viewer. In union, they become more expressive than they would be alone. United in harmony, darkness and light act as meaning-makers on both apparent and hidden levels.

When an alchemist like GK examines the patterns of light and shadow in a photograph, he perceives more than just the obvious representation of a scene. He sees silver, fixed into a coagulated form, expressing itself as various shapes and patterns. GK believes all photographic images are made possible by sunlight (even if it is an artificial aspect of sunlight), which corresponds to gold, and thus, to Ra. The visual constructs in the photograph are understood to be a product of the union of gold (sunlight) and silver (moonlight). It is also intuited that the fixed silver, most interpreted as superficial imagery, conceals secrets. GK informs us that silver is the only one of the seven alchemical metals whose rays are said to shine inward.

Picture 14.1 Mirrors of Fire (Twelve mirrors with which man tries to see God) 1610. Artist unknown.

In contrast, gold radiates its luminance outward. The alchemical symbol for silver is a crescent moon, a lunar phase that reveals only a small part of the satellite. Even when full, the far side of the sphere remains shrouded in darkness. GK specified, "It is only by the sun's rays that we know the moon exists and that we, as metaphysical explorers, may come to know its hidden depths."

In 1839, photographers joined a long and expanding lineage of explorers of light. From antiquity onward, priests, philosophers, and alchemists fervently sought knowledge of light's diverse and multifaceted dimensions. Egyptian priests recognized light as divine in all its attributes. The first magi perceived light as a magical energy that could be manipulated through extraordinary means. Philosophers associated light with wisdom and truth. Essentially, they explored light in the intellect of the mind, as well as from divine revelation. The alchemists regarded light as a sacred emanation. Some also viewed it as the fundamental source and manifestation of all things in existence, including the prima materia.

"Empyrean light" is claimed by alchemists to be a celestial force that radiates throughout the cosmos. Photometric instruments cannot detect it. It is an emanation of the inconceivable source, which GK refers to as a "god without prior theogony, the arche supreme, self-born luminary, Ra." Although the Egyptians saw Ra as one of many gods, he was recognized as "phosphoros," the bringer of all light and life. "Ra's enduring, generating principle produces an infinite spectrum of light through his actions, thoughts, and words," professes GK, "because he wishes all living entities, in all dimensions, to see this reality the way it truly is!" GK accepts that the divinely created light has two states: one called *dynamis*, or "state of becoming," and the other, *einai*, which means "to exist."

Whether visible or undetectable, the origin of all light is dynais, "the state of that which is not yet fully realized: power, potentiality" (Dynamis Definition & Meaning, 2022). Alchemists viewed this as a transitional state in which light actively evolves, changing from pure primal energy into whatever it is destined to become (einai) as it enters this realm of existence. The first-century Egyptian Basilides taught, "All evolution commenced by the working of the ineffable, absolute, Divine, upon [the source material]. His eternal thought is the origin of all created things...the Dynameis proceeding from him" (Freiherr von Bunsen, 1854, 118). GK makes it clear that, "This dynamis that Ra causes to evolve into being with his outward radiating thought, to manifest as the luminous einai, is known by many names, but it is what I call, *empyrean light*."

The way GK describes "empyrean light" is similar to what some Western Mystical Traditions call "astral light." The concept of astral light was developed primarily by Éliphas Lévi, who described it as: "an agent which is natural and divine, material and spiritual, a universal plastic mediator, a common receptacle of the vibrations of motion and the images of form, a fluid and a force, which may be called in some way the Imagination of Nature...The existence of this force is the great Arcanum of practical Magic" (Guiley, 2006, 20).

Furthermore, Israel Regardie identified astral light as vibrating at a different rate of motion than the gross substance of the physical world. Thus, existing on a higher plane, the Astral Light contains the builder's plan or model, so to speak, projected downward by the Ideation or Imagination of the Father; the plan on which the external world is constructed, and within whose essence lies the latent potentiality of all growth and development. Regardie drew correspondences between the concept of ether, the collective unconscious, and the astral light. The astral light also corresponds to the Akashic Records, which hold the records of all things, as all acts, thoughts, and emotions of all forms become impressed upon it for eternity. Levi said that life can be destroyed by the sudden congestion or withdrawal of the astral light (2006, 20).

Paracelsus designated this divine light the "Lumen Naturae." He believed it to be an essence of existence that could be liberated through the transformative processes of alchemy. Regarding the Lumen Naturae, he stated that

> it comes from nature which contains its manner of activity within itself. It is active during sleep…for things have spirit which is active for them in sleep…So, too, are these innate spirits in man…for it is the Light of Nature which is at work during sleep and is the invisible body…But there is more to be known than the mere flesh, for from this very innate spirit comes that which is visible…the Light of Nature which is man's mentor dwells in this innate spirit (Paracelsus, 1571, 113-114n6).

He accepted that the luminous mentor, dwelling in the spirit, continues to teach even after death. Furthermore, Paracelsus proclaimed that this divine light is hidden in all matter, the forces of nature, and throughout the universe.

In Abraham Kingswood's note-filled copy of Edwin D. Babbitt's 1878 volume, *The Principles of Light and Color*, one can read his revelations at the beginning of the first chapter. Here, Babbitt is the herald of light, as he asserts,

> LIGHT reveals the glories of the external world and yet is the most glorious of them all. It gives beauty, reveals beauty and is itself most beautiful. It is the analyzer, the truth-teller and the exposer of shams, for it shows things as they are. Its infinite streams measure off the universe and flow into our telescopes from stars which are quintillions of miles distant. On the other

hand, it descends to objects inconceivably small, and reveals through the microscope objects fifty millions of times less than can be seen by the naked eye. Like all other fine forces, its movement is wonderfully soft, and yet penetrating and powerful. Without its vivifying influence vegetable, animal and human life must immediately perish from the earth, and general ruin take place. We shall do well, then, to consider this potential and beautiful principle of light and its component colors, for the more deeply we penetrate into its inner laws, the more will it present itself as a marvelous store-house of power to vitalize, heal; refine and delight mankind (Babbitt, 1878).

GK indicates, "Babbitt's words emphasize those important aspects of light which make the world discernible to the eye and visible to photography's silver halides, those rays that fill the limited, detectable spectrum of light energy. Moreover, there is a spectrum that can't be measured in degrees Kelvin or nanometers. It is the light within the light, the essence of radiance that is undetectable by the conventional senses or other means. With gratitude, we have the capacity to know it exists. The alchemist must regard the coexisting and interconnected subtler aspects of light that can only be perceived by those organs of awareness sensitive to that inconspicuous light. It is in seeing those elusive forms, only made visible by empyrean light, that we can realize this world is much more populated than we realize! There are far more beings than the eyes or the camera would have us believe!"

In the late 19th century, Sir William Crookes, an expert in spectroscopy, theorized that a realm inhabited by unseen beings might exist, suggesting that their reality overlaps with our material world. He concluded that, "It is not improbable that other sentient beings have organs of sense which do not respond to one or any of the rays to which our eyes are sensitive but can appreciate other vibrations to which we are blind." The alchemist understands this to refer to empyrean light. Crookes goes on to say that

> Such beings would practically be living in a different world to our own. Imagine, for instance, what idea we should form of surrounding objects were we endowed with eyes not susceptible to the ordinary rays of light, but sympathetic to vibrations concerned in electric and magnetic phenomena. Glass and crystal would be among the most opaque of bodies. Metals would be more or less transparent, and a telegraph wire through the air would look like a long narrow hole drilled through an impervious solid body. A dynamo in active work would resemble a conflagration, whilst a permanent magnet would realize the

dream of medieval mystics, and become an everlasting lamp with no expenditure of energy or consumption of fuel (*Century Illustrated Monthly Magazine*, 656).

GK wholeheartedly agrees with Crookes' speculation about an unseen realm that operates contrary to the world's physical laws, where other beings do perceive the effects of empyrean light. It is no more or less unusual or unlikely than the fact that glass in this world is transparent or how the lens of a camera obscura projects an inverted image onto its back wall. This inversion could be a metaphor for how the indiscernible otherworld and its light mirror and interpenetrate what humans perceive in this overworld reality. The lesson of the camera obscura is that, like the upside-down image one sees, living beings exist in a realm where their perception of light witnesses countless illusions, and where phantoms of light move through space on a ground that seems real.

"The trick is to cultivate 'double vision' … A sense of metaphor, of translation — of two worlds interpenetrating — must be maintained. But this is also the essential movement of the imagination. We see through the literal world to the shape-shifting Otherworld behind" (Harpur, 2011, 47). GK elaborates,

By doing so, one sees what is rarely understood: that this corporeal plane, a realm we regard as material, is merely a dimension inhabited by phantoms of light — which are *us*. We are phantoms, surrounded by imaginary manifestations that we all agree constitute the myriad things of the world, of substance and matter. We are illusory forms of light, enveloped by a cosmos of light, appearing in its multitude of forms. From this perspective, it is entirely credible and even knowable that the undiscovered country of the otherworld exists. If so, the human light is never extinguished but merely transformed from one manifestation of luminance to another.

From an alchemical perspective, the difference between life and death is merely two different aspects of light. In one aspect, light coagulates to form the body and then dissolves after death, only to reform as an ethereal substance. The energy of life animating the body is yet another aspect of light, which the ancients regarded as part of the lumen naturae. GK tells, "This light is the active principle, the vivifying force of the body and soul and, by its very nature, seeks a purified atmosphere through which it can shine."

    [Alchemists] discover[ed] that in the very darkness of nature a light is hidden, a little spark without which the darkness would not be darkness ... the *lumen naturae* is the light of the darkness itself, which illuminates its own darkness, and this light the darkness comprehends. Therefore, it turns blackness into brightness, burns away "all superfluities," and leaves nothing but...dross and scoriae and the rejected earth (Jung, 2023, 160-161).

GK states,

> Suppose one imagines preparing for the transition to a life beyond death. In that case, one need only look to the wisdom and advice of the Egyptian Book of the Dead and philosophers such as Phaedo, Plato, Socrates, and Porphyry. It was Porphyry who professed wisdom when he said, "there is a twofold death; the one, indeed, universally known, in which the body is liberated from the soul; but the other peculiar to philosophers, in which the soul is liberated from the body. Nor does the one entirely follow the other (Porphyry, 1823, 169n9).

Moreover, Atwood stated that upon a man's death,

> He shall discover the miraculous conspiracy that is between the Prester [Priest] and the Sun, the external and internal fire of life, the thing desiring and the thing desired. He shall know the secret love of heaven and earth, and why all influx of fire descends against the nature of fire, and comes from above downwards, until having found a body, it reascends therewith in perpetual interchange (Atwood, 2005, 99).

"But remember, as Porphyry has told us," GK informs, "that for this fiery ascension of the soul to happen, its obscuring constituents must be purified during its time on Earth. Otherwise, one's soul's light is unable to shine forth and thus is faced with the Great Unknown."

"Another aspect of light which should be discussed," GK presents, "is the purely conceptual notion that light and darkness are somehow in opposition to one another. I believe it will help in the demystification of alchemy to address the idea of good versus evil and the union of opposites." In ancient Persia, somewhere between 1500 and 1000 BCE, Zoroaster asserted that there was a creator deity and a powerful evil being, and that the "two opposing forces: Ahura Mazda (The Light of Illuminating Wisdom) and Angra Mainyu (Destructive Spirit) were locked in conflict." These dualistic, contrasting principles promoted the notion of spiritual equilibrium, which became entrenched in several religious doctrines across the world. Consequently, photography, "as a metaphor, has generally been restricted to an age-old set of binaries that place light in opposition with darkness. Good/evil, knowledge/ignorance, action/inertia, inclusion/castigation, truth/falsehood, and redemption/sin—these oppositions have become synonymous with that of light/darkness" (Miller, 2013, 219). Furthermore, the symbols of the opposed, balancing concepts tend to enlarge the ideas of *light as good* and *darkness as malevolent*.

To temper the perceived conflict between the forces of light and dark, photography can offer the alchemist a more harmonious view. Light and shadow act as two essential principles that function in complementarity, forming a symbiotic partnership that enriches human perception with a sense of depth, texture, dimension, and space. These effects of light may seem opposed, yet they represent mutually beneficial endpoints on the infinite visual spectrum of tonality and contrast. They embody synergetic principles, not a dichotomy of good versus evil, but two aspects arising from a single, unified source: light.

Art critic Carol Armstrong underscores,

> light is only half the story, for darkness—the obscurity in the camera obscura—is also needed to make a photograph: both the darkness of darkrooms and camera interiors, and the occlusion of light that is necessarily part of any photographic inscription…The obscure and the occult are almost synonymous with one another, sharing a sense of the dark, of the secret and mysterious, the hidden and imperceptible. What the occult adds to the mix of obscurity is the experimental and the magical, as well as forms of 'science' that belong either to the past (alchemy, for example) or to the future (much of modern physics, say, from Einstein on) (Armstrong, 2005).

Furthermore, photography historian Aaron Scharf added, "Throughout the history of the camera obscura and the many other like devices, that effigy on the retinal glass, or in the prism or the viewfinder, has never entirely ceased to generate a reverence for its magical character, and a possessiveness for the magic itself" (Scharf, 10).

GK observes, "All shades of darkness are concealed within Ra, and by being the brightest and all-pervasive source of light, it is said that Ra has never seen a shadow." It's true that although a shadow is merely an effect produced by the absence of light, it is something that can't be seen from the vantage point of its source. One must move away at an angle

Picture 14.2 Ascension to the Aperture Gate, composition by Garin Horner, 2020.
Based on an illustration in the Anotomia Auri by Joannis Danielis Mylii, 1628.

from the light position, to witness the independent phenomenon called
shadow, an area with varying degrees of diminished or no illumination.

Creatures with a sense of sight use the discernible appearance of shadows to perceive the light-dark contrast necessary for navigating the tangible world. Light and the darkening shadow convey important visual cues on which our perception depends to interpret and move through the surrounding environment. The differences between these two contrasting visual cues inform one's awareness of their relationship to the world. The eye detects the subtleties in the gradation of the umbra, penumbra, and antumbra, using that knowledge to confirm the form of its subject and highlight it by noticing it, thereby setting it apart from its environment.

In the Bible's cosmology, as in Egyptian cosmology, the book of Genesis asserts that the dark void of chaos preceded the creation of light. God's words produced the illumination, which birthed and created the cosmos. In the center of this cosmos was the Earth's sun. Light became a metaphor for divine guidance and assimilation with all that is good and holy. Therefore, darkness assumed all the dimensions of evil. Much like Zoroaster's revelations of Ahura Mazda and Angra Mainyu, God and Lucifer, the Morning Star, were seen as antagonists. From GK's discerning vantage point, how could there be an eternal argument between light and dark when Ahura Mazda (or God) is the all-powerful supreme creator god, and Angra Mainyu (or Lucifer) is an inferior adversary, merely an aspect of the stronger deity's creation?

GK said hesitantly,

> At the risk of sounding like a heresiarch#, luminance and darkness should not be reduced to the polarized symbols representing good and evil. In truth, they harmonize as universal principles. When one understands their correspondences with night and day, that which is revealed in relation to that which is hidden, the sun and moon, or the noble metals of gold and silver, life-changing revelations become possible. A more accurate picture of the universe is understood, taking the philosophical aspirant, or *mystes,* one step higher toward the aperture gate over the top of the Great Pyramid, the *Akhet Khufu.*

15. The Sacred Union of Alchemy and Photography

Nineteenth-century writer Joseph Conrad proclaimed, "All creative art is magic, is evocation of the unseen in forms persuasive, enlightening, familiar and surprising, for the edification of mankind, pinned down by the conditions of its existence to the earnest consideration of the most insignificant tides of reality" (Conrad, 2015, 4543). Prior to the invention of photography, many artist-painters took an interest in alchemy, both as a field of study and as subject matter for their art. Some of these painters included Jan Brueghel the Elder, Lucas Cranach the Elder, Hendrick Goltzius, Rembrandt van Rijn, Adriaen van Ostade, Johan Moreelse, Peter Paul Rubens, and David Teniers the Younger. Artist and writer, Dr. Marcus Bunyan penned, "In the pre-Enlightenment era both artists and alchemists laid claim to the ability to not only imitate nature but to even perfect it" (2014).

Alchemists, as early as Nicolas Flamel, recognized the importance of art as a means of expressing their inspiration while also using it to advance their spiritual pursuits. They found,

> The work of art could do more than just exemplify the Hermetic principles of harmonious proportion and balance. "Once the pictorial imagery had entered alchemy it was set on a course of advancement which made it almost like a religion" (Burland, 1968, 37). It could act as a talisman. "In other words, it could be an active agent, a dynamic element, in the magical operation — could indeed constitute in itself a magical act" (Beigent & Leigh, 1997, 208–209) …Hermeticism endorsed the notion of interconnectedness of all things. This concept of interrelationship was believed to extend to art, music, and architecture (Edson, 2012, 220–222).

GK adduced, "When I set out to do any kind of photographic work, I wear a consecrated medallion that bears the image of Ra. It was one of several plaquettes# that were distributed among members of the Order in the 1890s. The talisman reminds me that I am connected to Ra, that my actions are for a high purpose, and that the pictures I take are an aspect of Ra's mystery."

As an act of intentional magic, alchemists produced a genre of allegorical artworks, mentioned in previous chapters, called "emblems." In many ways, these artworks resembled graphic versions of photographic compositions. Before 1800, pictures were significant because their portrayal of fables and myths bridged the gap between the penumbral language of alchemy and other forms of visual, poetic

Picture 15.1 De cavernis Metallorum occultus est, qui Lapis est venerabilis Hermes.
De cavernis Metallorum occultus est, qui Lapis est venerabilis Hermes by
Alexandre-Toussaint Limojon de Saint-Didier, 1745.

communication that could convey meaning beyond spoken language. The creative ideas for emblems addressed the challenge that alchemists faced in secretly expressing their thoughts and insights without using words. They believed the "visual language of alchemy is just as important as its verbal expression and is sometimes more accessible" (Ramsay, 1997, 32–33). This was especially true when the imagery used was polysemic# or had multiple meanings. They fabricated portraits of kings and queens, the sun and moon, snakes and dragons, the phoenix, and an entire menagerie of other animals. The Roman god Mercury also played a central role in the composition of emblems.

Abraham Kingswood saw photography as a medium to carry forward the marriage of art and alchemy. The camera was a powerful tool for creative expression. Few alchemists could paint like Rembrandt, yet most could learn how to take a photograph. Kingswood recognized that the fundamental operations in alchemy aligned with the four main stages of photography. For example, in Carl Jung's interpretation of the internal alchemical process, he enumerates them as: Nigredo, Albedo, Citrinitas, and Rubedo. Respectively, these were defined as: Catharsis, Illumination, Education, and Transformation (Centre of Applied Jungian Studies, 2023). The four corresponding steps in photography are: creative awareness, latency, revelation, and fixation.

Since the first alchemical experiments with photo-reactive and photoluminescent substances, a long-forgotten dialogue has existed between alchemy and photoreactive discoveries. Written histories of photography seldom mention alchemy. The observations and epiphanies of alchemists laid the foundation for the chemical processes that led to the discovery of photography. Their knowledge also planted the seeds for what would later evolve into an awareness of light and shadow, aiding in the development of the photographer's vision, so they could place "head, heart, and eye along the same line of sight" (Cartier-Bresson, 1976, 333) to capture their world, even the cosmos, in pictures.

Eighth-century alchemist Geber and thirteenth-century Albertus Magnus both studied the photosensitive properties of natural materials.

> The development of silver photography itself was presaged in the period up to the invention by presentiments of its arrival that related to the mysteries of alchemy and the occult…Christoph Adolph Balduin [an initiate in the Great Work] had dissolved chalk (calcium carbonate) in nitric acid, this then formed another substance called calcium nitrate. The interesting property of this substance for Christoph Adolph Balduin was that it was deliquescent, that is, it absorbed moisture from the air. Believing he was close to acquiring the Philosopher's Stone, he discovered that the substance glowed in the dark after heating and cooling.

As a result, he called this substance hermetic phosphorus [which means: bringer of light]…However, [in 1727] Johann Heinrich Schulze's experiment, the nitric acid was contaminated with silver…The compound turned a deep purple colour on exposure to light…Schulze named this substance 'Scotophorus' (which translates to 'bringer of darkness'), and his results would have been perceived as a prima materia — the 'dark materials of alchemy where the presence of "hidden treasure" was suspected (Webster, 2019).

As part of Michael Maier's alchemical study, in 1617 he created an allegorical emblem titled "Sol et ejus umbra perficiunt opus," or "The sun and its shadow bring the work to perfection." This prophetic artwork alludes to the Great Work of the Hermetic Arts, offering valuable insights for photographers who, over two centuries later, would strive for the perfection of their own art. Maier aided photographers by sharing his observations about the interplay of the sun and its shadow:

> The Sun being placed in the vast Arch of Heaven illuminates with its Rays all the concavity of Heaven, and those Bodies which are contained in it that are Diaphanous and capable of receiving light; that is all the Stars, both the Wandering and the fixed, except where the Thickness of the intermediate Earth prohibits it. For there a black shade or Darkness, which is called Night, remains so long till it is driven away by the Sun, and light is poured out and beheld in its stead. Shade therefore, or Night, is the Privation or absence of Solar Light, and Day on the contrary is the irradiation and Circumfusion of it. Shade is that which cannot endure the aspect of the Sun, and therefore absconds itself, and avoids it, sometimes in this, sometimes in another part of the Earth, according as the Sun is in opposition to it. The Sun and Shade never yet saw one another, although if Nature would admit it they might do it every moment.

Then, Maier addresses alchemists and their pursuit of spiritual illumination when he says,

> the Philosophers have observed that their Sun likewise has a black cloudy flying shadow. Hence Hermes saith, 'My sun, extracts its shadow from the Ray.' That is, see that you bring your Sun round about by the Primum Mobile over which Vulcan presides, that that part of the earth which is now covered with a shady night may enjoy the clear light of the Sun (1618, 134).

More than a century later, in 1761, alchemist Tiphaigne de La Roche wrote a surprisingly accurate description of the photographic process,

Picture 15.2 Michael Maier's emblem titled, *Sol et ejus umbra perficiunt opus*, or, *The sun and its shadow bring the work to perfection,* 1687.

nearly 80 years before Louis-Jacques-Mandé Daguerre announced his discovery!

> You know that the rays of light reflected from different bodies form a picture and paint these bodies on all polished surfaces, on the retina of the eye, for example, on water, on mirrors. The "elemental spirits" sought to fix these fleeting images; they have composed a very subtle matter, very viscous and very quick to dry out and harden, by means of which a picture is made in the twinkling of an eye. They coat a piece of canvas with this material and present it to the objects they want to paint. The first effect of the canvas is that of the mirror. One sees there all the neighboring and distant bodies whose light can bring the image. But what a mirror cannot do, the canvas, by means of its viscous coating, retains the simulacra" (Amar, 1997, 3).

In response to de La Roche's commentary, photo historian Aaron Scharf specified that, "This astonishing piece of prescience seems supernatural itself, and it no doubt echoes the age-old pleasure in prophesying that by some fabulous means it would one day be possible to peel off the image on the looking-glass and freeze the evanescent reflection on the surface of water" (Scharf, 1976, 10).

Then,

> In 1777 C. W. Scheele discovered that when silver had been dissolved in a strong acid, the surfaces steeped in the solution became encrusted with minute particles of the metal, which in this state was darkening with increased rapidity. These facts were first ascertained and recorded in regards of chloride of silver, or silver combined with chlorine. The first more or less stable images were obtained in 1824 by Nicéphore Niepce, a French physicist, using glass plates coated with a dispersion of silver salts in bitumen (a coal derivative). In the early 1830's, Niepce's partner, Louis Daguerre, discovered by accident that mercury vapor was capable of developing an image on a silver-plated copper sheet that had been previously sensitized by iodine vapor" (Millesima, 2023).

Furthermore, 21st-century writer Giordana Charuty stated, "In the composition of these sensitive and 'revealing' substances lies the secret of each operator; and the great treatises on photography continued, in the 1880s, to impose on the practitioner the preparation of silver nitrate – the infernal stone" (Charuty, 2005, par. 32).

The French chemist Gaston Tissandier wrote in his *History and Handbook of Photography*, "The alchemists have often been the subject of calumny…[yet] it must not be forgotten that a large number of the philosophers of the middle ages, men of indefatigable research, were possessed with a real love of their art." One of those honorable men,

> [a] disciple of Hermes, was named Fabricius [Johann Christian Fabricius 1745-1808]. One fine day, buried probably in the confusion of his laboratory, after having conjured up the devil and all the imps of darkness, after having in vain ransacked the books of magic, which swarmed the middle ages, for the formula of that panacea which was to prolong life, cure all ills, and transmute the metals, he threw some sea salt into a solution of nitrate of silver and obtained a precipitate (chloride of silver) which the alchemists of those times gave the name of "Luna

cornea" or horn-silver.' He collected it, and what was his astonishment when he perceived that this substance, as white as milk, became suddenly black as soon as a ray of sunlight fell on its surface! (1877, 6-7).

These noble researchers and their findings teach us that the history of photography extends far back in time, beginning in 1822 when Niépce invented Heliography. GK responds,

> There are lines of unexplored histories that converged in 1826 at Saint-Loup-de-Varennes, France, where the "View from the Window at Le Gras" was made. Those notable historical discoveries leading up to the 18th century laid the groundwork for the chemistry and science of the 1800s. Furthermore, I assert that inquisitors like La Roche, Scheele, Niepce, and Daguerre built upon the foundations of alchemists to popularize their discoveries. Additionally, they strayed from the previous insights of alchemical figures like Geber by focusing solely on the physical properties of their elements. This narrow focus caused them to overlook the metaphysical attributes that contributed to their experiments, rendering them blind to the infinite possibilities for discovering causes and effects in an unseen realm.

Thus, the progression of scientific inquiry continued into the 19th century.

The early 1800s saw many visionary inventors across Europe, all racing to grasp what would eventually evolve into a new discipline of creativity. This collective obsession sought one aim: solving the puzzle of granting images of light the virtue of permanence. They aimed to freeze the subject in a way that could capture the artist's perception in a continuous present moment. In Oliver Wendell Holmes' *Doings of a Sunbeam*, he said that "photography is extending itself to embrace subjects of strange and sometimes fearful interest" (Wendell Holmes, 1863). Explorers of chemistry and light longed to provide an immortal state of fixedness to the strange, the fearful, the beautiful, and everything the human eye could behold.

GK speculates, "Though we have always been content with the transient beauty of a rose, we could never come to terms with the notion of a short-lived photograph."

Maybe it's because the rose symbolizes sensory pleasure, which is fleeting, while the idea of an everlasting photograph addresses, in some way, our deep desire for the prima materia's promise of immortality. Photographs are thought to help us attain that goal, if only slightly, by promising that through a viewer's extended gaze, we will not be forgotten. Even better, we may be remembered as an image of our best selves, in the prime of our youth! Moreover, there is the alchemical essence of the portrait acting as a gateway to the subject's eternal soul.

Even in modern times, there remains an emphasis on the fixation and longevity of photographic images. Scientific research continues to introduce new archival methods in print production. Perhaps it's because light impressions are seen as memories that should not be forgotten. Photographs have become dependable signifiers of an experience or even substitutes for the memories of an occasion. Like memories, photographs are inherently fragile. They deteriorate, fade, burn, and expire over time. Photos may outlast the lives of their makers, but like all things that exist within the realm of time, they are transient.

In the photographer's mind, the blazing field of ambient light imparts life to an image. Yet, it is also the light that destroys it. From its inception, the fixed photograph is gradually devolving into its original components, and for its purpose, into the primordial state of its basic parts. To the pragmatic alchemist, the photographic image is in a constant state of transforming into something else. Whether it degenerates or evolves is a matter of opinion based on the viewer's perspective. The alchemist observes the natural process and asks, "How can this process be used in service of the Great Work?" As it turns out, there are many applications.

The valuable resources offered by the fugitive image are largely overlooked. Much like the beauty of evaporating frost shadows or a dying rose, there are enchanting and desirable properties of decay that attracted the attention of alchemists. The fleeting qualities of the devolving image heighten the sense of preciousness for the artifact-print and, consequently, its ephemeral arc of power. The experience of decomposition becomes part of the story, lasting just long enough to embed a memory in the viewer's mind. Then, like the predictable conclusion of the sun's daily rise and fall, everything goes dark. But wait! A filament of light still connects to what remains of the photograph! That umbilical strand has become a secret embedded in the smooth surface of blackened silver.

In 1992, novelist William Gibson wrote the 300-line poem "Agrippa (A Book of the Dead)." The story was distributed as a digital copy. When a virtual page was turned, the text on that page disappeared permanently. The eminent 16th-century alchemist Cornelius Agrippa would likely have been excited by the concept of such a publication. Today, the value of the disappearing image has gained popularity on the social media platform Snapchat, which compels users to share pictures that disappear after the viewer closes the image. Likewise, users of high magic have traditionally caused evanescence# upon their photographs through the intentional acts of burning, dissolving, shredding, burying, submerging, and defacing. The desired outcome of their spellcraft dictates the method of their demise.

Looking back, as early as 3100 BC, the transient nature of art was a consideration for users of spells. "In Egypt, for example…drawings functioned as tools of magic. This is why Egyptian pharaohs wore sandals with soles that depicted the ritual annihilation of their enemies. By placing their foes beneath their feet, they could magically trample them daily" (Modiano et al., 2017, 136). With each day, bit by bit, as the images wore off the bottoms of the sandals, physical, mental, and even spiritual harm was expected to befall the enemy. Additionally, the slow destruction of the image foretold the enemy's name being forgotten over time, a horrible curse among Egyptians.

The bonds between alchemy and photography are rooted in antiquity, when few or no distinctions existed between the crafts of art and magic. Alchemy adhered to ancient traditions where imagery, whether two-dimensional or three-dimensional, served as a language to communicate ideas. At the same time, it acted as a medium for magical energies. Kingswood's traditional use of photographs is no different from the Egyptians' use of paintings as tangible mediums, infused with human spirit, that could serve as points of union where the material and immaterial worlds could interact. Through art, the two distinct realms become interconnected, allowing for the possibility of magic. In 1912, the painter Franz Marc echoed this belief when he stated that art is "the bridge into the spirit world" (Christie's, 2022). Likewise, French sculptor, painter, and poet Jean Arp wrote in a 1915 essay, 'Art should lead to the spiritual and the real…[to] a mystical reality.'" (quoted in Gizzarelli, 2022).

Seventeenth-century painter Thomas Wijck sought to understand alchemy through his artistic practice by creating paintings of alchemists. Unlike other painters of the time, whose works depicted alchemy in a negative light, Wijck focused on the noble artistry behind this mystical science and portrayed the alchemist as "a respectable and virtuous…scholar-artisan." His alchemists inhabit painted worlds that

> resemble the real world outside their frames: the cluttered studios, busy workshops, and shared kitchens through which artists, artisans, and alchemists all moved…a scenario intimately recognizable to countless other early modern artisans, including metalsmiths and textile workers, but also artists…Such a persona aligns closely with the ideal alchemist presented by alchemical writers, but also with the qualities of the ideal artist and artisan (Drago, 2019, 97-98).

15.3 The Alchemist by Thomas Wijck, late 17th century.

As image-makers, alchemists and photographers work toward a single purpose, sharing light and shadow as their primary subjects. Their separate yet parallel disciplines search for expressions that lead to revelations or ultimate truths. The one medium they all use for their aesthetic and revelatory quest is *light*.

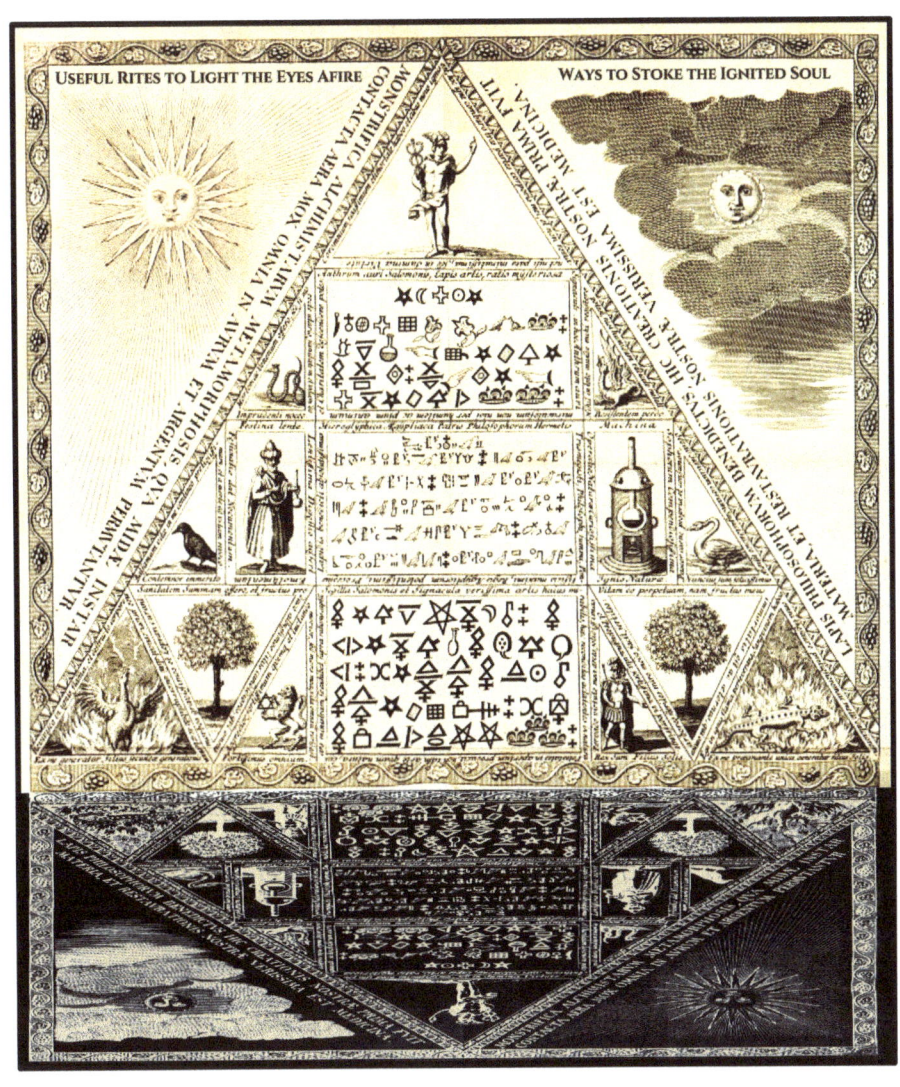

PART 2: Useful Rites to Light the Eyes Afire & Ways to Stoke the Ignited Soul

16. Divination: Catching Sparks of Future's Flame

Nineteenth-century astronomer Camille Flammarion said of divination,

> We wished first of all to prove that there really are manifestations from the dying, psychic action from a distance, mental communications, and a knowledge of things by the mind without the intervention of the senses. We may *see without eyes* and *hear without ears*, not by unnatural excitement of our sense of vision or of hearing, for these accounts prove the contrary, but by some interior sense, psychic and mental. The soul, by its interior vision, may see *not only what is passing at a great distance, but it may also know in advance what is to happen in the future*. The future

Picture 16.1 John Augustus Knapp, Consulting the Oracle of Delphi – courtesy of The Philosophical Research Society, Inc., all rights reserved, 1853-1938.

> exists potentially, determined by causes which bring to pass successive events. POSITIVE OBSERVATION PROVES THE EXISTENCE OF A PSYCHIC WORLD, as real as the world known to our physical senses (1900, 481).

Flammarion is credited as the first person to use the word "psychic" in its modern form (Morris, 18). He took the word from the Ancient Greek, *psykhikos*, meaning "of the soul, spirit, or mind" (Hall, 63). In more recent references, the Greek *Oracle of Delphi* is reported to be one of the oldest psychic diviners, dating back as far as 1400 BCE. She was called the "Pythoness, or Pythia," a title given to the female hierophant of the oracle, [which] literally means one who has been thrown into a religious frenzy by inhaling fumes rising from decomposing matter (Psychic (Adj.)).

She would sit inside a specially constructed seat called the Delphian Tripod, which concealed the priestess from view. Within the structure, she would enter an excited state of divine passion, partly influenced by noxious fumes that rose from a fissure in the Earth. In this altered state of consciousness, the Pythoness would offer prophecies to those who visited her. Her powers of divination were renowned throughout the ancient world, attracting visitors such as Alexander the Great, as well as the rulers of Greece, Persia, Macedonia, Rome, and Egypt. Her epiphanies were extensively documented by Aristotle, Diodorus, Euripides, Plato, and many others.

Divination was even included in the Old Testament of the Bible. Isaiah sought knowledge of the future through divine quarry when he reported, "See, the former things have taken place, and new things I declare; before they spring into being I announce them to you" (Isaiah 42:9). The ancient and sacred art of pre-vision continues to be an important tool for helping alchemists by providing knowledge that can support their efforts with the Great Work. Whether through dreams, visions, insights, or special tools, there are well over a hundred known ways for an alchemist to acquire information about events as they arise and fade away through the stream of time. Only the most prominent methods of divination are presented here, psychic mysteries that have been particularly significant to the Kingswoods, used to gain insight for their spiritual practice.

The methodologies used in Kingswood's lineage of alchemy aim to gain both inner and outward knowledge with the help of ethereal allies, such as ancestors and particularly the luminary deity, Ra. This practice always involves at least two participants: the querist and a willing, supernatural partner. It can be likened to how an off-camera strobe functions in a dark studio. There exists an alliance between a transmitter and a receiver. When everything is in place and the timing is right, the on-camera transmitter communicates with the flash's receiver, and in an instant, the scene is illuminated — in a burst of light, everything suddenly becomes clear! Similarly, divination opens a channel of communication to unseen forces, making the querist the receiver.

The purposes of divination may include seeking guidance, obtaining advice on the best course of action, gaining a deeper understanding of an issue, maintaining contact with a spirit ally, or forecasting important details about future events. It can also serve as an exercise to sharpen one's intuition and instincts, or to enhance one's psychic abilities and powers of perception. "Divination is a nonlinear process of accessing the totality of who you are in the truest sense of the word. Divination allows your perception to be adjusted like a lens on a camera that zooms in and out" (A. Hall, 2019).

At any given moment in history, there are few living spiritual masters from whom one can obtain wise counsel. Most of the time, they aren't available for conversation, so practitioners of the Hermetic arts have long discovered alternative methods to receive the guidance they need. One who performs divinations assumes the role of oracle, which means "to speak" or "to answer." Egyptian priests learned that by sleeping in consecrated spaces, they would receive dreams that offered profound teachings directly from Ra. They also discovered that the deceased could connect with them through dreams and visions, even if the sources were from the otherworld. GK reports from his own experience that, "Meditation, when combined with divination, can open the mind, helping one recognize the difference between mental/emotional distractions and the authentic responses received in response to the heartfelt need to know."

Mantic# methods of divination most preferred by the Kemetic Order include interpreting dreams, astrology, black mirror scrying, gazing, and psychometry using photographs. One of the tools of sortilege# most favored by Abraham Kingswood was either tarot cards or oracle cards. GK also prefers cartomancy over all other forms of divination but often relies on dreams, visions, and photo-psychometry.

Photomancy
Abraham Kingswood wrote, "A photograph is an orchestra, all of its compositional elements unified in their performance, working together to achieve as a single, meaningful voice." Kingswood considered photography a prophetic medium. He defined it as "the art that clearly reveals knowledge of the self, insight into the cosmos, and thus, illumination of the divine mysteries." However, photographs are not limited to expressing revelations solely to their maker. Susan Sontag believed that viewers, like herself, could find the photography of Edward

Weston "...prophetic, subversive, revelatory" (Sontag, 2001, 96). When she further stated that, "Photographers reveal to others the world around them...showing to them what their own unseeing eyes had missed" (2001, 96), she may have been discussing the art's ability to offer its audience a chance at seeing the revelations that photos, like Weston's, could reveal.

Twentieth-century photographer László Moholy-Nagy realized that conventional ways of seeing could be expanded once photography became an established art form. The "new kinds of vision he attributes to photographer are: abstract seeing (photogram), exact seeing (reportage), rapid seeing (snapshots), slow seeing (prolonged time exposures), intensified seeing (micro-photography, filter photography), penetrative seeing (radiography), simultaneous seeing (transparent superimposition), and distorted seeing (optical jokes)" (Scott, 1999, 19). Such an observation, GK elaborated, was a revelation for photographers, but Moholy-Nagy highlighted the inherent limitations that exist when one solely relies on the physical sense of sight. For GK, seeing with the eyes is just the first level of contact. A deeper, more profound level can only be revealed by awakening other organs of perception. In this way, one gains an extra-normal awareness of making and looking at photographs that brings deep understanding and insights.

The camera is a tool that works with all types of sight to help people recognize their innermost selves and their relationship to the cosmos. It's also "a discourse emanating from divine inspiration and declaring the purposes of God...or revealing things hidden" (Red Door Sentinel, 2011). In the hands of a hermetic artist, the camera is especially valuable for exploring questions about the past, present, or future. The seeker finds answers as the camera responds to their own query. Answers emerge. Making photographs sets into motion a "discourse emanating from divine inspiration." GK affirmed, "The responses to the questions aren't so much hidden in us, the world, or in photographs as much as they are obvious and waiting to be found. One needs only apply the appropriate methods of inquiry to find revelation. Even the most prosaic scenes reveal knowledge."

In the late nineteenth century, Reverend Alexander Keith embarked on a journey to photograph the "holy land" to prove that biblical prophecies about the landscape of Palestine had come true (Beaumont, 2018). His mission was to use daguerreotypes to provide irrefutable evidence of the past, present, and predicted future of biblical truth. Keith concluded that "the camera's accuracy was like the clear prophetic eye/word of God" (Beaumont, 2018). Keith's photographs were understood by the faithful to reaffirm both the veracity of the Bible's historical words and the foretelling of future events that would impact their spiritual lives.

Contemporary artist Sam Nightingale developed an abstract photographic process that uses the "inherent photochemical abilities of plants to produce images". He calls this process, *Para-photo-mancy.* His purpose for the images was to,

> explore the ancient art of augury (divination), examining how we might divine or sense signs from the organic and inorganic worlds that we are a part of but that also operate beyond rational human knowledge." Accordingly, he asks the viewer to, "consider how Para-photo-mancy might enable a different order of visuality, one that privileges a nonhuman aesthetic and makes it perceptible to sensory experience as a form of divination. (Nightingale, 2019).

Tarot

The typical tarot deck consists of 78 different symbolic, divinatory images. This collection is divided into five parts, including the major arcana and the minor arcana, which is separated into four suits: cups, wands, swords, and pentacles, also known as coins. Additionally, the minor arcana corresponds to the four classical elements: fire, air, water, and earth. In addition to a deck's meaning saturated imagery, author Charles Williams related the tarot to the four elements when he said, "that the shuffling of the cards is the earth, and the pattering of the cards is the rain, and the beating of the cards is the wind, and the pointing of the cards is the fire. That's of the four suits. But the Greater Trumps, it's said, are the meaning of all process and the measure of the everlasting dance" (Williams, 1950, 20).

The word "tarot" comes from the tarocchi decks, which were invented in the mid-1400s. However, their use for cartomancy didn't gain popularity until the late 1700s. When its otherworldly capacity for delivering knowledge was discovered, it was "an alchemical revelation, revealing the descent and ascent of Hermes, Mercurius Thoth" (Campbell and Roberts, 1982, 41). It was found that when a question was posed, the imagery could respond, speaking through the reader's imaginative intuition. GK remarked, "It seems a game of chance, but cartomancers believe that unseen forces influence the position of the cards in the deck so as to guide the reader to a certain understanding, a particular story."

In the late 1800s, Abraham Kingswood found this Tarot-image-based form of divination instrumental for aspirants in the Great Work. At one point, he diverged from known deck designs and composed his own tarot-like deck. His notebooks record detailed descriptions of the universal imagery (later called "archetypes") on the fronts of his card designs. Today, this kind of deck would be called "Oracle" or "Divination" cards. Kingswood wrote, "The faces of the cards represent universally shared exemplars that exist in the microcosm of worldly life, while the backs display the macrocosm: the realms of gods and the cosmos. When both sides are viewed as a relationship between one another, the cards tell a story regarding a specific query for each particular [card] draw."

Picture 16.3 Example of a Kingswood Oracle Card and its Back. The two sides represent the microcosm and macrocosm. Designs by Garin Horner, 2023.

Kingswood also wrote that he had commissioned an artist to create woodcuts illustrating the divinatory decks, which were distributed to members of the Kemetic Order. For instance, there were Victorian woodcuts of various animals, including a snake, a candle, the moon, and an eye. Additionally, there were line-art illustrations of people, such as a king, teacher, artist, and warrior. Along with his collection of images, there were also 13 *intium*, or inhabited capital letters cards. The intium were used as significators#, to clarify questions, to represent the querent, or as an aid to invoke allies who could facilitate the reading.

"I regret to report," GK says in a tone of remorse,

that none of the Kemetic Order's decks exist. Currently, I am referring to my great-grandfather's notes to have the designs remade. The deck that my ancestor envisioned was quite different from popular tarot imagery, such as the Rider-Waite-Colman Smith deck. Its ingenious, archetypal imagery could effectively open intuitive and spiritual portals of perception, revealing knowledge. I envision the 78 portal cards as divination tools rather than oracle or tarot cards. Each card invites the reader to look beyond the common symbols represented and into readily understandable, divinely inspired interpretations.

GK notes that he prefers to use Godfrey Dowson's Hermetic Tarot until he recreates a version of his family's deck.

Dreams

Father of psychotherapy, Sigmond Freud believed, "it possible to interpret dreams, and that…every dream will reveal itself as a psychological structure, full of significance, and one which may be assigned to a specific place in the psychic activities of the waking state" (Freud, 1911, p. 1). Freud's approach is one investigation of dreams in which imagery from one's night visions originates solely from the dreamer. Another important aspect, which relates to divination, involves external forces that either influence the happenings in the dreamer's dreams or generate the narratives entirely. In Western mysticism, it is reputed that oneiromancy offers invaluable wisdom and actionable knowledge about one's internal and external universe.

As early as the second century BCE, the Egyptians wrote on papyri about instructions for dream interpretation. In fact, the old Egyptian word for "dream' not only refers to "see something in a dream" but also means "awaken," representing dreaming as a special state of consciousness—something like 'watching during sleep" (Botterweck and Ringgren, 1974). Many prophets of old relied on dreams as opportunities to receive divine knowledge, as seen in the biblical story of Jacob's Ladder. In Jacob's vivid and transcendent dream, he saw a ladder stretching from the earth to the heavens, interpreted as representing the unmediated, direct connection between man and God. In 44 BCE, Calpurnia, the wife of Caesar, presaged his death in a dream. Nicolas Camille Flammarion, in his book, "Premonitory Dreams and Divination of the Future,' states: 'I do not hesitate to affirm at the outset that occurrence of dreams foretelling future events with accuracy must be accepted as certain" (quoted in Miller, 1995, 9).

The forefather of alchemy, the Egyptian Zosimos of Panopolis, experienced a series of dreams that revealed to him enlightening knowledge about alchemy and himself. The dreams, or sleeping visions, were also interpreted as an allegory for the significant contributions he would make to the field of alchemy. In recounting the colorful phantasmagoria, he saw a priest and,

> listened to the words of the one atop the bowl-shaped altar then asked him who he was. He answered me in a quavering voice: 'I am Ion, hierophant of the innermost sanctuary and I have endured unbearable violence. At dawn, I was overtaken and dismembered by one wielding a sword. He chopped me apart according to the strictures of harmony. He gripped his blade, scalped me, and gathered together my bones and flesh. Then he burned them in the numinous fire until I learned to become spirit through transformation of the body.' I compelled him and after he spoke these words his eyes turned blood-red and he vomited up all of his flesh. I saw him as a deformed, tiny homunculus, gnashing at himself with his own teeth while he disintegrated (Barrett, 2015).

Zasimos took this esoteric reverie to mean,

> The sky gives and the earth receives. Thunder yields flashing fire. All things are interwoven and unravel. All things mingle and fuse. All things mingle and disperse. All things moisten and dry. All things flower and bloom in the bowl-shaped altar. For each, the conjunction and separation of all occurs through method, measure and the weight of the four elements. There is no chain of being without this method. Inhalation and exhalation are the method of Nature. The order of the method is preserved through expansion and contraction. Simply, when all things unite and separate in harmony and no part of the method is neglected, then Nature is transformed. Nature rotates and cycles back upon itself. This is the chain of being and the nature of the Art for the whole cosmos (Barrett, 2015).

Kingswood believed that the revelations of Zasimos' dreams and visions were delivered directly by Ra. GK concludes, "Ra may either send an emissary to appear in one's dream or could even appear himself as one of countless mytho-poetic forms. In either case, the purpose of his appearance is to deliver previously unperceived wisdom." Neo-Platonic philosopher Synesius of Cyrene (CE 370 CE - 413 CE) wrote, "If dreams are prophets, and if the visions seen in dreams are riddles of their future fortunes to anxious men, they would in that case be full of wisdom, though certainly not clear. In sooth their lack of clearness is their wisdom" (Livius, 2020). Dreams are valued in the Hermetic arts as visions that emerge from the deepest depths of the sleeper's being.

Another source of prognostic dreams may stem from those magicians who are adept in the art of dream-casting.

> Ancient Egyptians priests or magicians performed rituals to cause other persons to have a specific dream. A legend concerning Alexander the Great credits his divine origins to a sent dream. According to lore, Nectanebo, the last native king of Egypt, used dream magic to cause the Greek queen Olympias to dream that the Egyptian god Amun would make love to her and she would bear a god. Nectanebo accomplished this through sympathetic magic, by pouring the extracted juices of various desert plants over a wax effigy of the queen and reciting a spell (Occult World, 2022).

Some dreams have been cast to evoke lust. For example, the Papyri *Graecae Magicae* states that the sender should invoke Selene to

> give a sacred angel or a holy assistant who serves this very night, in this very hour . . . and order the angel to go off to her, NN ("so-and-so"), to draw her by her hair, by her feet; may she, in fear, see phantoms, sleepless because of her passion for me and her love for me, NN, come to my consecrated bedroom (Guiley, 2006, 82).

GK advises that, "To realize the full potential of dreams, the alchemist is advised to make one's questions and purpose clearly defined and to earnestly ask for a visitation from Ra or an allied spirit. It can also be beneficial to connect with the spirit of a past oracle, or one who had strong psychic abilities while they were still in an embodied form on earth. Aspirants rely on divination from oracles or even deities to gain higher self-knowledge and self-awareness during their ascension."

Religious scholar Lee Erwin states, "some dreams are a basis for the development of psychic and mystical states which can subsequently impact the dreamer and shift or reorient his or her worldview and value constructions. Dreams of this higher, more impactful type may be a basis for significant human development when those dreams are assimilated into new conscious attitudes or behaviors" (Irwin, 2002, 2). Furthermore, the knowledge delivered in dreams can contribute directly to one's spiritual evolution. For, "if any one deems the way upward a great undertaking, but disbelieves in the imagination…let him listen to the sacred oracles which tell of the diverging paths…for the ascent, in virtue of which it is possible to make the seed within us grow. It is written: 'To some he gave the revelation of the light to be a lesson, Others even in their dreams, He made fruitful with His courage'" (Livius, 2020).

GK remarks,

> It's quite common for individuals to seek information from various sources, such as tarot readings, in addition to their dreams. There can be such a torrent of insights within a dream that the mind struggles to process it all quickly. Consequently, one may even experience unexpected visions during waking hours as a result. It's important to remain open and particularly introspective for some time after the communication appears to have concluded.

Carl Jung once said, "Your visions will become clear only when you can look into your own heart. Who looks outside, dreams; who looks inside, awakes." When Jung uses the word "awakes," he likely refers to awakening to the divine, natural occult truths hidden within both the corporeal body and mind, as well as the various aspects of this reality.

Since dreams communicate using the language of imagery, one of the sacred missions of the dreamer is to learn how to interpret the enlightening messages conveyed through their visual symbols, metaphors, and allegories. While some imagery is highly specific to the dreamer, much of it can be universally meaningful. For instance, "imagery takes place in an inner realm of existence, free of time and space, where we access a 'vertical axis' beyond the constraints of gravity. Spiritual seekers have acknowledged [this as] the axis of freedom. Imagery always attempts to put us in connection with this vertical axis enabling us to escape the ordinary limitations of earth-bound living" (Federoff, 2012, 9).

> This limitless realm is the golden land where allies are free to reveal their benefactions to recipients, as was given to Zosimus, using meaningful imagery to convey imperative, beneficial insights about the past or present, or the foresight needed to progress in their spiritual pursuits. It is advised that the passionate alchemist pay close attention to their revelatory dreams, thus never missing the chance to receive a personally beneficial message sent by a god. (GK)

Visions

A spiritual vision is defined as a "trance, or religious ecstasy, especially a supernatural appearance that usually conveys a revelation" (Vision Definition & Meaning, 2023). These visual events often foretell future occurrences, typically referred to as *prophecies*. At times, visions can be difficult to distinguish from dreams because they seem to communicate through the same creative sight impulse. Visions may arise during the transition from sleep to wakefulness or vice versa. Authentic visions are said to be more vivid than dreams. Sometimes, like dreams, these experiences may include disembodied voices, originating from an unknown source. For example, Joan of Arc heard supernatural voices, which her accusers claimed were demonic.

Another name for visions is the "gift of sight," referring to their tendency to appear as visual imagery. GK puts forth, "It is the inward-looking eye that is sensitive enough to perceive transcendental, prophetic imagery." And although the occurrence of visions has always been quite common among mystics, the first-hand experience of the future is a rare happening for most people. Israel Regardie indicated that among common folk, "there seldom comes that flash of spiritual light making descent in splendid tongues of flame like the Pentecostal Holy Ghost, radiant with joy and the highest wisdom, pregnant with spontaneous inspiration" (2013, 26).

The following is an example of a vision from the Oracle at the Temple of Apollo at Delphi, as recorded by Porphyry. It concerns an inquiry into the condition of Plotinus' soul, some time after his death. In the translation by Thomas Taylor, the Oracle describes Plotinus' after-death experience:

> While in the middle of its boist'rous waves
> Thy soul robust, the deep's deaf tumult braves;
> Oft beaming from the Gods thy piercing sight
> Beheld in paths oblique a sacred light:
>
> Whence rapt from sense with energy divine,
> Before thine eyes immortal splendours shine;
> Whose plenteous rays in darkness most profound,
> Thy steps directed and ilium in 'd round.
>
> Nor was the vision like the dreams of sleep,
> But seen while vigilant you brave the deep;
> While from your eyes you shake the gloom of night,

The glorious prospects burst upon your sight (Taylor, 1895, 66–67).

During the life of the medieval Benedictine mystic Hildegard of Bingen, it was recorded in hagiographies# that she had a series of lapses into visionary states. To describe one of her experiences, she wrote

> In this vision my soul…rises up high into the vault of heaven and into the changing sky and spreads itself out among different peoples, although they are far away from me in distant lands and places. And because I see them this way in my soul, I observe them in accord with the shifting of clouds and other created things. I do not hear them with my outward ears, nor do I perceive them by the thoughts of my own heart or any combination of the five senses, but in my soul alone, while my outward eyes are open. So I have never fallen prey to ecstasy in the visions, but I see them wide awake, by day and night…The light which I see thus is not spatial, but it is far, far brighter than a cloud which carries the sun…I call it "the reflection of the living Light (Newman, 1985, 164-165).

Visions can have a lasting impact on one's perception and consciousness, lingering for minutes, days, or even years. For instance, "the great German Mystic, Jacob Boehme, who, after his divine beatific vision, walked into the green fields close to his village, beholding the whole of Nature ablaze with so glorious a light that even the tender blades of grass were resplendent with a divine loveliness and beauty that never had he seen before" (Regardie, 2013, 25). Boehme's transcendent experience awakened a new, enduring sense of "Sight" which enabled him to perceive the outpouring of the world's empyrean light.

Black Mirror
The Black Mirror, also known as the Scrying Mirror, is one of the oldest methods of divination in Egyptian culture. Traditionally, this forecasting tool was made of obsidian as black as a raven's head. GK tells, "The black mirror is a unique object because its surface has two opposing properties. It has the capacity to absorb light, whilst at the same time reflecting it." Instead of the traditional obsidian tool, GK uses an 8 x 10 sheet of fully exposed and processed film, which is framed so that the reflective acetate side faces the viewer. The film he uses, "has been exposed with scenes from all events, past, present, and future."

The process begins with the querent asking a question. Next, they gaze into the dark, glassy surface until they receive a response. From one vantage point, the plane of darkness is like a screen upon which spirits appear or other images emerge as projections. The manifestations then deliver some kind of answer. Another way to understand the mirror is as a black portal looking into a receding abyss. From there, forms of the past and future can arise out of *nothingness*. It is up to the alchemist to interpret what the imagery means in relation to the question.

Photo-Psychometry

Photo-psychometry is the divinatory practice of receiving information about a person, place, or thing through physical contact with a photograph, by supernatural means. With this form of clairvoyance, the alchemist can psychically gather knowledge about the past, present, or future concerning the subject matter in the photo. This is accomplished by using empyreal filaments that create connections between the diviner, the photograph, and whoever or whatever is in frame. Information can also be gathered regarding the physical object itself. Those who have developed this ability receive visual impressions in their mind and do not need to look at the photograph. By simply holding the object, one can successfully divine relevant information.

> If the photograph is of a person, the divinatory information obtained by the psychometrist may include insights about the individual's character, various moments in their life, or their current emotional state and opinion of a particular situation or person. At times, information about the person's recent location may also be gathered, making psychometry a valuable tool in cases involving missing individuals. Some psychometrists merge their skills with traditional body reading and face reading when applying their art to photographs of people.

>> If the photograph is of a house, a gravestone, or a piece of land, the information which the psychometrist receives may include information about people or animals who lived there, what spirits reside in the location, and whether the home is haunted by ghosts or negative entities.

>> The photo of a house or grave site of a deceased person may also be used in an to attempt to make contact with the spirits of the dead when no photographs of the people themselves are available, but this is not, strictly speaking, divination through psychometry; rather it is a form of image-assisted mediumship (Readers and Rootworkers, 2023).

GK read that Abraham Kingswood was 24 when he encountered the concept of *psychometry*. Soon after, he attended a gathering featuring a psychometric demonstration by Cornelia H. Buchanan. Kingswood then learned that he was an adept psychometer, or *photo-psychometer*— a term used among members of the Order, derived from the Greek words *"photos,"* meaning light, and *"psyche,"* meaning soul, and *"metron,"* meaning measure. The translation is *to measure the soul with light*).

In 1850, poet and Unitarian preacher John Pierpont wrote the following poem, a yellowed copy of which was tipped into one of Kingwood's personal notebooks. In it, Pierpont's prose responds to the question, "What is psychometry?" The following excerpt is from the "Manual of Psychometry: The Dawn of a New Civilization."

> But much, Daguerre, as has thy genius done
> In educating Latona's son,
> In thus educing, in the god of light
> The power to paint so, at a single sight,
> BUCHANAN has transcended thee, as far
> As the sun's face outshines the polar star.
> Thine *art* can catch and keep what meets the eye -
> His *science*, subjects that far deeper lie.
> Thy skill shows up the face, the outward whole -
> His science measures and reveals the soul.
> Thy subjects must be present - his may be
> Sunk in the depths of the mysterious sea;
> Their bodies may have mouldered into dust,
> Their spirits long have mingled with the just,
> Made perfect: Yet if one has left behind
> A written page, whereon the living mind
> Has but pour'd out, through pencil, paint or pen
> That written page shall summon back again
> The writer's spirit; pressed upon the brow,
> Or by the hand of many, living now:
> It shall the writer's character disclose,
> His powers, his weaknesses, his joys, his woes,
> The manly air, the sycophantic smile,
> The patriot's valor, and the traitor's wile,
> The fire that glowed beneath the snows of age
> As in the "Hero of the Hermitage,"
> When he claimed (methinks I hear him still),
> "By the Eternal, I will not, or will!"
> All is revealed! The prompting spirit threw
> Itself upon the paper - and the few

"Spirits that are finely touched to issues fine"
Will move the hand, thus touch'd, along the line,
And catch the soul that issues from it yet,
(As fishes taken in an evil net),
And the detecting spirit shall declare
"The form and pressure" of the soul that's there,
With greater truth than e'er a Sybil sung.
And with as great as fell from prophet's tongue!
Mysterious science! That has now displayed
"How fearfully and wonderfully made"
Is man, that even his touch can catch the mind,
That long has left material things behind!
Fearful the thought, that when my clay is cold,
And the next Jubilee has o'er it rolled,
The very page, that I am tracing now,
With tardy fingers and a care-worn brow,
To other brows by other fingers prest,
Shall tell the world, not what I had deem'd,
Nor what I passed for, nor what I had seem'd,
But when I *was*! Believe it, friends, or not,
To this high point of *progress* have we got,
We stamp ourselves on every page we write!
Send you a note to China or the pole -
Where'er the wind blows, or the waters roll -
That note conveys the measure of your soul!
(Buchanan, 1885, 1-3).

Pierpont's words capture the fascination of the time with the new metaphysical technology of psychometric divination. It expresses the sense of wonder that people felt about the rapid pace of technological progress. In just a few years, many world-transforming inventions emerged, like photography, gas lighting, phonotypy, phonography, telegrams, and new printing processes. This period also marked a historic spiritual revolution when ritual magic, spiritualism, psychic phenomena, and divination entered the collective consciousness of the public. "By 1897, there were eight million followers of the spiritualist belief in the US and Europe - mainly the middle and the upper classes" (Duell, 2017). Historian Janet Oppenheim said, "Spiritualism and psychical research were never monopolized by any one class of British society" (Oppenheim, 1985). Similarly, psychometric abilities emerged randomly among the rich or poor, young or old, and were not influenced by whether the receiver was male or female.

Ignem

17. The Great Pyramid: Stairway to The Everburning Light

As one of the Seven Wonders of the Ancient World, the Great Pyramid of Giza is the largest existing ancient structure, built approximately 2500 BCE, just outside Cairo. "The word pyramid is believed to be derived from πυρ [pyr], fire, thus signifying that it is the symbolic representation of the *One Divine Flame*, the life of every creature...Both pyramids and mounds are antitypes of the Holy Mountain, or High Place of God, which was believed to stand in the 'midst' of the earth" (M. Hall, 1928, 44-45). The structure is entirely composed of limestone and granite.

One of its purposes was as a tomb for the pharaoh, Khufu. Manly P. Hall wrote, "Eloquent in its silence, inspiring in its majesty, divine in its simplicity, the Great Pyramid is indeed a sermon in stone" (1928, 41). In 1880, British Pyramidologist Charles Piazzi Smyth described the Gizean edifice as "a gigantic cairn, as it were; but of strikingly crystalline figure on the whole...[with] almost mathematical truth and perfection" (1890, 19-20). Once called the "Pyramid of Light" (Adams, 1895) and "the House of Hidden Places" (Adams, 1985), the edifice has always been shrouded in mystery and has been the subject of research by alchemists, including Sir Isaac Newton. In fact, "The searching out of ancient occult secrets was a central trope of alchemy, a subject which Newton studied deeply...[he] was interested in the cubit, a unit of measurement used by the Great Pyramid's builders. He believed that it could [ultimately] hold the key to understanding the biblical apocalypse" (Southeby's, 2022).

Expanding on Newton's studies of the shape and dimensions of the pyramid, Hunter Havelin Adams III wrote in his 1987 essay, *African and African-American Contributions to Science and Technology*, about the mathematical marvels of the Great Pyramid. Adams calculated that the dimensions of the Great Pyramid contain: "the value of pi, the principle of the golden section [sic], the number of days in the tropical year, the relative diameters of the earth at the equator and the poles, and ratiometric distances of the planets from the sun, the approximate mean length of the earth's orbit around the sun, the 26,000-year cycle of the equinoxes, and the acceleration of gravity" (Adams, 1990).

Manly Hall envisioned the pyramid as much more than just a tomb for a pharaoh. He believed the

> Pyramid emphasizes anew the fact that it was in reality the
> supreme temple of the Invisible and Supreme Deity. The Great

Pyramid was not a lighthouse, an observatory, or a tomb, but the first temple of the Mysteries, the first structure erected as a repository for those secret truths which are the certain foundation of all arts and sciences. It was the perfect emblem of the microcosm and the macrocosm and, according to the secret teachings…Through the mystic passageways and chambers of the Great Pyramid passed the illumined of antiquity.

They entered its portals as men; they came forth as gods. It was the place of the 'second birth,' the 'womb of the Mysteries,' and wisdom dwelt in it as God dwells in the hearts of men. Somewhere in the depths of its recesses there resided an unknown being who was called 'The Initiator,' or 'The Illustrious One,' robed in blue and gold and bearing in his hand the sevenfold key of Eternity. This was the lion faced hierophant, the Holy One, the Master of Masters, who never left the House of Wisdom and whom no man ever saw save he who had passed through the gates of preparation and purification. It was in these chambers that Plato--he of the broad brow---came face to face with the wisdom of the ages personified in the Master of the Hidden House (1928, 45).

The shape of the Great Pyramid represented "rays of sunlight, further connecting the pharaohs with Ra, the sun god" (1928, 45). "The triangular geometry of the Pyramid is also similar to the posture assumed by the human body while sitting during the ancient meditative exercises (RA: The Sun God of Egypt, 2023). The corners at the base were also viewed as the four corners of Ra's throne. The perfect, radiant structure appears as an architectural polyhedron. Its four faces, which face the four cardinal directions, are congruent triangles. Its capstone, the pyramidion, which is missing from the Great Pyramid, would have pointed up toward the cosmos. Far below the peak, it sits on a flawless square base, designed as the quadrature of a circle. The 1st century BCE Greek geographer "Strabo declared the building looked as if it had descended from upon its site ready formed from Heaven, and had not been erected by man's laborious toil at all" (Smyth, 1890, 41). GK regards, "Its design is a perfect synthesis illuminated in a single symbol, which serves to gather the discriminating intellect, the spirit, and the will, to amplify and project them upward toward the embrace of the divine mystery which is Ra: the creator, the preserver and the transformer."

Consequently, there was another aspect of the pyramid that Newton, Adams, and Hall had not considered. When GK discusses the Great Pyramid, he is not only talking about the physical structure that pilgrims travel to. Many times, he refers to the *Mer*, an ethereal form that serves as an eternal reflection of Khufu's tomb. It can only be found on a spiritual plane, in the otherworld. It would be more accurate to say that the pyramid at Giza is a double or shell of its metaphysical construct. It is more than a metaphor because it is understood as real in the visualizations of alchemists – even more real than the wondrous, previously mentioned creation in Egypt.

The Mer's Four Corners

The load-bearing corners of the base that support the entirety of Giza's physical pyramid are the Mer's basal cornerstones of *courage*, *silence*, *will*, and *knowledge*. These four admonitions are similar to the "Oaths of the Magi," or the traditional maxim of Western ceremonial magic traditions, which say that,

> To attain…the knowledge and power of the Magi, there are four indispensable conditions – an intelligence illuminated by study, an intrepidity which nothing can check, a will which cannot be broken, and a prudence which nothing can corrupt and nothing intoxicate. TO KNOW, TO DARE, TO WILL, TO KEEP SILENCE – such are the four words of the Magus, inscribed upon the four symbolical forms of the sphinx (Lévi, 1896, 3).

GK reveals that part of the ancient Hermetic initiation included vows established on these foundational principles. They symbolize the base of the pyramid because the alchemist must understand the enormous weight of these four requirements. One needs to contemplate them as part of their very first step on the ground level course of stones. It's where the aspirant begins their spiritual journey. One must internalize the four requirements before proceeding on their ascent. This preliminary activity is necessary before any progress can be made as the initiate works to move up the steep risers, pursuing the narrowing arris lines as they converge toward the apex.

Courage (Aude)

The first cornerstone of *courage* urges the aspirant to take action and to confront both rational and irrational fears. Courage is essential when facing the transformational processes of one's material and spiritual existence. In situations that seem dangerous or harmful, a person's body and mind respond with fear. The instinctual choices appear limited: fight or flight.

> The mystes must make a different choice. One learns that courage is not the absence of fear; rather, it is acting while feeling it. The

aspirant does not respond with pusillanimous# reactions but instead takes a deliberate risk, fully aware that such an act could lead to spiritual reward or, possibly, death. This is how progress is achieved in one's transformative evolution. Such self-empowering choices enhance one's level of self-confidence and courage. (GK)

Silence (Tace)

The second cornerstone is *silence*. This principle is not defined as a state of calmness achieved through quieting the mind, concentrating, or through some form of meditation practice. Silence, in this context, refers to the resolve to proactively <u>refrain from</u> communicating anything about one's path of ascension in the Great Work. Additionally, one must avoid speaking about the alchemystical aspirants they associate with. Similarly, offering spiritual advice to others or displaying occult wisdom is particularly forbidden. Silence requires not showing any visible indications that one is anything but a regular, normal person operating within their worldly station, while engaging in activities and interests typical for someone at their societal level. This includes never allowing others to view one's ritual sanctuary or altar. In the presence of others, the aspirant should blend in and avoid drawing attention to themselves as someone with any practical or academic interest in mysticism. Kingswood did add the caveat that "the practice of silence does not apply to interactions with one's initiated brothers and sisters in one's Order."

Silence generates a powerful, raw energy field that enhances one's ability to collect and manipulate magical energies. One can feel the visceral quality of this potent energy when a situation arises in which they desperately want to reveal a secret, especially during a conversation that seems like the perfect moment to say something! There is a sense of tension. The body and its energetic field become excited, much like the way the atmosphere feels just before it releases a lightning bolt! The atmosphere radiates with empyrean light, almost as if it has produced a miniature sun within one's chest! It's an uncomfortable sensation, filled with anticipation and potential. The longer one holds the feeling of wanting to share the secret, the brighter their radiance becomes — so bright that it could captivate the eye of Ra! "Hence," GK expounds, "by spilling the secret, one would feel the energy quickly dissipate, along with any lambent, thaumaturgical light-energy. The mystes is left empty and feeling discouraged knowing that, through casual actions, they squandered their power and broke their vow."

In the Kemetic Order, silence was an absolute requirement for membership. Abraham Kingswood stresses the importance of maintaining confidentiality as a sacred practice that can either support or hinder an aspirant's spiritual efforts. One's ability to uphold the tradition of secrecy directly influences the individual's spiritual health and impacts the group's metaphysical wellbeing. For example, an inability to be discreet could negatively affect the numinous and rarefied aspects of group members' lives. Kingswood wrote extensively about intentionally using silence to create a container for the magical energies and connections that arise during daily practices, rituals, and ceremonies. "The deliberate undertaking of silence," Kingswood scribed, "generates a protective barrier within which the miraculous result of the Great Work can most successfully express itself. Inside the protective sphere, the alchemist will have an unequaled opportunity to profit from the quality and effect of their rituals, practices, and invocations."

Will (Vole)

The third cornerstone is *will*. This fundamental force concerns one's growing capacity for patience, persistence, and perseverance. The idea embodies having the discipline to do what must be done to achieve the desired result. It also refers to keeping promises and commitments to others, especially to fellow aspirants, as well as to oneself. One who masters their will masters self-control and self-discipline. They cannot be persuaded to break their promises, or, more importantly, their vows. The more one exercises their will, the stronger their physical, emotional, and psychological stamina becomes.

GK divulged that four of the most fundamental mystical disciplines are to "make your bed, keep your room clean, go to bed and wake up at the same time every single day." He presents another challenge to anyone wishing to test their will. The task is to commit to taking a single, consciously considered photograph each day for a week. If the candidate can achieve it without fail, they should attempt the same challenge for a month. Then six months. Then a year. This exercise, GK claims, is one that he has adhered to for over 50 years. It is a self-made vow he continues to uphold to this day. He also speculates that with the rise of digital cameras and cellphone cameras, this practice for the 21st-century alchemist-photographer becomes technically easier. However, the common obstacles that prevent one from fulfilling their commitment do not stem from their camera but from their resistance to change.

Knowledge (Vide)

The fourth cornerstone is the principle of *knowledge*. The aspirant of the mysteries professes, "May the intention of my magic be aligned with the intentions of Ra. I wish to know in order that I may serve!" The purpose of knowledge is essential so the mystes can better understand how *to serve* the divine mystery. While acquiring knowledge is a vital part of the alchemist's spiritual journey, one must build upon this cornerstone by taking actions that integrate the information into a transformative understanding, which can only be gained through experience.

Knowledge is the *understanding* of alchemy, its mysteries, tools, and practices. At the same time, one should recognize that while knowledge is essential for progress, it serves only as a starting point. Consequently, understanding guides the alchemist's evolution. GK instructs that,

> Anyone can read the ancient Hermetic books, study alchemical manuscripts, and even memorize all the Order's grimoires and writings. However, all that accumulated information won't elevate them any higher on their ascent toward dissolution into the divine light of gnosis than they were before beginning their research. The disciple of Hermes must apply the knowledge and gain hard-won experience to realize the goal.

The four cornerstones together support the highest, divinely inspired principle: *creativity*. GK offers his insights,

> This vivacious state of being manifests as radiating light, an instinctively active energy that exists to fulfill its potential: to create. It is the ability that was directly inherited from humanity's most generous ancestor and progenitor. Creativity is a bond that connects the divine to the seeker. The same creative impulse that gave rise to the universe is what drives all species to reproduce. It compels the artist to make and the aspirant to pursue. This same creative impulse motivates and excites the artist. It rises in the alchemist as a need to know, a need to transmute, from cell to soul, into their highest potential. Humans have been granted the possibility for evolution, the ability to dissolve and re-form into who and what they are.

> The apex of the pyramid, representing the divine pinnacle of creativity, can be seen as an arrow that points the way for those who are climbing toward fulfilling the soul's potential. That same pointing arrow, used as the primary symbol for the four elements, also signifies the ultimate spiritual goal of alchemy. The equilateral triangle serves as a two-dimensional representation of the Great Pyramid, containing all history and significance within that form.

GK clarifies the mystical aspects of the pyramid.

To understand what the eyes perceive, one must find evidence to support what they believe they see. This process confirms the reality they accept, based on information gathered through the distortions of their perceptual lens. Life experiences, emotions, psychology, spirituality, and beliefs shape these aberrations. For instance, one person may look at the Akhet Khufu, the Great Pyramid, and arrive at a conclusion based on their appreciation of its awe-inspiring physical properties. They may admire its structure as a perfect example of ancient engineering and design. Another viewer might see it as a good backdrop for a photograph. Others might perceive it as a mountain-like form that presents a climbing challenge. A treasure hunter could envision it as a giant, multi-sided container, possibly filled with treasure.

But when I look at the pyramid [pause], I perceive a microcosm of a supersensible#, multi-dimensional universe. I see a gateway through which souls may be purified to become *Maa Keru* – true of voice and action. The pyramid is the portal through which the purified soul may travel beyond this life, ascending through the aperture opening above its apex and continuing on to the divine mystery. Alternatively, one's spirit may pass across the threshold of one of the architecture's interior "false" doorways and descend through the pyramid's base, where it reflects the same edifice, leading to a new life in the otherworld.

Many people accept the world at face value, relying solely on what their senses affirm. It seems to be a realm that is lacking in transcendent mystery, stripped of miracles, and devoid of magic. GK challenges this perspective with probing questions.

Aren't the uncreated sparks of life-force living on the planet proof of magic? Isn't the vastness of the cosmos, the wonder of the majestic oceans, the infinite, living complexities of the earth, and the life-giving qualities of the sun all miraculous? It's so easy for our eyes to become inured to the magic that surrounds us. If one can't live in a state of awe for the miracles happening in every moment, then one certainly won't appreciate the wonders that magic can manifest. Surrounding us is a universe expressing itself as the ever-changing flow of divine processes. They are the teachers who can guide an aspirant to a miraculous state of gnosis.

My identification with alchemy and the Great Work shapes the lens through which I view the world. I also recognize that the distortions of my perceptions influence me. That's why I diligently polish the lens of my inner eye until it becomes a transparent conductor of pure light-reality, allowing me to reach the Supreme Vertex of the pyramid, known as AZOT (first and last). Upon arrival, I will be lifted through the aperture-gateway to the Divine Ocean of Limitless Light-Matter. With clear vision and a purified soul, this represents the highest attainment of my alchemical journey. On this matter, I am of one mind with the Neoplatonic philosopher Porphyry when he said, 'It is necessary…that the soul, when purified, should associate with its generator' (Porphyry, 1823, 169, n. 34]. In doing so, I will become inseparable in identity with the source of all light and witness the cosmos, as the divine mystery knows it.

Others, looking at the same universe, might see an entirely different reality, mediated by the biases of their subjective lenses, and not feel compelled to pursue the supreme goal. Their intellect may not be able to penetrate other spheres. Therefore, they may perceive the universe as a place with only physical properties, where everything in it is quantifiable and measurable, where stars and planets are composed only of their physical elements, all moving meaninglessly through a vast, chaotic expanse of space. In contrast, I understand that all things in the universe hold secrets. They communicate their knowledge through an intimate connectedness of filaments of light. Others see themselves and all things as distinctly separate entities, independent from all other things. The mystic identifies with whatever exists at the end of each filament in the network, which ultimately leads back to the original center of the entire cosmic network. There, one will discover the welcoming point of the genesis of all light, the source of the soul.

Plato described the essence, purpose, and goal of the alchemist in the Great Work when he said,

"The soul" …in the *Theaetetus*, "cannot come into the form of a man if it has never seen the truth. This is a recollection of those things which our soul formerly saw when journeying with Deity, despising the things which we now say *are*, and looking up to that which REALLY IS. Wherefore the *nous*, or spirit, of the philosopher (or student of the higher truth) alone is furnished with wings; because he, to the best of his ability, keeps these things in mind, of which the contemplation renders even Deity itself divine. By making the right use of these things remembered from the former life, by constantly perfecting himself in the perfect mysteries, a man becomes truly perfect – an initiate into the diviner wisdom" (quoted in Blavatsky, 2006).

What GK is undoubtedly an initiate of the mysteries. In every aspect of his life, he has immersed himself in the study and practice of mysticism. Rudolf Otto supports my theory by explaining that

> Mysticism is the *identification*, in different degrees of completeness, of the personal self with the transcendent Reality. This identification has a source of its own…and springs from moments of religious experience which would require separate treatment. "identification" alone, however, is not enough for Mysticism; it must be Identification with the Something that is at once absolutely supreme in power and reality and wholly non-rational (1957, 22-23).

Collectively, GK, Plato, and Otto describe how a mystic dwells in a reality that is entirely different from the collective human understanding of reality. It is a transcendent realm grounded in the alchemist's profound belief that the surrounding world is a magical realm, composed of light and filled with hidden knowledge. Moreover, with this knowledge, the transformative process of the Great Work promises to restore them to a state of unity with the godhead. This concept can be metaphorically understood in the esoteric cosmology of the Great Pyramid, Godhead, or *unio mystica*. In this cosmological framework, just beyond the highest point, above the Golden Summit, lies perfect Union, where one's spirit, purified by their art, may ascend through a divine aperture and be exalted.

GK confesses,

> When a truly hyper-perceptive viewer examines a photograph, they can interpret what the composition communicates in a multi-dimensional way. With photodynamic awareness, they can also delve into the image to understand the underlying aspects of the photographer who took the photo. They can superinduce new levels of illumination to look beneath the bidimensional surface and find meaning. The evidence is there, pointing to the story beyond the obvious. Similarly, to grasp what GK refers to as the Great Pyramid, one must look beyond and imagine how the shape and form of this magical structure relate to the various aspects of the Great Work.

"On a spiritual plane," GK continues,

> Imagine the Mer Pyramid as a five-sided, sacred edifice. In terms of dimensions, shape, and form, it closely resembles the Great Pyramid at Giza. Its exterior features a series of steps that ascend toward the sky, gradually disappearing from view. Ultimately, the path culminates at an inconceivably perfect shape at the top, known as the Golden Pyramidion. This point serves as the intended destination for the alchemist. It is where all things are transmuted into gold. Above the pyramidion, there is a gateway shaped like an iris [a mechanical aperture] that opens and closes. This gateway is called the Eye of Ra. For the alchemist to fully transition into a state of Divine Knowledge, they must rise above the apex and pass through the opening. The paradox is that the closer the aspirant gets to the luster of the pyramidion, the smaller the portal gateway becomes.

When one balances on the sharpest point, the Eye's portal is so small that Kingswood wrote, "not even a thought could pass through." On the other side of the Eye, Ra awaits to lift up, receive, and embrace the purified soul. Only Ra can facilitate one's passage through the impossibly tiny portal. Zoroaster once said in the Chaldean Oracles, "the mortal who approaches the fire shall have light from God, for to the persevering mortal, the blessed immortals are swift to come" (Sacred Texts, 2022, 158).

A novice once asked Abraham Kingswood if reaching the goal could only be accomplished through a painful series of transitions. "Yes," he replied, "It is the same suffering the new sparrowhawk feels when it breaks out of the shell of its limited understanding." He elaborated, "Whether one experiences pleasure or pain, they are both opportunities to learn how these experiences can serve one's spiritual progress. If your focused intention is the Golden Pyramidion, you will receive heaven and earth. If your focused intention is the earth, you will receive neither." He also wrote about how it is the destiny of all non-aspiring souls to drop, like meteorites from the sky, as they transmigrate into the Great Mer pyramid. There they will live again in the otherworld.

In the spiritual dimension, the inner area of the pyramid's base plane is covered by an impenetrable veil through which material forms cannot pass. It is an unyielding membrane, except for those recently disembodied souls that flow through effortlessly, transitioning from this reality into the otherworld. Once in the otherworld, most spirits, in their transitional state, cannot pass back through to the material realm.

The Egyptians claimed that there were spirits who could "always ... enter and leave the netherworld / Always speaking to the living ones / Proven to be true, a million times" (Abt & Hornung, 2003, p. 144).

Picture 17.1 Pyramid Mysteries by Daniel Martin Diaz,
courtesy of the artist.

For those who were fortunate at their time of death, they were buried with items that included a petitioning spell. It "was often inscribed on jade heart scarabs that were placed with the deceased. The spell appeals to the heart not to weigh down the balance or testify against the deceased to the keeper of the balance. Part of the spell gives instructions for making the heart scarab:" (Carelli, 2011, 86-87) "Lo, make for thyself a scarab (of) nephrite (set in) and adorned (with gold and put) within a man's heart, and perform (for him) the (ceremony of) opening the mouth, it (i.e. the scarab) being anointed with myrrh" (Allen, 1974, 39-40). Once the rite of judgment was completed, the soul was guided to the region of the otherworld where it would most appropriately belong.

Waiting on the other side of the barrier at the base of the Inverted Great Pyramid is the exalted Egyptian psychopompos, the god Hermanubis. He is known as the "collector of souls." It is he who escorts spirits that have recently become disembodied. Holder of the great Hermetic Caducean

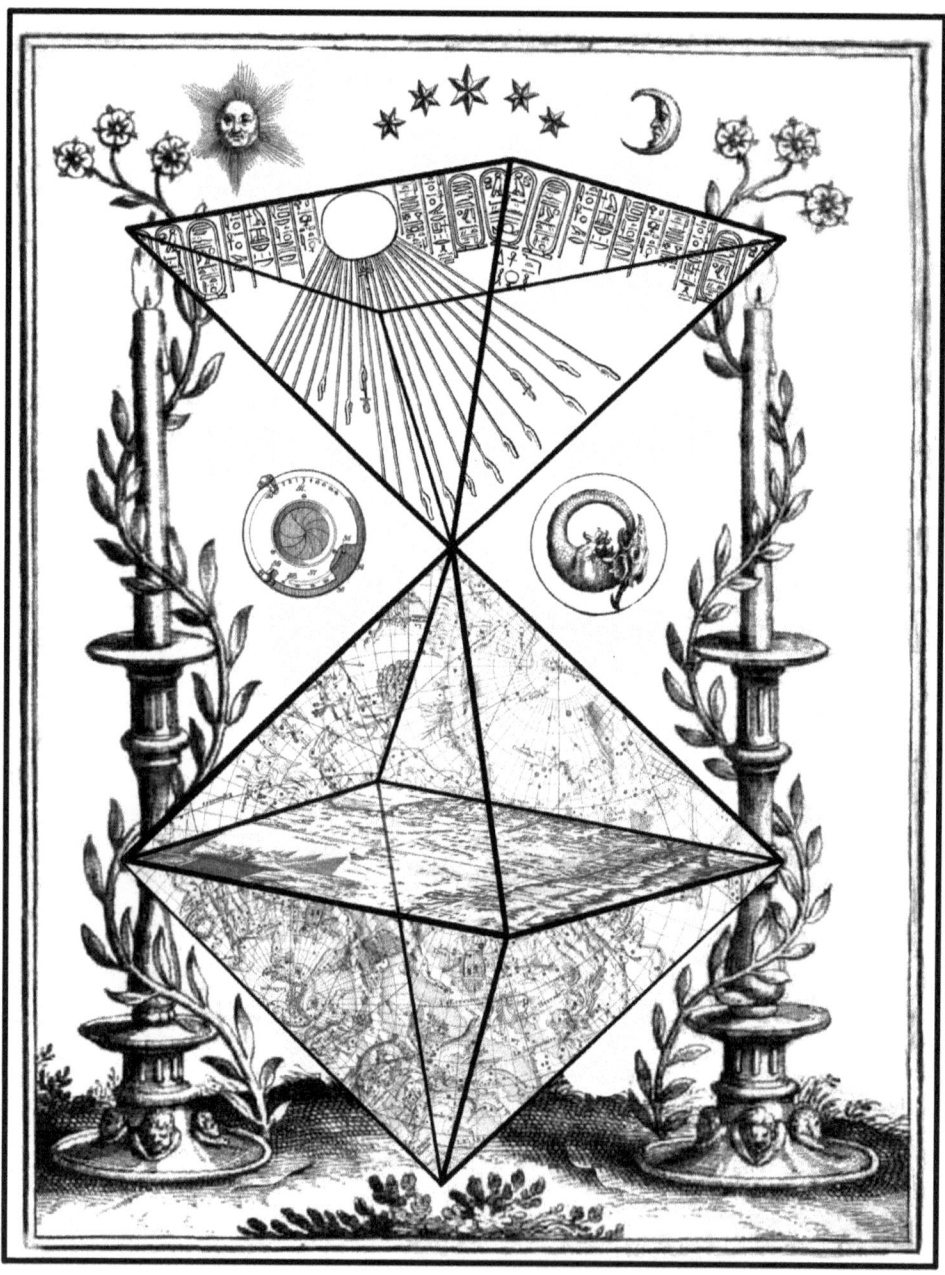

Picture 17.2 The Great Mer Pyramid of Light. Composite illustration by Garin Horner (2023), from Joannis Danielis Mylii, Anatomia auri, 1628.

Rod, the god evaluates the earthbound lives of each soul by measuring the intensity of their radiance. He then guides them accordingly to their following assessment.

GK believes that the actions one takes in life will largely determine where one's soul will naturally travel after death. In Egyptian mythology, it was believed that after the soul (Akh) separated from the body, it embarked on a journey to a new realm of existence. Carried on a current of light, most would find themselves on the path to the underworld, where they would enter the *Hall of Judgment*. In the Hall, the soul would be met by gods who were waiting to perform the weighing ritual. Anubis, Thoth, Ra, and Ammit would all be in attendance.

Picture 17.3 Hall of Judgment - Unknown artist in Giza, Egypt. Papyrus from the collection of George Kingswood.

The heart of the recent deceased was placed on a balance scale and weighed against the feather of Ma'at.

> Ma'at was the goddess of truth, balance, justice, harmony, as well as many other concepts. If a person's heart was equal to, or lighter than, one of Ma'at's feathers, then that person has led a life full of what she represents and passes the first judgment. If the heart was heavier than the feather, that person was condemned. Egyptians had no concept of hell or eternal torment. Instead, those that failed would be devoured by Ammit. She was the devourer of the unworthy dead, and was part lion, part hippopotamus, and had the head of a crocodile. Those who were devoured simply ceased existing. There would be nothing more for them, and they would never be reincarnated or enjoy eternal life (George, 2022).

Those spirits who endure the trials of judgment continue to exist in the realm of the otherworld.

Given the right conditions, those otherworldly spirits can travel back through the barrier-veil to visit the earthly plane. One opportunity arises when a spirit is called to come through, which is how one's allies traverse the barrier when summoned by a magician. Other spirits appear to be able to move freely between realms, interacting with people in this world. For example, in August of 1799, Napoleon Bonaparte journeyed to Cairo and chose to sleep in the King's Chamber of the Great Pyramid. He was determined to do so because legendary conquerors before him, like Alexander the Great and Julius Caesar, had done the same and received insights from visiting apparitions.

"The Great Napoleon spent around seven hours inside of the Great Pyramid and just at dawn he 'came out of the pyramid' pale and frightened. When a few of his most trusted men asked Napoleon what had happened inside of the Pyramid, Napoleon replied: 'Even If I told you, you would not believe me'" (Ancient Code Team). Rumors among those close to Napoleon believed that he had been confronted by spirits from the underworld who showed him visions of the future. What he learned, "changed his life forever…Countless legends were formulated on Napoleon's experience, including one that suggests Napoleon had some kind of vision where he saw himself as being the greatest emperor ever to live on the planet" (Ancient Code Team, 2022).

18. ᴀLTAR OF THE SUN

The word "*altar*" originated from the Latin root, *altārium*, meaning "high" or "high place." It is also associated with the Latin word "*adolere*," which means "to ritually burn or sacrifice'" (Cerwinske, 2000, 78). Artist and scholar Kay Turner maintains that "from the very beginnings of human consciousness," spiritual altars were created because they "assuaged the terror of separation by creating a special site to serve the human desire for relationship with unseen gods and spirits." (Turner, 1999, 7).

Turner says, "An altar makes visible that which is invisible and brings near that which is far away; it marks the potential for communication and exchange between different but necessarily connected worlds, the human and divine" (1999, 7). Author Laura Cerwinske explains, "The earliest altars were likely considered by their makers as access routes through which spirits could enter and leave the world. Used for sacrifice, consecration, and prayer, they were erected as sites where the presence of divinity was indicated by a natural formation — at a spring, under a shade tree, or...wherever the mystical manifestation of a deity appeared" (2000, 78).

Another interesting word related to altars is the term' *focus*,' which once meant *'hearth'* but also referred to an *altar*, or specifically, *a hearth altar*. This concept of *focus* as an *altar* can be found in the 21st-century definition of the word: "the center of interest or activity" or "the state or quality of having or producing clear visual definition" ("Define Focus", Google). As such, the altar serves as the point of critical focus from which one's acts of vision are realized and brought into being. Cerwinske says an altar is "a site of power. It is a place where eyes are drawn, where prayers are *focused*, where offerings are made, from where utterances of the supplicant arc takcn hcavenward" (2000, 78).

The altar functions as an access point, a sacred space where believers commune with higher powers and ethereal beings, and in this case, connect to the Egyptian god of light. It is a portal for accessing and interacting with spiritual realms. It's a place where one encounters the "wholly other," or what Rudolf Otto referred to as an experience of the "mysterium tremendum." He described it as

> The feeling of it may at times come sweeping like a gentle tide, pervading the mind with a tranquil mood of deepest worship. It may pass over into a more set and lasting attitude of the soul,

continuing, as it were, thrillingly vibrant and resonant, until at last it dies away and the soul resumes its 'profane', non-religious mood of everyday experience. It may burst in sudden eruption up from the depths of the soul with spasms and convulsions, or lead to the strangest excitements, to intoxicated frenzy, to transport, and to ecstasy. It has its wild and demonic forms and can sink to an almost grisly horror and shuddering. It has its crude, barbaric antecedents and early manifestations, and again it may be developed into something beautiful and pure and glorious. It may become the hushed, trembling, and speechless humility of the creature in the presence of-whom or what? In the presence of that which is a *Mystery* inexpressible and above all creatures (Otto, 1957, 12-13).

Picture 18.1 George Kingswood's Apothecary. Photograph by Garin Horner, 2021.

In addition, "The altar is an intimate spiritual site of power. A space where the mind can be converted from its self-imposed smallness to an experience of light expanding without boundary." GK reveals,

I maintain several altars located in my library, apothecary, laboratory, and photography studio. Throughout the house, there is also a collection of resplendent shrines. My primary altar is located in the temple room, the same place where my great-grandfather experienced transmutational ecstasies while he received divine knowledge from Ra. I am now the keeper of the altar. This room is the core manifestation of the creative alchemical arcana, the well-nigh indescribable locus where I offer myself to the "mysterium tremendum" of Ra.

GK's altar functions as a metaphysical focal point that amplifies his practice, a place where even a secular visitor can sense the energizing

Picture 18.2 George Kingswood's Temple Room. Photograph by Garin Horner, 2022.

atmosphere, alive with a vital potency resulting from over 130 years of continual magical and alchemical practices.

Additionally, in the temple chamber, a lamp hangs. On it burns a flame. It's in front of a large, full-scale painting of Ra. GK claims that his great-grandfather lighted the lamp and continues to burn without assistance to

211

this day. In his notes, Kingswood wrote about the creation of *divine water*, which he placed in the lamp. Within the same writings was a quote attributed to H. Khunrath (Heinrich Khunrath 1560-1605): "that the ether in this praeter-perfect aqueous body will burn perpetually, without diminution or consumption of itself, if the external air only be restrained." GK declares,

> This light symbolizes my soul, its lamp filled and lit by the eternal fire of Ra. It is my birthright to watch over it so it burns beyond my death and into eternity. The brilliance of our home star, Sol, has never shone in this temple; nevertheless, it is illuminated by an alternate sun, which has learned its art from Ra's sun and will continue to cast its light perpetually.

Each morning, GK adds new offerings to his ancestral altar. One can find cameras, candles, luminaires, fruit, incense, and various other gifts on any given day.

> This is the threshold where the most honored supernatural guests appear. They are celestial Kings and Queens, and accordingly, I offer them the highest level of adoration. I greet them with gifts that they would find delightful. There is a protocol for envisioning offerings. To Ra, the god, 'Anubis, Governor of Amenti [the underworld], giveth thee thousands of cakes, thousands of vessels of beer, thousands of vases of oil, thousands of oxen, thousands of changes of apparel, and thousands of bulls.' Since the magnitude of these offerings is unrealistic for most aspirants, one can use magical methods to multiply the scale of their gifts. Just as an infinite number of prints can be made from a single negative, from one candle I telesmatically project plenitudinous astral treasures of light. A photograph of a beautiful cake may become Everest-sized mountains of cakes! Offerings, like incense, music, and nectar, should be expanded to fill the entirety of the cosmos! To a god, offerings become *Sa*, (Budge, 1898, 146) a divine nectar that bestows health, vigor, and eternal life. Those who are disciples of Ra are advised to use the same multiplication method.

GK provides guidance on how to create a proper altar to Ra, enabling aspirants to make offerings in their own sanctum sanctorum.

> It's best to place one's altar in an area that serves as a sanctuary, a protected space where no other people are allowed to enter. In this private location, known as one's Solar Temple, the altar

should be positioned altarwise against the eastern wall. The specific spot along the wall should be near a window to allow natural daylight to enter and illuminate the sacred site. Having four obelisks of any size is desirable, with one placed in each corner of the room. Photographs, illustrations, or two-dimensional representations of obelisks are perfectly acceptable.

When building the altar, it should have a square block or box as its base. The three visible sides of the cube should be decorated with artworks depicting Ra's cartouche, the ankh, the eye of Ra, and images of the standing or sitting forms of Ra. Appropriate messages in hieroglyphics may also be inscribed upon the altar. The center of the front panel should feature a black aperture with five leaves, outlined in either silver or gold. The top of the cube should be covered with a mirror, representing the veil between worlds at the base of the Great Pyramid. Having done so, all the sacred objects arranged on the altar surface will perfectly reflect the otherworld altar. In keeping with the geometric form, install a square backboard made of black material, the same size and dimensions as the altar's top. It should be positioned so that its base meets fully across the back width of the surface mirror. Upon the black square, there should be an orange or red triangular shape, pointing up to the cosmos. Its foundational side should span fully across the width of the altar top. It is common for the black areas of the background to feature gold, silver, or phosphorescent five-pointed stars. When completed, the temple and altar should be consecrated as *Akhetra*, "The horizon of Ra."

GK provides further details in his instructions,

Upon the altar-top mirror, the alchemist envisions four lines—two running front to back and two from left to right, forming a tic-tac-toe pattern that divides the surface into nine equal portions. It should resemble the talismanic square of Saturn. This design, known as the *rule of thirds diagram,* outlines the five power positions on the altar. The most dynamic location on the diagram is at the center of the central square. It is the primary focal point, where one places a statue or a photographic image depicting Ra. The other four power points are located where the imaginary lines intersect, or at the corners of the central square. Typically, offerings are placed near these locations in the four corners of the quadrants. The area in front of Ra's statue is designated for a talisman representing one's camera. Additional offerings, such as elemental items, a bell, luminaries, pyramids, and other small statues, may be arranged in the remaining areas of the base.

One should personalize the sacred design by incorporating spiritually significant objects into its overall composition to enhance this guidance for fashioning an altar. In doing so, one should be discriminative, choosing only those items that can open the gateway connecting the ritualist with Ra. Meaningful objects should have an established filament connection with Ra, or the aspirant may choose to establish and deepen those connections. The objects one places on their altar ought to contribute to the spiritual life-force that flows between the alchemist and the deity.

Altar items must be consecrated before they are added to the sacred installation. Anything used in rituals, such as regalia or books, should also be made hallowed. This spiritual act will transform tools, objects, and people through a magical transition, changing their mundane function into a new, higher purpose within a sacred space. From that point forward, anything that is consecrated and remains in one's sanctuary is understood as supremely sacrosanct. Abraham Kingswood wrote, "The camera used for magical purposes and all its accessories should be consecrated and ritually empowered as instruments in the service of the Supreme Deity of Light."

Consecration involves blending one's intentional energy with a deity's energy and fixing it upon an object, such as a photograph or camera. Part of the intention should be to purify and prepare the object for use in the Great Work. Other, more specific intentions should also be included. Each intention may be unique, depending on the purpose of the ritual. As part of the rites, Ra is invoked to awaken the objects with empyrean light energy and bestow divine powers upon them.

There is also a matter of timing. For instance, choose times based on either a solar or lunar calendar. Determine the optimal month, day, and hour for performing a consecration ritual. Using astrology, the alchemist identifies a timeframe that is most auspicious. Astrology can also assist in decision-making, such as determining how long an object remains on one's altar or the duration of the energy from the consecration. Installed energies may be set to last only for the duration of a ritual or until the spell is terminated. If objects aren't assigned a timeframe of potency, then from that point onward, sanctified objects will perpetually radiate empyrean light. They will be recognized as having been imbued with a divine, eternal life force. Mystical adept Franz Bardon reminds,

> As we have learned from the history of the Egyptian mummies, such fixed forces continue acting for thousands of years. If a talisman or an object destined and individually loaded for a definite person falls into the hands of someone else, he will not experience the least influence. But if this object returns to the true owner, this influence will go on acting (Bardon, 1971, 57).

In addition to the altar, another sacred space is significant for engaging in the Great Work: the magic circle. GK's main circle is located in his studio, where he depends on it for protection while casting spells and summoning spirits. He advises that anyone planning to cast spells and enter a circle of protection should first be consecrated while standing before their altar. The same applies to any venerated objects that will be brought into the circle. Here's an example of a priestly consecration ritual from an ancient Egyptian papyrus:

> Keep yourself pure for seven days, and then go on the third day of the moon to a place which the receding Nile has just laid bare. Make a fire on two upright bricks with olive-wood, that is to say thin wood, when the sun is half-risen, after having before sunrise circumambulated the altar. But when the sun's disk is clear above the horizon, decapitate an immaculate, pure white cock, holding it in the crook of your left elbow; circumambulate the altar before sunrise. Hold The cock fast by your knees and decapitate it with no one else holding it. Throw the head into the river, catch the blood in your right hand and drink it up. Put the rest of the body on the burning altar and jump into the river. Dive under in the clothes you are wearing, then stepping backwards climb on the bank. Put on new clothes and go away without turning around. After that take the gall of a raven and rub some of it with the wing of an ibis on your eyes and you will be consecrated (Butler, 1979, 10).

Though parts of the above sacred ritual are similar to those used by the Kemetic Order of the Silver Sun, GK claims that the Order never sacrificed animals. When people kill living creatures, the offerings emit a distinct kind of emotional light-energy that could attract undesirable supernatural beings that feed on death. Instead, the alchemist offers gifts that generate vital forces of devotion, love, gratitude, and generosity. The qualities of these influences attract specific types of benevolent beings, like Ra. His attention, along with that of other entities, is captured by the energy plumes created from the offerings and the supplication felt while giving the gifts. In response, the beings approach one's altar and consume the banquet of energetic nectars, which they find nourishing, pleasurable, and delicious. GK highlights, "The filaments that join the ritualist to supernatural beings grow and are made stronger."

Offerings that Ra particularly appreciates include candles and lamps, through which he manifests. These luminous gifts are living aspects of Ra's consciousness. Plus, phosphorescing firelight tends to ward off undesirable entities. Beeswax candles are the most beloved to Ra; they evoke memories of the temples in ancient Egypt where priests burned them over 5000 years ago. If beeswax isn't available, white luminaria, saffron, or ruby red candles are preferable to other jewel tones. GK mentions that Ra, "is partial to all the hues of the heliotrope#."

He continues to share that he has seen Ra in the flames of his altar lights on many occasions. GK also reports that a candle can significantly increase the chances of prophetic dreams. One should gaze into the flame and pray to Ra for clairvoyant insight and clarity. Ra finds the burning of frankincense, myrrh, Kyphi, and Kapet pleasing. Feasts of red, yellow, and orange fruits, along with pale or amber beers, are also attractive to him. Ra revels in a calm style of acoustic music when played as an offering. In addition to oblations, petitions can be written on small pieces of papyrus or other paper and posted around the altar. After nine days, the supplicant burns the paper in a small cauldron.

When an altar is "turned on," with its candles lit and lights ablaze, adorned with beautifully displayed offerings in abundance, it becomes "a point of intersection between art and religion where the sacred is apprehended…in relationship with the Divine" (Turner, 1999, 27). Kingswood taught, "Using handsome offerings, decorative finery, and attractive ornamentation, one's altar should be made to be as beautiful as possible, as a hallowed work of art that should excite the eyes of its beholder. For when Ra inhabits the space, he will be a beacon who looks back into the eyes of his devotee and blesses their capacities for transformation in the Great Work."

19. Imagination's Wellspring

The word *imagination* comes from the Latin root, *imago*, which means *image*. Furthermore, philosopher Nigel Thomas maintains, "*Imagination* is a word of power" (2010, 1). The term that evokes the idea of ultimate freedom, where the mind has a limitless potential for creation. Yet, some may assume that *imagination* is synonymous with the *fanciful*, *fictitious,* or the realm of *fantasy*, and that it opposes reason. After all, fiction and make-believe are born in the imagination.

The seeds of magic find fertile soil in what Henry Corbin called *Mundus Imaginalis*, "The intermediary between the world of Mystery…and the world of Visibility…that can only be the Imagination" (1969, 193). Corbin says, "the Active Imagination carries out the divine intention, the intention of the 'Hidden Treasures' yearning to be known" (1969, 189).

The 19th century pioneer of the imagination, A. Kingswood, wrote,

> It's through the language of mental pictures that transcendent knowledge is understood. It gives rise to impressions on the golden screen of the receptive mind. Only in the prolific imagination can gnosis, unmediated divine transmission be received and understood. Thus, when imagination is mixed with Ra's transfer of light, it is beatific genius! In the mind dwells the 'soul's eye…the glass of visions and the apparatus of magical life" [Lévi, 1896, 6]. Its father is *light's creative possibility*. Its mother is *expanding perception*. Their children are *art, photography, mythology, and magic*.'

In the book Transformative Imagery, Leslie Davenport demonstrates that

> References to the primary language of image are made in Genesis (1:26), where it is stated that we are made in the image and likeness of God. The creation of the world is considered a work of art created by the Master Painter who created His unmatched visual spectacle. We emulate the Master when we use the corresponding gift we are born with called 'imagination,' of which mental imagery is one function. Thus our world was and continues to be birthed through this creative process (Davenport, 2016, 61).

Similarly, philosopher Alexandre Koyré stated

> The notion of the imagination, magical intermediary between thought and being, incarnation of thought in image and presence of the image in being, is a conception of the most importance (Koyré, 1955, 60)...on the one hand the notion of the *Imagination* as the *magical* production of an *image*, the very type and model of magical action, or of all action as such, but especially of creative action; and, on the other hand the notion of the image as a body (a *magical* body, a *mental* body), in which are incarnated the thought and will of the soul (Koyré, 1955, 59-60).

In these examples, people are not only born in the "image of God". They are also bequeathed the infinite treasure of imagination, through which each human being can make and project creative worlds.

Mary Anne Atwood stated

> All things are thence arisen through the Divine Imagination and do yet stand in such a birth, station, and government. The four elements have likewise such a ground or original; but the understanding and capacity is not in nature's own ability without the Light of God; but it is very easy to be understood by those who are in the Light, to them it is easy and plain (Atwood, 2005).

The three initiates of *The Kybalion* stated that the first Hermetic tenet is the "Principle of Mentalism." Its axiom is, "The All is Mind: the Universe is Mental." This means that everything in our reality exists as a product of the All Mind's imagination, the same imaginative power in all human minds. Though the Kybalion describes the All as "Absolute, Eternal and Unchangeable," it's also an ever-transformative space, a fiery athanor where ideas, memories, and experiences constantly undergo the processes of calcination, conjunction, and coagulation to produce novel ideas and new revelations (Three Initiates, 2017, 21-29).

Imagination is the matrix from which ideas emerge. It's also where the mind interprets images. French philosopher Bernard Stiegler posited, "There have never existed physical images...without the participation of mental images, since an image is one that is seen (is in fact only one when it is seen). Reciprocally, mental images also rely on objective images in the sense that they are...the *rémanence* [afterglow] of the latter" (Stiegler, 2002, 145). It could also be said that photographs depend on the viewer's imagination to interpret what is seen, in a way that accesses one's understanding of reality. It's akin to how one navigates the world, by recalling memories of everything that lies beyond one's field of vision. Imagination, then, is a critical part of interpreting, understanding, and knowledge production.

To imagine is to conjure. It's an act that brings thoughts to life in a mental space. Philosopher Nigel J. T. Thomas describes imagination as,

> what makes our sensory experience meaningful, enabling us to interpret and make sense of it, whether from a conventional perspective or from a fresh, original, individual one. It is what makes perception more than the mere physical stimulation of sense organs. It also produces mental imagery, visual and otherwise, which is what makes it possible for us to think outside the confines of our present perceptual reality, to consider memories of the past and possibilities for the future, and to weigh alternatives against one another. Thus, imagination makes possible all our thinking about what is, what has been, and, perhaps most important, what might be (quoted from Manu, 2007).

GK explains that imagination consists of a "dynamic and volatile light-energy that can be harnessed as ideas that mix within a content rich storehouse." He describes,

> When creative visualizations take form, the mage fixes them through focused concentration. Imagination's evocative qualities, its active influence over human perception, its power and freedom to 'produce,' and its capacity to fabricate make it an essential faculty for accomplishing magic. More importantly, imagination is "an organ of perception through which the imaginal world can be perceived." Its role is not to make up these images; rather, through its perception, it transforms them, giving them more solidity and depth, as well as a deeper relationship to the human who perceives them. Perception is creation in this way. However, the entities experienced through the imagination have their own autonomy and reality–they are not the products of imagination (Raff, 2019, 278).

In other words, imaginative visualization allows the ritualist to summon entities, such as the solar god. By projecting light outward into the form of a light-vessel, it becomes a container in which an aspect of the god may reside. The ethereal being is given a means of agency in the material realm. GK clarifies, "Projected light will return to the mage's eyes, deiformed. Imagination enacts every part of the process while the intellect observes, finds meaning, and understands. Even more happens in this ritual act that is far beyond what the magician perceives or can comprehend! The experience transcends the familiar, common happenings of the waking day and is more akin to a vision or dream."

There is no place where imagination thrives more than in dreams. GK further explains,

> The reason why humankind has and will always believe in magic is that we sense that we can make real whatever we can imagine. In support, we are reminded nightly of what is possible when we surrender our consciousness to the imagination during our sleep. In dreams, we learn to use thoughts to transform our reality. We can fly, communicate telepathically with others, and overcome our greatest fears and obstacles. Lucid dreams are the *will* made real at the speed of thought. If the alchemist desires, they can instantly transform lead into gold!

> Dreams suggest that we can make this fixed material reality as fluid and changeable as the dream realm. We intuit that the secret to success lies in the imaginative, liminal space between dreaming and waking reality—an exalted space of lucid intention, imagination, and the magic trinity. We want to believe that imagination has the potential to empower us, granting us control over our own fate and the world. It seems logical that the force of our intention, propelled by the rigidity of will, could bring about tangible changes in the alchemist's environment. As it turns out, it is possible.

"The imagination can also be a frightening space, where nightmares are populated by tormenting demons and threatening monstrosities." GK pauses in thought. "Phantoms may appear to haunt the explorer, who can become trapped in an emotional spectacle of fear." If one struggles with these kinds of recurring visitations, then GK suggests performing a banishing ritual before going to sleep. "Even better," he proposes, "is to perform the ritual whilst in the dream! Alchemists can formulate an elixir allowing them to raise consciousness. When ingested, one will be able to, in deep sleep, enact the ritual of raising protective magic."

In addition to the aid of an elixir, GK explains that there is another way for the alchemist seeking a limitless capacity for their magic: to banish, invoke, transform, and transmute during sleep. One can learn to dream lucidly, thereby retaining a continuity of consciousness whether awake or dreaming. "Given that the average person is asleep for one-third of their lifetime, it's a good opportunity to carry out spiritual endeavors. If one can become aware during a portion of those hours, they will gain full control over their will and intention, whilst also being able to manifest them."

> As with the waking reality, dream reality also has its properties and systems. For instance, waking life maintains a strong sense of continuity with the phenomena of time and space. This is not the case in the dream realm. Even if one soars from one mountaintop to another, no distance is crossed, and no time is spent. The absence of time-event-space integrity enhances the potency of magic during dreamtime. Magic becomes the foundation of that reality, where all things are possible.

Some theorists propose that, like the mind, the imagination possesses multiple levels of consciousness. For example,

> Anthropologist Michele Stephen…hypothesized the existence of the 'autonomous imagination,' a part of our imagination that appears to operate independently of our conscious control. It produces a constant stream of mental imagery that helps process experience. This stream of imagery can enter consciousness through dreams, trance experiences, hypnosis, and altered states of consciousness. More freely creative than ordinary waking thought, it mixes material from the cultural register with elements from the ordinary world and our memories, in a way that produces vivid hallucinatory images that feel extremely real. Stephen theorizes that this faculty is particularly strong in individuals with a religious or spiritual role in society, such as shamans, or priestesses/priests (Herdt, 1989, 45).

Likewise, the "autonomous imagination" of the Hermetic artist opens a welcoming environment for visitations, particularly for muses who enjoy appearing in dreams. Synesius of Cyrene wrote,

So then, if any one, in his dreams, receives the present of a treasure, I shall not be at all surprised; or if a man quite uncultured should fall asleep and, meeting the Muses in his dream and exchanging question and answer with them, should become a cunning bard. This has happened in our own time [3rd century] and does not seem to me very astounding…But whenever a dream open up to the soul a path conducting it to the most perfect points from which to view existing things, a soul that has never yet aspired, nor has given its mind to the assent, [Plato, Republic 517B.] it would be indeed the climax of the occult force in existing things that this dream should override nature and unite to the realm of the mind the man who has wandered so far from it that he knows not whence he has come (Synesius, 400AD).

GK states, "Creative artificers across time have conspired with muses. Historically, they were an ancient mythologem# who collaborate with artists by serving as wellsprings of inspiration, filling their minds with unthinkably ingenious ideas. They have appeared as spirits, gods, and goddesses to deliver inspiration in the form of images." Because "the image cannot be perceived by other bodies until it is embodied… [furthermore] the image does not really become an image until it is animated by a beholder. Bodies, though, can also produce images internally, in dreams, visions, and memory (Wood, 2001, 371).

Even today, muses visit the fertile minds of creatives. They elevate the artistic capacity of those most likely to act on their messages and revelations. It could even be said that Thoth, as the "Creative Heart of Ra" and "Voice of Ra's Divine Words," served as a muse to the Egyptian priests when he taught them hieroglyphics. It follows that Ra was Abraham Kingswood's muse when he instructed the alchemist on the poetry of magical incantations. And when Ra emitted pictures of light, it inspired Kingswood to celebrate photography and honor its divine possibilities. GK once gave counsel to photographers, "Due to the bountiful projections of Ra, those artists who embrace and obey their muses will feel an enlargement of their imaginative capacity. Without warning, they will experience overwhelming paroxysms# of creativity!"

Abraham Kingswood surmised that "Imagination impresses on the alchemist that magic is real, while coeval fueling the inventive mind of the master photographer. In this time, the artful populace is collectively appalled by the notion that photography has any relationship whatsoever to man's creative soul." He believed that the culture's disapproval perpetuated an atmosphere that spread these ideas. Kingswood observed, "The uncreative mind is a plenum into which imagination's desires to fabricate the impossible are unwelcome. Thus, those who lack imagination have no chance of elevating their lives to a visionary or magical existence. They have no chance for evolution."

Those nonbelievers regarded the camera as a mechanistic tool whose products were reflexive, mirrored representations of reality. They viewed the photographer as a witless automaton who was limited to merely making visual documents, products of empirical evidence that provided access to the human visual circumstance. Photographs were perceived as objective representations of reality. Furthermore, there was a "tacit agreement, a compact, or covenant, that a viewer observes when viewing an image…in order to believe, some legitimate claim to truth to be affirmed" (Morgan, 2005, 76).

The societal consensus was that photographs held no inherent aesthetic value beyond being visual references for true artists. Few recognized that a picture could spark a viewer's imagination. "Since the middle of the 19th century, painters used photography as an optical aid the way previous generations had used the camera obscura and other such devices. While photography's very ability to reproduce appearances more accurately, more realistically, and more objectively served the artist, these qualities also threatened painting's supremacy in the same manner that digital imaging does today. Imaginationless critics of the time dismissed the notion that a photographer could use the camera alongside their creativity to interpret reality in the unique way they each perceived it. Artists commonly believed it would be a waste of time for any divine muse to visit a maker of photographs" (Ostrow, 2013, 180).

In the late 19th century, attitudes began to change. After Dr. Alexander Keith returned from his 1820s photographic expedition in Egypt, he published many of his photographs in books. In the 37th edition (1859), he included an updated opinion of photography. He wrote, "As soon as photography began to take its place among the wonderful arts or inventions of the present day, he anticipated a mode of demonstration that could neither be questioned nor surpassed: as, without the need of any testimony, or the aid of either pen or pencil, the rays of the sun would thus depict what the prophets saw" (1859, 3). Dr. Keith's recognition helped elevate photography to the status of a legitimate art form. This was just the beginning.

New approaches to photography flourished. It began to transition from a purely commercial endeavor into one of visionary, luministic art. Pictorialist photographers, such as Henry Peach Robinson, George Davison, and Alvin Langdon Coburn, sought control over the technical and aesthetic potential of the visual medium. They were convinced the camera served as a means for creative and spiritual expression. In the book, *Art and Alchemy*, Laurie Dahlberg deduces that, "in discovering…their connection to the mystical, spiritual, and chemical strivings of the alchemysts, pictorialists like F. Holland Day and Alvin Langdon Coburn not only revived the handcraft of early photography…they focused the content of their pictures upon a transformation of the imputed brute realism of photography into the product of pure invention and imagination" (Dahlbert, 2006, 96). This new breed of photographers understood the art's unique capacity to convey the wondrous aspects of the human spirit. They leveraged the art's potential to produce dream-like, ethereal, and metaphysical interpretations of the world. They embraced photography's enchanting qualities, like those attributes of poetic ambiguity.

Meanwhile, public perceptions of photography evolved to see it as an art form. This was mainly due to the ongoing creative and artistic revolution that photographers were advancing. The imagination of the image-maker could not be stopped in the 19th century any more than it can today! GK understands that

> Pictures open a dialogue with the viewer's imagination. One feels a need to understand what they're witnessing…even through apperception# they must invent an understanding by awakening memories that force recognition. That same creativity invites the artist to look beyond the boundaries of their reality, encouraging a partnership of light and film, urging imagination to conform to one's previsualized ideas, or allow for the creative license to re-visualize (post-visualize) at any time. Creativity should be allowed to control the process. To grant the photographer's muse the liberty to spontaneously point those crosshairs in the narrow sight of attention, toward that enchanting element in a scene that, when recorded, will reveal a new piece to the puzzle of who and what a photographer is. It could even impart insights about who they might become.

Alchemists spoke of a "secret fire." Paracelsian Martin Ruland the Elder (1569-1611) identified it in his *Lexicon Achemiae* as *imaginatio* [imagination]. The term is further defined as "the star in man, the celestial or super celestial body" (Tucker, 2016). In other words, the star within man is the sun. It is also the creative source of empyrean light. Photographers of the 20th century thrived in a state of inspiration derived from that same imaginatio-sun. GK proposes that,

> For photographers seeking to venture beyond the typical, mundane practices of exhibiting, selling work, and documenting weddings, imagination can illuminate the path. It serves as the arc of light connecting the mind's poetic side, where photographic vision resides, and where imagination shares its role as a co-creator. To the other querying and resolute side, across the divide where alchemy and magic maintain a reputation for their non-rationality, uncertainty, doubt, suspicion, and, as some might say, lunacy, stands the creative alchemist-photographer. They face a choice: to squander their imagination on conventional, unprofitable routines or to cultivate knowledge that brings intellectual restoration and spiritual rejuvenation. This leads to renewal through the Great Work!

In Kingswood's writings, he believed that,

> Imagination is the starry matrix in which the energy of creativity grows and gives birth to ideas. Imaginativeness manifests through a spark of recognition, as rising thoughts are new, unformed, and inspired. Before that, the creative idea existed only as potential. It is nebulous light-energy and has no locus point of existence. It is in the latent states of *becoming* and *changing*. The attentive photographer will hear the call and respond to the flash of inspiration! Using the intentional camera, they facilitate the birth of an idea. In the camera (temple, womb, athenor), the creative idea dawns into physical form. In flash, the image embarks into the earthly plane of existence.

> When the light of consciousness connects with something greater than the mind, a new level of imagination becomes accessible, 'in which we experience an influx of meaningful insight and higher inspiration. This altered state of consciousness reveals the true alchemy of a person's life' (Carty, 2007, p. 53).

In GK's experience, "Imagination mixes with awareness and the axiom, *as above so below, as within so without,* lifts imagination to actualize unlimited inspiration from which it can compose creative ideas. What is imagined in the mind is also imagined in the cosmos."

GK continues the conversation, "Everything that can and can't be photographed becomes subject matter for the artful vision of the mind. The penumbral expression emerges from the imagination and becomes a cyclic, ouroboros link connecting the photographer to their pictures, to the viewer's experience, and back to the photographer's imagination …where the head meets the tail." This circulatory action mirrors the cosmic cycle, where all creation emanates from the highest empyrean realm of Ra, down to the heavy solidity of the mortal realm. From there, the soul's imaginative desire is driven to return to its origin.

Abraham Kingwood reported that the Hermetic photographer's imagination can be understood as the prima materia, the unseeable formless substance that resides in all things. He said, "After all, the essence of the photographer is the luminous imagination." Hermetic Qabalist William Gray discusses the visionary creation of "telesmic" Imagery (1978, 13). The word telesmic derives from its root, "telesma," a Renaissance alchemical term for the Philosophers' Stone. Furthermore, Egyptian mystic Zosimos Alchemista (the "Crown of Philosophers") was the first to discuss the Philosophers' Stone in the late second century, using "dichotomous paradoxes: 'This stone which isn't a stone, this precious thing which has no value, this polymorphous thing which has no form, this unknown thing which is known to all'" (Brill, 2005, 25). Kingswood also claimed that the stone was made of coagulated light. Even Atwood supported his conclusion, writing, "And that ray of motive Light, pure, vital, and efficient, we have shown to be the true Form of Gold, the alone universal principle of increase and perfection, the same which in the circulatory system, becoming dominant, is made concrete in life; and is the transmutative ferment --- even the Philosophic Stone" (Atwood, 2005, 245).

These enigmatic clues may suggest that the creative impulse growing in the imagination, used to envision spirit vessels during ritual incantations, is much more than a simple mental faculty used to manifest intention. The active principle of creative desire is light. It is synonymous with the philosopher's stone, an imaginary yet powerful catalyst that drives evolution, serving as a vehicle for creating anything that can be thought of or dreamed of. If this premise is true, it affirms the fact that thoughts have far-reaching power, especially those visionary formations that emerge from the deepest, divine depths of imagination's wellspring.

20. Telesmic Projection from The Lantern of Wisdom

Telesmic "projectualizations," as GK refers to them, originate from a very particular part of the imagination that GK calls the *"Fons Oculus Fulgur,"* which translates to *"the fountain of eye lightning."* Though lightning implies a short-lived but intense flash, GK further clarifies the metaphor that

> The lightning, which is more akin to a spark, serves as the source—the ignition that launches the storm of light flowing from the fountain and projected into space, taking the form of a visualization. "Alkindi, author of the *Theoria artis magicae*, explained these material effects by supposing that the imagination has 'rays' similar to those of the stars and operating in the same way upon reality, to impress on an external object conceived in the imagination" (Beyer, 1978, 89).

> Alkindi wasn't entirely wrong. The visionary point in space where the imagination's 'rays' are fixed is the location where the self-generated projection appears, at the place where the alchemist's attention comes into focus and where the ethereal being arrives so that the two can meet. That locus is where one invites and perceives spirits and gods. It is also the site from which one is seen by those invoked. As Susan Sontag once said, "The photographer projects himself into everything he sees, identifying himself with everything in order to know it and to feel it better" [Sontag, 2001, 116].

During the visualization process,

> the eyes of the [image or artwork] are ritually opened so that the deity may see its devotees – this is deemed to be a very powerful gaze. The exchange of sights between devotees and the visible God, at the time of worship, is [an] auspicious vision…It entails approaching them with respect, bringing them offerings: by seeing them with humility, and [being] seen by them, one gets their blessings (Tarabout, 2011, 2).

As the being observes with visual awareness, an exchange begins where the appearance can communicate with the caller. The phantasmal event becomes an interaction that increases what anthropologist Tanya Luhrmann refers to as one's "porosity," or "'how a person might receive thoughts, emotions or knowledge directly from outside sources.' These might include divine inspiration, divination, telepathy or clairvoyance" (Feder, 2021).

Visualization can be described as transforming one's environment into a favorable atmosphere for a summoned being. The alchemist aims to achieve mastery over their telesmic abilities to create welcoming, compatible, and desirable environments for their guests. Furthermore, the more skillful the alchemist is with visualization, the more likely they are to receive divine inspiration and revelation. GK said, "It is miraculous that a god or spirit could manifest in a mentally projected image of light. Yet it happens regularly as part of the primary spiritual practice of magicians." Esotericist, Ben Joffe added,

> One could say that to 'pull the eye' of spirits is to make use of the creative imagination to produce a 'pleasure garden' of resonant, affectively-charged images through which the mind becomes a sort of miraculous [exhibition], filled with unfolding displays of visual and other sensory delights that pull in spirit visitors and coax them to stay a while. [This is achieved with] visuality, visualization, imagination and emotion [while]…sensory attunement and affective/attention training are a key component of…ritual magic practice (Perfumed Skull, 2017).

Photography is a perfect medium for developing telesmic skills. It helps strengthen attention, memory, and imagination, all of which are supportive techniques for visualization. By directing attention to photographic imagery, individuals can enhance their ability to maintain focus. With a sustained gaze, an aspirant embeds imagery into their brain's neural network. This embeds information deeply into long-term memory, where it becomes an asset for the imagination. To "imagine' is to exercise the ability to visualize and cast light-based images.

One begins the practice by selecting a photo with which one feels an attraction. Next, one envisions a transparent pyramid resting on the surface of the photo. The image serves as the base of the pyramid, and the peak extends away from the print, reaching out into space toward the viewer's right eye. The height of the pyramid should match the distance from one corner of the print to its opposite diagonal corner. When the alchemist's eye is at the apex of the imaginary structure, the observer's point of view is positioned at the "god's eye view." This represents the correct distance from which to survey and study the image.

After that, one looks closely, taking inventory of the subject matter in the composition. By focusing on the main subject of the photo, one examines the attributes of all the compositional elements: light and shadows, colors, patterns, textures, and any other elements that are present. Then, with eyes closed, the viewer tries to remember the details, mentally reproducing small portions of the image. When the image fades or one gets distracted, they should open their eyes and start again. Once one gains confidence in their ability to reproduce the composition they see mentally, it's time to incorporate other surrounding elements in the foreground and background. The visualization practice is repeated until the entire image can be accurately remembered and envisioned. The final stage is to open one's eyes and project the visualization, complete with all its details, into space, approximately three feet in front of the eyes. Success is achieved when the projection remains stable, without fading or distraction, for at least a minute. Lastly, one practices going beyond their limitations by increasing the duration of visualization to five or ten minutes.

Eventually, the alchemist can achieve consistency in their visualization. At that point, it is time to practice projecting an image vessel for Ra. To proceed, Phil Hine reminds us,

> Visualization…requires that the practitioner is familiar to some degree with (a) the image (b) the mythic narratives which relate to the deity, and (c) the theology – both general and particular – in which the deity is embedded. It is relatively easy for outsiders to the traditions to collect information on the particular signifiers relating to a deity; to read the major (and minor) narratives in which a deity appears, and to find a wealth of material relating to the theologies & philosophies with which one can begin to understand a deity within a particular context. However, it is in practice that all these "pieces" are brought together and made meaningful – which can be a long process. Visualisation is more than simply a matter of memorising images or reciting words – it requires actively incorporating insights and realisations which arise out of practice – those sudden flashes of "oh, I get that now" which make all the difference (Hine, 2016).

In his sage advice, Hine insists that the key to creating an effective visualization suitable for invocation is to become well acquainted with the intended subject. One must bring

into mind a whole relationship, a chain of connections rooted in [one's] personal history. [Think about how] …how much you do this in love relationships – in the first flushes of a relationship, there's a continual bringing to mind of the beloved. There's also that which might arise spontaneously – (similar to practices like skrying) if one hits the right angle of relaxation…one is 'rewarded' with images that spring into the mind unbidden, that give new insight into the practice and your relationship with the deity (Dan, 2016).

GK emphasizes that,

> Only by forming a relationship with a spiritual entity can the ritualist successfully create a visionary container that is inviting and effective. The radiance produced by feelings of desire, openness, and supplication will ultimately attract Ra. The same methods apply for summoning allies. In addition to unifying these practices during a stable visualization, one gains confidence by contemplating the four cardinal obelisks of photography, which correspond to the obelisks of alchemy. They are vision, imagination, determination, and insight, which spell out the acronym *VIDI*, meaning *to see* in Latin. The four obelisks represent aspects of perception that the photographer-alchemist utilizes to invoke and internalize divine inspiration.

Table of Correspondences:

Obelisks of Alchemy (VIDI)	Oaths of the Magi	Senses	Cardinal Points
Vision	Courage (Aude)	Sight	Eastern obelisk
Imagination	Silence (Tace)	Speech	Southern obelisk
Determination	Will (Vole)	Touch	Northern obelisk
Insight	Knowledge (Vide)	Hearing	Western obelisk

Telesmic images can be projected at any size since imagination isn't limited by scale. An incorporeal appearance can be as small as a grain of sand or as large as the universe. Regarding one's allies, GK suggests that they be envisioned slightly smaller than the height of the ritualist.

Conversely, when visualizing a god, the form should be appropriately larger and impressive in size.

> One maintains a fluid state of expectation, open enough to embrace and welcome whatever forms arise alongside the telesmic projection. Occasionally, atmospheres of light and unimaginable configurations also become visible. It appears two worlds occupy the same space simultaneously — not because the alchemist's mind makes it so. It offers a glimpse of the true reality in which we exist.

The alchemist

> lives in this malleable universe, in that his visualization creates surreal landscapes projected upon the very fabric of reality; his private realm of freedom and power is indeed an echo of Breton's rhetorical question, "What if everything in the Beyond is actually here, now, in the present, with us?"...This provocative surrealist model, however, gives only a limited analogue for the total collapse of the boundary between the public and private universes. What the surrealists call their 'magic' indeed increases the repertoire of awareness, adding the imaginary to the objective at the same ontological level. But where the surrealist image is thrust upon a reality already given in experience, the [alchemist] sees the complete and absolute interpenetration of the two unitary fields. His image and his object are not superimposed, but rather are primordially one, and this is what makes possible his magical ability to manipulate the universe (Beyer, 1978, 87-88)

In addition, scholar Harold Goddard professed that, "the imagination is not a faculty for the creation of illusion; it is the faculty by which alone man apprehends reality" (Barkley, 2014, 29). Furthermore, Éliphas Lévi went on to say, "Imagination, in effect, is like the soul's eye; therein forms are outlined and preserved; thereby we behold the reflections of the invisible world; it is the glass of visions and the apparatus of magical life" (Lévi, 1896, 34).

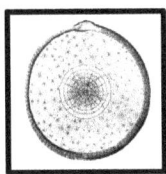

Aquam

21. Ritual: Acts of Power

Alchemical rites and rituals strengthen a concordance of mental, emotional, and physical actions to unify the senses of the physical body (voice, mind, and soul) in pursuit of an intended goal. When the proceedings of a ritual elevate the thaumaturgic intensity of empyrean light, a transition occurs in which the light begins to work through the ritualist's five harmonized sensory connections: sight, sound, taste, touch, and smell.

The magic that is channeled was described by the ancient philosopher Proclus as a "power higher than all human wisdom, embracing the blessings of divination, the purifying powers of initiation, and, in a word, all the operations of divine possession" (Arcana, 2006, 51). GK maintains that even though this power, as light, never crosses the limen# of corporeal senses, those organs of perception more spiritually attuned become aware of its presence. The ritual actions that have been repeated for thousands of years resonate through their performance over time, evoking the same powers today as the ancient priests did in the Great Solar Temple.

Jesuit scholar Athanasius Kircher wrote,

> The early priests believed that a great spiritual power was invoked by correct and unabridged sacrificial ceremonies. If one feature were lacking, the whole was vitiated, says Iamblichus. Hence they were most careful in all details, for they considered it absolutely essential for the entire chain of logical connections to be exactly according to ritual. Certainly for no other reason did they prepare and prescribe for future use the manuals, as it were, for conducting the rites. They learned, too, what the first hieromancers--possessed, as it were, by a divine fury--devised as a system of symbolism for exhibiting their mysteries. These they placed in this Tablet of Isis, before the eyes of those admitted to the sanctum sanctorum in order to teach the nature of the Gods and the prescribed forms of sacrifice. Since each of the orders of Gods had its own peculiar symbols, gestures, costumes, and ornaments, they thought it necessary to observe these in the whole apparatus of worship, as nothing was more efficacious in drawing the benign attention of the deities
> (quoted in Hall, 1928, 57).

The practice of formal rites requires patience, persistence, and determination. GK recommends that rites be performed with "constancy, attention to detail, and regularity" if there is any hope of success. He continues, "Taking on the role of an alchemist who employs magical rites requires a quality of discipline that is shunned by most. It is easy for the aspirant to become indifferent, bored, and disappointed from lack of results. Instead of giving in to emotions that cause reluctance, the alchemist recognizes these feelings as opportunities and uses them as subjects for ritual transformation. The darkness of averseness is transmogrified into the light of action. Of dedication!"

GK advises the reader to

> Be prepared for the fact that becoming fluent in magic and gaining proficiency in ritual may require as many as 10,000 accumulated hours of practice in rites before a divine response or success can be expected. These upward steps of progress rise at a steep angle as the arris lines on either side converge, narrowing the path as one climbs higher.

Knowing this, GK recommends that one should be completely honest with oneself about whether they believe they are among the rare individuals who are hopelessly drawn to the summit of mysteries and the gateway to the sun. Only a few seekers may choose to undertake the initiatory tests, which represent their own death and resurrection.

Furthermore, the initiation process provides guidance on how to embody the state of courage needed to attain self-knowledge. It also emphasizes that there is no progress without both. Mastery over one's mind is achieved by gaining self-insights through the practices of introspection, self-reflection, and self-observation. Martin Heidegger, German philosopher, said, "Reflection is the courage to make the truth of our own presuppositions and the realm of our own goals into the things that most deserve to be called into question" (Heidegger, 1938, 115). Twentieth-century mystic Thomas Merton found photography to be a consummate practice that endowed "a time for stillness, solitude, and self-reflection" (Patnaik, 1980, 11).

GK found that

> Seeing serves as a function of one's spiritual camera, which looks in two directions to achieve revelation and insight. The act of *muesis* involves the aspirant closing their eyes, symbolizing the turning of one's lens toward the inner self to observe more clearly

the mental and emotional qualities that obstruct spiritual progress. When the outer lenses are closed, the inner lens can see into the chasm of the inner landscape. Lenses magnify what is in the frame, isolating and clarifying what obscures truth and confuses vision. The purpose of looking inward is to learn. Looking with intention shines a light into the depths of one's forgotten shadows. This is how one uses self-knowledge to gain self-control. Identifying hidden negative qualities for what they are, whilst knowing that they contain the seeds of gold. Regularly contemplate the correspondences between encumbering patterns and the elements.

Franz Bardon wrote that recognizing the relationships between internal spiritual obstructions and the elements could provide deeper, more meaningful insights. "For instance, you will ascribe jealousy, hatred, vindictiveness, irascibility, and anger to the fiery element; frivolity, self-presumption, boating, squandering, and gossiping to the element of air; indifference, laziness, frigidity, compliance, negligence, shyness, insolence, and instability to the watery element; laziness, lack of conscience, melancholy, irregularity, anomaly, and dullness to the element of earth" (Bardon, 1987, 36). GK recalls,

> Plato said that we must learn by looking inward with '10,000 eyes', since only with it can the truth be seen" (Plato, In the Republic VII). Only by seeing one's own faults, failures, harmful passions, offensive instincts, self-limiting behaviors, and destructive habits can the dross that incrusts the soul be purified enough for the divine light to stream forth as the midnight sun — while simultaneously as the noonday sun!

Mary Anne Atwood prioritized looking inward as part of the Great Work.

If we may believe the experienced, we are not cut off from this fountain [Universal Nature], but attracted out from it; which supplies all things with life perpetually, so that we are what we are by its influence; but in turn receiving the impressure of foreign forms, passions, accidents, and evil generations, the passive purity is defiled and obscured, and unconscious of that inner light which lives in reality; of which the present life is a mere vestige and a comparative diminution of existence, an imitation, as it were, of that which is absolute and real; whose spontaneous revelation in a purified soul imparts virtue with understanding, and universal knowledge, health of body, and long length of days; riches as from the Causal fountain of all things, and felicity in communion with all. It also emits light accompanied with harmony of intellection, and finally exhibits a form of such rarified effulgence that the eye of mind, all the while faithfully regarding, is drawn to contact suddenly, unable longer to sustain itself alone. This is the method and arcane principle of Self Knowledge, and the narrow way of regeneration into life; and so great is the tenuity and attractive subtlety of the Divine Nature (Atwood, 2005, 108-109).

"The alchemist is a Miner of Gold." GK stresses, "To discover the precious material, one works the picks and shovels of observation. First, there is a significant amount of undesirable material: soil, rocks, and debris. One may even encounter false treasure, artifacts believed to be gold," what Manly P. Hall called "those finer traits of character buried in the earthiness of materiality and ignorance" (Hall, 1928, 53). At the same time, one takes account of their noble psychological qualities as they correspond to the elements.

Namely, "you will assign activity, enthusiasm firmness, courage, and daring to the fiery element, diligence, joy, dexterity, kindness, lust, and optimism to the air element, modesty, abstemiousness, fervency, compassion, tranquility, tenderness, and forgiveness to the watery element, and respect, endurance, conscientiousness, thoroughness, sobriety, punctuality, and responsibility to the earth element" (Bardon, 1987, 36). The energy of these qualities can also be harnessed in service of the Great Work. They are characteristics that energize and promote one's ascension in their practices.

Another topic to review is the aspirant's analysis of the photographs they take for practice and pleasure. Photographs are windows into their creator's minds; yet for them, photos can seem opaque and difficult to see into and understand. One tends to be sightless when it comes to the intricacies of self-knowledge in their own work. This is why conventional photographers seek critique from their peers. Critique helps photographers uncover personal insights about their intentions, motivations, thought processes, preferences, and worldview that might otherwise go unnoticed. "I have discovered over time," said GK, "that my photographs tend to be smarter about me than I am." One's own photography has much to teach, but it takes a perceptive and insightful person to recognize the lessons it offers.

GK argues,

> The lesson here is that photographs, unlike magic, don't always emerge from a seed of conscious intention. Sometimes they

spring forth freely when the photographer feels compelled to act, as if a "must" whispered in their ear, "You *must* gather this photo, right now! You can't see the knowledge and beauty in this scene at this moment, but if you act now, you will thank me later!" One should not miss the opportunity to act on such an impulse.

One could argue that this kind of "impulse" may also stem from a photographer's unrealized intention or from a sympathetic muse. In contrast, the performance of magic requires a clear, defined intention.

The origin point for all creation myths is a single driving force that sets everything into motion: conscious intention. Intention is the first spark needed to ignite the firestorm of ritual. Only then can it transform into the narrow, targeted flame of magic. GK advises that to clarify one's intention, the Hermetic artist should clearly write their thoughts along with their desired result. Similar to divine petitions, it is inscribed on a piece of papyrus or parchment, or in a book of shadows —a consecrated notebook used by an alchemist. Once documented as an act of "writual," it is kept with the mage up to and during the sacred performance. When one is finally sealed inside the magic circle, immersed in the ritual's magical activities, they can glance back at their written words to support clarity of purpose, helping keep the ritualist focused and on track.

In preparation for the physical aspects of a ritual day, the alchemist prepares the terrene# body by eating meals intentionally. Food and drink should be beautiful and flavorful, designed to awaken and seduce all the senses of the body. When the dish is ready, it should be enticing enough to attract the deity of light and one's allies, to whom the meal is offered before eating (Ra first, then allies). A second gift is a photograph that captures the final presentation of the meal. In doing so, the delicious elements should be arranged in an appealing composition, with supporting elements like flowers or candles added to enhance the overall context of the composition.

Dramatic lighting will also help take an aesthetically beautiful photo. As an additional oblation, one can print a small photograph and place it on the altar during the formal ritual. GK notes that the Egyptians believed spiritual beings could derive pleasure from eating the enticing images of food, so they depicted feasts on their tomb walls. If the Egyptians had had cameras, they would have hung elaborate still-life images of irresistible banquets on their walls.

To further prepare for the ritual, physical exercises are suggested to ready the body. One begins by clearing the mind and allowing the body to work in unison with the camera during a brisk photo walk. This type of activity, combined with breathing exercises, helps nourish the muscles, blood, and organs while invigorating the brain. As the lungs fill deeply with oxygen and nitrogen on the deep inhale, carbon dioxide, nitrogen, and even thoughts are released on the exhale. This activity raises the heat of the fire element in all aspects of one's being. During the vigorous walk, the mind should be as empty as possible, allowing creative perception, muses, and Ra to flow through the connections made between the eyes and the passing scenes.

GK recommends,

> One invites Ra's empyreal light to flow from the eyes, traveling into the surrounding phenomenal world in a manner that perception readily accepts and embraces everything on exhibition. At various stages in the practice, light from the retinas will frame and capture a subject, even before the camera is raised. It is a moment of awareness where the eyes briefly pre-visualize a composition, anticipating the photograph that will exist in the future. This passionately disciplines the mind. It is a form of invocation and offering to Ra, who is invited to take pleasure in the seductive interplay of brilliant rays, radiant hues, highlights, and bold shadows. GK says, "Know also that supernatural beings enjoy the emotional energy produced by the delightful aesthetic experience of the alchemist.

> When the mystes is properly conducting the photo-walk, Ra will act as a muse to enkindle an impulse within the aspirant. He will guide the eyes toward something noteworthy, signaling that one should pause and focus their attention on framing a composition. With the intention of making an offering to the immeasurable Mystery of Light, one proceeds by taking as many photos as desired, shifting vantage points, and broadening one's awareness of the scene's surroundings. In doing so, additional photographs may present themselves. Then, like a rock released from a sling, the mage sets off again in whatever direction intuition points. After the walk, which should last at least an hour, the aspirant showers with hot water, using soap to cleanse the entire body.

These preparations take place on the day of the ritual, while some rites necessitate more time for preliminary practices. It is a Hermetic tradition that, prior to a major ritual, intentional activities and washing are performed daily for 40 consecutive days. In fact, *The Book of the Sacred Magic of Abramelin the Mage* (1458) prescribes patience and endurance during a rigorous, multi-month purification practice that readies the magus for,

> the invocation of good and evil spirits to accomplish some very worldly goals, including acquisition of treasure and love, travel through the air and underwater, and raising armies out of thin air. It also tells of raising the dead, transforming one's appearance, becoming invisible, and starting storms. The key to this is a set of remarkable magic squares, sigils consisting of mystical words which in most cases can be read in several directions (Mathers, 2016)

Corporeal cleansing and purification, like the physical exercises mentioned above, serve as a starting point for numerous high rituals. Some aspirants fast, some choose celibacy, and bathe at varying intervals. Around ancient Egyptian temples, "there were sacred lakes or pools for priests to bathe in, and water was poured over them in the 'House of Morning'. Officiating priests were even required to rinse out their mouths [and put on] Clean linen clothes and new sandals made from reeds or palm fibres were put on after washing."

The priestly vestments were specifically reserved for ceremonial rites. They were consecrated and stored in a special place. GK reveals, "I store my ritual regalia with other sacred implements in large camera cases in the sanctuary of my temple room. By doing so, I increase the intensity of energy flowing through the filament connections and correspondences that interconnect everything in that sacred space. The collected light energy, then, can flow through the intentions of the rituals, while supporting their intended success" (Pinch, 2006, 77).

For several years, the Order's magical implements included a large camera obscura. For example, GK explains,

> Part of the initiation rites into the Kemetic Order of the Silver Sun required a freestanding camera obscura of prescribed dimensions. Its inner chamber could accommodate as many as 9 people. The dark space assumed a sense of sanctity, serving as an important ritual site that expanded the original design of the dark room into new, magical realms. Sacred artworks and beautifully crafted ritual tools were sequestered in the chamber. Often, the creative pieces were site-specific, much like the paintings Neanderthals created on the walls of their caves. Artworks were crafted inside the room to help contain and maintain their energetic potency. Once the artist finished their work, it was

decreed that the pieces would never leave the chamber, never crossing beyond the threshold of the holy preserve.

John Berger asserts that alongside the alchemist's magical space,

> The visual arts have always existed within a certain preserve; originally this preserve was magical or sacred. But it was also physical; it was the place, the cave, the building, in which, or for which the work was made. The experience of art, which at first was the experience of ritual, was set apart from the rest of life — precisely to be able to exercise power over it...During all this history the authority of art was inseparable from the particular authority of the preserve (Berger, 2008, 32).

To uphold the authority and significance of the artworks placed in the Order's ritual camera obscura sanctum, it was prohibited for anyone to photograph them.

The Order's nineteenth-century initiation ritual began with a pre-initiation that took place at sunset, nine hours before the sunrise of the winter solstice. During this time, the initiate entered the camera obscura dressed as a common person. Once sealed in the room, he (there were no female initiates at that time) remained inside to perform a ritual until sunrise, all in complete darkness. Outside the camera-adytum, five facilitating alchemists conducted their parts of the initiation rites, occasionally engaging in a call-and-response with the person in the dark chamber. This part of the rites symbolized the process of death or entry into the otherworld.

After the first three hours, the initiate disrobed and remained naked for three more hours. At the end of the second segment, they stood in a designated location within the chamber. Slowly, an aperture opened on the east wall. Through the iris light flowed, carrying images of magical symbols that fell perfectly onto the initiate's chest, right over the heart. At the end of this second three-hour phase, the novice clothed themselves in virgin white linen robes. Following several hours of prayer, incantations, and visualizations, a spiritual transformation was anticipated to occur. Finally, the initiate emerged from the camera obscura, reborn as a new member of the Kemetic Order of the Silver Sun.

The ritual was complete when the initiate was bestowed with a new and most sacred name. Alchemist Johannes Helmond explains,

Giving a 'NAME' was a magic operation, because within a name was the expression of the designation, the target, the reason for being. Therefore, with a change of name, the character and the nature of an object or person changed. For this reason, the Neophyte was given a new name when he was admitted into a religious order, which usually was connected with baptizing. This was not only indicative of being symbolic in regards to a fundamental transformation of the character and a conversion into a new psychic-spiritual existence, but it was also nothing short of its magical effect. With the name, the character of the Neophyte changed" (Helmond, 1996, 32). Furthermore, "Having received such a spiritual name represents a high and holy obligation, because through this name, the Human Being should be reminded of his true intended purpose and his higher mission. This name should be his ally, his energy in opposing his cravings for doubt. This Name should raise the Human Being out of the animalistic and material world and should give him the consciousness that he is carrying God's Power within him. (Helmond, 1996, 32)

The newly named alchemist, reborn into a higher state of consciousness as a new being, was then granted privileged access to sacred documents, such as the Order's five books of Ra.

In 1895, the initiation ritual underwent significant changes. It incorporated a new ceremony in which each initiate's likeness was recorded by producing a daguerreotype. Henceforth, portraits became part of the Kemetic Order's doctrine that one's photographic image should be cast in silver halides. This practice intentionally created an energetic thread between the photographer, the photograph, and the subject. With the physical artifact of a print, a person could benefit from a spell cast upon their image, regardless of the distance separating the photographer from the faithful likeness. Photographs became important magical tools, used by group members to coalesce and focus incantations, prayers, and magical currents, thereby assisting one another in achieving their goals as part of the Great Work.

Terram

22. The Grand Circle of Evocations

When a photographer chooses to use a high-quality mat and frame for a print, it isn't just any photograph they select. It is an image worthy of framing that effectively conveys its maker's vision. It likely possesses visual qualities that attract the viewer's attention, draw them into its emotional sphere, and transport them beyond their everyday existence. Framing is, therefore, an intentional act. Photographers go to great lengths to prepare their work for final presentation with precision and care. This widely accepted exhibition practice is intentionally designed and serves several practical purposes.

Mats and frames protect prints while also providing a way to hang artwork on a gallery wall. They add a dimension of visual interest to the overall presentation, transforming a picture's flat, two-dimensional plane into a three-dimensional object that reaches out from the wall. It demands attention! However, the primary reason artists seek this form of presentation is that it creates a sense of spectacle. It asserts the photograph's autonomy by isolating it on the wall, like a lone star in the night sky. Even though the framed photo interacts with the wall, it claims its defined territory, establishing an independent space. This creates a negative space between other framed images, where "it is not just the images that matter, but the space between them that causes an ice/fire frisson#" (Bunyan, 2014).

Another form of framing is the decorative outline around doorways and windows. By framing entry and exit portals, such as a gallery doorway, one feels as though they have passed through a threshold and entered a separate space. The interior design of a gallery evokes a sense of contrast between its framed walls and the aesthetic realms inside the boundaries of framed artworks. The configuration of a gallery is a deliberate act, aiming to direct the spectator's attention away from the space their body occupies. This frees their awareness, inviting it to enter the artwork's frame-threshold that leads somewhere beyond. Photographer and social anthropologist Thera Mjaaland talks about the photograph in terms of "beyondness: as an indexical fragment of the real, always pointing back to a reality beyond itself as image and indicating, in a metonymic sense, a continuation of space and time beyond its own frame" (2017, 2).

"For magical workings," GK advises, "the theurge structures a circular, metaenergetic# enclosure called the Grand Circle of Evocations." The shape functions, in many ways, like a frame around a portal or a photograph. For a thaumaturge, the circle functions, in many ways, as the frame around a picture or a portal. It establishes a conscious, intentional distinction between here and there, inside and outside, as a perimeter without beginning or end. Typically, an event horizon is a boundary beyond which light cannot escape. (Event Horizon: Black Hole, 2023) In this case, the razor-sharp outer edge of the magic circle is an energetic boundary, a borderline between dyadic# dimensions. This perpetual line is designed to separate two distinctly different cosmoi.

Outside the circle, the secular reality persists into which the alchemist's body was born. Inside is a realm of knowledge, possibility, protection, and an imaginarium of creative potential. Its quality of separateness envelops the rites performed therein, helping to shift the consciousness of the ritualist into a state of sublime creative dynamism. It provides a safe, sacred space where one's abilities, skills, and talents are magnified and enhanced without fear, knowing that the boundary cannot be trespassed. Being inside the frame reminds one of the ideas that as without, so within; the alchemist's soul reflects the reality within the circle, which acts as a miniature mirror of all the cosmos outside the circulating orbit of protective energy.

The idea of the Grand Circle is also a topic for meditation in which historian of religions Jonathan Z. Smith suggests that it is an opportunity to reflect on the disjuncture between what is and what ought to be; it is a 'focusing lens' through which people can attempt to see, or argue for, what is significant in real life (quoted in Bell, 2009, 11). GK agrees with Smith:

> It is a shape without beginning or end, it is a timeless symbol of cosmic cycles: birth, life, death, and afterlife. Spiritually, it encourages reflection on the mystic's transformative movement, coiling up and around toward the evolutionary peak. These points of contemplation are beneficial for centering and focusing the mind before ritual. This practice points toward a larger context for the magical work that is about to begin.

Before the ritual, the alchemist determines the location of all the items needed in the space. Where things are placed is important, especially in relation to the main circle of protection. For instance, the circle needs to be cast in a way that, if one were standing inside, all the ritual instruments, imagery, and elements are within the line of sight. To illustrate these instructions, GK described his studio dedicated to invocation (Picture 22.1). He mentioned a large white circle placed on a black floor, inside which he has a 4x5 view camera on a tripod. The camera, as he stated, was used to invoke specific allies, which, when called, were contained within a separate, outer circle. In the room, there was an altar dedicated to Ra, along with plenty of 120 and 4 x 5 film in boxes, shelves filled with books, and a substantial collection of statues of Egyptian gods and goddesses. One wall, he explained, was covered with heavily curtained windows that could let in the light of the North sky.

Picture 22.1 George Kingswood's Studio of Invocations.
Photograph by Garin Horner, 2021.

The wall opposite the windows is adorned with enshrined photographs of people with whom his family has had spiritual connections over time. After entering the room, GK approached the wall and walked its length, greeting many of the images individually, some in languages other than English. He leaned in close to each photo, asking questions and pausing as if receiving a response. It seemed that GK listened to their answers, as if the spirits of these long-dead friends were reaching out to his attentive ear. GK noted that the spirits endured in a state of anticipation, ready and waiting for the next ritual to begin. While the room's walls formed a cloak of protection around us, the photos served as portals through which ghosts entered from unseen realms.

On that same day, GK took me on a tour of his studio. My first thought upon entering was that, like many of the rooms in his house, this one was a cabinet of alchemical curiosities! Opposite the wall of windows was a collection of *carte de visite* photos, enshrined on display from floor to ceiling. They were small portraits of people with whom GK's family had, over time, established spiritual connections. While my eyes tried to take in as much as they could, GK proceeded to walk along the south wall, greeting many of the images individually. He leaned in close to various photos, asking questions and pausing as if he were receiving a response. It was as if the spirits of these long-dead friends were reaching out to his eager ear. GK said the spirits remained in a state of anticipation, ready and waiting for the next ritual to begin. While the room's walls formed a fortress of protection around us, the photos served as portals through which ghosts entered from realms unseen by most human eyes.

GK explained, "During ritual activities, the alchemist's consecrated vestments function as their cuirass, an energetically reflective armor of protection." In addition, ritual regalia or

> Costumes become a conduit for the supernatural, and importantly, their magical properties are perceived as real in much the same way as air or water might be. The ... author [of this quote] was initiated into an occult society that often used costumes to assist its members in exploring alternative visions of reality. The Hermetic Order of the Golden Dawn sought to discover, translate, and practice the magical and religious traditions of the ancient world, and adepts ... followed complex rules of dress that were thought to add efficacy to certain magical rituals [in which] costume could become an important bridge between the material and immaterial world. (Laska, 2015, 73)

Among Egyptians, magic was called heka. "The ancient Egyptian language did not have a word for religion, as we know it, only magic [heka]—and more precisely, magical power. Everything in Egyptian life was classed according to its perceived amount of magical power" (Stavish, 2006, 4). For instance, the alchemist's scepter was a tool of the priestcraft and is still used today as an instrument that controls heka, or the luminous flux of magical force. It can regulate the energetic potency of spells, install adamantine energies to form magic circles, and serve as protection against unwelcome spirits. GK claimed that by reading the papyrus of Weret-Hekau, "the great of magic," any of his scepters or scepter emblems could be transformed into venomous cobras, directed by his command. On the ethereal plane, those same scepters would be

Picture 22.2 The Kingswood family's collection of five hermetic scepters.
Courtesy of Sage Billups, 2023.

perceived as solar wands of power or flaming swords, used to scribe, open, or close the boundary of a magic circle.

Picture 22.3 Scepter Emblem by Garin Horner, 2020.

With the magician inside, the circle is drawn and closed. It solidifies, connecting with all cardinal directions to form the alchemist's primary defense barrier. To achieve this, one begins in the direction designated as east by the invoker (the point from where Ra ascends on the horizon) and traces the circular frame in a clockwise, deosil, or sunwise direction until it meets the starting point. A hermetic seal is established. Suppose there is a secondary circle for invoking and manifesting allies. In that case, it is constructed outside the first circle and positioned in front of the eastern axis point of the alchemist's circle of protection.

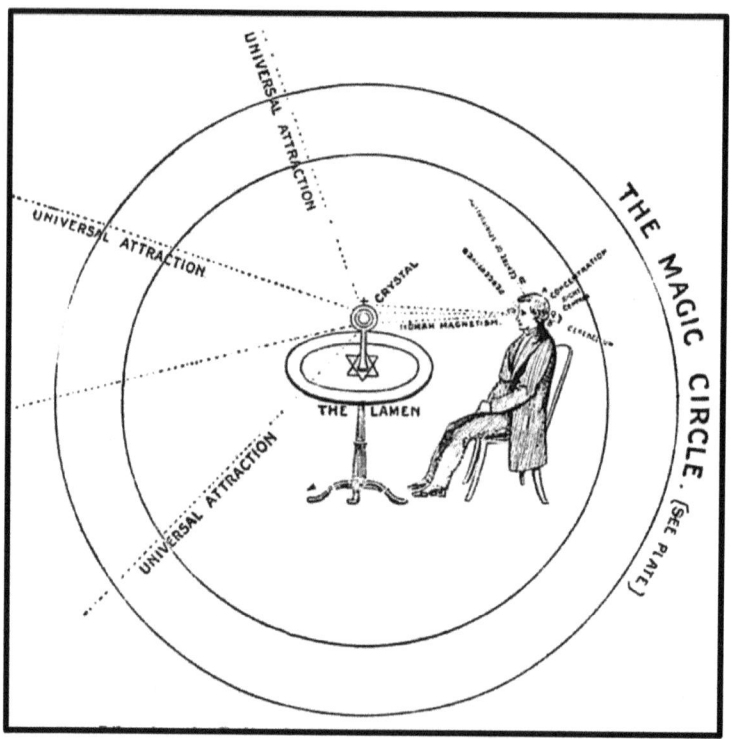

Picture 22.4 The Magic Circle. From Crystal Gazing and The Wonders of Clairvoyance. W. Foulsham & Company, 1910.

Before calling upon an ally, Ra is invoked so that the Monarch of Light may oversee all proceedings. With the alchemist either standing or sitting in the circle, the invocation begins. The ally is invited to appear in their separate circle. The alchemist's field of vision should include only the world within their circle and those of their allies; nothing outside the circle's predetermined depth of field should exist with any visual, mental, or spiritual clarity. Everything else in the outer worlds remains irrelevant and outside the field of focus. Everything that exists beyond the ritual area, extending to infinity, is part of a dream-like illusion, known as the *circle of confusion.*

23. THE ELEMENTS: SILVERY WATER & STARRY EARTH

In the beginning, there was nothing but a primordial darkness called the Waters of Chaos. Then, Ra emerged from a ray of light, self-created, as "the magnificence and sovereignty of the Light" (Helmond, 1996, 49-50). He was perfect in his unity, without boundaries and without end. In the next moment, Ra "discovers the mystery of being in the experience of his own being" (Corbin, 1969, 184). Ra is thus

> the unconditioned Imagination…The initial theophanic operation by which the Divine Being reveals Himself, 'shows Himself' to Himself, by differentiating Himself in his hidden being, that is, by manifesting to Himself the virtualities of His Names with their correlata, the eternal *hexeities*# [unique one-ness] of beings, their prototypes latent in His essence…this operation is conceived as being the creative Active Imagination, the theophanic Imagination (Corbin, 1969, 186).

As Ra's fiery luminance expanded, he "moved downwards, descending from the Eye of the Light, as if a cloud should come from the sun" (Vaughan, 1652). Ra spoke, and a Primeval hill formed from which several other gods emerged. His resplendent words took shape as the cosmos, giving birth to all the elements. When this creation was complete, Ra shed sparkling tears of joy that fell to the earth. Upon mixing with the fertile soil, humankind rose from the damp, muddy spots. "The Light is the first Materia of all things, and all Corpora inclusive of the Body of Human Beings will only then be fully restored to their first dignity, when the Light will again shine out of them from within" (Helmond, 1996, 186).

Ra's imagination was regarded as the fountainhead of all magical power, and he harnessed the potency of his candescent force to create the cosmos. All stars, planets, the Earth, and its multitude of creatures were formed from the radiant activity and transmutations generated by his heka. In this cosmology, each person is considered special because a vital part of that source-magic is manifested in every human soul. In this way, the soul and all its hidden complexities are inseparable from the magic that is Ra.

According to Egyptian funerary texts, when Ra created souls from pure light, he endowed them with nine divine aspects:

Khat - the "physical body"

Ka - the "double-form or astral self"

Ba - 'soul' which continued to receive offerings.

Shuyet - the "shadow of the soul" or "*shadow of Ra*"

Akh - "was the immortal, transformed, self which was a magical union of the *ba* and *ka*."

Sahu - the spiritual body or ghost that could appear in dreams

Sechem - the 'magical power, form' of "vital life energy" which could "control one's surroundings and outcomes."

Ab - The heart, which holds all the good and evil acts of its host

Ren - One's secret name(s) and true identity, bestowed by Ra (Mark, 2017).

The ancients viewed Ra as the ultimate source of magic. He used his heka to summon the elements and bring all things into existence. Thus, the most fundamental, indivisible essence of everything is the magic from which it originated. It was particularly true that the highest form of elemental creation was the human being, a blend of magical elements, infused with Ra's eternal light.

GK points out that the first philosophers didn't accept the creation stories on faith. They sought to know, with certainty, the truth about the origin of elemental and spiritual existence. They theorized that by reverse engineering, they could uncover the truth behind the legend while also discovering the single, hidden essence common to all creation. The first step was to break this reality down into its most basic constituent parts, which were understood as the four elements. In the *Aureus,* also known as the *Golden Tractate of Hermes*, Hermes Trismegistus instructs philosophers on how to approach their explorations of spirit and matter. "Understand ye, then, O Sons Of Wisdom, that the knowledge of the four elements of the ancient philosophers was not corporally or imprudently sought after, which are through patience to be discovered, according to their causes and their occult operation" (Yarker, 1886).

A multitude of stories have emerged throughout time about how the cosmos was created. For the Kingswoods, there is no doubt that it was Ra, known by many names, who performed miracles by manifesting the four elements from light: fire, air, water, and earth (*ignis, aeris, aqua,* and *terra*). For alchemists and photographers, these divinely produced materials hold an irresistible allure. GK claims, "Few have ever been able to resist taking pictures of a setting sun as its passionate fusion of fire and air blaze above the open horizon. Waterscapes of oceans, lakes, and rivers are a perennial attraction for the photographer's compositional attention. Image-makers can't resist the sensuality of landscapes, including those of mountains, plains, and valleys. They long to capture the likeness of the elements, to display the majestic and awe-inspiring body of the Earth. And at the top of the list of favored artistic themes is human subjects, the embodiment of all the material elements and heka."

"Photographers simply don't understand why they are so attracted to the elements," GK remarked as he turned the pages of an album containing some collected photographs.

> Or why do they continue to get so excited by how a scene looks, knowing its photographic representation will fall short of the impact they initially felt at first glance? When faced with sublimity, the camera is somehow destined to fall short, especially when compared to how the artist envisioned the exalted appearance in the photo. This attraction stems from the divine elements and the captivating way the subject matter appears when it interacts with light. They are seduced by the expression of the elements' radiant divine essences. Without realizing what enchants them in a scene, like a siren's call, they feel compelled to act. They must respond to the enchantment with their camera.
>
> Photographers intuitively sense that there is something transcendent about what they see. Some quality compels the artist to engage with and embrace the source of their inspiration. The aware image-maker becomes a moth to the flame, not only because they witness that beautiful performance of corporeal phenomena with their eyes, but also because they intuit a connection to the hidden, divine aspects of which they catch glimpses. Photographs are destined to fall short of their aesthetic goal, as it is beyond the art's capacity to literally represent the philosophical, energetic, and divinely hidden light essences that shine out from beneath the surface of things. Those rays are Ra's revelatory emissaries. They cannot be captured on film! Rather than merely expressing themselves through visible light, they extend luminous fingers and touch the photographer's eyes as invisible, yet knowable, enchanting intelligences.

"The function of Light as a cosmogonic agent begins in the world of Mystery. It's Light which reveals to the Divine Being the latent determinations and individualization contained in His essence. That is to say, the eternal hexeities# which are the contents of the Divine Names" (Corbin, 1969, 170). "At the same time," GK informs, "light (*lucis*) is dispatched by Ra to enthrone those glittering beams as the spirit of life!

That shining element, the spark in all things, restlessly longs to *become*, to take *form*, and to *act*." In the mid-1600s, Thomas Vaughan wrote from Heliopolis, Egypt. He discussed the way this light essence, or primary matter, flirtatiously co-mingles with the elements. He said,

> The eye of man never saw her twice under one and the same shape; but as clouds driven by the wind are forced to this and that figure -- but cannot possibly retain one constant form -- so is she persecuted by the fire of Nature. For this fire and this water are like two lovers: they no sooner meet but presently they play and toy, and this game will not over till some new baby is generated (Vaughan, 1651).

GK reports that the lessons of creation etched upon the Emerald Tablet mention, by name, three of the four elements: fire, earth, and wind. Water is understood to represent the moon. From the alchemist's perspective, the cosmos is the divine matrix. It is a never-ending container filled with myriad things, all formed from the materials, energies, and essences of the *four elements*. The Divine Principle animates all *things,* and it is only through *their* mastery that one discovers how to master themselves. The biblical Solomon was granted divine knowledge about the fundamental integrants of the universe, which would help guide him for the rest of his life.

In the King James Bible, Solomon said, "For he hath given me certain knowledge of the things that are, namely, to know how the world was made, and the operation of the elements" (Wisdom of Solomon, KJV). Almost 3000 years later, Ra's voice was received by the thoughtful ear of Abraham Kingswood. The deity made a promise to deliver the "desideratum of knowledge" to gain control over the elements:

> I am the eternal *woubah* (Shining light of the sun) who weighs the goodness of all hearts, who sees all into being, who knows the thoughts of all minds. Whosoever calls upon me, I will move the waters. Whosoever calls upon me, I will drive the wind. Whosoever calls upon me, I will raise the fire. Whosoever calls upon me, I will make life grow from the Earth. Whosoever calls upon me, I will cast my light before them as a guide through all darkness and even during the time between death and new life. (Abraham Kingswood)

Kingswood's encounter with Ra affirmed the importance of elemental magic. Ra attested that the use of natural forces would aid the alchemist through their mastery in the Great Work. Even in the Egyptian magic of antiquity, the elements were understood to be gods—important allies included in spellwork and rituals. The elemental gods were represented by sacred tools or substances on Ra's temple altars. The alchemists who followed sought the knowledge of Ra so they could work with the elements to master their physical and spiritual properties. The great 15th-century alchemical sage and magician, Henry Cornelius Agrippa, in his Three Books of Occult Philosophy, wrote:

> The Number and the Nature of those things,
> Cal'd Elements, what Fire, Earth, Aire forth brings:
> From whence the Heavens their beginnings had;
> Whence Tide, whence Rainbow in gay colours clad.
> What makes the Clouds that gathered are, and black,
> To send forth Lightnings, and a Thundring crack;
> What doth the Nightly Flames, and Comets make;
> What makes the Earth to swell, and then to quake:
> What is the seed of Metals, and of Gold
> What Vertues, Wealth, doth Nature's Coffer hold
> (Agrippa, 1898, 3).

Elemental implements play an essential role in the Magician card of tarot. It's the first card in the major arcana. He is depicted with a wand (fire), a sword (air), a cup (water), and a pentacle, or coin (earth). These consecrated items are the instruments used by traditional practitioners of magic, although other corresponding items may be employed in different magical systems. GK tells, "Along with symbolic implements, I use natural elemental specimens on my altar, such as lighted candles, suffumigation of aromatic incense, water from the Nile, and black sand from Heliopolis. As a photographer and user of magic, I also include the four elemental items of the light-based art."

For GK, photography provides tools that correspond to the elements. Film is represented by fire because it is the medium, receiver, and holder of fire as light "burns" upon its surface. Air expresses its aspects through the body of the camera, the container of dark air that holds the *potential* of space. The lens corresponds to water because of its glass spillway, with its aperture being the valve that controls the flow of light. The tripod, a permanent fixture for the view camera, is a tool of earth, anchoring the device to solid ground. When the camera is securely fastened to the platform's head, it provides stability and equilibrium for the entire body of the instrument. Its center post points from the camera to the very heart of the Earth's core, allowing the photographer to take absolute authority over all the photographic elements.

To gain control over the qualities of the four basic elements, one must first gain insights from the knowledge they are meant to impart. GK elaborates, "One aspect of the element's wisdom can be seen when examining how these vital elements function individually as the building blocks of the universe. Each is a unique phenomenon with the capacity to unite in harmony or to rise up as destructive forces. In both cases, the elements dynamically interconnect to perpetuate the cycle of new forms. Another part of gaining their knowledge will be found by studying how the fundamental intelligences correspond with the numerous aspects of one's inner and outer worlds. The elements reveal secrets about their divine seeds. They teach about the relationships that exist between the alchemist's inner states and their outer environment, as above and so below."

The 4th-century BCE Greek mystic Empedocles elaborated, in hexameter poetry, on the nature of the elements:

> HEARKEN and learn that four, at the first, are the sources of
>   all things:
> Fire, and water, and earth, and lofty ether unbounded.
> Thence springs all that is, that shall be, or hath been aforetime.
> JUST as men who the painter's craft have thoroughly mastered
> Fashion in many a tint their picture, an offering sacred;
> When they have taken in hand their paints of various colors,
> Mingling skillfully more of the one and less of another,
> Out of these they render the figures like unto all things;
> Trees they cause to appear, and the semblance of men and
>   of women,
> Beasts of the field, and birds, and fish that inhabit the waters,
> Even the gods, whose honors are greatest, whose life
>   is unending:—
> Be not deceived, for such, and nowise other, the fountain
> Whence all mortals spring, whatever their races unnumbered
> (Campbell).

Empedocles theorized that there exists a primordial phenomenon considered the most basic, fundamental component of a whole. The mystic proposed that there were four elements, which he called the "four root powers": earth, water, air, and fire. He argued that the natural forces causing them to mix, combine, and separate were love and conflict. He said, "Sometimes by Love all coming together into one, sometimes again each one carried off by the hatred of Strife" (Kingsley & Parry, 2020). Empedocles' classical doctrine remains the foundation of contemporary mystical ideas about the elements. His four categories represent active qualities rather than physical attributes. They were: Fire = combustibility, Air = vaporosity, Water = fluidity, and Earth = solidity. He also went a step further with the idea that elements were intelligences, identifying them as deities: fire = Hades, air = Zeus, water = Persephone, and earth = Hera (Kingsley & Parry, 2020). Alchemists of old also equated the elements with processes: "Just as calcinatio pertains to the element fire, coagulatio to the element earth, and sublimatio to the element air, so solutio pertains to water" (The Alchemy of Elements, 2018).

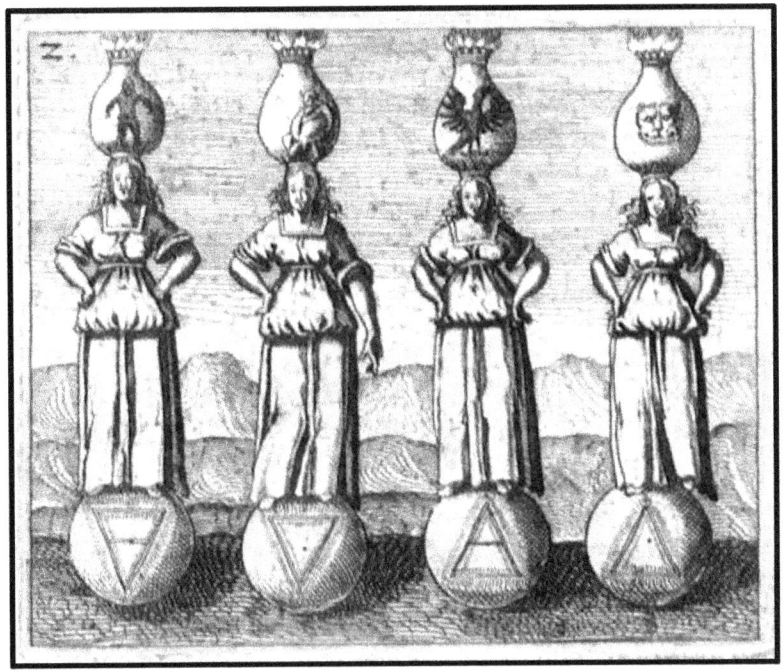

Picture 23.1 Viridarium Chymicum by Daniel Stolz von Stolzenberg, 1624.

GK elaborates further,

> Modern science teaches that the four elements are not fundamental; instead, there are 118 known root elements. Nonetheless, the concept of the four elements holds significant importance in magic. For instance, each of the four elements corresponds to psychological, physical, and spiritual aspects of existence. They also relate to photography. A photographer uses their intuition and awareness to identify corresponding patterns in their outer world, which are based on their inner-world perceptions. The four elements relate to all that exists in this material plane and the otherworld.

It's almost an obsession for alchemists and occult philosophers to create charts based on associations they learn from the elements. Abraham Kingswood was no different. He devised a map founded on his realizations and experiences with correspondences. His charts record critical correlating information needed for performing his spiritual practices, including spells, rituals, divination, incantations, meditations, and even his photography.

Today, correspondence charts based on the four elements typically begin with Aristotle's proposition of four physical, "simple bodies," along with a fifth element that he postulated was the *quinta essentia*, or element of "aether." Aether, also called the *spiritus*, was "the pure essence that the gods breathe" (Helmenstine, 2021) and was considered, at one time, to be a deity itself. Aristotle perceived the first four basic elements to be telluric materials, while the aether was an unseen force, a pure, celestial, primigenial element. Around the year 1500, Benedictine abbot and occultist Johannes Trithemius contemplated aether in relation to spirit when he wrote in his epistle:

"Not the bright stars of the skie, nor flames of hell,
But the Spirit begetting all doth in us dwell" (Atwood, 2005, 73).

Here, GK speaks of quintessence:

> I don't consider aether a fifth element since it is an intrinsic natural phenomenon. It pervades each classification in the traditional tetrad of elements. Rather, one could view it as part of a different order of element. Like light, it is a fundamental essence of all four elements. Both aether and light are rarified, luminiferous, primary essences, or *ousiai*, that pervade and sustain all parts of this realm and others. As such, aether is an essential partner to the heart of light; it is critical in the coagulation of photons and necessary for the generation of all physical things, including the philosopher's stone. Understanding aether as a fundamental essence of the elements allows one to comprehend how it interacts with empyrean light while regulating "the correct mixture of the sublunar elements, when forming terrestrial things from prima materia" (Kotansky, 2005, 19).

Quinta Essentia
In the physical sciences, quintessence is characterized as "dynamical, time-dependent, and spatially inhomogeneous" (Caldwell, 2000). It was once thought to be a medium that propagates light as it travels through space; however, it was later discovered that light is self-propagating. In

the occult sciences, it is described as a spiritual energy that, among other things, Pythagoras believed made up the soul. In 1498, Raymond Lully wrote that aether:

> preserves the body from corruption, strengthens the basic constitution (elementativa), pristine youth is restored by it, it unifies the spirit, dissolves the crudities, solidifies that which is loose, loosens the solid, fattens the lean, weakens the fat, cools the inflamed, heats up the cold, dries the humid, humidifies the dry; in what way soever, one and the same thing can perform contrary operations, the sole act of one thing is diversified according to the nature of the recipient, just as the heat of the sun has contrary effects, for it dries the mud and liquifies the wax (Pseudo-Llull, 1498).

Paracelsus proposed a theory that aligns with Kingswood's understanding. He believed the elements have a more fundamental hidden aspect within their material forms. Paracelsus said,

> that each of the four primary elements…consisted of a subtle, vaporous principle and a gross corporeal substance. Air is, therefore, twofold in nature-tangible atmosphere and an intangible, volatile substratum which may be termed spiritual air. Fire is visible and invisible, discernible and indiscernible--a spiritual, ethereal flame manifesting through a material, substantial flame. Carrying the analogy further, water consists of a dense fluid and a potential essence of a fluidic nature. Earth has likewise two essential parts--the lower being fixed, terreous, immobile; the higher, rarefied, mobile, and virtual. The general term *elements* has been applied to the lower, or physical, phases of these four primary principles, and the name *elemental essences* to their corresponding invisible, spiritual constitutions. Minerals, plants, animals, and men live in a world composed of the gross side of these four elements, and from various combinations of them construct their living organisms (Hall, 1928, 106).

Kingswood and other alchemists claimed that the unseen essence is an invisible light. He posited that it was "only visible to itself." This light is the secret, spiritual energy from which all things take form; that aether is merely a matrix upon which light actively coagulates and adopts whatever specific elemental paradigm is assigned. Thus, when exploring elemental symbols in Western magical traditions, one will find the upright pentagram representing the shape of the elemental matrix as it corresponds to the elemental collective, "man." On the typical pentagram, the topmost point represents aether or spirit, while the remaining points represent the four elements. For the Kingswoods the top point is equivalent to the pyramidion, which symbolizes the divine source of and embodiment of light.

Picture 23.2 Elemental Pentagram with pyramidion.
Composite by Garin Horner, 2021.

Lucis

Alchemists maintain there are two dimensions to every element: a corporeal form and a vital essence. GK introduces a third dimension. It's an all-pervasive, foundational essence that is light. The 16th-century alchemist Johannes Helmond agrees when he wrote,

> Fire's nature is articulated through an extrovertive expression of light, but the most basic essence of all matter, solid, liquid, and gaseous phenomena, from which all things are created and made to exist, is an introverted quality of esoteric light. Fiery, inward-

lustrous light is the true elemental and essential inspiration of alchemists and photographers alike. Some alchemists call it the Son of the Sun, the Soul of the Elements, and the power of the imagination (Helmond, 1996, 23).

GK adds, "Thus, the photographer's daily worship is one in which the devout seeks out and captures the exoteric radiance of those luminous scenes that will perfectly express one's singular vision as an offering to the solar deity. Light's beauty and mysteries motivate the photographer to capture that moment when short-lived rays reach their peak of evolution. In the same way a shaman embodies the spirit of an animal, photographers invoke the insights of light to become, themselves, more insightful and aware. They become more perceptive about what the partnership of light and shadow communicates about themselves, the photographer, and their relationship to the universe."

Mary Anne Atwood concluded that the Philosopher's Stone is made of aether. She believed it was formed from the active and essential principle of light when she wrote,

> The sense of all these philosophers is the same and from their gathered evidence we may infer that their stone is nothing more or less than the pure Ethereality of nature, separated by artificial means, purified and made concrete by constriction and scientific multiplication of its proper Light --- the preparation, generation, birth, specification --- all proceeding…on the hidden basis of its primal eduction. Earliest and easiest it attains to the perfection of the mineral kingdom; and the seed of gold, says the adept, is a fiery form of Light inspissate, and this is the Stone of Fire…Thus nature, by the help of art, is said to transcend herself, and Light is the true fermental principle which perfects the Ether in its proper kind (Atwood, 2005, 45).

In 1654, alchemist Eirenaeus Philalethes wrote in his treatise, "*The Marrow of Alchemy*," about the unseen dimensions of his temporal form:

> This form is light, the Source of all Central heat,
> Which being clothed with matter begetteth a Seed:
> Which Seed is no sooner produced, but it assayeth to bring
>   Matter to a change,
> whereon having stampt it Character the Matter becomes living,
> and wonderfully co-operateth with the Form, to attain the End…
> For all Things live according to their Kinds, whose Life is

259

Light which lieth hid in them, and is only discerned by the
Eyes of superior Minds (Philalenthes, 1993, 11).

Abraham Kingswood was one such "superior mind" who immediately
recognized the vital correspondences between alchemy, light, and
photography. He viewed photography as a means to identify, observe,
and record the truths graven on the Emerald Tablet, "the performing of
the miracles of the One Thing whence all the rest proceed by adaptation"
(Gumm). In short, GK points out,

> These miracles the tablet speaks of are the marvels of light, the
> prolific wonders of the skillful artificer, the coruscating# face of
> Ra as displayed through countless material appearances and
> occulted forms across the cosmos, all of which are infused with a
> vital spirit, a nourishing light. All have been written into
> existence by the pure, self-multiplicative adaptations of his
> luminance. For those photographers of superior mind, who are
> interested in their evolution, open your perception to the treasures
> of light and be aware of the one who is sphered in the magian
> circle of his own light: Ra.

GK expands on the idea.

> Light, a creative fire in potentia, is the treasure sought by both
> alchemists and photographers. It is the common, radiant seed, the
> essence that cannot be fully grasped by the five physical senses.
> Through perception granted by other extraphysical, more aware
> sense organs, one simply *knows* that ethereal (ether-real) light
> exists. This *knowledge* motivates the artist to explore every
> shadowy and illuminated place, both within themselves and
> throughout the world. They seek a *shining through* of the divine
> incandescence.

Sixteenth-century alchemist Michael Sendivogius declared:

> That nature, having her proper light, is by the shadowy body of
> sense, hidden from our eyes; but if, says he, the light of nature
> doth enlighten any one, presently the cloud is taken away from
> before his eyes, and without any let, he can behold the point of
> our lodestone, answering to each center of the beams (viz. of the
> sun and moon philosophical) for so far doth the light of nature
> penetrate and discover inward things; the body of man is a
> shadow of the seed of nature; and as man's body is covered with
> a garment, so is man's nature covered with the body. Man was

created of the earth, and lives by virtue of the air; for there is in the air a secret food of life, whose invisible congealed spirit is better than the whole world. Oh, holy and wonderful nature! Which knowest how to produce wonderful fruits by water, out of the earth and from the air to give them life! The eyes of the wise look upon nature otherwise than the eyes of common men. The most high Creator, having been willing to manifest all natural things to man, hath even showed us that celestial things themselves were naturally made; by which his absolute power and wisdom might be so much the better known; all which things the philosophers in the light of nature, as in a lookingglass, have a clear sight of; for which cause they esteemed this art of Alchemy, viz., not so much out of covetousness for gold or silver, but for the knowledge's sake; not only of all natural things, but also of the power of the Creator (Atwood, 2005, 68).

Elemental Correspondences:

Category	Fire (Ignis) Flame/Light	Air (Aer) Wind/Breath	Water (Aqua) Pool/Vapor/Ice	Earth (Terra) Rock/Sand/Clay/Soil
Elements of Photography	Line & Lead Space	Color & Space	Texture & Pattern	Shape & Form
Principles of Photography	Movement, Variety, & Emphasis	Negative Space, Unity, & Hierarchy	Repetition & Rhythm	Proportion, Contrast, & Balance
Rule of 3rds Power Points	Top Left	Top Right	Lower Right	Lower Left
Rule of Thirds Lines	Left vertical	Top Horizontal	Right vertical	Lower Horizontal
Egyptian God/Goddess	Sekhmet - Goddess	Shu - God	Tefnut - Goddess	Geb - God
Alchemical Action	Combustion	Evaporation	Mixation	Decomposition
Photography	Creative Vision	Intellect	Intuition	Intention
Tarot	Wands	Swords	Cups	Coins
Photography	Film	Camera	Lens	Tripod
Direction	South	East	West	North

Picture 23.3 Ignis Seal.
Composite by Garin Horner, 2023.

Ignis

Philosophers professed that "alchemy is a Science of Fire. They instruct: 'Above all seek first for the Fire'" (Hartmann, 1890, 91). Those same philosophers said that Fire,

> is the purest and most worthy of all the elements, and its substance is the finest of all; for this was first of all elevated in the creation with the throne of Divine Majesty. This nature is of all the most quiet and like unto a chariot, when it is drawn, it runs; when it is not drawn, it stands still. It is also, in all things indiscernible. In it are the reasons of life and understanding, which are distributed in the first infusion of man's life, and these are called the rational soul (Atwood, 2005, p113).

GK advises photographers to kindle their fire and heed his counsel, "Above all seek first the light." After all, the radiance of the burning sun is the very material that photographers pursue to trace their images upon the medium's silvery emulsion. Without fire, there is no visible light. There are no perceivable and, possibly, no imperceptible things. Without light, there is no photography, which is the beating heart of this alchemical lineage.

Kingswood wrote, "Fire is attracted to fire for the sole purpose of assimilation." Inherently, fire forms the elemental bridge between the material and spiritual worlds, between mortal humans and Ra. It is believed to be divine because it is the only element that both gods and humans can create. It is the radiant luminance from this element that Ra is credited to have used, not only to create himself, but to manifest all the elements and the things made from their combinations, throughout the cosmos. Fire, it follows, is the most divine of elements. It exhibits a universal, powerfully transformative principle that cannot be separated from its manifestations of light and heat. The heat it produces sustains life. Lack of it invites death. People of the Earth experience warmth, both from the sun and a radiating force from within the core of the human body.

GK tells an anecdote that he heard from his father about the Kingswood patriarch, Abraham. As the story goes, on a freezing and snowy night in England, one of Kinswood's disciples spied his teacher in a clearing on the home's grounds. Dressed only in a long, white cotton tunic, he sat in a chair positioned in the center of a large circle, defined by a line that divided several inches of snow and inside, a wet earthy interior where the snow had melted. There was a bright, full moon. It and Vesper# hid high above the cloud-covered sky. With ample ambient light, Kingwood was somehow reading from a book. He held it open with his left hand. In his right hand, he lifted an ornate scepter to the luminous sky. When Kingswood finally returned to the house, his disciple met him at the door. "Master", he said, "you were sitting in the bloody cold for hours, without a greatcoat — how are you still alive?" "My body generated a shrouding troposphere of heat — fueled by the fervor of my incantations. It was my steadfast covenant with the sun of Ra that set my heart ablaze and warmed me!"

The ancients both respected and feared fire. Its sight served as a reminder that their eternal souls were at risk of burning forever in the Lake of Fire. Contemporary Egyptologist Richard H. Wilkinson wrote that,

> According to the Coffin Texts and other works, the underworld contained fiery rivers and lakes as well as fire demons (identified by fire signs on their heads) which threatened the wicked. Representations of the fiery lakes of the fifth "hour" or "house" of the Amduat depict them in the form of the standard pool or lake hieroglyph, but with flame-red "water" lines, and surrounded on all four sides by fire signs which not only identify the blazing nature of the lakes, but also feed them through the graphic

"dripping" of their flames. Some temple texts and modern books have said that the Lake of Fire in the Egyptian Religion is the lake that Ra would pass through in his daily journey in the Duat (Wilkinson, 1992, 161).

Magic, religious fervor, prayer, and divinity have all been related to fire. The Book of Exodus states that the biblical God appeared in Egypt as a pillar of fire, serving as a guiding light for Moses and the fleeing Israelites. 17th-century alchemist Johannes Tritheim wrote,

> God is an essential and hidden fire in all things, and especially in man. That fire generates all things. It has generated them, and will generate them in the future, and that which is generated is the true divine light in all eternity. God is a fire; but no fire can burn, and no light appear within nature without the addition of air to cause the combustion, and likewise the Holy Spirit in you must act as a divine 'air' or breath, coming out of the divine fire and breathing upon the fire within the soul, so that the light will appear, for the light must be nourished by the fire, and this light is love and gladness and joy within the eternal deity (Hartmann, 1890, 86).

Moreover, Mary Anne Atwood said of God, "no mortal man can see God, or come to Him naturally. For that Fire which is carried the seal and majesty of the Most High, is so intense, that no eye can penetrate it; for Fire will not suffer anything that is compounded to come near to it: but is the death and separation of everything that is compounded" (Atwood, 2005, 113).

Paulo Coelho, author of *The Alchemist*, is said to have composed this hopeful, poetic prayer, to invoke a fire of transformation for the evolution of all humanity:

> I came to set fire to the earth. And I am watchful that the
>   fire grow.
> May the fire of love grow in our hearts.
> May the fire of transformation glow in our movements.
> May the fire of purification burn away our sins.
> May the fire of justice guide our steps.
> May the fire of wisdom illuminate our paths.
> May the fire that spreads over the Earth never be extinguished
> (Attributed to Coelho).

GK assures that light is the expressive soul of fire, and that fire and light each contain their own unique, divine essences. French art historian Marcel Augert said, "God is light, and light gives beauty to things; essential beauty must be identified with brightness which, together with harmony and rhythm, reflects the image of God" (Aubert, 1959, p. 52). Ra, as the solar god, is inseparable from all aspects of fire and light, along with their corresponding principles of passion, creativity, sexual impulse, electricity, and revelation.

GK further posits, "When the limitations of human sight prevent one from seeing the ethereal fire, its radiant qualities can be understood by its knowable principles, such as its abilities to illuminate, penetrate, expand, and enlighten. For every aspect of the invisible light's living, hallowed sparks, there are counterparts in the visible world that take the form of fire, its radiance, or descending daggers of lightning."

Ra, both the physical and spiritual sun, has inspired civilization's early ancestors to invent new methods of harnessing fire and creating light. More than 200,000 years ago, there is evidence that early humans first learned to produce fire. Much later, in 4500 BCE, candles and oil lamps emerged. In 1792, to gain control over fire, gas lighting was conceived. At each progressive stage, creative thinkers harnessed fire's newfound radiance to enhance their innovative capabilities. Then, in 1879, the lightbulb was invented, opening "the potential for a new revolutionized way to use light as not just a subject but a medium. It wasn't until several decades later in the 1930s that light was used in its purest form by Lazlo Moholy-Nagy" (Choppara, 2021).

The photographic artist was the first to create an object-based light sculpture as part of the wildly imaginative Dada movement. He projected colors and white light onto his sculpture, *"Light Prop for an Electric Stage (Light-Space Modulator),"* spurring a range of shadow effects as the piece rotated. His work prompted future artists to adopt a new approach to lumino-kinetic art using an unprecedented medium: light. He demonstrated that art can employ light to convey emotion, conceptual thought, or make a statement; it transcends language" (2021). Moholy-Nagy conjured the element of fire, and with the help of Ra's fiery bulb, he helped emancipate photography from the limiting confines of public opinion and into the realm of art.

In his book, *Where the Wasteland Ends,* modern scholar and artist Theodore Roszak includes a prophetic poem about the transformative power of fire. He encourages readers to act and embrace the divinely radiant element; otherwise, the fleeting chance for gnosis will be lost.

Unless the eye catch fire,
The God will not be seen.

Unless the ear catch fire,
The God will not be heard.

Unless the tongue catch fire,
The God will not be named.

Unless the heart catch fire,
The God will not be loved.

Unless the mind catch fire,
The God will not be known (Roszak, 1989, 296).

GK reflects on Roszak's lines: "For those who are called to climb the steps toward light, who are not afraid of dissolution and rebirth through coagulation, who seek evolution through trials by fire, I advocate for the transforming stages and sum of the Great Work."

Picture 23.4 Aeris Seal.
Composite by Garin Horner, 2023.

Aeris

Air, like water, possesses fluid qualities. It is the gaseous substance that fills the lungs and sustains animal life. GK elaborates, "It expands to fill the dark space of anticipation inside the camera obscura. Its quality of transparency allows the lens to see with far-reaching clarity. Images of surrounding scenes arrive at the eye, having traveled through air on beams of light." In addition to sight, air supports the senses of smell and hearing. Scents travel to the nose as they are carried and dispersed by the currents of air. The sounds of words move through the density of air as vibrations and waves. In this way, air supports the acquisition of knowledge because spoken language facilitates the human ability to communicate, teach, and learn.

In the air, thoughts hold creative power, especially when words are cast as spells or told as stories and myths. Egyptian priests claimed that Ra created all existence through the movement of his breath in the form of luminous words. GK underscores that,

> In the case of Ra's spiration#, his words possess the ultimate power of creation. It is his breath upon which they are formed. It is the element of air that allows them to travel to their destination. Thus, air supports creation. As Ra sails in his barque, from horizon to horizon, across the vast blue arc of the sky, he does so on the tides and currents of air.

"Air has been connected with the soul in many cultures, and this is seen particularly in Western magickal languages with examples such as *Ruach* (Hebrew) meaning '*spirit*', '*breath*', or '*wind*'; *Psyche* (Latin) is derived from *psukhe* (Greek) meaning '*breath*', '*life*', or '*soul*'; and *Pneuma* (Greek) meaning '*breath*', '*soul*' or '*vital spirit*'" (Rankine & d'Este, 2008, 22-23). The ancients recognized a connection between the unseen, animated vitality of air. Henry Wadsworth Longfellow wrote of his perceptions regarding the correspondences between air and spirit:

> The spirit-world around this world of sense
> Floats like an atmosphere, and everywhere
> Wafts through these earthly mists and vapors dense
> A vital breath of more ethereal air
> (Longfellow, 1858).

In the antiquity of both India and Egypt, meditators discovered various breathing techniques that could harness magical, energetic forces. In doing so, they found that meditation offered health benefits while heightening one's spiritual awareness and level of consciousness. From Egypt, there is a practice known as "Kemetic Yoga" or "Smai Tawi," which is inspired by Ancient Egyptian hieroglyphs and emphasizes breathing patterns, incorporating the philosophies of self-development, mind-body-spirit healing, and self-discovery (Bové, 2022). Methods of yogic breathing are practiced,

> in order to stimulate the parasympathetic functions of the mind and physiology, to develop concentration and self-control, and to properly facilitate the flow of internal life force through the energy channels. [The Kemetic breathing exercise] consists of inhalation, void (holding of the breath for 1 to 2 seconds), exhalation and another void before the next inhalation. Our goal over time is to experience the void or empty space for an extended period of time during meditation. This void is called Sep Tepy in the Kemetic creation story and signifies the void in universal time before the process of creation and thus time began (Hotep, 2014).

For Yirser Ra Hotep, the air in the vast blue sky is a source of vital life-force that, when inhaled and exhaled in these ways, has the capacity to transform the whole body, mind, and spirit. (Burch, 2023). The air in the Earth's atmosphere is a source of vital life-force that, when inhaled and exhaled in these ways, can transform the whole body and mind.

The Egyptians learned to harness the power of air by appealing to the spirits that lived in it, moved through it, and were formed by air. The following is a prayer called the "Secret Inscription" from the Greek Magic Papyrus of Paris, which calls forth the spirits of air and pays homage to the "God of the Aeons," Ra:

> Greetings, entire edifice of the Spirit of air, greetings, Spirit that penetrates from heaven to earth , and from earth, which abideth in the midst of the universe, to the uttermost bounds of the abyss, greetings, Spirit that penetrates into me, and shakest me, and departest from me in goodness according to God's will; greetings, beginning and end of the irremovable Nature, greetings, thou who revolvest the elements which untiringly render service, greetings, brightly shining sun, whose radiance ministereth to the world, greetings, moon shining by night with a disc of fickle brilliance, greetings, all ye spirits of demons of air, greetings, ye for whom the greeting is offered in praise, brothers and sisters, devout men and women! O great, greatest, incomprehensible fabric of the world, formed in a circle!

> Heavenly One, [Ra] dwelling in the heavens, aetherial spirit, dwelling in the aether, having the form of water, of earth, of fire, of wind, of light, of darkness, star-glittering, damp-fiery-cold

Spirit! I praise thee God of gods, who hast fashioned the world, who hast established the depths upon the invisible support of their firm foundation, who hast separated heaven and earth, and hast encompassed the heavens with golden, eternal wings, and founded the earth upon eternal bases, who hast hung the aether high above the earth, who hast scattered the air with the self-moving wind, who hast laid the waters roundabout, who callest forth the tempests, the thunder, the lightning and rain: Destroyer, Begetter of living things, God of the Aeons, great art thou, Lord, God, Ruler of All! (Preisendanz, 2001)

As Earth's protector, the sky resides as a shielding blanket of air that safeguards its surface from the dangers of outer space. Meanwhile, the atmosphere provides the nourishing, oxygen-rich compounds that sustain and energize life across the planet. The Earth's breath creates gentle breezes that can bring pleasure to the skin, evoking feelings of happiness, contentment, and joy. This gentle movement of air can calm both the body and mind, while its potential for speed and force can also bring devastation and death. When it manifests in its most aggressive form, it can instill panic and terror. For this reason, air is an element that must be respected for its dual role as both creator and destroyer.

Picture 23.5 Aqua Seal.
Composite by Garin Horner, 2023.

Aqua

Water is the medium for all photographic chemistry. In its pure form, water is the last step in darkroom processes, acting as a purifying agent for film and paper by washing away all contaminating reactive substances. During the wash phase of his darkroom prints, GK uses a large metal print washer to circulate water around the images. After the prints are cleansed and removed, they are placed in a final tray that contains a very specific kind of water:

> In the last tray, I wash the ordinary water away with consecrated water, which contains an infusion from various sources. I use water from the Dead Sea, the Ganges River, the Nile, the Jordan River, the Themes, Marne and Seine Rivers, to name a few. Each has its own unique metaphysical qualities and supernatural properties.

As another example of the use of sacred waters, photographer Tomiko Jones used water from Rattlesnake Lake to wash her film, "as an invitation of the lake to merge physically into the image" (Yonker, 2019). "From an alchemical perspective," says GK, "Jones recognized that her print, titled 'Rattlesnake Lake,' could evolve. It did so by absorbing a particular watery element and establishing new empyrean filaments; it could be transformed into a higher state of being. Its thirst to become *more* was quenched."

From its metaphysical, physiological, and psychological perspectives, the concept of water carries an instinctual imperative of *need* or *thirst*. GK claims,

> The element has an enduring impact on the human psyche in its relationship to the biological impulse of thirst. This longing is a stimulus that overwhelms the mind and taps into the primal instinct to survive. Philosophers connect the thirst for water to their *thirst for knowledge*, which is equally necessary and urgent. Like the photographer Jones, there exists an unquenchable desire to capture, possess, and feel satiated. This desire, or need, drives both the alchemist and the artist to seek perpetually because there is an undeniable, compelling impulse. The feeling insists that reaching the goal is a matter of life and death.

Humans are a species that has both physical and metaphysical sympathy with water. This is logical, given that the human body consists of approximately 60% water, and seventy-one percent of our habitat, the Earth's surface, is composed of water. GK teaches, "Water is a precondition for life. Life on this planet originated from the fertile influxions# of primal waters around 3.5 billion years ago. Alchemists reinforced science's conclusions about the origin of life when they proclaimed that water is the womb-source from which all life continues to emerge. It's also the element from which rebirth is possible."

In the 16th century, Elizabethan occultist Simon Forman wrote of water as the matrix of life:

> *The Sprite of the Lord moved*: Here by the sprite of the Lord is meante the holy ghoste…which moved upon the face of the depe or upon the waters, to put severalle ydees [ideas, i.e., archetypes or patterns] and virtues [efficacies or properties having power] of diversity of things and of all Creatures therein (bothe into the earth and also into the waters), that afterward they should bringe forth every severalle creature…For the [be]ginning of all Influences, powers, virtues, graces, and good gifted com of and from the sprite of god, which is the holy ghoste…And this was the cause which the holy ghoste moved upon the waters: because waters ar liquid, apt and able to take impression of all forms…Therefore is water the first begininge and originalle of all Creatures, and from thence they growe to a harder form, as the Earth that was first begotten of the water. (Schuler, 2013, 61).

Understanding that life originates from water, the alchemical process of *solutio* seeks to uncover the common life-essence of elements by sublimating or reducing them to their original watery source, the prima materia.

> Solutio symbolism is rich and varied. The solutio is a way of dislodging stuck complexes and also the solutio is linked to chemical liquefaction. All that is stuck is put in solution to allow movement. It is used to symbolize softening or melting processes. It is representative of dissolution, dispersal, and even dismemberment. It is about the containment of a lesser thing by a greater. It can be the return to the primal state or womb. Solutio is about rejuvenation, immersion in the creative energy flow, and as its word root implies, the solution of problems. It is also symbolic of a purification ordeal. These various aspects overlap and mingle in a single experience (The Alchemy, 2018).

GK promotes the idea,

> Though the solutio process is a physical action, there are psychological and spiritual correlations that can be explored around meditations on water, a potent symbol of the conscious mind and the fluid depths of the unconscious. It is in these

dreams that the alchemist encounters their psychological and spiritual self, often focusing on bodies of water, including pools, rivers, rain, fountains, waves, and waterfalls.

Sigmund Freud wrote, "The conscious mind may be compared to a fountain playing in the sun and falling back into the great subterranean pool of subconscious from which it rises" (Levinson, 1971, 185). Carl Jung identified water as "the very source of the creative impulse" (1928, 117). Jungian Analyst Brian Collinson says, "As with bodies of water, we often see the surface, but cannot easily see into the depths. Also, the vastness of the ocean symbolizes the vastness of the unconscious mind. Jung observed long ago that the unconscious mind was much vaster than the conscious portion" (2021). Those depths, both in the oceans and in the mind, remain largely unexplored mysteries.

As a metaphor for the mind, water symbolizes states of meditative calmness and depicts transient states of turbulence, upheaval, and agitation. Literally, water can be defined by its qualities and actions. The coolness of water invigorates and refreshes; its wetness lubricates, its softness soothes, its purity cleanses, and its holiness purifies. Its fluidity teaches as it flows and conforms to the shape of its container. The tides rise and fall under the influence of the moon, with gravitational forces endlessly reconfiguring shoreline boundaries. In essence, water is a symbol of transformative change. Through temperature variations, it can take on different forms, easily adapting to its natural environment by converting between liquid, solid, and gaseous states. Its changeable nature in the Earth's *water cycle* was illustrated by the 8th century alchemist Theophrastos, who wrote:

> O progeny of splendor, light and worth!
> O robe with gold and silver overlaid!
> O double-folded mantle bright as snow!
> O metal which with gleaming silver teems!
> O clear refreshing river of the sea!
> O water than the loosened earth more free!
> O ether rising far above the earth!
> O clouds transformed from blackness into white!
> O brilliant coloured glory of the heaven!
> O light which shines to all beneath the sky!
> O system and bright circuit of the stars!
> O lunar light reflected from the sun!
> O sun whose darting beams engender gold!
> (Theophrastos, 11th Century, 2023).

Egyptians regarded the waters of the Nile (Iteru-aa) as a life-providing and life-sustaining substance. Its waters were worshiped as the god *Nun*, whose name means "primeval waters." Nun "represented the waters of chaos out of which [Ra]-Atum began creation. Nun's qualities were boundlessness, darkness, and the turbulence of stormy waters." However, the god associated with the Nile was called *Hapy*. In their Hymn to the Nile (dwAw Hapy), Egyptians sang,

> Hail to thee, O Nile, that issues from the earth and comes to keep Egypt alive!...The bringer of food, rich in provisions, creator of all good, lord of majesty, sweet of fragrance…Entering into the underworld and coming forth above, loving to come forth as a mystery…When the Nile floods, offering is made to thee, oxen are sacrificed to thee, great oblations are made to thee, birds are fattened for thee, lions are hunted for thee in the desert, fire is provided for thee…So it is "Verdant art thou!" So it is "Verdant art thou!" So it is "O Nile, verdant art thou, who makest man and cattle to live!" (Anonymous, 1350).

This divine water of the Nile, whose mysteries are largely unknowable, is also a metaphor for the essential water sought by the alchemists, which, "Thales of Miletus believed…was the prime matter. The flow of water and its central role in the growth of plants and animals convinced Thales that all matter was originally composed of water." It is the water of the Hermetic doctrine, the root element from which all other elements were born at the beginning of time.

> Hermes said that the separation of the ancient philosophers is made upon Water, dividing into four substances, that it is not the common elementated water to which he alludes; any more than did Thales when he said that all things were generated from thence, or Moses when he taught that the Spirit of God moved creatively upon the face of the same. This water they speak of is not the fluid with which in this life we are conversant, either as dew, or of clouds, or air condensed in caverns of the earth, or artificially distilled in a receiver out of sea fountains, either of pits, or rivers, as the empirical chemists formerly imagined --- but it is the ethereal body of life and light which they profess to have discovered, --- a certain tortured water, having suffered alteration by art and becomes corporified. Oh, how wonderful, exclaims the Arabian [Geber], is that thing which has in itself all things which we seek, to which we add nothing different or extract, only in the separation removing superfluities! (Atwood, 2005, 41).

Terra

The Earth element represents solidification. The firmament upholds itself as rocks, sand, soil, hills, structures, and mountains. Earth, composed of cosmic material, takes the form of one's physical body and the bodies of all living things. It is the fundamental element to which all these temporary bodies will eventually return. Earth embodies density, weight, and physicality. It also symbolizes strength, endurance, and patient determination. Earth provides shelter, food, and stability, generously offering its bounty to all, including the lunar metal of silver and the perfect solar metal, gold. It connects all human beings to the planets in the cosmos and serves as the home planet for the human species, as well as its orbiting satellite, the Moon. The earth element can be nurturing but also possesses destructive qualities through volcanoes and earthquakes.

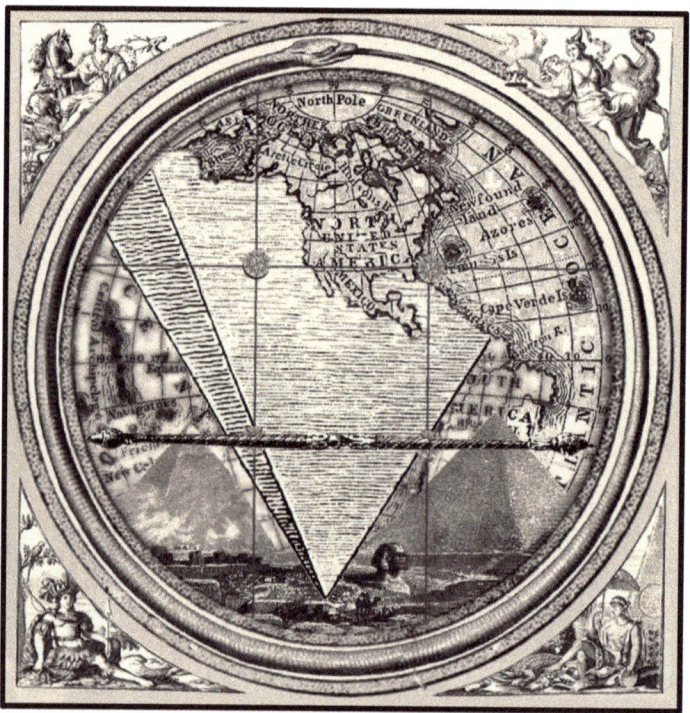

Picture 23.6 Terra Seal.
Composite by Garin Horner, 2023.

The physical tools of the photographic art are linked to the Earth element. The materials used for making cameras and prints are derived from earth. They exemplify the earth element through the solidity of their construction. For example, Abraham Kingswood's cameras were made from mahogany, leather, and brass. Film cameras were subsequently constructed from aluminum and copper but may have also included small amounts of titanium, silver, and gold. Modern cameras, however, are designed to feel sturdy yet lightweight. To achieve the quality of lightness, the latest cameras are primarily made of plastics, which originate from crude oil. Additionally, modern photo prints include plastic (resin-coated), though most use wood fiber as their base material.

"I would also maintain," says GK,

> The most crucial tool of photography is the human body. The body is the point of origin for all photographs. It's the mind's vehicle that moves through space while its physical senses interpret the surroundings. Suppose one understands the photographer's eye as the lens. In that case, the brain can be appreciated as the original camera, recording into memory those visual experiences that catch attention and make a memorable impact. The only reason one needs a camera to capture an image is to preserve a scene as a permanent artifact. By doing so, one can share a unique experience that could change how others see the world.

From the microcosm's vantage point, the earth element appears strong, stable, durable, and dependable. In contrast, the macrocosmic view of planet Earth tells a different story. On Christmas Eve in 1968, the Apollo 8 spacecraft was about to make an unexpected discovery that would alter the collective human perception of the Earth. The mission aimed to orbit the moon and capture high-resolution photographs of the lunar surface, enabling NASA to identify the best possible landing sites for future missions. As the spacecraft rounded the dark side of the moon, light flooded onto its crater-covered surface. Then, on the crest of the lunar horizon, in the blackness of space, rose the luminous sphere of Earth. Astronaut Bill Anders hurried to remove the black-and-white film magazine from the camera so he could load Ektachrome color film into his Hasselblad 500 EL. Using a 250mm telephoto lens and with his camera set to 1/250 sec at f/11, he quickly captured the iconic image of the blue and white planet, dwarfed by the barren celestial body in the foreground and the dark infinity of the background (NASA, 2018). The latent images remained concealed in the camera until they returned to Earth.

After the film was processed and revealed, the impact of the legendary image was felt in the collective consciousness of all observers on Earth. The photograph transformed the common understanding of the planet from a circle drawn on a chart, surrounded by other non-scale circles, to a more realistic photographic representation of Earth and its relationship to the moon and space. "Earthrise" transformed the archetypal understanding of the Earth as a secure, protective sphere of immobility. In contrast, the photo taught humans that Earth, from a macrocosmic view, was small, fragile, and delicate in the context of the vast cosmos.

GK expands further: "The four elements mix and intertwine to give form to the spirit of the universe in which all beings live. Ra's fiery manifestation as a solar body, floating in the open sky, embraces the earth to create life. That same Theophrastos who wrote, "O progeny of splendor," wrote:"

> He makes his circuit in the dozen months
> Which form the year and sheds his light on all
> Beneath the sky. The splendor of his beams
> Fills all the earth with mild increasing warmth;
> With rapid course he summons things to life
> And makes with gentle heat all trees to bud.
> From him the moon receives her gleaming light
> And all the wandering stars, the planets seven,
> And likewise those whose shifting orbs are fixed
> (Theophrastos, 11th Century, 2023).

Union of Elements

Existence tends to establish and maintain harmony among elements. It does this by creating cyclic patterns of unity, harmony, and balance. This sympathy can also be observed in a vast multiplicity of forms, spirits, and the singular essence. The alchemist enacts this divine purpose in their lives, both literally and symbolically. The aim is to discover the knowledge of the singular divine essence in all things—the original creative spark. The Thrice Blessed Hermes passed along his wisdom on the matter when he said that:

> All things descend from Heaven to Earth, to Water and to
> Air...Tis Fire alone, in that it is borne upwards...Tis Earth alone,
> in that it resteth itself...That, then, from which the whole Cosmos
> is formed, consisteth of Four Elements — Fire, Water, Earth, and
> air; Cosmos [itself is] one, [its] soul [is] one, and God is one
> (Mead & Hermes, 2001, 310-311).

Fifth-century antiquities scholar John the Lydian wrote on the concept of alchemical elements from an ancient Chaldean perspective. In *De Mensibus*, his retelling highlights how the Chaldeans brought the elements to life by associating them with the four heads of the goddess of the crossroads, representing the four directions, through surreal imagery of fantastical mythical creatures. This creative, symbolic narrative evokes images that stir the imagination! The ideas were handed down as

> the mystical doctrine concerning the four elements and four-headed Hekate. For the fire-breathing head of a horse is clearly raised towards the sphere of fire, and the head of a bull, which snorts like some bellowing spirit (daimonion), is raised towards the sphere of air, and the head of a hydra as being of sharp and unstable nature is raised towards the sphere of water, and that of a dog as having a punishing and avenging nature is raised towards the sphere of earth (Lydus, 1967, 41).

The mythopoetic symbols encourage the imagination to visualize the elements as fierce, untamed forces of dreams or nightmares. Simultaneously, there is an artistic, terrifying quality to the description of the goddess that evokes Surrealist paintings or visionary photographic manipulations.

As GK discussed, the four elements have always inspired the creative mind. "The photographer's perception is forever lured toward connecting with and understanding the unifying harmony of the elements. Image makers sense the binding thread of light, born of divine inspiration, that runs through physicality. It is the quintessence, the element of spirit present in every scene and in the composition of every photo. The ancient philosophers of alchemy point one finger to the sky and the other to the earth, leading aspirants toward an understanding of the universal elements, their unique qualities, and their unifying essence. The sages claim that what seekers search for is in plain sight. That said, it's difficult to capture and know."

Aerem

24. Allies: A Gathering of Spirits

The perennial question about spiritual allies, guides, gods, and a metaphysical ecosystem is whether they exist. At the end of his life, Kingswood wrote about an evening when he spoke on behalf of the members of the Kemetic Order. His topic was *The Light of Ra*. He jotted down a question asked by a novice: "Are gods and ghosts real?" He replied, "Ra and his company of ever-present spirits…and magic are as real as you are. I'll say no more until we meet at the crown of the golden pyramid. Then we will discuss this further." After a pause, he resumed.

> This isn't a question that the working alchemist would ask because they have developed the faculty of suprarational perception, where interworking in partnership with the *universum supernaturalis* is a daily occurrence. We have a legacy of direct interaction with supra-physical beings. It isn't a type of psychotomimetic# episode or the bubbling up of juvenile fantasies. We intercommunicate with entities that dwell in unseen realms intimately connected to our own. This would be like asking today's creative photographers if what they produce is art. They would say, "yes, of course" because they experience something in their work that others may not be able to see or believe exists, especially those who claim the highest authority in the art world. I'll add that one must not simply believe what any boasting scholar tells them but must find out for themselves and trust in their own experience.

During the same period that Kingswood wrote those words, struggles were occurring. Photographers worked diligently to gain credibility and recognition within the broader arts culture. English and American societies debated the certainty or impossibility of the existence of spirits. Regarding the spirit question, Doctor, James Martin Peebles expressed his own sense of logic when he wrote that since the early days of Christianity, church councils have "promulgated decrees against enchanters, astrologers, soothsayers, magicians, and necromancy (talking with the dead). Right here the inquiry arises, if there was no possibility of converse with the dead - that is, with spirits - why should the church condemn it?" (Green, 1901, 208).

Another question people asked was, "If there are spiritual allies, where do they come from?" The ancient Greek philosopher Porphyry provided an answer when he explained the soul's actions after the death of the body. He said that if the soul still possesses a spirit turbid from humid exhalations, it then attracts to itself a shadow, and becomes heavy; a spirit of this kind naturally striving to penetrate into the recesses of the earth, unless a certain other cause draws it in a contrary direction. As, therefore, the soul, when surrounded with this testaceous and terrene vestment, necessarily lives on the earth; so likewise when it attracts a moist spirit, it is necessarily surrounded with the image…When, however, the soul earnestly endeavours to depart from nature, then she becomes a dry splendour, without a shadow and without a cloud, or mist. For moisture gives subsistence to a mist in the air; but dryness constitutes a dry splendour from exhalation (Porphyry, 1823, 32).

Furthermore, within the context of Kingswood's philosophy, the soul must ultimately proceed alone, either continuing its holy ascension or descending into the otherworldly realm.

Picture 24.1 Saul and the Witch of Endor by Washington Allston, 1851.

Like the solitary spirit, both the hermetic artist and the photographer tend to work alone. GK highlights, "There is much that can be accomplished on one's own regarding creative problem-solving, self-exploration, and the freedom to pursue one's own interests. Even so, when performing magical work, it increases the odds of success when done in concert with others. For instance, for my spellcraft, I rely on the assistance of benevolent spiritual beings," which he refers to as 'allies' or 'the glorified." Photographers can have allies too. For challenging projects, image makers may choose to enlist the help of assistants, marketing experts, and professional editors. This alliance of people coordinates with the photographer to more effectively accomplish important goals that a solitary photographer may not have the resources to complete.

The difference between photographers and alchemists is that the latter calls on allies dwelling in the spirit realm. The great benefit of working with glorified beings is that, with paranormal support, one can unite forces. Allies can align their intentions to focus their combined energies on achieving a challenging goal. Typically, one's allies lend their unique abilities to support the purpose of the conjurer. The accumulated light energy from various sources improves the likelihood of the alchemist's aim becoming a reality. Spiritual allies, claims GK, "are essential to the alchemist's work because they bring upon the endeavor, an inflowing light of favorability.

Henry Wadsworth Longfellow, in an excerpt from his poem *"Haunted Houses,"* wrote about the material and ethereal realms and the interactions between their residents.

The spiritual world
Lies all about us, and its avenues
Are open to the unseen feet of phantoms
That come and go, and we perceive them not,
Save by their influence, or when at times
A most mysterious
Providence permits them
To manifest themselves to mortal eye.

Though I close mine eyes,
I am awake, and in another world,
Dim faces of the dead and of the absent
Come floating up before me.

So from the world of spirits there descends
A bridge of light, connecting it with this
(Green, 1901, 205).

It is helpful to understand that supernatural beings are categorized into several different types of entities. Egyptologist Gerald Massey further clarifies that,

> Egyptians designated *"the Gods and the Glorified."* The gods are superhuman powers, whether elemental or astronomical. The glorified are the souls once mortal which were propitiated as the spirit-ancestors, here called the Manes of the dead. Not that the Egyptian deities were what Herbert Spencer thought, "the expanded ghosts of dead men." We know them from their genesis in nature as elemental powers or animistic spirits, which were divinized because they were superhuman, and therefore *not* human. (Massey, 2007, 121).

GK illustrates for aspirants, "Spiritual ascension is nearly impossible to complete on one's own. It's necessary to accumulate a constellation of supernatural beings as one's allies, who can serve as guides and clear obstacles. Only then can one accomplish their aspirations in the Great Work." The Hermetic artist is advised to regularly practice the skills necessary to summon and invite otherworldly spirits and deities to be present, manifesting within a designated space. This includes verbally expressing one's intentions directly to images of their allies. Speaking to a connecting photograph enlivens its filaments, sending light energy back through space and time, and even through the locked door that separates life and death.

When followers of Ra call on allies, they are never evoked. Evocation is an aggressive action in which a conjurer takes a position of authority over the entity being called and seeks to dominate it into submission. Its purpose is to establish a hierarchy in which the ritualist reigns over and assumes control of a spirit, forcing it to follow the alchemist's commands. It takes the form of a powerful, necromantically-driven monologue. Instead, visitants# should be invited with an *invocation*, which is more of an entreaty to attend. It's a formal request to join the cooperative undertaking of a ritual ceremony. Allies respond more consistently to an earnest, humble, and respectful request. At the same time, it must be noted that allies, including gods, are unpredictable. Sometimes they don't respond. The same can be true for earthly assistants who have been repeatedly called upon for favors!

When choosing allies, it's essential to consider the qualities and abilities that would be most advantageous. One should consider each ally's strengths and weaknesses. In turn, the alchemist must offer something in exchange for spiritual assistance. Contacting a spirit can start a lifelong partnership, so it's best to thoroughly scrutinize whom one chooses to connect with. To seek help, one may call on angelic beings, ascended spiritual masters, ancestors, or others with whom they feel a strong bond. GK offered sound advice when he warned,

> I can't stress strongly enough that any practitioner of magic should reject malevolent beings, such as greater or lesser daemons, poltergeists, crossroad dwellers, spirits of malice, spirits seeking revenge, or spirits of those who suffered traumatic deaths. Additionally, avoid contact with any supernatural being that requests living sacrifices. Form bonds only with those ethereal beings who are attentive to one's spiritual progress.

> There is a common fallacy that when someone has passed on to the other side, it means they are knowledgeable, wise, and all-seeing. This isn't true. Spirits tend to resemble the people they were in earthly life, possessing many of the same characteristics, flaws, and attitudes. The preferences, peculiarities, and idiosyncrasies they embodied in this physical realm accompany them into the afterlife. It is wise to gather information about the personal traits, faults, and interests of the spirit with whom one is considering connecting. Investigating whether those spirits possessed good character, were intelligent, generous, helpful, and whether they learned from their mistakes can be beneficial. Was there a bond between the seeker and the spirit in life that would make them more inclined to respond to a request? Did they contribute to society and provide sound counsel and guidance to others? Were they thoughtful and wise? These are all valid questions to consider, as the quality of one's allies will shape the merit of their magic.

In a summoning ritual, GK recommends that the aspirant provide suitable gifts to attract chosen advocates. For example, if one wants to collaborate with one of the most outstanding landscape photographers of all time, they might play Beethoven's Moonlight Sonata as an offering. Joseph-Nicéphore Niépce can be approached by offering heliographic substances such as objects made of pewter, bitumen of Judea, and silver chloride. Wine, preferably French, is also appreciated by Niépce. It's advised to research one's chosen advocates to discover what they may have liked when they were alive. Additionally, it would be helpful to include some firelight, such as lanterns or candles, with one's gifts as an offering to Ra.

When requesting the presence of supernatural beings, the alchemist should use names associated explicitly with each being. Religious historian Georges Gontenau highlights the importance of using a name in spellwork and invocation when he wrote,

> Since to know and pronounce the name of an object [or being] instantly endowed it with reality, and created power over it, and since the degree of knowledge and consequently of power was strengthened by the tone of voice in which the name was uttered, writing, which was a permanent record of the name, naturally contributed to this power, as did both drawing and sculpture, since both were a means of asserting knowledge of the object [or being] and consequently of exercising over it the power which knowledge gave (Contenau, 1955, 164).

"In many ways, a photographic portrait is like a subject's visual signature and, to some degree, also the photographer. Even with this being the case," GK maintains, "sometimes the spirit that arrives isn't the one that was called." The Byzantine Greek monk-philosopher Psellus wrote about these phenomena as he

> describes the apparitions procured by the Chaldaic rites…called superinspection, when he who celebrates the divine rites sees a mere apparition, as, for instance, of light in some form or figure, concerning which the oracle advises, that if anyone sees such a light, he apply not his mind to it, nor esteem the voice proceeding thence to be true; sometimes, likewise, to many initiated persons, there appear lights in various forms and figures. These apparitions are created by the passions of the soul, in performing divine rites, mere appearances, having no substance, and therefore not signifying anything true. Which vaporous estate of universal-being, the poets also fabulously concealed under the satiric form of Pan, who exhibited himself in every variety of atrocious disguises of wild beasts, and monsters, and demoniacal appearances, that he might affright those who would captivate him…For it is the imaginative spirit which is the maker of these images, as in dreams, only more intense (Atwood, 2005, 94).

Therefore, the language used for invocation should be as precise as possible. Additionally, other non-verbal languages can be utilized for rites and ritual invocations:

> Since art was language in Egypt", GK explains, "drawings and sculptures were imbued with verbal correlations. For example, I

have a photograph of my most cherished ally and ancestor, Abraham Kingwood, hanging in every room of my home. I also carry his name. For the Egyptians taught that a name, being essentially a word, is also a locus of power. In ancient times, names that were written on papyrus could only be handled by priestly experts familiar with the dangers of this power. This is why pharaohs possessed one secret name, and why their cartouches were essentially hieroglyphs bound by the magical power of a knotted rope (Modiano, 2017, 137).

GK suggests incorporating both spoken and visual language in rituals to enhance specificity, helping to prevent any confusion in the minds of the ritualist or those in the spirit world.

Third-century Neoplatonist philosopher *Iamblichus* wrote about his observations on the esoteric practices of the Egyptians in his manuscript, *On The Mysteries*. In it, one is encouraged to heed his wise remarks on methods, or "species" of prayer, for contacting a god. He said,

> that the first species of prayer is *collective*; and that it is also the leader of contact with, and a knowledge of, divinity. The *second* species is *the bond of concordant communion*, calling forth, prior to the energy of speech, the gifts imparted by the Gods, and perfecting the whole of our operations prior to our intellectual conceptions. And the third and most perfect species of prayer is *the seal of ineffable union with the divinities*, in whom it establishes all the power and authority of prayer; and thus causes the soul to repose in the Gods, as in a never failing port. But from these three terms, in which all the divine resources are contained, suppliant adoration not only conciliates to us the friendship of the Gods, but supernally extends to us three fruits, being as it were three Hesperian apples of gold. The *first* of these pertains to *illumination*; the *second*, to a *communion of operation*; but through the energy of the *third*, we receive *a perfect plenitude of divine fire*. And sometimes, indeed, supplication *precedes*; like a precursor preparing the way before the sacrifice appears. But sometimes it *intercedes as a mediator*; and *sometimes accomplishes the end of sacrificing*. No operation, however, in sacred concerns, can succeed without the intervention of prayer. Lastly, the continual exercise of prayer nourishes the vigor of our intellect, and renders the receptacles of the soul far more capacious for the communications of the Gods.

Gods, for the most part, are associated with prayers rather than invocations or spells. From GK's perspective, they are, in many ways, the same. Spells that are domineering and demanding, seeking to seize and restrain spirits, lie at the opposite end of the spectrum from spells or prayers that invite spirits, offer adoration, and make a respectful request for a cause. Spoken or written, they are all petitions to supernatural beings. Prayer, then, could be seen as a type of spell. Alchemist Basil Valentine wrote, "the mystery of all great things…shews how available Prayer is for the obtainment of things Spiritual and Eternal, as well as Corporal and perishing… and when Prayer is made with a Heart not feigned, but sincere; you will see that there is nothing more fit for the acquiring of what you desire" (Valentinus & Kerckring, 1675, 5).

Iamblichus went on to explain that prayer, as invocation, "is the divine key, which opens to men the penetralia of the Gods; accustoms us to the splendid rivers of supernal light; in a short time perfects our inmost recesses, and disposes them for the ineffable embrace and contact of the Gods; and does not desist till it raises us to the summit of all" (Taylor, 2018, 271-272).

GK illustrates further, "A prayer is in no way limited to the use of language, written or spoken." Photographer Harry Calahan once said, "a picture is like a prayer" (Coleman, 1976, 76). However, GK asserts that a picture isn't *like* or *equivalent* to a prayer. With intention, it *becomes* a prayer. It is the photographer who can make it so. Minor White made this realization, as evidenced when he said, "Spirit selects its own photographer. All we can do is to be open to Spirit" (White, 1964) and "…prayer uses the same energies that creativeness and photographing [do]" (White, 1942). Based on this knowledge, GK offers the guidance: "Whatever methods one uses to call their allies, I recommend that before one pulls on a filament, one had better know for sure what is on the other end!"

GK believes,

> My alchemical chariot is full of allies. Their likenesses are recorded in books, drawings, etchings, and photographs. They have accompanied me for much of my life, but when this life ends and the new one begins," GK trusts, "when I die, all these thousands of photographs and other images that are bound to my being will be scattered hither and thither across the world. Most of the portraits are not the faces of anyone in my ancestry. Of course, they are images of allies and gateways through which I perform the Great Work. In the hands of outsiders, these

likenesses will be nothing more than aged curiosities, prompts for the fancies of the viewer's imagination. Yet, wherever they go, they will follow my life force through the connections I have established with my magical efforts. Each sitter's story, which is inexorably intertwined with my own, will go on to expand their network of light filaments, perpetually creating their own new chapters. Who knows, in the future someone may reach through those ever-lengthening bonds of contact and call upon me to serve as their ally.

The relationship one establishes with allies is deeply personal and transactional. The alchemist makes offerings and does favors for allies. For instance, an ally may request support and assistance with issues that persist in the material plane, or they might need help in their incorporeal realm. For example, two ways that GK serves his spiritual allies are by establishing filament bonds that don't exist between people or things. Secondly, and much more frequently requested, is to extinguish destructive filaments that cause pain or keep them tethered to a place, person, or something they would rather be free from. "Severing filaments that connect to photographs is easy. There are some *surefire* ways to find success." GK clarifies, "The word, *surefire,* in itself describes how to break bonds."

When I first met GK, he burned a portrait of a young woman. Now, he shared with me why he had done so. "It was the last action in a magical process which destroyed a filament connection that had existed for over a hundred years." He looked up and said, "The bond is broken."

"Burning a photo and all its copies achieves compelling results for removing filament bonds. Forming or extinguishing filaments between people or spirits must be approached differently, with magical means." With the knowledge and ability to do so, GK becomes a valuable intermediary, representing this realm among the other realms of ethereal beings. Consequently, it is one of many ways GK can fulfill his allies' wishes, typically receiving their gratitude and willingness to assist him in his ventures.

Another type of ally invocation is described as *mediumship*, which was very popular throughout the 19th century. Oxford Languages defines medium as, "the intervening substance through which impressions are conveyed to the senses or a force acts on objects at a distance" (Define: Mediumship). In other words, instead of projecting a vessel of empyreal light in which a supernatural being will dwell, the ritualist uses their psychic abilities for conjuration and submits their consciousness-body as a container. If the human medium undergoes a telestic initiation, they may become the host for the god or goddess to whom they were ordained. The idea is like the way light-sensitive emulsion on film is commonly referred to as a medium. "Fitting the definition, distant light approaches and interacts with the silver halides in the emulsion, while its effects take up residence on the film. As a result," GK says, "the image speaks through the medium."

In human mediumship, a particular spirit is "channeled," establishing filament connections that allow it to possess the consciousness-body of the human host. The channeled spirit exerts a certain level of control over the medium's actions, especially their voice. In daily life, spirits are unable to speak due to their disembodied nature. However, they can utilize a medium's ability to vocalize in the material realm. Mediumship persists to this day, and from these practices has emerged a movement called "Spirit Art," where artists act as mediums, allowing supernatural beings to provide knowledge and creative inspiration for producing artwork.

Using clairvoyance, the medium channels the being or Divine Energy and responds by creating artwork through various creative disciplines, such as paint, clay, ink, or photography. The medium may also engage in automatic writing or dance. The resulting works become collaborative focal points for insights and inspiration. The intended recipients of the produced artworks could be the medium, an audience, or a specific individual. Creative works may also be designed for use in rituals or as centerpieces for meditation.

25. Motivation as Fuel for the Fire

The alchemist and the photographer share many similarities. For example, both are aesthetes who deeply appreciate art and beauty. They tend to be naturally curious, and both fields originate from a sincere sense of curiosity. They are explorers; they seek to answer the question: *what if?* However, like many noble pursuits, *the desire to know* has been overshadowed by *the urge to possess*. Ultimately, the study of alchemy became synonymous with greed, attracting seekers driven by promises of wealth. The pursuit of riches has been, and continues to be, common in the realm of photography. The English inventor of photography, William Henry Fox Talbot, aspired to wealth by selling the rights to his photographic process and promoted the craft as a lucrative career. To this day, few photographers would turn down an opportunity for their art to generate substantial income. How wonderful it would be to engage in what one loves most: transforming their talents and photographs into a fortune of cash—i.e., gold!

Historically, alchemists were regarded as being motivated by the desire for fame, not just in society or popular culture of their time, but within the ranks of fellow alchemists. Even today, some find great joy in receiving acclaim from those they consider skilled in the hermetic arts. Additionally, some photographers would admit that they seek a high level of recognition from their academic and artistic peers. It is a common aspiration among photographers to have their names mentioned alongside those of Diane Arbus, Man Ray, Cindy Sherman, and Paul Strand.

Another impulse for alchemistic users is the allure of gaining control over their lives and environments. The motivation for the Kingswoods has been to achieve spiritual elevation. While some alchemists have motives of power and control, some photographers also seek those same things through their actions. Philosopher Susan Sontag points out that,

> Photographs really are experience captured, and the camera is the ideal arm of consciousness in its acquisitive mood. To photograph is to appropriate the thing photographed. It means putting oneself into a certain relation to the world that feels like knowledge — and, therefore, like power...help people to take possession of space in which they are insecure... [and photography] is mainly a social rite, a defense against anxiety, and a tool of power (Sontag, 2001, 3-4).

Both paths possess a forceful and assertive quality. The alchemist and photographer deliberately impose their wills on their circumstances. The alchemist uses high magic to intentionally alter the natural course of events for personal gain, even if the actions are taken in service of the Great Work. Similarly, the photographer acts resolutely when they "take" photographs. GK posits, "Without consent or consideration, they propagate filaments of energetic light, attaching to subject and image, connected with purpose, while a piece of the subject matter is gathered, appropriated, and carried away. In their compositions, photographers also intentionally "conceal information by abstracting its subjects to an irreversibly two-dimensional plane, and by permitting the viewer access to only those facets deemed worthy by the photographer's flashlight' (Turner, 2012). Make no mistake, the motivated will of the alchemist, as well as that of the photographer, manifests as acts of power."

For the sincere alchemist and the authentic photographer, these identities are more than pastimes; they are ways of life. The labels they use describe not only what they do but also who they are. For instance, the words *"alchemy"* for an alchemist and *"photography"* for a photographer encapsulate everyone's unique worldview, with all their actions reinforcing those views. Every action they take expresses those labels. GK feels the significance of the term "alchemist" down to the finest genetic code of his being. He submits,

> The words people use to characterize themselves are many times partial truths. The distinctions and titles they attach to their names, which have always been a popular tradition among the English, are primarily used to influence how others perceive them. Being a bona fide alchemist or photographer is not something one performs only when it's most advantageous. These terms motivate and define who they are. These identities shape every thought and action in their lives.

Alchemists and photographers embrace the urge toward, "The conscious exercise of skill and creative imagination" (Define Artist). GK suggests that the divine impulse is common to both practices because they are sacerdotal# arts, inspiring a deeply felt need to bring something inspiriting into existence, something that has never been seen before. This could be an event or a material object, like a photograph. These artists derive pleasure and satisfaction from performing their art and achieving the desired result. Sometimes, they fail; at other times, the outcome is far more successful than anticipated…a happy accident!

26. THE ALCHEMISTICAL PHOTOGRAPHER-MAGICIAN

To understand the concept of the "Alchemystic Magician," GK feels it would be helpful to examine the first card in the Major Arcana of a traditional tarot deck, *The Magician*. This card, like the entire visual and artistic canon of the tarot, speaks through an archetypal system, a penumbral language. Much of the tarot's symbolism connects to the Western mystical tradition, which includes alchemical iconography. In their design, the cards feature patterns of visual imagery in the form of emblems that convey messages in a way that words alone cannot express. For example, "when the alchemist speaks of gods and goddesses, plants, animals, and astrological elements those connections do not necessarily refer to actual substances but to spiritual essence" (Edson, 2012, 223).

The Mercurial pictures created by an alchemist employ imagery in a similar manner. For instance, the compositions in the tarot are designed to generate meaning through the relationships between compositional elements deliberately. Those associations convey messages. The content resonates with those who are perceptive or intuitive enough to notice and gain an understanding.

Uninitiated viewers may see beautiful pictures in the arcana of the tarot. They might even connect with a card like the Magician, admiring its fascinating artwork, while its deeper meanings remain elusive. In this case, the viewer is hindered from engaging with esoteric pathways to humanity's highest aspirations. Conversely, someone like the analyst Carl Jung understood the imagery on the Magician card; for him, it embodied significant archetypal meaning. One of the most popular Magician cards is found in the well-known Rider-Waite-Coleman Smith deck (Figure 26.1). The standard image is filled with hidden knowledge, containing symbolism rooted in ancient Hermetic teachings that are central to the Western Mysteries. Hermetic occultist and author Israel Regardie wrote of the card:

> 1st KEY-THE MAGICIAN This is a young man, with the Caduceus on his chest vestments, facing the altar on which are the four elemental weapons...They are depicted here exactly as they are in the document describing the making of the four elemental weapons which have almost a universal application.

They not only represent the four suits of the Tarot, the four Worlds of the Kabalah, the four Beasts of the Apocalypse -the

Picture 26.1 The Magician.
From the Rider-Waite-Coleman Smith Tarot Deck, 1910.

four Kerubic signs - they represent the four letters of the Tetragammaton and so are the vice-regents of the Holy Name (Regardie, 1995, 132).

In Godfrey Dowson's Hermetic Tarot Deck, the equivalent Magician card is called *The Magus of Power*. It was designed in stark contrast to the traditional imagery of the Magician. In Dowson's card, the Magus is not a novice but is older, more experienced, and knowledgeable, symbolizing mastery over the wisdom of the ages. He is the authority over all magic, the adept who holds valuable lessons for all users of magic. A venerable teacher, he is sought by those on the path that leads to perfection in the Great Work. This noble and revered mage is an exemplar because he has achieved the goal of alchemy by transmuting the soul's scoria# of ignorance into the gleaming, golden perfection of gnosis.

GK slides the card toward me across the tabletop with his index finger and says:

> He stands within the camera obscura of the divine mysteries, his feet upon the Great Lens, a circle of protection. Surrounded by

The Magus of Power

> ritual implements, his right hand holds a scepter of dominion, proclaiming ultimate knowledge of the essence hidden in the elements. Pointing toward the universe, the magical scepter illuminates the scene, defining the space against the surrounding darkness. His left hand holds a scroll, which he points toward the

earth. It is the key to all the ancient Egyptian mysteries and confirms that he has internalized their secrets. His pose exudes a commanding presence that proclaims, 'as above, so below.' This position indicates that the magician, as alchemist, is aware of the complex network that binds all things together. He knows how to wield his own will over that network of empyreal light filaments, changing the destined course of events. The character understands that the creation and dissolution of filaments on both a cosmic and microscopic scale influence the ebb and flow of all natural and supernatural events.

The magician is engaged in the act of ritual invocation, making offerings of water, a flower, burning incense, and a lit candle to the divine mystery. As a result, an astral aperture opens. Emanating from its center, his ally appears in the form of Hermes-Mercury-Thoth. Above him is the winged Behdety#, a symbol associated with Ra and his emanation of

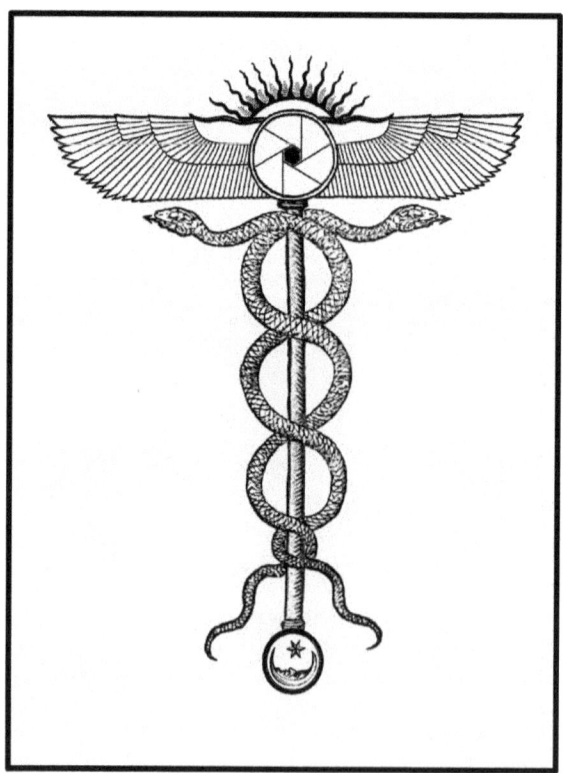

Picture 26.3 Kingswood's Caduceus. From George Kingswood's collection.

divine wisdom. Inside the solar circle is the alchemical symbol for mercury. The robed master wears a winged hat corresponding to the Behdety above, the top of the caduceus rod, and the winged boots of Hermes-Mercury.

"This is the most important card within the tarot collection," GK reveals as he lifts the card off the top of the deck and turns it to face me.

This image is the nexus point from which all other cards radiate and correspond. Here lies the universal archetype of the alchemist-magician, serving as the central node of connection where all points of place and time in the cosmos converge. This solitary subject exemplifies what alchemists aspire to become. The card is, in my opinion, a vessel of secrets, one of the gifts delivered by the Great Teacher of divine knowledge. It is up to the alchemist—or anyone for that matter—to respond as they wish to these gifts. Insightful understanding of the divine mysteries is an experiential vehicle that takes one nowhere unless it is guided by contemplation of its meaning.

One advances to the next level by applying the lessons learned. Anyone who resonates with the titles magician, alchemist, hermetic artist, or magus is continually ongrowing their sense of Sight. They aim to become skilled at discerning, interpreting, and applying divine knowledge. If such a theurgist also incorporates photography into their high art, they specifically seek the hidden wisdom of fire and light, the esoteric essences of Ra. For this is the only path to access the indescribable gems of wisdom that illuminate the ascent toward enlightenment and perfection.

The magician seeks completeness, compelled by the feeling of being pulled by the current of force moving through knowledge, flowing upward toward the divine artist. Thoughts of returning home evoke joyful emotions, creating a sense of coming full circle to the wondrous place where it all began. Sometimes, descriptions of alchemy and magic, even my own, may sound too down-to-business and joyless, as if the Work is merely a steep climb of endurance, sacrifice, pain, and will. That would be rather dreary, indeed! Nothing could be farther from the truth.

There is delight and pleasure in every moment of the Work. I live in a perpetual sense of awe! The Work offers a deep understanding of meaning and satisfaction that nothing in this mundane world can provide. Evolution, though sometimes painful, doesn't bring meaningless suffering. Instead, it offers rewards that far exceed those discomforts. If there may be a little discomposure# when Ra's brilliant rays burn away the unwanted emotional, psychological, and spiritual refuse, then let it be so, that the phoenix of the soul may rise from the ashes!

GK continues gazing off into space,

> The alchemist is a multi-dimensional traveler of the triple worlds: life in the terrestrial plane, the transcendent spiritual reality that interpenetrates this realm, and the otherworldly domain of the afterlife. On Earth, the alchemist's public life closely resembles that of anyone else. We have jobs, friends, and even families. Like everyone else, they are at the mercy of life's uncertainties. What sets the magician apart from the fumbling populace is that they don't fear unpredictability. They improve their odds when it comes to uncertainties. They take full responsibility for their situation and, with clarity, steer the direction of their lives in a very purposeful way.
>
> Alchemists leverage their knowledge. They utilize their magical abilities to stay on course, creating beauty from the truth found in the Great Work. The alchemist indeed lives in a world that others see as mundane. While those with Sight perceive it differently, viewing it as a realm filled with awe-inspiring marvels and mystifying wisdom, there is nothing mundane about it! The alchemist chooses to perceive the world in this way because, as it turns out, this perspective aligns more closely with the way things actually are.
>
> The source of wisdom and truth is the divine mystery. Although deep understanding is necessary for one to ascend the steps toward gnosis, success is impossible without Ra, who casts a guiding light over the mind, spirit, and the precipitous path. The ultimate goal is his illumination, where one's internal subtle flame moves toward its attraction to the divine flame, allowing one to inherit and actualize ageless wisdom.

Additionally, Franz Bardon states, "Wisdom does not depend on mind and memory but on the maturity, purity and perfection of the individual personality. Wisdom could also be considered as a developmental stage of the ego. Therefore, insights are not passed on through the mind, but – and this particularly – through intuition or inspiration. The degree of wisdom is therefore determined by the state of development of the individual" (Bardon, 1971, 26).

"It is the same impulse that leads the aspirant to the pyramidion," GK continued as he demonstrated by joining his thumbs and index fingers to form a triangle. "When the alchemist-photographer feels their attention seized by the puissant# impulse to make a photograph, it is the soul's need to reach through those darkening superfluities so it can unite with both the visible rays and unapparent empyrean light radiating from the source. And through the act of capture, made possible with awareness and intention, taking a photograph contributes to the ecstatic purification of the photographer's indwelling spirit."

Artist Eric Kim acknowledges the photographer's sense of immediacy when the soul's light resonates with a captivating composition.

> You know the feeling. You see a person, a scene, or some light— and you feel this urge in your chest to make a photograph. You can't explain it. It doesn't come from any rational part of your brain. It just seizes you — like a ship being seized by a massive wave. The feeling is from another world. I am starting to see photography more like a spiritual act. Photography is about finding beauty in the world— through either natural or man-made objects. Photography is about finding more gratitude in the world. Realizing that anything can be beautiful — if we just look closely enough. We need to listen to our photographic impulse. This is where all creativity comes from. To ignore your photographic impulse is like a small death. It is when you betray your artistic self. To not make a photograph when you feel so compelled to is almost like choking yourself. You cannot breathe without making that photograph" (Kim, 2017).

GK rejoins, "Life, death, and light make up a single interconnected enigma that neither the alchemist nor the photographer can turn away from. Since the mystery lives through them, even in death, in such a way that its penetrating calls for evolution and liberation—which stir the eyes to open—simply can't go unseen or unheard."

Lapis

27. The Alchemist's Camera — The Dark Room Temple

The Camera Obscura and the Camera Lucida are the oldest ancestors of the camera's family tree. From that root appeared the Solar Megascope (1780), the Physionotrace, and the Graphic Telescope (1812). Some of the first generations of photographic devices followed: the Agatograph, Diagraph, Hyalograph, Quarreograph, Pronopiograph, and the Eugraph. Additionally, there were the Graphic Mirror, the Periscope Camera, the Meniscus Prism, the Universal Parallel, Panoramas, the Eidophysikon, and the Phantasmagorias (Scharf, 1975, 11). Abraham Kingswood built a simple view-camera to accommodate the accessories of ground glass, bellows, film backs, and a lens he purchased from France.

The component that made the modern camera so capable was its lens. The glass provided a high level of sharpness and clarity while also offering options for depth of field. The ancient Egyptians are credited with the invention and development of lenses, but it was the ancient Greeks who advanced theories on light, vision, and optics. Their research furthered the evolution and production of more refined camera lenses.

Picture 27.1 Turn-of-the-century view camera. Picture by Frédéric Dillaye, 1907.

The word *optics* was coined to define the study of lenses, originating from the ancient Greek term meaning *sight*, *seen*, or *visible* (Define: Optic). Additionally, the word "*focus*" entered the photographic lexicon. The word was used, "in post-classical times for 'fire' itself; taken by

Kepler (1604) in a mathematical sense for 'point of convergence,' perhaps on analogy of the burning point of a lens" (Define: Focus). The first cameras and their predecessors are products of ancient discoveries, many of which stem from alchemy. GK tells, "Since its invention, the camera has been a compelling apparatus, designed to replicate the attentive projection of the photographer's retinal image. As an impartial instrument, it is neither inherently good nor bad. In any photographer's hands, a camera can be a machine used to help or harm."

In the hands of James Nachtwey, the camera shines a light on social injustice and atrocities around the world. As a result, he gains allies in the fight for justice for these causes. In the hands of an unscrupulous predator, the camera can be used to exploit, demean, and damage the fundamental human dignity of others. GK adds, "For my purposes, the camera is a vehicle of magic that, when used to focus its burning point, ignites the ignescent# imagination! In the context of alchemy, it serves as a consecrated instrument for the most exalted purposes."

The 35mm camera is a perfect device for magical practices on several levels. First, one notices the quality of its physical shape, a hexahedron. The camera body is a compact representation of a box form whose four base points symbolize the alchemical elements: earth, fire, water, and air. Its six sides represent a force of balance among the elements. Additionally, six is the number of all heavenly bodies known as "suns" and is regarded as the number of ultimate creativity since the Bible (Genesis 1:31) states that man was created on the sixth day.

GK continues,

> The camera is a powerful tool, well-suited to manifest one's inner experiences as a tangible artifact. As mentioned previously, the observant alchemist uses a photograph as a window through which they can see far beyond the superficial interpretations provided by the uninitiated. They achieve this by delving deeply into the representations of experiential complexities. An alchemist can honestly examine a photograph and perceive the subject matter uniquely, from angles that aren't accessible to the average photographer or the lay viewer. They can identify profound dimensions of meaning that aren't comprehensible to most people whose perspectives are narrowly confined to this physical reality.

As Steven D. Foster noted,

Making photographs is for me a way of interiorizing the world, a way of "listening." Through intuition I see the things of the world as photographic images with potential symbolic meaning. Once the vision has been given pictorial form, I can then contemplate the image and begin to unveil its hidden treasures … The practice of contemplation is a kind of intuitive, imaginative, meditative journeying into both the symbol and us simultaneously. It requires of us a highly active, conscious state of one-pointed attention in which we interiorize an image such that we can "see" it or imagine it through the eyes of the heart. When we are in our heart, the very center of our soul, we are in the Silent World. (Foster, 2010).

For example, GK decided to show me how a photograph is more than what most perceive. In the parlor, we stood face-to-face, about three feet apart. GK centered himself. He closed his eyes, and I felt a stillness envelop the room's atmosphere. He lifted an old photograph between us,

Picture 27.2 The Pyramids of El-Geezeh, from the Southwest
by Francis Firth, 1857.

blocking my view of his face. The composition I saw was taken in landscape orientation. A finger and thumb pinched their hold on the aged margins on each of the short sides of the print. The picture depicted a desert landscape with four Egyptian pyramids. A few people and a horse appeared in the foreground to convey a sense of scale to the enormity of the forms. The print was an original Francis Frith photograph from the mid-19th century.

When I looked into the scene, it seemed to morph into a summertime image of my childhood home, like a portal opening to a different landscape beyond the print's surface. Everything looked as I remembered it! Surrounding the print was a halo of light. The photograph had somehow transformed into a window opening onto the depths of a memory. The tonality remained faithful to its original monochrome presentation, yet its sense of detail was extraordinarily sharp. As I moved closer to peer inside the threshold, the photograph reverted to its original Egyptian scene.

I was dumbstruck! It was uncanny! My rational mind raced to find an explanation for what had just happened. Did the photograph change before my eyes? Or was my perception of the artifact somehow influenced by whatever was occurring in this situation, like hypnosis or mesmerization? Was it an illusion, the retrieval of a memory, or some mystification? Was I dreaming? I asked GK about what had just occurred, seeking a logical explanation so everything would make sense. Yet, this man, who was always enthusiastic about providing thorough responses to questions, was uncharacteristically silent on this matter for the rest of the day.

I brought up the subject again a couple of days later. GK said,

> Photographs relate to the photographer's recent experiences, while also having the capacity to awaken the viewer's distant memories. The viewer's knowledge can be overwhelmed by dream-like imagery that displaces the immediate encounter of viewing a photograph. It's as though all of one's attention shifts toward a photo album opened in the mind. This is what happened to you, and for a moment, all your thoughts ceased racing, and your mind became still as you fell into a memory.

> The only question that has merit is self-reflexive. Like, 'What did this experience teach me about who and what I am?' You ask me for information that will help explain your experience, but you must realize that it's hard for me to communicate your perception because it's very different from my reality. It is difficult for me to see the world as you do, just as you cannot see the world through my eyes. As great-grandfather Abraham used to say, 'The eyes can never be forced to see things as they are, because one always has the freedom to look away from the light. Or close their lids.'

For Minor White, "the photograph was a 'mirage' and the camera was a 'metamorphosing machine'" (Photopedia, 2021). "White's purpose for photography," claims GK, "was to transmute ideas into shapes and patterns of light, bringing them into this physical reality as both a contemplative act and as artifacts used for inward reflection. His use of the camera for his creative-spiritual activities, which the alchemists call *projection*, sought to transform his perception of the world, aligning it with his spiritual vision. This world was physically manifested as compositions of the divine mystery's empyrean light energy."

White, who seems to have an affinity for alchemy, viewed the camera as a sacred instrument of creation. For Ra's adherents, it represents a profound and hallowed architectural structure, understood to be a temple topped with a lustrous silver or black pyramidion, akin to a viewfinder prism. GK states, "Regardless of the kind of camera one uses, when it is consecrated to the god of light, an aspect of the god dwells within. The alchemist causes the miniature *temple of light* to take on new meaning and purpose, as a nexus point where the aspirant and Ra can commune and perform acts of wonder among the four elements."

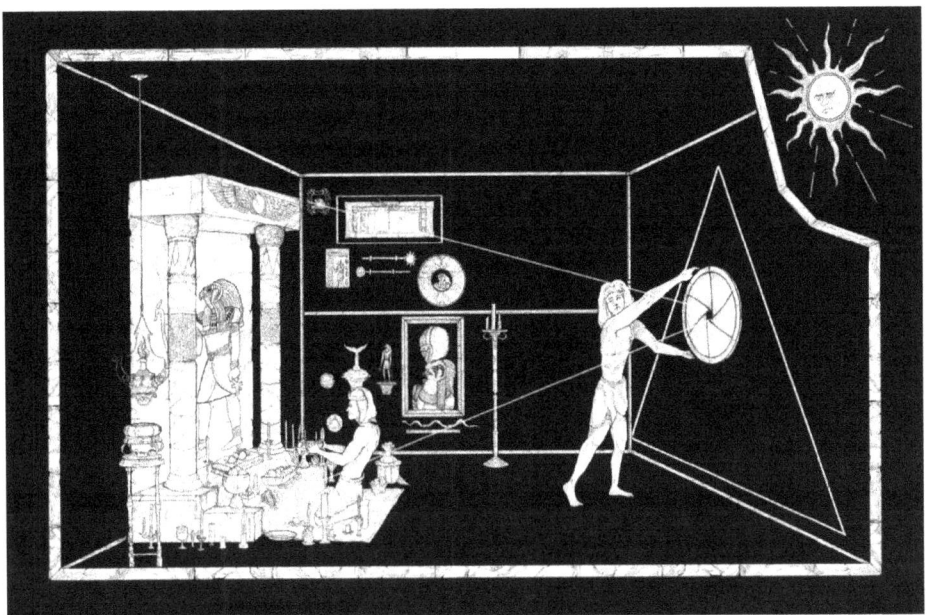

Picture 27.3 The Egyptian Camera Obscura Temple, courtesy of Enes Gücük, 2023.

Delving deeper into the relationship between the four elements and the camera reveals it as a creative tool for experiencing the earth. As such, it reflects aspects of the earth element. The camera body is composed of both common and rare-earth metals. At one time, they even used mercury to make their mirrors reflective. This practice ceased in the 1840s. Nonetheless, a magical correspondence remains between the quicksilver mirrors and the more recent, highly reflective convex mirrors used in SLR cameras. When the photographer holds the camera, its body connects with the human body, functioning as an appendage. The two bodies work in unison to create images. When on a tripod, the camera sits at the apex of a sacred tetrahedron, anchored to the earth.

Picture 27.4 The Camera Temple, courtesy of Lee Cushard, 2024.

The *fire* element manifests in the camera as latent energy derived from the fiery construction of its frame and lenses. GK points out, "The camera could never exist without fire." The metals in the camera were all forged in fire. The lenses of the camera are made by heating sand (silicon dioxide) in a furnace. At temperatures exceeding 3000 degrees Fahrenheit, the silica transforms into a molten liquid. As the substance cools, it solidifies into glass. Another example of fire as an elemental component of the camera is its design to receive and capture light, an expression and extension of the fiery source, the sun. The lenses guide the light into a portal, through the aperture, and into a chamber of darkness where the film anticipates exposure's flame.

The *water* element is reflected in all the glass components of the camera, including the lenses. While glass shares characteristics of a solid, it is a liquid in a frozen state, like ice. The features of its liquid and random molecular structure allow it to be poured into slabs, cut into disks, ground, shaped, and polished into its final concave or convex lens form. Over an extended period, the structure of the glass changes as it slowly flows, succumbing to gravitational forces.

The element of air manifests as the intangible energy of thoughts, atmospheric emotions, and immaterial visualizations. It is a focal point where the alchemist's intentions mix with divine energies, interpenetrating the camera's inner chamber. Ansel Adams once said that "Visualization is the single most important factor in photography" (Adams Adams Gallery, 2020). Visualization takes place in the minds of both the alchemist and the photographer. It is where they envision the resulting photograph even before it is captured. Hidden from the curious eye, a mental, immaterial intention translates into a tangible object. This all occurs inside the camera, where the welcoming atmosphere of air gives shape to thought and light. The air element collaborates with the other elements to manifest material artifacts … crystalline, silver halide images and paper.

All the elements co-mingle around the inner sanctum of the camera's chamber of anticipation, the locus terra. It's the point on earth where all the elements perform in harmony to give birth to those objets d'art made in their creator's image—born from their creator's imagination. It is the womb in which light penetrates the dark potential to awaken life in the moon's metal. GK lifted a Hasselblad camera from a black, boxy case and turned it to reveal a line of Latin words etched on its body. "I have inscribed on all my cameras the fiat, Ego Video Esse, or I see it into being. It is the fertile space of the air element in which the mind, light energy, and divine sanction collaborate in the act of creation.

Occultus

28. An Ancient & Everlasting Magic

The term *magic* originates from the name of the ancient Zoroastrian priests who tended the eternal flame. These priests were known as *magi*. The ethereal energy that fueled the eternal flame was thus referred to as *magic*. To the Egyptians, the radiant force was *heka*.

Picture 28.1 A Zoroastrian priest reads from a book while performing a Sacrifice, by Bernard Picart (1673–1733).

Another word for magic as the power of god and connected with heka is *akhw*. This idiom covers the performative character of heka, mainly in the form of verbalized spells. Heka is said to have existed prior to the first moments of creation, empowering the whole process. Therefore, this magic could be seen as one of the creator gods. Another explanation is that heka as power or concept was conceived by the creator god's heart at the beginning of time, enabling him to start the creation process (Ritner, 1993, 192). Heka appeared even before the creative word *Hu*, the first creation of *Re-Atum* [Ra], the creator god; therefore magic was already in the world when the gods and the cosmos were shaped (Zinn, 2012, 31).

In a text known as the *Instruction for Merikara*, which may have been written as early as 2000 BC, heka is described as a gift from the creator to humanity 'to ward off the blows of fate" (Pinch, 1994, 47). The predominant belief was that in an ethereal realm, "The gods, the pharaoh, and the deceased were the three most highly active sources of heka" (Edson, 2012, 159). In the earthly realm of Egyptian civilization, magicians were involved in an array of activities relating to all aspects of life. They were often called upon to deal with supernatural beings "from major deities and their emanations or messengers, to creatures of the underworld, from demons, and malicious ghosts" (Pinch, 2006, p. 47) ...Magic and mysticism had a particularly important role at the time of death (Cavalli, 2016, 59).

Egyptians incorporated heka as a practice for both life and death. It was invoked for its transformative potential, including the process of mummification.

There is etymological evidence specifically linking alchemy with mummification. In any case, it seems clear that taking something as 'corrupt' as a corpse and transforming it into an eternal home for the soul is, by any definition, an alchemical procedure ...Herbs, oils, and ointments were used for ritualistic purposes to help in this transition; small talismans and amulets were folded into the mummy bandages for protection and help in the afterlife...magical spells, instructions, rituals, and maps were provided to help guide the deceased through the underworld (duat) (Cavalli, 2016, 59).

Furthermore, Egyptologist Edmund Meltzer claimed that "transmutation of the body in mummification was a prototypical alchemical act" (Cheak, 2013, 82).

Photographer Hollis Frampton suggests that photography has become a modern metaphorical and, at times, physical equivalent of mummification, in which

the process of photographic representation amounts to a preservation or embalming process. The lost presence of the photographed thing, person, situation is invoked through a mummified echo, reduced to a husk of the light that once revealed it. The photographic likeness bears a distant, partial, decolorized or muted resemblance to its subject; at the same time, it has unique qualities of its own, which are entirely independent of what it depicts" (Lin, 2015).

"And like mummification," said GK,

There is a corresponding use of *solve et coagula* in which one form dissolves so that a new form may arise. For example, the same scene can never be photographed twice. This is because, from instant to instant, the scene changes, and so does the photographer. All things are mutable in the flowing current of time. After the shutter fires, the original scene dissolves into light and becomes reformed. It's embedded as the image on the surface of the film. That imagery undergoes a process of preservation, akin to mummification, within the film's emulsion. And like mummification, that image tells the enduring story of its indweller. Those who take the time to photologically "unwrap" the subject matter that has *re-arisen* from light will be rewarded with stories about the subject, the photographer, and the viewer.

Nearly five thousand years after the first mummies were entombed, photographer François Arago traveled to Egypt to gather his gems of knowledge in the form of photographs. He claimed, "No other kind of relic or text from the past can offer such a direct testimony about the world which surrounded other people at other times" (Berger, 2008, 10). On November 7, 1839, Arago captured the first photograph in Egypt, depicting the *Ras El Tin Palace.* Shortly after, he began exhibiting his work in France. "During that time, in the Victorian era," GK pointed out, "alchemist Éliphas Lévi took an interest in acquiring treasures that came out of Egypt, including Arago's photos and Napoleon's publications, *Description de l'Égypte.*"

Lévi's interest in the relics of antiquity was rooted in his studies of the history and spread of magic. In his book, *Dogme et Rituel de la Haute Magie*, Lévi emphatically averred,

> There was and there still is a potent and real Magic; all that is said of it in legend is true after a certain manner, yet – contrary to the common course of popular exaggeration – it falls below the truth. There is indeed a formidable secret, the revelation of which has once already transformed the world, as testified in Egyptian religious tradition, summarized symbolically by Moses at the beginning of Genesis…They are terms which must be understood in their proper sense; they formulate the varied applications of one and the same secret, the several aspects of a single operation, which is defined in a more comprehensive manner under the name of the Great Work (Lévi, 1896, x-xi).

Lévi was an educated man and a student of classical philosophy. In his studies, he learned about the priestly heka of Egypt. He became obsessed with archaic knowledge of the esoteric mysteries. The author of more than twenty books on occultism, he explained, there exists in Nature a force which is immeasurably more powerful than steam, and a single man, who is able to adapt and direct it, might change thereby the face of the whole world. This force was known to the ancients; it consists in a Universal Agent having equilibrium for its supreme law, while its direction is concerned immediately with the Great Arcanum of Transcendental Magic (Lévi, 1896, 6-8).

As part of his practice, he discovered that while the natural forces of magic could be used for good or ill, they were, in and of themselves, morally and ethically neutral.

Parapsychologist Dean Radin says,

Real magic falls into three categories: mental influence of the physical world, perception of events distant in space or time, and interactions with nonphysical entities. The first type I'll call force of will; it's associated with spell-casting and other techniques meant to intentionally influence events or actions. The second is divination; it's associated with practices such as reading Tarot cards and mirror-gazing. The third is theurgy, from the Greek meaning 'god-work'; it involves methods for evoking and communicating with spirits (Radin, 2018, p1).

Radin's definition captures the type of magic that alchemists, such as the Kingswoods, have employed in their life-transmuting practices.

Though belief in spirits isn't required for traditional, laboratory-based alchemy, it is part of the fundamental belief system for practitioners of magic. GK explains that "Regarding magical energies, supernatural beings, and gods, there is a common belief in a metaphysical ecosystem. I attest that each novice must seek supernatural experiences for themselves, using their abilities to cast spells, conjure spirits, and partake in the performance art of ritual." Many occultists believe in the existence of an active universal force of nature. Some see it as the same force that Christian, Jewish, and Islamic alchemists would refer to as god. From that perspective, any rituals conducted as part of one's practice would aim to invite the attention of their god(s). The ritualists become the performers, while each god is a singular, heavenly audience.

GK elaborates.

Ritual is the highest and most illustrious form of performance art! It is a spectacle, a production aimed at the highest of beholders, the all-powerful god of eternal light! While theater presents to a passive audience, ritual engages its audience in action! To elicit an active response, the four elements should be intentionally prepared to coordinate in the demonstration of the high magic ritual. A mysterious atmosphere or dramatic mood of theatricality should be established. It becomes not only an ethos but also a unique *mise-en-scène* characteristic of the hermetic arts.

Mise-en-scène refers to the design of a ritual space that emphasizes the alchemist's position of ascendancy. It creates a sense of ambiance where the rites are performed. "Designing and exploiting mise-en-scène are basic to the art of production…props, costumes and lighting make up the visual substance of the world in which we set…our story. They constitute the reality that we conjure for our empyrean gathering" (Douglass, 1996, 119).

Mise-en-scène also incorporates other qualities, such as how the space almost becomes a living being or character that mirrors the alchemist and their magical intention. This is achieved through the drama of lighting, the intentional placement of the Grand Circle of Evocations in relation to the overall space, the ceremonial attire of the magus, and the way all these separate components come together to establish a specific aesthetic context. All elements unified by purpose create an atmosphere of "beyondness" or "otherworldliness." Such attention to the environment enhances its evocative potential, creating a magical frame of mind for the ritualist.

A good example of mise-en-scène is the photography darkroom. When one goes through the light-safe portal, they leave the outer world and enter a cave-like, sequestered environment. There is a shift in sensory stimuli. One's awareness transitions into a strikingly different setting. It's like going from noon to midnight in an instant. The dramatic, twilight ambiance heightens the senses. One's pupils adjust to the dimness of the amber-red scene. The air fills with the sharp vapors of the stop bath. There is the sound of trickling water from the wash basin. The space is charged with an energized sense of expectation.

Additionally, the inscrutable setting creates its own sense of time. Hours seem like minutes during the ritual activity of printmaking. The outside world disappears as one focuses their attention on willing the trapped light in a negative to appear on the print. As a result, all these sensual qualities of the mise-en-scène support the photographer's intentions during image-making.

"When skillfully executed," adds GK,

> mise-en-scène awakens something primeval in the perceiver. For instance, the darkroom environment harkens back to a time when our ancient ancestors lived in the sanctuary of their shadowy caves, where they used red and black pigments to depict visionary images of animals. With firelight and ritual intention, those creatures, skillfully executed on soot-blackened walls, came alive to offer their corporeal flesh to their hunters. In our collective unconscious, there exists a connection between the ambiance of the cave and the darkroom, where artisans must access the darkness to create with light.

Picture 28.2 Turn of the Century Darkroom by Frédéric Dillaye, 1907.

Oliver Wendell Holmes evokes the unique mise-en-scène of the darkroom experience when he writes,

> Then we replace the slide in the shield, draw this out of the camera, and carry it back into the shadowy realm where Coeytus flows in black nitrate of silver and Acheron stagnates in the pool of hyposulphite, and invisible ghosts, trooping down from the world of day, cross a Styx of dissolved sulphate of iron, and appear before the Khadamanthus of that lurid Hades. Such a ghost we hold imprisoned in the shield we have just brought from the camera (Holmes, 1864, 4-5).

"When that 'imprisoned ghost' is released from Holmes' darkroom as an act of creation, it goes back out into the world as a talismanic object," GK reveals.

> The force of intention focused during processing makes those activities magical acts within the context of the alchemist's darkroom. This sensory impact illustrates how mise-en-scène can facilitate worldly changes that extend beyond the site, reaching beyond the alchemist's physical and magical context. The atmosphere also transports the ritualist's mind to another place, another dimension of consciousness.

> All the elements of ritual work together to enhance one's extrasensory sensitivity. However, spiritual experiences that alter the ritualist's consciousness can vary depending on the type of magic employed. For instance, Hermetic magic differs significantly from shamanic magic. Enochian magic produces different experiences from witchcraft. Even within Western mystical traditions, there are numerous ways to perform rituals. Each method depends on the administrator's goals and desired outcomes.

Significant rituals require the Grand Circle of Invocation, but other rituals may only need visualization, driven by a well-defined intention. There are also daily rituals used to maintain contact with allies. Some rituals are intended to offer or sanctify meals. For GK, specific rituals are designed for photographing, film processing, printing, and all activities related to making prints. Additionally, other rituals are associated with the laboratory and are tailored to the creation of photochemistry as well as the formulation and production of unique ingestible elixirs and tinctures.

> He that would seek Tincture most specious
> Must needly avoid all things wild and vicious.
> The philosopher's worke does not begin
> Till all things be pure without and within
> (Atwood, 2005, 215).

The laboratory aspect of alchemy involves formulating elixirs to enhance spiritual practices. GK clarifies that, "The purpose of the elixirs is twofold. First, they are broadly defined as curatives for perception-degrading hallucinations the alchemist suffers while trying to navigate this reality. Secondly, they accelerate one's evolutionary process. The formulas for the chemical and spiritual amalgams take advantage of each ingredient's distinctive physical and metaphysical properties." During this conversation, he removed the cap from a small glass bottle containing less than a teaspoon of amber-colored fluid. He lifted the vessel to his lips, tilted his head back, and drank its contents.

> To anyone else, this would be a deadly toxin. Yet for me, small amounts can yield profound psycho-spiritual benefits. Most elixirs have benign effects on the body, although some formulations I devise are poison — from an ordinary perspective. Elixirs are essential, supplementary agents for my practices. Some of my mixtures even require ingredients like photographs or negatives that have been distilled to their elemental essences. Some recipes ask for the ashes of burned prints, including one I am currently developing. Susan Sontag once said that 'Images consume reality', but in my alchemical practice, it is the other way around!

The alchemist's use of harmful substances doesn't surprise me. It reminded me of a conversation I had with Shelby Lee Adams in 2009. The celebrated photographer began photographing members of the Appalachian Holiness Pentecostal Church in 1983. Members of the congregation drank strychnine not only to prove their piety but also to strengthen their faith in God. They received the instruction to do so from the Bible's Gospel of Mark 16: 17-18, "In my name they will drive out demons; they will speak in new tongues; they will pick up snakes with their hands; and when they drink deadly poison, it will not hurt them at all." This religious practice is said to be transformative for the devout. By participating in it, one's soul is uplifted, exalted, and brought closer to one's creator. For others, drinking the substance would kill them.

GK's operations exemplify a long-standing convention in laboratory alchemy involving the ingestion of chemical substances, potable metals, written spells or prayers, and imagery. Sixteenth-century philosopher Paracelsus stated: "Of all Elixirs, Gold is supreme and the most important for us... gold can keep the body indestructible... Drinkable gold will cure all illnesses, it renews and restores" (Paracelsus, 1988, 320). Contemporary alchemist Rubaphilos Salfluĕre explains in an interview, "Potable Gold is the next best thing to *Elixir Vitae*, or the elixir of life. It's a rejuvenative but it also alters the mind, like all of these [alchemical] preparations do. If they are made properly, they take you into an altered state. And it's not the kind of altered state that you would experience from taking recreational drugs" (Kaminsky, 2013, MS17). GK claims that his practice "Prepares the vistiment of body and spirit for the ordeals of the Great Work." He also burns, he dissolves, shreds, and even powderizes photographs to make them consumable.

Similar consumption practices exist in both Islam and Christianity.

> There are many…instances worldwide in which people drink or swallow sacred texts…religious artifacts and devotional objects for pilgrimages used to offer "*Schluckbildchen*": sheets of postage-stamp sized prints, mostly depicting Mary. These prints had to be blessed and then swallowed…Early mentions of drinking the Quran from around the turn of the 20th century firmly place the practice in the realm of "folk Islam" or "magical practices"…The most popular and powerful verse for use in amulets and drinking is the "Throne verse" (2:255) (Wilkins, 2013, 244-246).

A biblical line is written on a piece of paper that is placed in water. As the ink dissolves, the script dissolves. Then, the water is sipped until it is gone. The words become intermixed with the believer's entire being.

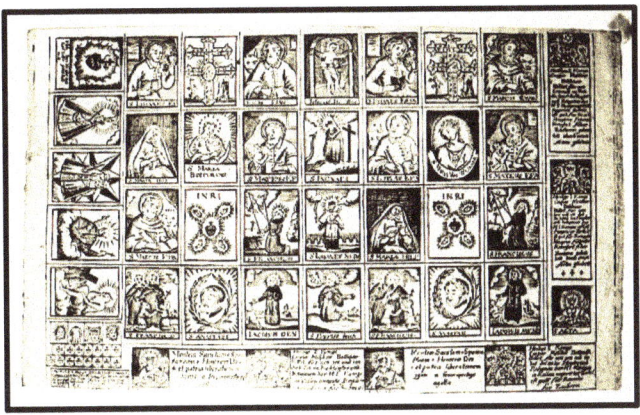

Picture 28.3 Schluckbildchen, 1780.

There is also a method for assimilating mentally fabricated pictures. In his practice, GK installs or embeds telesmic images into the core of elixirs. In the visionary projections, Ra can appear standing, sitting, or walking, or he might appear as a brilliant red disk of light.

> This powerful visionary ingredient catalyzes a transubstantiation of the commixtion's# chemical components. It activates the spiritual properties of the elixir, endowing it with magical properties. Without embedding this deific, miraculous essence, the decoctions would most likely be harmful, even to me.

One thing I must bring to the fore," injected GK.

> Ordinary people should not attempt these practices. Again, some of these ingredients and processes are noxious and can cause serious side effects, even death. One time, I imbibed an elixir and suffered physical blindness for nine days as a result. I knew this would happen and was also aware that a penetrating, supernatural sense of vision would awaken as the outcome. On the tenth day, my eyes were restored, and their sight was integrated into the new Sight, producing a heightened sense of awareness. This was the purpose of the elixir. Now, I can see the world in its multiple dimensions—simultaneously as it appears and as it truly is. For someone who lacks divine preservation, magic, and allies, they surely would have lost all forms of sight.

Personal, magical, and artistic transformation can also be fostered through the consumption of radiant light energies from physical artifacts. In this practice, the alchemist absorbs unseen forces directly from objects that exist in the material world. It's similar to how spirits and deities partake in the energies produced by making offerings. GK, for example, can absorb the vital power that emanates from masterful and spiritual artworks. It is an empyrean light energy that travels through corresponding filaments, from divine inspiration, through the artist's hand, to the artwork, and into the ritualist. The Alchemist-Adept Rudi (Swami Rudrananda) was able to absorb the radiant energy from ancient, handmade artworks. He could then transmute that power into extraordinary self-transformative abilities (Mann, 1987).

While sitting across from GK in the Kingswood drawing room, I noticed him glance to my left at an ornate painting of Ra:

> When one engages energetically with an artwork, they discern the natural animating forces that are the same energy from which magic is composed. Photo-Alchemists absorb the radiant yet invisible firelight that comes through art via a kind of photovoltaic# effect to gather the energy needed to launch profitable magic. What one consumes is transformed through the body's fires, converting into usable energy and manifesting as actions and living flesh. There is no way to create energy; one can either receive it from a source or utilize it through action. Alternatively, one can transfer energy from a thought or an emotion to an intended recipient.

29. Protection from Friends and Enemies

In our human realm, malicious forces are at play for all of us. Everyone has enemies, no matter who they are or where they live. Harmful, chaotic energies in the universe also impact every person alive. It's unavoidable. In this 21st century, like in all other times, life gives rise to murderous insanity, disease, war, terrorism, and violent political and religious divisions. Like all things in nature, these energies flourish and are compelled to survive and reproduce. They seek connection with others so they can multiply their impact. Their very existence attracts those entities that dwell as phantoms, specters, shades, and demons. Such tormented spirits feed on the dark, negative energies emanating from unfortunate, tormented life forms. All these beings play their parts in an ecosystem perpetuated by fear and venomous anger.

GK indicates that,

> Though the veil between life and death is a barrier that prevents the transfer of material substance from one realm to another, all the malignant energies that humanity propagates flow freely into the ethereal realm, where they thrive. The tormented spirits of those who lived lives filled with anguish and suffering—those consumed by overwhelming hatred, anger, resentment, and violence—naturally carry these states of being with them into death. This is precisely why one casts a circle of protection when working with spirits. When summoning an ally by name, it's like calling out across a far-reaching crowd. One's ally may respond, but so might a hostile visitant. Therefore, it's essential for the thaumaturge to be prepared and protected, even in daily activities, when operating outside a circle of protection.

GK recounts an anecdote about one of his father's close friends, Charles. This gentleman was a novice alchemist who, one evening, had to attend a meeting in Southwark, a notably dangerous area of London. It was a place most people avoided at night, and Charles felt very uneasy about going there. To help reassure his friend, GK performed a protection spell to ward off various dangers.

As the late afternoon light faded into the setting sun, Charles arrived at his destination without incident. However, it wasn't long after his meeting that he faced a "dodgy encounter" on the street. He was confronted by an aggressive, intoxicated man. Though afraid, Charles trusted George's ability to gather forces that would protect him. The drunk man continued to harass and threaten as Charles quickened his pace along the cobblestone street. The situation escalated when the drunk man hurled a liquor bottle against a brick wall beside the fleeing Charles.

Picture 29.1 Circle of Protection with unfriendly spirits, 1715.

The bottle shattered on impact, sending shards of glass onto the right side of Charles's face. In the end, he escaped with only a few cuts and a bloodied collar.

The next day, GK was visited by Charles, who showed up very agitated. Charles was upset that the protection spell hadn't worked and couldn't understand how such a thing could have happened to him when he was supposed to be safeguarded. The alchemist consoled his friend, explaining that the spell had, in fact, worked. Furthermore, GK told Charles that he couldn't imagine the tragedy that would have occurred had he gone there without the protection spell. Charles was speechless; he hadn't considered the alchemist's viewpoint on his unfortunate encounter. He paused to think about the possibility that the protecting spirits were indeed there. In a state of panic, he believed he was alone and helpless, doubting that there were forces acting on his behalf. In hindsight, Charles realized that what George had said was true: he had been protected from the moment he left the Kingswood house.

GK emphasizes that "Protection magic is unfortunately necessary."

> Harm to our beings can come in myriad forms, from both friends and enemies. It has been said that no one can hurt us more than those we love. For instance, Mercurius, beloved friend to all alchemists, defines the parameters within which his relationships with alchemists must adhere to. He stated, "Know this: I, Mercurius, have here set down a full, true and infallible account of the Great Work. But I give you fair warning that unless you seek the true philosophical gold and not the gold of the vulgar, unless you heart is fixed with unbending intent on the true Stone of the Philosophers, unless you are steadfast in your quest, abiding by God's laws in all faith and humility and eschewing all vanity, conceit, falsehood, intemperance, pride, lust and faint-heartedness, read no farther lest I prove fatal to you…Obey me and I will be your servant; free me and I will be your friend. Enslave me and I am a dangerous enemy; command me and I will make you mad; give me life and you will die" (Harpur, 2008, 17).

Most of the time, malefic energies don't come from outside forces; they arise from within oneself. For instance, a significant difference between the Harry Potter world of magic and our own is that the pain one suffers daily rarely comes from black magic or sinister enemies; it comes from one's own mind. The Alchemist fully utilizes magic to protect themselves from the parts of their mind that are mean, resentful, angry, cruel, selfish, filled with shame, judgmental, ungenerous, and generally very unhappy.

Emotions manifest as specific forms of psychological and bodily energy," GK maintains.

> They mix with, influence, and shape the energy we gather in our magical work. One can imagine, even without being an alchemist, that humility, kindness, devotion, and trust yield very different qualities of energy compared to aggravation, bitterness, hostility, and self-doubt. Yet, the alchemist must engage their entire being, remaining aware of the states of consciousness that arise during magical work. Some aspects of oneself will resist the conscious intention to transform because they are living parts of the magician's being. All hostile energies, like anger, resentment, and hatred, will rebel against forces that seek to change them into compassionate and loving people.

There is a widespread belief among Alchemists that inner protection should be the primary concern before initiating any form of outer magic. Protection clarifies intent while cleansing unconscious ambitions that harbor hidden negative motivations and harmful intentions. Self-awareness is key to recognizing that it likely isn't one's enemies who are conjuring demons and creating curses to cause harm. One's nemesis is probably not the source of destructive motives that hinder success. In reality, it's the negative thoughts in one's own mind that undermine efforts in working with magic, preventing progress in the Great Work. Protection magic ultimately assists the alchemist in transmuting irrational, self-destructive behaviors into intentional, constructive habits essential for spiritual growth. Aspirants learn to identify the behavioral patterns that no longer serve them in their evolutionary quest and discover how to transform those patterns into ones that do.

GK advises that Alchemists should remember that no place within them, including their intent, is the origin of magic. Magic comes from a divine source and works through the Alchemist. Concentrated intention merely gives form to the energetic arrow of light and directs it toward a target. The reservoir of magic is the universal, all-pervasive light energy that created the cosmos and everything within it. It manifests as countless generators in the World and the Otherworld. It draws from the origins of higher power, such as Ra, Hermes-Thoth, Horus, Vulcan, Lucina, and all the many generous gods and goddesses.

30. Keys to the Principles of Magic

The principles of magic can easily conflict with empirical science. Nevertheless, in some cases, the principles of alchemy align with physical laws. For instance, alchemists utilize the physical *Laws of Photology*, especially those relevant to photography. Alchemist and father of modern science Sir Isaac Newton formulated the three *Laws of Motion*. The first principle perfectly aligns with alchemical spellwork and magic. It states that, "Every object in a state of uniform motion will remain in that state of motion unless an external force acts on it" (Smith, 2022). This axiom is a shared law. It equally applies to magic since it describes the action of magical energy as the "external force" that changes the trajectory of the object in question.

Each field of study relies on its own foundational set of laws. Laws serve particular purposes in the operations of both the macrocosm of the universe and the microcosm of one's life. Spiritual and physical laws exist in coordination with each field's worldview, as seen through the differing lenses of alchemical magic and science. When viewed through the lens of magic, one sees that the Laws of Science possess their own implicit strengths and limitations, and vice versa.

For example, science presents a very useful *inverse square law* that helps photographers calculate the relationship between the intensity of light in a scene and how that intensity is affected by its distance from the light source. However, this law falls short for magical purposes because it doesn't assist the alchemist in calculating how the intensity of a spell is affected by the distance between the place of origin and the intended destination. The point is that magical energy, although it is understood as light energy, is (so far) imperceptible by scientific means, and its intensity is not affected by distance.

Science doesn't invalidate the existence of magic because it is incapable of proving or disproving anything in the metaphysical realm. Analytical tools can't measure the energetic aspects of magic, spirituality, or even religion. For instance, the instruments of science can't gauge the intensity of Ra's luminance. It would be like trying to assess the brightness of the sun using a measuring cup. The laws, tools of practice, and units of measurement differ completely between hard science and the spiritual aspects of alchemy. "One need," as counseled by GK, "use the appropriate laws and tools for the context in which they most suitably apply."

Photologist J.W.N. Sullivan highlighted in his book, *"The Limitations of Science,"* that

> these laws are purely descriptive laws. They are just statements of fact, like saying gold is yellow. Kepler gives no reason why his laws should be as they are. The observations and recording of laws is the first step in scientific procedure. Science begins by hunting for uniformities amongst natural phenomena. The scientific man finds, for instance, that light is propagated in straight lines, that unsupported stones fall to the ground, that heat passes from a hotter body to a cooler one. In this way he introduces a sort of order into whole groups of happenings. And this sort of knowledge is often quite sufficient for practical purposes. Indeed, in many cases of great practical importance science has not yet advanced beyond this knowledge (Sullivan, 2018).

GK leaned in closer, as if to emphasize what he was about to say.

> The laws of magic assert that there is a functional process within the ever-changing context of magic. They seek to explain how magic is understood to operate within this reality. The first law is the *Law of Knowledge*; for if one understands all the laws, it will aid them in grasping the principles of magic and thus support their inner and outer alchemical practices. If one aspires to be an alchemist-photographer, they must gain control over their craft and technique by obtaining the experience and knowledge required to master their image-making tools. To be successful, one must also learn as much as possible about oneself. Knowledge of photography, the universe, and self-awareness is crucial if one wishes to achieve prosperity on this path.

The Law of Cause and Effect is a physical law that also applies to metaphysical actions. In both domains, it is universally acknowledged that causes produce effects. In alchemy, it is believed that actions will always yield a result. The sixth law of Hermetic Philosophy is "The Principle of Causation," which states that, "Every cause has its effect; every effect has its cause; everything happens according to law. Chance is but a name for law not recognized. There are many planes of causation, but nothing escapes the law" (Carty, 2007, 6). In most cases, it is believed that the effect produced is proportional to its cause. However, GK thinks that "The effects of a spell which Ra has successfully received may be amplified many-fold, between being directed toward and reaching its intended destination.

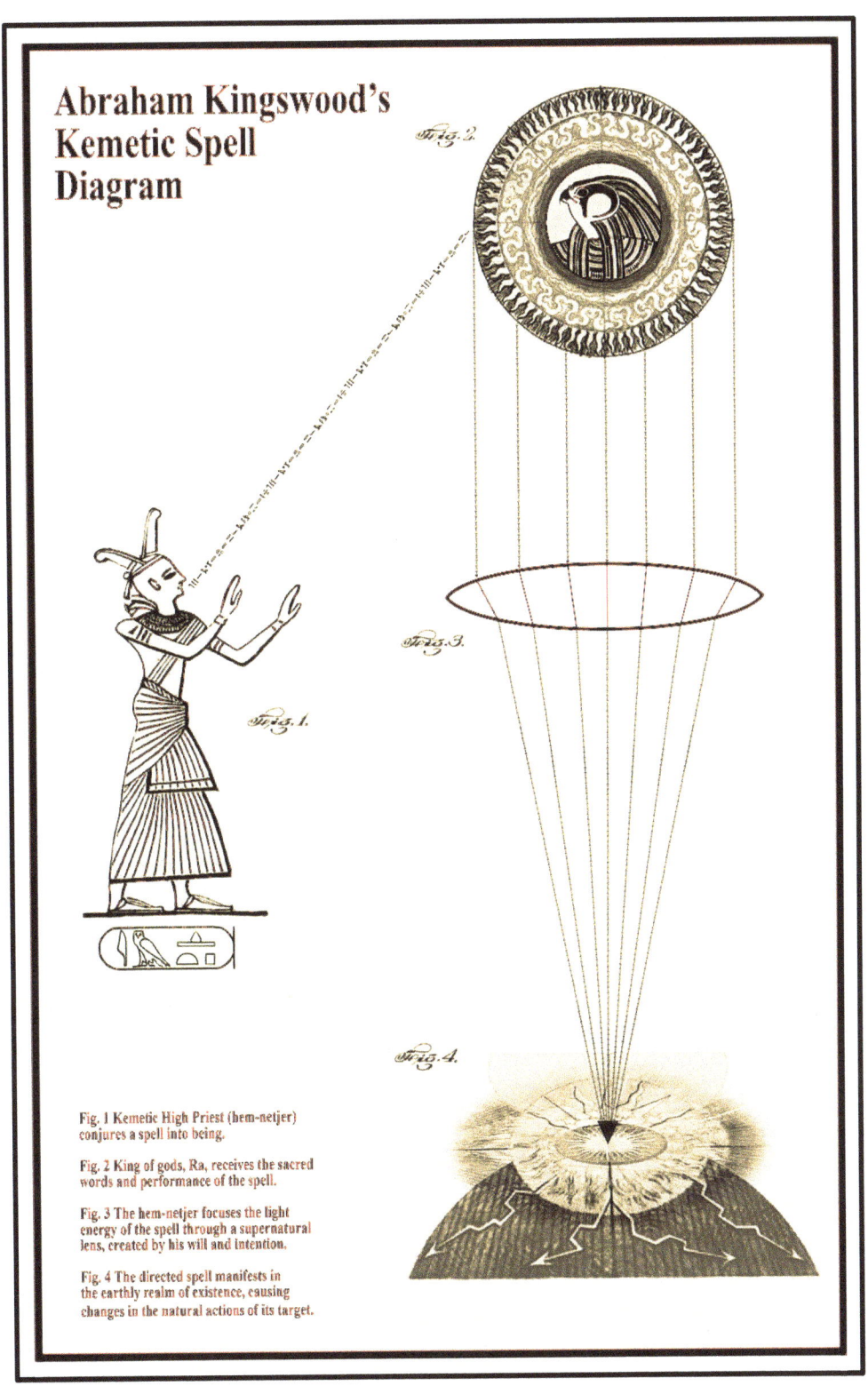

Abraham Kingswood's Kemetic Spell Diagram

Fig. 2

Fig. 3

Fig. 1

Fig. 4

Fig. 1 Kemetic High Priest (hem-netjer) conjures a spell into being.

Fig. 2 King of gods, Ra, receives the sacred words and performance of the spell.

Fig. 3 The hem-netjer focuses the light energy of the spell through a supernatural lens, created by his will and intention.

Fig. 4 The directed spell manifests in the earthly realm of existence, causing changes in the natural actions of its target.

Picture 30.1 Spell Diagram by Garin Horner, as described by Abraham Kingswood.

323

"If one presses their shutter release," GK lifts his hands as if to hold an invisible camera.

> One expects to hear the responsive click-clack of the shutter opening and closing. As a result of this action, a photographic exposure is created. There is a predictable cause-and-effect relationship. However, if the intention behind the same act is to cast a spell or move energy as part of a magic ritual, there will be an additional outcome. Still, its aftereffect will not be as predictable as simply pushing a button to obtain a photo. In a magical context, initiating an action like taking a picture may or may not lead to the specific desired outcome. Magic offers numerous opportunities for collaborating forces to influence the result. Since magic involves a synergistic effort with capricious ethereal beings and unpredictable forces, it doesn't always produce the consistent outcomes that an empirical scientist would anticipate.

Truth be told, there is also an element of unpredictability in the art of photography. A photographer can anticipate the mechanics of the camera, using the aperture to control the amount of light and the lenses to reproduce what the photographer sees in the viewfinder faithfully. Still, the photograph may lack the visual impact that its maker expected. If the desire is the intention and cause for a previsualized image, the result will be a photograph. However, the outcome may not be the picture that the photographer imagined! In fact, in most cases, it probably isn't. This suggests that the success rate of *cause and effect* for alchemistic magicians and photographic artists may be quite similar!

GK continues,

> Sometimes, when people test the waters of their abilities to conjure and cast, they do so with unrealistic expectations. Not every picture taken by a skilled photographer will be a masterpiece, and the same goes for spellcraft. It can take hundreds, or even thousands, of exposures to produce a photograph that elevates its subject far above the ordinary. Similarly, an alchemist succeeds by mastering an incantation to the point of excellence. This process requires awareness, insight, and effective practice. Over time, through the hard work of rehearsal and training, successful outcomes become more frequent. Small-scale spells should be performed as training during the periods between the successes of one's magnum

opuses. It is expected that these exercises will yield questionable results until one achieves a degree of mastery.

Magical disciplines subscribe to the *Law of Contagion*, or, as Abraham Kingswood referred to it, the *Law of Interconnection*. This law states that once contact has been made between two things, a linkage or connection is formed that perpetually remains. James G. Frazer recognized that, "Things which have once been in contact with each other continue to act on each other at a distance after the physical contact has been severed." (Frazer, 1925, 11). For example, when a photographer takes a portrait of a person, an intangible bond is established among the photographer, the subject, the camera, and the photograph. Even when the subject has been separated by time and distance, connections persist. All parties and objects involved in the event become interconnected. Moreover, if the photographer's intention is to form such bonds, the filaments may become reinforced.

Next is the *Law of Similarity*. The idea behind this law is that there is a strong relationship between things and their images. The law implies that, in many respects, appearance is inextricably linked to reality. This doesn't mean one would mistake a photo of a person for the actual person, but it recognizes an undeniable link between the two. Using the example of the portrait above, a photographic image is connected to the photographer through the Law of Connection. The photo is also linked to the subject because it shares reflective similarities with both the subject and the scene in which that image was captured. The photograph becomes an artifact that is physically, visually, and energetically bound to the subject in the picture. In other words, the similarities they share in appearance create a robust correlation between those things that look so much alike. As part of the Law of Similarity, the portrait becomes more than a mere effigy of a person. To an alchemist, the photograph transforms into a physical and energetic extension of the person.

Another fundamental precept is the *Law of Sympathetic Magic*, which encompasses the Law of Contagion and the Law of Similarity. The Law of Sympathetic Magic is the most ancient law of magic, with far-reaching implications for the operation of magic. The axiom, *like produces like* or *the image equals the object*, lies at the heart of this law. It functions by seeking out and recognizing the universe's connective patterns that act as conductors for magic-light-energy. Part of this recognition involves identifying similarities among people, places, things, and ideas. These similarities form the basis of patterns and sympathetic bonds. By working with items that resonate with one another, the alchemist can enhance the energetic field of light in which their focus lies. Its effects can be likened to using a hundred candles to illuminate a scene rather than just one, where light intensity increases

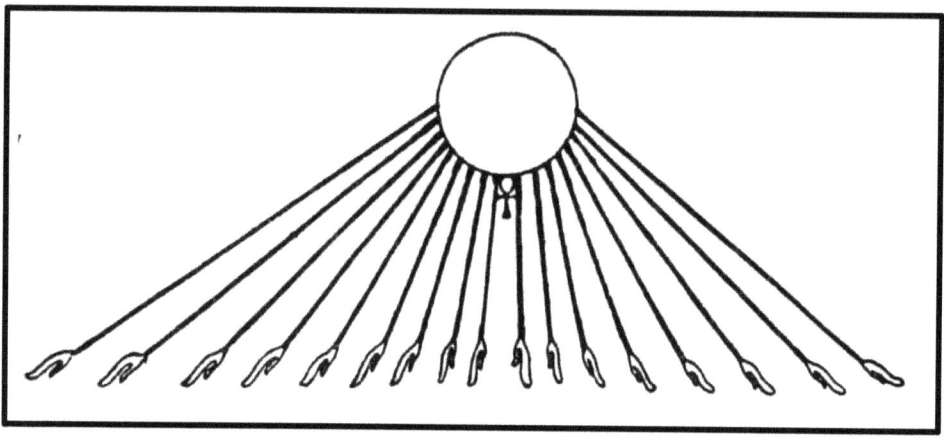

Picture 30.2 Ra's Life Bestowing Rays composite by Garin Horner.
Based on Akhenaten Worshipping the Sun, 2019.

the potential for creative possibilities rises as well. More options become available when adjusting ISO, aperture, and shutter speed. And magic.

In his article, *Sympathetic Magic: The Power of the Image*, Graham Collier wrote,

> Essentially, the term 'sympathy' signifies the urge and ability to enter into another person's or creature's mental state…and feel both an affinity with, and a compassion for, the state of their existence… If we go back to what we previously thought were the earliest man-made prehistoric images created in the cave complexes of Altamira in Spain, and Lascaux in France—say 20,000 to 15,000 B.C.—the paintings of animals discovered there displayed an acuity of visual perception, a drawing skill, and expression of 'feeling' for the animal, that can certainly be described as 'Sympathetic'… And one of the world's most distinguished anthropologists, Henri Breuil, added the word 'Magic' in describing them, denoting the archetypal belief held by many so-called 'primitive' societies, that to possess the image of an animal (so vital for the hunter's own survival), ensures a degree of human control over the animal's destiny when it comes to the hunt. In addition, pre-hunt rituals involving the image were intended to assure the animal spirit that it would not be hunted without mercy (Collier, 2014).

31. A Brief Note on the Laws of Time

Alchemy has always harmonized with the phenomena of time, particularly since it is the art of change over time. Scholar Gary Edson explains how the perception of time varies significantly between the average person and the mystic.

> All things change, therefore time is itself an element of transformation. Although the concept of time is critical in human life, the time duration process is conceptual instead of real…Mysticism has an invariable role in the understanding of time, since time has no naturally preferred direction (forward or backward). Time can be taken out of context (and often is), thereby causing the event or sequence of events to converge or diverge. The shaman, soothsayer, conjuror, oracle, or mystic transcends time by moving forward or backward (intellectually or emotionally) to live or relive relevant activities…This puzzlement calls attention to one of the peculiarities of mystical activity: the shifting sense of time as it relates to physical or metaphysical events. (Edson, 2012, 27-28)

Edson continues, saying, "It is possible with ritual practice to recreate the fundamental relationship between humans and deities and to reorder that relationship" by changing one's point of view from a phenomenon of "profane to sacred time" (2012, 27-28).

In an effort to speed up one's evolution while simultaneously extending their life, some alchemists set out to formulate an Elixir of Immortality. With such a concoction, they aimed to secure a permanent home for the everlasting soul. "Blood-red cinnabar and gleaming gold; fickle mercury and fiery sulphur: these were the ingredients of immortality…They are also deadly poisons" (Soth, 2018). The historical record shows that instead of extending life, many found their lives had been cut short by ingesting their malevolent formulations.

> But even without the toxic elixirs, internal alchemy was dangerous. After days without food or rest, [one account warns], "your clever spirit will leap and dance. You will sing and dance spontaneously, and utter crazy words from your mouth. You will compose poetry and will not be able to be restrained." If the alchemists weren't careful, demons would latch on to them and lead them astray with wild visions: phoenixes, monsters, jade maidens, pale-faced scholars. If they responded when these

figures called, they would be caught in the demon's trap, and all their diligent effort wasted (2018).

Even alchemists of old understood that time seems to stop when one's consciousness is enraptured by supernatural splendors, or when engaged in meditation. Time also appears fleeting during periods of focused study and research. Like contemporary alchemists, they knew, "The sacred manifests itself in time and space, so that time and space themselves become diaphanous indications of the holy.
(Encyclopedia Britannica, 1995).

The mechanism of holiness or sacredness generates an imperceptible, rapid flow of moments in which the world appears before the eyes. Each instant swiftly blends into the next, only to vanish into the past. It is a self-replenishing, self-renewing process that persistently reforms the perpetual now. For the smallest perceivable increment of analog measure, one notices that everything seems fixed. Then it vanishes, before the next sequential moment quickly arises. This is why the vanishing present is often represented in alchemy as a flash of lightning. It is very much like the frames of a movie film passing between a light source and a lens, projecting a simulated reality before one's eyes. The frames, like moments, blend together into a continuous stream of reality. The phenomenon is known as *persistence of vision*.

Photography, like filmmaking, theater, dance, cooking, music, and the alchemical art, is all based on the phenomenon of time. In other words, these creative ventures rely on time as one of their principal considerations. It's what photographer Henri Cartier-Bresson called the "decisive moment." It could be described as when, in a heartbeat, the flow of energy, the choreography of actions, and events reach their pinnacle of performance, the peak of their collective presentation.

Everything comes together in an instant of perfect circumstance. It is a temporal yet transcendental convergence to a unique point in time that the photographer appropriates as an act of recognition. Such an act serves their journey. Witnessing the subject's performance, the photographer anticipates everything aligning perfectly in the frame at precisely the right moment. Just as the action peaks, with a reflex action, one pushes the shutter release to capture time and space. Author Deba P. Patnaik describes the paradoxes of this photographic event to be "Momentary yet everlasting, unremarkable yet noteworthy, worthless yet invaluable" (quoted in Duggan, 2022).

Another paradox that exists is the relationship between the fleeting moment and eternity. Image capture is the first act of *fixation*. Photography became possible through the invention of a process for the second act of fixation. Chemical fixing endows the photographic image with longevity, granting it an illusory sense of eternal existence or immortality. Since the initial desire to make photography a reality, image-makers and inventors have agonized over the archival quality of their photographs.

Philosopher Martin Hägglund offers a different perspective. He says, "What's interesting about photography is that it tries to seize a moment that is fragile and fleeting, and to preserve it or trace it in some way, not to make it eternal, so that it can live on for the future and be taken up again…it's not about eternity — it's about connecting across time and space (Hägglund, 2019, 34). Photographers tend to ask, "How long will this print last?" or "What is the time frame in which these fugitive colors will lose their vibrance?" Due to the variables of cause and effect, no one knows the answers. No one knows how long an image will remain "taken up again" by the viewer in the future. One thing is sure: all images are impermanent, and it is only a matter of time before they dissolve back into their constituent elements.

As a magical tool, the camera allows the alchemist to pinpoint specific instants of "now" within the stream of light as it flows through time. Art critic Hal Foster understood, "There is no simple Now: every present is nonsynchronous, a mix of different times. Thus, there is never a timely transition, say, between the modern and postmodern: our consciousness of a period not only comes after the fact, it is also always in parallax" (Foster, 1993, 5-6). In this way, photography is an art of the past because its product is always a record of the past. The ability to catalyze a creative representation that freezes energy in the flux of time at a specific moment greatly increases the chances of an alchemist's intent successfully taking shape.

Like photography, the precise timing of a spell's execution can enhance its effectiveness and increase the likelihood of positive outcomes. Whether pressing the shutter release or casting a spell, timing leverages the buildup and peak of potential energies to achieve beneficial results.

GK presents,

> The most favorable window of opportunity to cast a spell can be found in several ways. The first step is research. Auspicious times can be discovered by studying the web of analogies and

correlations through astrology and divination. For instance, astrology's charting system of correspondences with constellations and "houses" is essential for providing information about the benefits and disadvantages of specific points in time to gather and cast energies. Depending on the type of spell being cast, the most advantageous time can be pinpointed for any magical work by examining the relationships formed by the positions of the sun, moon (waxing or waning), planets, and how these times relate to the equinoxes and solstices. I believe celestial influences are of utmost importance. Consider that the emergence of a spell, or a photograph, is like the birth of a person and will be influenced by the confluence of energies present at the time of their creation. Each is represented by its corresponding astrology chart. The energetic qualities present at any given moment are naturally imprinted on all generative acts and will influence many aspects of their time in this world.

Prayers and petitions to spiritual allies can also aid an alchemist in choosing an auspicious time. When someone asks for advice, they can gain information about timing that can't be found anywhere else. Details may be delivered through dreams, as part of divinations (like tarot or gazing into a black mirror), or through an unexpected flash of insight. To support this idea, GK read from one of his great-grandfather's notebooks, "If Ra bestows knowledge about when magical proceedings should occur, such guidance supersedes all other sources of information."

When a spell is cast at the right moment, the trajectory of magical energy rides a wave of rising light energy, while manifesting in the present moment. At the point of critical focus, as the wave crests, the stream of events reshapes itself into the magician's intent. If all goes as expected, the results appear. Maybe the outcome is that an opportunity for a solo exhibition arises. Or perhaps the natural lighting during a photo shoot suddenly becomes perfect. It could even be that a friend you haven't heard from in ten years calls out of the blue. Whatever the spell, one will either see results or they won't. Conversely, poor timing catches the moment's wave too early in its rise or the act of dissolution, thus making the manifestation of the alchemist's intention less effective.

Timing with spellwork is as important as timing is in photography. Lighting, the scene, vantage point, aperture, shutter speed, and ISO all need to work together to create a successful photograph. "Each and every shooter is capable of great work if he is willing to work toward excellence. When shooting, have patience and wait for the moment.

Arrive early and stay late…Try to spend enough time with your subjects so they will soon become comfortable with your presence; that is when the real moments will begin to happen" (Zakia, 2007, 452). The relationship between the photographer's eye (vantage point) and all the elements in the frame should also create a desirable composition. Just as one needs a heightened sense of awareness to respond at the optimal time to open and close the camera's shutter, there is also a need for that awareness of time, when, in a heartbeat, the delivery of magic is optimal.

Another aspect of time to consider is the certainty that everything exists in an ongoing state of flux. GK proposes that there are no nouns, only verbs, because everything that seems fixed, even photographs, is transitioning from what they appear to be into something else. This situation is a boon for photographers. Psychologists Philippe Gross and S. I. Shapiro called attention to the fact that,

> Impermanence, transition, transformation — each can be seen as a blessing by the percipient photographer. If things never changed, photography would quickly become a boring occupation — the photographer who has seen it all would quickly become jaded and starved for surprises. Impermanence, from this perspective, ensures that nature will continuously provide a supply of new images to the aware photographer. In a world that is inherently impermanent, wave after wave of photographic opportunities keeps rolling in (Gross, 2001, 183).

The alchemist hopes that the currents within the stream of time will carry forward the evolution of the entire cosmos. This includes photographers and their art. One reflects on the evolution of photography and how magic must likewise adapt and evolve over time to take advantage of new corresponding technologies. Richard Zakia wrote,

> Digital imaging is the next evolutionary step in providing for and advancing today's postmodern visual culture. With a world-view marked by new technologies, consumerism, and the media, its influence is simultaneously local and global, a further democratization of knowledge mediating contemporary human experience. Digital imaging claims for itself the sites of societal activity long recognized as those once sustained by photography. Building upon this groundwork, it draws other media into its expansive sphere, uniting the still, the filmic, and the televisual into the wide-ranging whole of hypermedia. The emergence of digital imaging and its accompanying technologies represents a

reconfiguration of the appearance, use, distribution, and meaning of pictures, both still and moving, for newly conditioned audiences of interactive users (Zakia, 2007, 29).

Abraham Kingswood was undoubtedly one of the first "cross disciplinary," "interactive users" of photography. And though his descendant, George, hasn't transitioned into the digital age, he does recognize its potential for alchemical and magical possibilities in the Great Work. GK remarks

> In many ways, we live in a *post-photographic* world, where there has been a decline in the use of film and its traditional processes (now called *alternative* or *historical* processes). There are still photographers who keep that tradition alive. They do so because of the interactive thrill, the anticipation felt before seeing the resulting image, the strange and exhilarating experience of using chemistry, and the sense of expectation that permeates the darkroom. They also believe that the hand-making process and viewing the luster of a physical print can never be replaced by editing a file on a computer screen.
>
> I must concede that the digital age may have its correspondences. For example, processing one's digital files may have parallels to the darkroom experience. Digital photography offers significantly greater creative freedom, allowing artists to exert their will on an image instantaneously. With digital editing tools, a photograph can quickly evolve into a refined and aesthetically pleasing vision of perfection. Photography is now a much more malleable and fictionalized medium. Many questions arise about how this new, evolved form of the art can contribute to its alchemical relative.

From GK's vantage point, he believes, "This inquiry is for the next generation of spiritually sound, able-minded, and visually literate photo-alchemists to interpret and experiment. They will harvest the benefits of their relevant discoveries. In doing so, they may encounter photography's transformative potential and unrealized mystical complexities. This art will certainly, over time, evolve both arts."

32. A Separate Reality

To understand the five bodily senses and their role in alchemy, it is necessary first to discuss what the Kingswoods have comprehended about the relationship between the physical senses and our common reality. The foundation of GK's notions is rooted in the certainty that sight, taste, smell, touch, and hearing have evolved over millions of years to serve essential functions in the survival and advancement of the human species. Subsequently, he explains that the sense organs help define the body's relationship with its surroundings. For example, sight allows one to extend one's awareness into the environment. It helps determine one's position in relation to the world, both within the immediate context and out into the spaces beyond. All the senses help individuals interact with their surroundings by interpreting the necessary information to make decisions that can have life-or-death consequences.

Picture 32.1 Allegorical representation with Heaven and Earth by Joseph Mulder, 1685.

In addition to the five most common senses, human beings possess other senses, such as spatial awareness and balance. There are also others, like those that "can detect underground water, lost objects, metal pipes, and less obvious things" (Green, 1983, 73). The entire human being is sensitive to various stimuli, including temperature, pain, pressure, gravity, hunger, and sexual attraction. Additionally, there are psychic senses that allow one to discern direction, feel intuition, sense when someone has passed away, and perceive when one is being watched. When a signal of danger is detected, a physical reaction occurs.

> The effect of the report of this sense is particularly noticed in the region of the solar plexus, or the pit of the stomach. It manifests in a peculiar, unpleasant feeling of 'gone-ness' in that region — it produces a feeling of 'something wrong,' which disturbs one in a strange way. This is generally accompanied by a "bristling up," or "creepy" feeling along the spine (Panchadasi, 1916, 33).

According to Kingswood, most of the "intricate gearwork of the senses" is designed to convince the perceiver that the information they gather and decrypt, without exception, must be trusted. They act like advisors who all corroborate each other's stories into a singular, believable narrative. The story told by the collective sensory input is convincing, and "the notion of reality must be gauged against the anthropocentric attitude that perceives it" (Edson, 2012, 10). For example, if someone is hiking in a desert and taking photographs, they can feel the heat pressing against their body. A thirst rises on their lips. They can smell the dryness of the air and see heat waves in the distance. They can also look at and feel the source of the discomfort. There is no doubt it's the unrelenting, blazing sun in the sky.

In this scenario, the camera's light meter indicates that the ISO setting should be lowered, the aperture should be closed, and the shutter speed should be increased due to excessive illumination. The meter and our senses work together to confirm this reality. There can be no doubt in the perceiver about what is happening. Several separate streams of information all converge to reach the same conclusion: I am in a desert, it is hot, I'm thirsty, and the energy from the sun is overwhelming. Furthermore, these messages can be distilled to their essence: I am awake, I am alive, and I exist.

Similarly, during dreams, the senses function to assure the dreamer that they are awake and that everything is real. The five senses turn inward during sleep and coordinate in much the same way as they do when one is awake. This is how they maintain continuity of trust in the perceiver. In dreams, as in the waking state, sight is the dominant sense, and it is through this organ of perception that dreams are projected as kinetic pictures, like movies.

Seeing is believing and believing is seeing. This chiasmus rings true when we stop to think about it. Seeing is believing and the reverse, are not separable. The image incident on our retina is not seen until our brain processes it. What we see, we see to some extent, by choice and by *expectancy* — a condition in which a person is more receptive to seeing what he or she anticipated or wants to see rather than what is…We see what we choose to see (Zakia, 2007, 468).

Additionally, similar phenomena occur in dreams because the visual cortex is highly active. Therefore, *sight* retains its status as the most dominant sense, both during sleep and while awake (Neuroskeptic, 2020).

Susan Sontag argued that we need "to have reality confirmed and experience enhanced by photographs" (Sontag, 2001, p. 18). GK adds,

One doesn't often consider how photography or one's senses work to confirm the existence of this reality. Then, the cut on their hand comes into contact with the wet acetum of the stop bath in the darkroom tray. That stinging burn sends a signal to the mind, "You know this experience is real because you feel the burn, and it hurts like hell!" What the senses are confirming is that *you are real*, that this *whole experience is real*, and *that this realm of existence* is real. Therefore, who would dispute this conclusion when all the evidence substantiates these apparent truths? The body's senses inform the brain that there is no need to worry; one can feel secure knowing this is all happening, just in case one doubts that maybe things aren't as they seem. But what if the physical senses of the recipient are a collective, genetically supported, synchronized hallucination of the entirety of what constitutes this material reality? If this theory is true—that there is something more real than what is felt through sensory information—then what is real?

Acclaimed author and perception researcher Richard Zakia said that

In the early 1900s, perceptual psychologists at the Berlin Psychological Institute were involved with research in how we see. Out of their research emerged a number of important and practical principles sometimes referred to as the Gestalt laws. They also put forth the concept of *ganzfeld*, a completely homogeneous visual field in which nothing exists, no objects, no surface texture — just light. When a person is subjected to such a visual field for a prolonged period of time he feels disoriented, may hallucinate, and some experience a temporary loss of vision. The eye must have something on which to fixate for the visual system to function properly (Zakia, 2007, 460).

In other words, when the sense of vision can't take charge of providing information to confirm this reality, it either pulls imagery from the imagination or completely relinquishes its role to the other senses.

In photography, the eyes hold total dominion over all the senses, with the expectation that they will guide the creative impulse in a truthful, trustworthy manner. The act of making photographs perfectly exemplifies the human compulsion to affirm what can be seen while figuring out what to do with the rest. It must either engage the imagination or completely disregard what can't be seen. For instance, when a viewer looks at a photograph of the Great Pyramid at Giza, they experience a photophysical response. A relationship develops between the visual stimuli experienced by viewing a picture and the sensory reaction that follows. In that reaction, the viewer likely won't notice that they can only see two sides of the monumental structure.

No matter the eye-level perspective from which the subject is photographed, only two of its four sides can be captured. Despite this, viewers still believe that two more sides exist, resembling those they can see, even though they aren't in the photograph. Similarly, the eyes gather evidence of a desert scene surrounding the pyramidal structure. It is automatically assumed that the scene continues far beyond the borders of the image. This brain activity is what University College London neuroscientist Karl Friston refers to as *predictive coding*. By drawing on memories and imagination, the perceptual mind instinctively fills in what the eyes can't see, predicting what it anticipates is most likely there (University of Glasgow, 2011). The result: viewers are compelled to trust in the existence of what they cannot perceive.

One cannot assume or trust that what the eye sees is real. A photograph can be like a quote taken out of context. Only by understanding the context can one hope to grasp what is perceived in the composition. The entire scene in the photograph of Giza could be a scaled-down version of a Hollywood set, where the backside of the pyramid is a framework of 2x4s and plywood. Outside the boundaries of the frame, there may be studio lights, film dollies, booms, and a parking lot. One cannot predict with certainty, based on sensory information, what exists outside the limits of the photographic frame.

Similarly, previsions, whether as acts of perception or divination, are never one hundred percent accurate because they must both employ information provided by the senses and rely on one's ability to interpret what is perceived. The interpretation is left to the viewer, who must ultimately decide what is true and what isn't.

Belief in this reality, as purported by the senses, helps the average person lead a life in which they feel comforted and engaged with the world. The same applies to the alchemist, but the former understands that there is a hierarchy to the senses.

> and the sense of sight is celebrated by all these, therefore, as not only beautiful and useful for the purposes of this life; but as a leader in the acquisition of Wisdom. For it is not that very light which in us looks out beaming on our eyes that, directed within, and being purified also, and scientifically inquiring, discovers at last that other light which is the substance of its own, until light meeting light apprehends itself alone" (Atwood, 2005, 101).

> While in the middle of its boiust'rous waves
> Thy soul robust, the deep's deaf tumult braves;
> Oft beaming from the Gods they piercing sight
> Behold in paths oblique a sacred light:
> Whence rapt from sense with energy divine,
> Before thine eyes immortal splendours shine;
> Whose plenteous rays in darkness most profound,
> Thy steps directed and illumin'd round.
> Nor was the vision like the dreams of sleep,
> But seen while vigilant you brave the deep;
> While from your eyes you shake the gloom of night,
> The glorious prospects burst upon your sight
> (Taylor, 1895, 66-67).

GK professes,

> Those words from the Roman-Egyptian philosopher Plotinus remind the alchemist that there exists a species of 'light' which the common eye cannot see. There is a subtle sense of 'Sight' that can perceive that very light! This 'Sight' and this 'light' are mysteries, as knowledge of their existence can only come from sources outside the physical senses. In writings on magic, mysticism, and alchemy, one is encouraged to lower the fortress walls of logic that guard against fearful beliefs about what is real, allowing the mind to embrace something unfamiliar and risky. Accepting the uncertainty of a different reality can challenge the presumption that everything the deceptive physical senses claim to be real is indeed

true. Such acceptance opens one to the subtle senses and the possibility of a different truth.

When a camera records a scene, it mechanically captures an accurate two-dimensional representation of the subject from the photographer's single punctum in space. When a person looks at that same scene, they do so with aesthetic, emotional, and psychological biases. James Elkins reminds us, "seeing is not an emotionally neutral, purely physical process. Although sight is often said to be the most rational of the senses, it cannot always be controlled by our conscious mind. It is, on the contrary, soaked in unconscious affect, closely connected with love and desire as well as with jealousy, possessiveness, violence or fear" (Haustein, 2012, 6).

As those influences take control of the act of looking, a mental-visual image is formed, shaped by those biases. The image transforms into a memory based on one's interpretation of the scene. This picture is recorded as a visualization that corresponds to that interpretation. When one thinks about or remembers the initial experience of the scene, they envision a memory —a mental picture of their interpretation of the scene. With each step in the perceptual process, the original experience shifts further away from the first-contact interpretation of the scene's apparent reality.

Furthermore, because the world is visually complex and confusing, human perception has developed strategies to navigate it more efficiently. Unfortunately, these strategies can prevent one from seeing what is right before their eyes. Photographer Freeman Patterson explained,

> We are so bombarded with visual and other stimuli that we must block out most of them in order to cope. Instead of seeing everything, we select a few stimuli and organize these. Then, once we have achieved order in our lives, we stick with the realities we have established. We seldom try to rediscover the possible value of ignored stimuli and are reluctant to do so as long as the old ones still seem to be working. We develop a tunnel vision, which gives us a clear view of the rut ahead of us, but prevents us from seeing the world around us (Patterson, 1979, 10).

Human beings believe and have faith in what their eyes tell them, just as they believe and trust photographs. Even though they know those images aren't authentic depictions of reality, they are mirages. Susan Sontag wrote, "despite the presumption of veracity that gives all photographs authority, interest, seductiveness, the work that photographers do is no generic exception to the usually shady commerce between art and truth" (Sontag, 2001, 6).

This human tendency to believe is called the illusory truth effect. It is a phenomenon in which the mind automatically accepts, for instance, a heavily Photoshopped image as real, even when the viewer knows it has been altered through digital manipulation. This explains how Hippolyte Bayard was able to convince an entire French populace that his self-portrait depicted him as a dead man, even though he was very much still alive. To misquote Barbara Kingsolver (Kingsolver, 1990), "A Photograph is a complex thing, a relative to the truth but not its twin." 1

The senses dissuade perception from questioning the apparent fixed properties of reality. Their job is to operate within the dynamic, confined, closed-loop system of perception, preventing it from perceiving what lies outside the circle. It resembles a circle of protection. What the senses conceal from normal perception is that, as Kingswood wrote in one of his personal journals, "The visible world and all its sensual qualities is only made possible by those mysterious processes that rely upon elements from the invisible world: calcination, dissolution, separation, conjunction, putrefaction, fermentation, and distillation. In turn, the alchemist uses those same processes to deconstruct substances to extract their divine essence." "What's more," adds GK, "great-grandfather emphasized that the active principle of the ethereal realms existed prior to the material realm upon which the senses are narrowly tuned."

One message conveyed by the five senses is that everything they perceive is real. Any other conclusion is unfounded. The senses operate in a manner that restricts awareness by shaping perception through one of five misleading lenses. However, one can consciously choose to embrace an understanding of other perceptions, such as those that reveal the presence of ethereal beings and deities. These spiritual entities can communicate through their existence, broadening one's awareness by serving as guides to the ecosystems of unrealized, latent realms.

Additionally, one may transcend one's perceived reality to understand it as it truly is. GK notes, "The mechanism of perception is the same across species. Therefore, each of its kind shares its grand delusion. Only humans have the possibility to see through the darkening myst."

Aristotle used his intellect to theorize.

> A thing only exists, when the 'form' (*eidos*) is added to "matter" (*hyle*). "Matter" is the passive principle in things, "form" the

motive, pure activity. One can even say that "matter" is pure potentiality (Gk. *dynamis*; Lat. *potentia*) which is realised through "form" (Gk. energeia; Lat. *actus*). Only formed matter is real as an individual thing and reality consists of such individual things making up "substance" (*ousia*). Aristotelian "form"means not just the external shape of things, but its essential form, its type. As an entelechy (*entelécheia*, something that contains or realises a final cause), it carries its own purpose within itself, which leads to the external form of the thing. In a universal hierarchy of purposes, each thing becomes "matter" again, once it reaches a higher essential form, as the seed becomes the tree (Kotansky, 2005, 17-18).

As he addressed the material substance of things, he also recognized an unseen yet sensed mystery alongside this reality.

What's more,

Augustine then distinguishes among three types of vision: bodily, spiritual, and intellectual (XII.6.15 and 7.16). Bodily vision is the actual physical sight of the eyes. Spiritual vision is, despite its name, the exercise of the imagination, by which we see physical things in the mind's eye as if they were present. The example is of a person standing in the dark and picturing the physical features of the surrounding world, even though it is too dark to make anything out. Both are rather prosaic forms of vision. But there is a third sort, intellectual vision. This is the exercise of the mental faculties, by which the intellect sees based upon mental images impressed upon the mind. This is the most excellent sort of vision (XII.10.21). It is the sort involved in contemplation of God and is independent from bodily and spiritual vision. (XII.24.51)" (Kennedy, 2005, 130-131).

Mary Anne Atwood describes the third type of sight (Sight) as the

third vision of the light is in Elysium: where the eye of mind, no longer as heretofore looking from without inwardly, beholds its object through the atmosphere of the natural life; but contrariwise, having passed through this, purifying to the center, is converted and raised; and, as a Unit, now regards the circumference transitively, including it as an understanding or reflector, as it were, to the focus of her light (Atwood, 2005, 107).

In the accounts above, the philosophers present their conclusions about how, apart from each of the five physical senses, there are corresponding, subtler, expanded, and refined kinds of senses. Additionally, these remain inaccessible to most people. For example, parallel to the physical sense of sight is the *eîdos*, or "Sight," an extrasensory faculty of clear and penetrating perception. The subtle senses, such as the eîdos, can provide information to one's cognition that conflicts with the reality described by the physical sense of sight. "The word *supernatural* is directly linked to the senses." GK says,

> It refers to that which appears to lie beyond the senses, something that the dull senses cannot detect. Only through the use of subtle senses can one expand one's supernatural perception to gain a broader perspective on what is truly occurring in this realm. For without the subtle sense of Sight, one is left blind, forced to depend on eyes that are easily deceived and, consequently, will quickly betray.

Nineteenth century occultist William Walker Atkinson wrote,

> The many familiar instances of optical delusions show us that even our sharp eyes may deceive us — every conjuror knows how easy it is to deceive the eye by suggestion and false movements. Perhaps the most familiar example of mistaken sense-reports is that of the movement of the earth. The senses of every person report to him that the earth is a fixed, immovable body, and that the sun, moon, planets, and stars move around the earth every twenty-four hours… and yet we know that this is merely an illusion, and that the facts of the case are totally different (Panchadasi, 1916, 15).

GK counsels, "The philosophers also advise that to find truth, one strives to penetrate the barrier of perceptual limitations imposed by the brain and its corporeal senses. One enlists the assistance of their self-intellect, self-wisdom, and that supernatural, luminous Source from which they emanate." Mary Anne Atwood further explains,

> The eye is not satisfied with seeing, nor is the ear filled with hearing, nor does any transitory good suffice to human desire; above all, there is no selfish object worthy the pursuit of Intellect; nor is any worldly recompense found corresponding to its need. But the proper object of the rational faculty is in its Source, which lies profoundly buried in this life of sense. And this it is the province of Hermetic Artifice to resuscitate and bring through self-

knowledge into the experience of life. For this same Root of Reason is Wisdom, and that saving Salt which philosophers were wont anciently to excavate and…to exalt. The diadem of Wisdom is with this Stone, which, as a halo or crown of light, the regenerate soul puts on as a new body, wherein it can rule over the elementary world and pass through it, overcoming evil and falsehood, and ignorance (Atwood, 2005, 248).

In a compelling voice, GK says, "It is the senses themselves that perpetuate those falsehoods and ignorance, leading one to question, what lies beyond the limits of the senses and what is actually going on here?"

Even when the senses play a role in supernatural experiences, "(most mystics) contend that visions beheld with ordinary senses such as eyes or ears are not to be trusted, as they can come as easily from a disturbed mind as from a divine source" (Raff, 2019, 276). Atwood digs even deeper by asking,

> For how should they, who have never glanced even in imagination toward the Causal Truth, believe in any other than remote effects [as confirmed by the senses]? The well out of which she is drawn is deep, and not therefore to be fathomed by the plummet of a shallow reason; he must ascend in thought who would, descending, hope to penetrate so far as to the superstantial experience of things. For there it is yet hidden, the true light shut up as in a prison, the fountain of Universal Nature separated off from human understanding by the external attraction of it through the gates of sense (Atwood, 2005, p. 79).

GK agrees with Atwood. "The dilemma here is how one can learn for themselves, to have suspicion for their undoubting confidence, their enduring belief in the messages of their senses so they may, instead, use deeper, subtler organs of perception to seek knowledge and experience of an unlimited perception of reality?"

Even though photography seems to offer immediate access to reality, it corroborates and supports the party line of the senses. Photos assert truth when the eyes gaze upon the world. Simultaneously, photography also has the potential to indicate what may exist beyond the limits of human perception. For instance, Graham Clarke, in his book *The Photograph*, discusses how some of the first witnesses of photographs concluded that they were illusions. He said that "'Illusion' is appropriate, for it recalls to us the extent to which the attempt to record and fix an image was seen as almost magical in its effect and suggestiveness: an alchemical process of transformation akin to revelation" (Clark, 1997, 11).

Nevertheless, few wonder whether the photograph and its scene are both illusions. The alchemists claim that although neither representation is real in the way one thinks it is, they contain obvious, self-hidden aspects that point toward the truth of what lies beyond the illusion. They maintain that the most familiar of the intuitive and discriminating organs of perception—often referred to as the third eye—is what many consider essential for *knowing what is real*. GK quips, "Sadly, we have yet to invent a camera with which the third eye can peer into this realm, seeing with absolute clarity through its discriminating viewfinder!"

Author Lyam Thomas Christopher said, "To see such systems in their true light, one must undo their hold. In order to make a difference in the lives of those who are enslaved, one must first be free oneself. And so begins the tedious process of untangling the soul" (Christopher, 2006, 7). GK mentions

> The alchemist's insights frustrate and disrupt the comfortable status quo of tyrannical senses. One should remember that it is through the senses that Ra experiences all the stories of this realm, including the breakthrough perceptions of aspirants in the Great Work. Ra indeed rejoices when one realizes that the senses are subordinates of the tyrant mind, which claims its high position through disinformation and subterfuge. In this scenario, we are born bondservants of the internal Pharaoh, who tries to make us believe that we are each the center of the universe and masters of our own destinies, while all the while the light within burns ever more dimly. Our goal is to recognize the deceit of the senses and, by doing so, enlist them as secessionists, making them our supporters in the Great Work.

The physical senses are quite limited in their range of ability when it comes to perception. Hermes Thrice-Great taught to "Leave the senses of the body idle, and the birth of divinity will begin. Cleanse yourself of the irrational torments of matter" (Copenhaen, 1995, 50). GK advises to "pursue emancipation from the five earthbound illusionists!" Atwood joined with her own advice, "There are many ways known and practiced of entrancing the senses, and the key of the Hermetic vestibule may be said to be already in our hands, which are able to dissolve the sensible medium and convert it to the experience of another life" (Atwood, 2005, 91).

Philosophorum

33. Seal of the Four Gates

GK contemplates the purpose and mission of his life deeply. This has intensified the urgency he feels to chase goals that appear nearly impossible to achieve:

> As a species, humans have always been drawn to stories. The reason is that deep down, we know we play supporting roles in the story of the Universe. Each person is the main character in a subplot of that larger narrative. One can see oneself as a central or minor character in that greater divine chronicle. This perspective allows one to shift attention away from the minor, mundane concerns of life's struggles to imagine one's place in the 'big picture.' This can help one confront feelings of insignificance regarding their perceived role in the cosmic scheme of things, while also embracing the hero's role in their own life. As a hero, the monotony of daily routines fades into the background. One feels they can overcome personal conflicts, tensions, and pain because they have become endowed with relevance, significance, and supernatural abilities.

> Myths and stories help one understand the wide range of possibilities for human life experiences. They help one realize that everyone has the potential to navigate the circumstances of their life competently.

> One of the purposes of each person's life story is to meditate on the divine spark that animates one's spirit, whilst submitting to its desire to live through us in a way that offers every human being the opportunity for a mythic narrative, worthy of the gift that has been given, to be fully awake and alive. One's spiritual legacy is the journey yet to be lived. It is the individual's choice to accept or reject the role of protagonist, to live their story in the manner they choose, in a way that is worthy of the gift. Part of the alchemist-photographer's saga is to bear witness to the world's story. To bear witness to cosmic evolution.

Life can be seen as the arc of one's storyline. It involves taking on the role of the lead character in a unique narrative, where the fullness of one's plot and conclusion remains to be lived and discovered. Ultimately, one's story appears to end with death, but from GK's perspective, it is simply a new chapter in an ongoing tale.

GK brought out a brittle, browning sheet of paper. Printed on it was a black-line image that illustrated a diagram of an equilateral cross within a square. If placed in a circle, the design would resemble an ancient sun cross, a symbol for the sun god worshiped by various names in prehistoric cultures. Even without a circle, the symmetrical arrangement represented a solar symbol meant to banish or ward off evil. It also signifies perfect symmetry, the four seasons, the four elements, and the

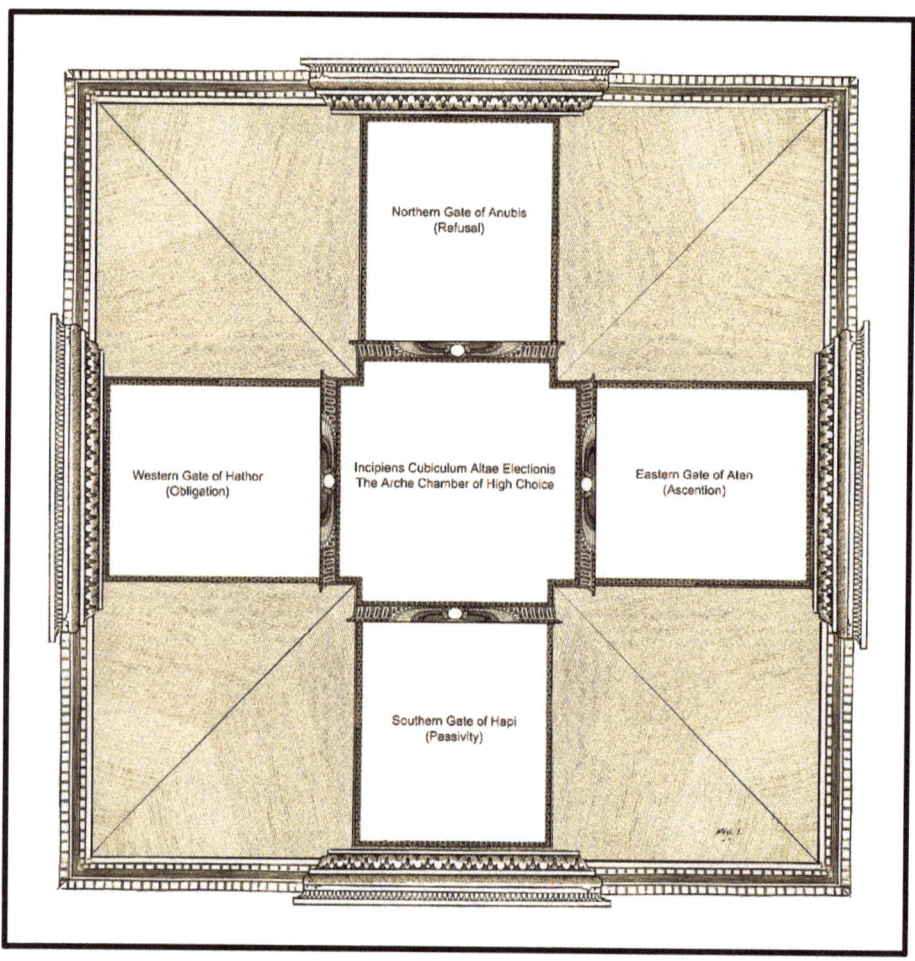

Picture 33.1 Emblem-Diagram of the Arche Chamber of High Choice.
Courtesy of George Kingswood.

the moon's phases. The symbol resembled a crossroads. In ancient Greece, one might think this drawing refers to Hermes, the god of the crossroads. Written on the sheet were the *FOUR GODS OF THE GATES*: Anubis, Hathor, Hapi, and Ra. A distinct space in the center was understood as a liminal site between the material and spiritual realms. It is a place where making an important decision can lead to life-changing consequences. GK noted that specific correspondences are important to observe when using the drawing for magical purposes.

> This emblem depicts a diagram of the divine pyramid's cross section, sliced parallel to its base. It illustrates the House of Eternity's deep inner rastau, a concealed network of hallways. Each arm of the cross symbolizes a hallway branching from the pyramid's central area, the 'Incipiens Cubiculum Altae Electionis' or *The Arche Chamber of High Choice*. If an aspirant stands at the center, where the halls converge, they face a profound choice: which of the four directions will they take to exit the inner pyramid? The hallway they choose and the life-gate they pass through dictate the fundamental premise of their living story. Among the four passages, only one will lead the mystes through the gateway to the Great Work.

GK continues to explain that each soul must decide how to compose the story of their lives. The four pathways that emerge from the pyramid's core differ in purpose and philosophy. For instance, the first gate faces north and extends upward on the diagram toward the Anubis Gate. This philosophy is based on the rejection of life altogether and is intended for those who refuse to engage with this realm of existence. There is a deep sense of abnegation regarding the ownership of one's embodied state. Few people choose this path, but those who do are resolute in their decision to leave the earthly realm.

The second passage guides the seeker to the eastern rise of radiant steps, leading to Aten's gate. It points toward the alchemist's goal: to promote the narrative of one's higher nature and become the hero of one's story. The individual taking this path feels compelled to undertake the Great Work and make their biographical odyssey about attaining the state of divine photognosis. Only the rarest electors pursue this path. Few are called to this life purpose, defined by the quest for wisdom and knowledge. They are driven by a unique sense of certainty that guides the seeker toward the fiery source of their own indwelling spark. It is the most noble and worthwhile story a person can create as an offering of gratitude for the divine gift that resides within them.

The 13th-century Sufi mystic Jalāl ad-Dīn Muhammad Rūmī offered advice to aspirants on the journey, "Set your life on fire. Seek those who fan your flames" (Rumi and Mary Foundation, 2023). Those who pursue this pathway exemplify the highest level of human spiritual evolution. Helena Blavatsky, Pythagoras, Dogen, Nisargadatta Maharaj, Georges Ivanovitch Gurdjieff, P. D. Ouspensky, and Thomas Merton are among those who climbed the upward course of this remarkable direction. Many others exist whose names we will never know.

Picture 33.2 Athanasius Kircher, Turris Babel, 1679.

The third passageway represents the conscious or unconscious choice to live one's life in a passive state. Those who select this option are willing to let external events and actions dictate the direction of their lives. Friends, adversaries, relatives, acquaintances, and influencers at large play an influential role in this story. They are all welcomed as either forces of order or chaos, each exerting influence over the chooser's life decisions. These persuasive forces lay the groundwork for the narrative of one's life and the resulting consequences of acquiescing to those choices. Those who live this life must often submit to feeling powerless, fearful, resentful, and angry in their approach to living. This exit way, which leads south, takes one through the Gateway of Hapi.

The fourth hallway, which exits to the west, leads to a path of obligation, where one seizes the opportunity to live their story. This orientation is chosen by those who seek fulfillment and meaning in their lives. This corridor is for seekers of love, happiness, contentment, and security, where they become the apparent directors of their stories. It's the most common of the four philosophies, as it offers what most people desire in their lives.

One person who exemplified this approach was Winston Churchill, who wrote 72 volumes about his life's achievements. Churchill is a perfect example of someone who grasped the importance of living a fulfilling and meaningful life. He was a dedicated leader, tirelessly working to bring prosperity to his people. His extraordinary story encompasses a full range of human experiences for his precious divine spark. For those who embrace this ideal as their purpose—to live life to the fullest during the time they have been given—they should walk down the hallway that leads to the Gate of Hathor.

"The equilateral cross in the pyramid diagram also corresponds to the 35mm camera viewfinder's pyramidal pentaprism, most of which used to contain crosshairs that marked the middle of the frame." GK continues speaking,

> Once one is aware of the connection, the viewfinder prompts contemplation of the choices that will shape their life. Even if one uses a camera without crosshairs, they can envision the symbol in the center of the frame whenever the subject is positioned in the middle of the composition. The cross may not be present, but one can visualize it into existence.

What isn't seen on the map of the cross are the fifth and sixth soul portals, which run perpendicular to its two-dimensional plane. These secret corridors can only be traversed by the soul (one's *Ka*), which has shed its worldly form. If the diagram were imagined as the ground level of a pyramid and viewed from the side, the unseen portals extend up and down from the center chamber. To visualize the iris portal, one would picture standing in the middle chamber, looking up toward the pyramidion.

Overhead, one would find the Gate of Ra, or Eye of Ra, an aperture portal through which the ka may ascend into the Eternal Sun of the Divine Mystery. It also acts as a barrier that prevents unprepared souls from entering. The aperture serves as a passage for those beings that left the pyramid through the Gate of Ra and, upon human death, returned through the gate to make their ascension.

Souls who either chose to live their life stories by exiting through one of the other gates or those beings that didn't achieve the necessary level of sublimation, transformation, and transmutation in life, pass as a diaphanous being (called the *ba*) through the spirit door at the base of the pyramid, the Osiris gate, directly beneath the central chamber. Once through, they awaken to continue their life in the otherworld.

The passageways of the Pyramid Base Emblem are also associated with the four cardinal directions. Because the design corresponds to an actual pyramid, GK deems it is valuable to mention that the Egyptians were intentional in their directional placement of the pyramid faces and the corners of their bases. For instance, scientists have long known that the Great Pyramid at Giza was built in such a way that "each corner [is] facing a different cardinal direction: North, East, South, and West. The alignment…is nearly perfect, only 0.067 degrees counterclockwise from perfect cardinal alignment" (Hugo, 2018). When one examines the relationship between the Pyramid Base Emblem and its directional passages, they will discover correspondences that provide further insight into composing an intentional and meaningful life story.

GK communicates:

> Life trajectories are rarely straight. They often curve or take sharp, unexpected turns. Each experience prepares the aspirant for the next challenge on the horizon. Know this: one's story doesn't stop with death. Life narratives continue in two significant ways. The first is through a transition into the next chapter of the story. Vital energies leave this reality and proceed into the otherworld spirit realm. The second storyline continues in all the artifacts left behind, which serve as physical objects that express their connections through filaments of radiating light.
>
> The makeup of one's personality and all their accumulated habitual odds and ends endure. One's material belongings maintain lasting filament attachments. The energetic lines create bridges across the barrier. Thus, objects like photographs

continue their journeys as they are passed on to relatives, change hands among strangers, are destroyed by water or fire, or end up at a resale shop. Wherever their stories lead them, they hold enduring connections that trace back to the photographer and the people whose likenesses were captured in the silver emulsion surface of the photo paper.

GK pauses for a moment to think in silence.

Everyone wandering through life in a state of ambivalence— going to work, caring for families, and fulfilling societal expectations—are consumed by a madness stemming from the numbing drive of their base instincts. In some ways, they are more dead than if they were spirits from the underworld.

Meanwhile, those whose bodies are buried in the ground—those who, when they walked the earth, transcended social and societal expectations, who lived life to the fullest and sought the highest levels of intellectual, emotional, and spiritual development— continue to exist in a state of boundless inspiration in the ethereal realm because they still follow the path they had set during their lives.

It is a rare person who is wise enough and compelled enough to look high upon the steps leading to the utmost goal and say, as Israel Regardie said, "I must return to my work and finish what I began, all the time praising my bountiful God, who hath called me into the Art of the Fire" (2013, 32). For I will leave this solid ground of comfort and security, confront my fear of unknown heights, and climb, all the while knowing the steep and narrow steps could lead to a fall at any time.

Regardie supports the idea of the uncommon, extraordinary person who is driven enough to seek their highest purpose. "Were only a few men to exert themselves to discover *what* they really are, and ascertain beyond all cavil the scintillating refulgence of bright glory and wisdom burning in the innermost heart, and discover the bonds connecting them with the universe then I think they will have accomplished not only their own individual purpose in life and fulfilled their own destiny, but, what is infinitely more important, they will have fulfilled the destiny of the universe considered as one vast living organism of consciousness" (Chandler, 1662, 462).

Adepts currently alive offer wise counsel on which life path to choose, depending on one's desired result. Contemporary alchemist David Chaim Smith provides honest advice to awaken the viewer-reader's sleeping eye of perception. "Human beings wade through an ocean of banal tedium punctuated with sensory pleasures, intellectual fascinations, emotional attachments, and temporary amusements. It all swirls amidst the foam, meandering aimlessly into infinity. The swirling morass reveals a gossamer play of textured luminosity presented as the solidity of earth, the cohesion of water, the transformation of fire, the motility of air, and the pervasion of space. This is the play of a groundless ground ... an empty dream without a dreamer. Right where we stand, the most precious resource awaits us, mixed in with the rubble and detritus of human experience. The discovery of this treasure is eminently possible once the proper sensibility has been cultivated. This is our birthright" (Smith, 2022). Smith indicates that the keys to the treasure of the highest path are available to anyone. One needs only to focus one's intention on changing one's perspective to align one's viewpoint and perception with the qualities and actions required to receive the treasure.

"Stories come and go while the earth revolves around its heavenly host. Out of all those countless stories, it would only take a handful of people across the world to choose to become living flames, to be sources of light for others," GK predicts, "Then the work in the microcosm could radiate across humanity and effect extraordinary changes throughout the macrocosm of the universe." What's more, Israel Regardie said, "In those individuals who constitute a minute, almost microscopic minority of the populace of this globe, willing and eager to devote themselves to a spiritual cause, lies the only hope for the ultimate redemption of mankind." (2013, 32). GK concludes,

> With this as the highest goal, one's *raison d'être*, the mystics of old implored spiritual candidates not to be disheartened by the fact that the objective of 'ultimate redemption' could surely take more than one lifetime. The wise advice of those mystics for the alchemist could also benefit the photographer. One should act as though the present life is the only life one will ever have. Therefore, the Sages throughout time emphatically urge, "There is no transformation without practice. Our time is short. We must begin the process straight away and not stop — because we have no time to waste! We are but dead stones determined to come alive through our philosophy!

CONCLUSION

It was mid-October 2022. I had recently given my first talk on GK and the book at the Midwest Society for Photographic Education conference in Cincinnati. During the drive home, I reflected on a couple of questions that were asked after my talk. One person asked if I had a spiritual relationship with GK and if I considered myself his disciple. Another asked why GK wanted a book written that would bring to light his family's secrets.

To the first question, I replied that I only considered myself GK's scribe and photographer, not his student. Then I thought back on some of our interactions. One day stood out. It was a moment when our roles as interviewer and interviewee had changed. There was an interaction when GK meant to draw me into his world. I didn't expect it when he assumed the role of a teacher. After showing me the photo that transformed from an Egyptian landscape into the scene of my old house, he asked me what the experience taught me. I believe this is a question a teacher would ask a student.

Over the last couple of years, I've contemplated GK's question. I concluded that the house I saw wasn't a childhood memory that was called up from an experience. It couldn't be. I was too young to remember anything from that time. Instead, it was a false memory. That picture had to be a mental projection, a flashback of my 3x4-inch black-and-white photo from an old family photo album. It became clear that all my earliest memories weren't based on recollections of events, people, or places. Instead, they were impressions left by sixty-year-old family photographs. Those pictures somehow became surrogates for absent memories. I realized my mind holds a gallery of images, relics of my parents' experiences. In place of my impressions, I saw how important those photos were in shaping my understanding of my history. I learned how those vicarious experiences deeply influenced my sense of who and what I am. As it turns out, I *was* GK's student, if only for a minute.

As I pulled into my driveway, my heavy pondering turned to delight! I was thrilled to find a familiar parcel waiting at my door. A box with frayed edges was mummified in bands of ragged tape. It was the same package I had sent when delivering a copy of the book's final manuscript to GK. The same stack of printed sheets was enclosed, having come full circle to return to where it all began. I looked inside to find some additional items stacked with my document. The first thing I noticed was a few handwritten notes from GK. The first page provided written approval of the book's final version, confirming that my understanding aligned with the information GK intended to impart. He felt that I had listened carefully, and as a result, my description of alchemy, the Great Work, and the Kingswood's arcane photographic practices was "satisfactorily accurate."

Coincidentally, the next page addressed the audience's second question about why GK wanted the book. In elegant cursive handwriting, he noted, "The only way this story can deliver magic into the lives of its readers is through the life energy I deliver through the printed words on the pages.

> Enspirited sheets bound between covers. Thus, this book can be held close to the heart or raised high above the head. It can be hidden or shared. The script on the pages can be felt with one's fingers. The paper leaves can sense the warmth of a hand. The ideas can be torn out, burned, or consumed. Matter, such as paper, book board, glue, and ink, serves as a perfect conductor for metaphysical energies.

> The unbroken filament of magical light moves from the printed words into the reader's eyes, body, and soul. It's a continuous line of energy that connects the holder to me and beyond, back to the origin of the universe. To Ra. The shapes of the text blocks are conduits through which the reader can draw inspiration to awaken creative abilities, such as the capacity to perceive knowledge during the act of taking photos, and once again, while seeing into a photograph.

I felt grateful that he had finally explained the book's purpose.

On the third page, GK stipulated that the project be finished as a bound book. There were also two prayers. The first request is that Ra continue to bless this project. The second was an invocation, attributed to GK as the translator of Abraham Kingswood's Latin text. The title of this book comes from the eleventh line of this prayer:

> Warm'd temple gates, now open wide
> Embrace the morn as you arrive.
> Approach this holy ground my king
> With solar crown, on hurried wing;
>
> With cobra wreath and glist'ning oil
> You journey round the season's coil

From beaming daybreak hear my plea
To find the door that sets souls free.

Oh falcon God, appear to me,
Your devout child who calls to thee!
A feather on your breath, am I
Surrendered to your open sky.

Rise from the dark-world strong and bold
To help transmute this lead to gold!
Accept this offering of pure flame
A brilliant blaze that speaks your name.

You soar above the world to find
Earthbound spirits lost and blind.
Remain until my earthly fall
And guide me to my next life's call.

Prepare me for a life below
So I may thrive and I may know
Knowledge of mysteries divine
Revealed through your auspicious signs.

Resplendent God of worlds unseen
Grant now your child with sight pristine.
I dwell in shadows day and night
Without your guidance or your light.

Endow me with your radiance,
Salvation from my ignorance.
I wish to know, to serve all days,
Teach your devout, the sacred ways.

Also, on that page, GK expressed his sincere gratitude for my "scholarly perseverance and indomitable spirit in seeing this project through to its completion." Furthermore, he emphasized the importance of our collaboration to him. In closing, GK mentioned that now that his part of the project was finished, he intended to return to his work. This meant GK would focus all his time on the extraordinary effort needed to accomplish the Great Work. I imagined him signing his name, refocusing his attention, and mentally departing this ordinary reality. I had a sinking feeling that this was likely the end of our friendship. At the same time, I was comforted by a sense of connection. I believed it was produced by a strong filament bond that GK had intentionally created between us.

Picture 34.1 Mayer & Pierson "Photographers of His Majesty the Emperor" Carte de Visite of Abd el-Kader, circa 1855.

Just beneath the correspondence lay a small antique envelope, its edges embossed with a raised floral pattern. Inside was a 20th-century Parisian carte de visite, featuring the likeness of Abd el-Kader, one of GK's most beloved allies. The image of the bearded man depicts him standing tall and attentive. He wore a white hooded cloak that partially covered the set of ornate Algerian robes underneath. He also displayed a sash, which held a French Legion of Honour medal. Kader's image represented him in his various roles, including those of warrior, emir, and Naqshbandi Sufi saint.

It was as if Kader's photograph was placed atop the manuscript intentionally. Perhaps GK requested that his ally safeguard the box during its journey back to me. Alternatively, the photo may have been sent as a thoughtful gift. In any case, I know GK had a specific reason for including this artifact in the box. For if there is one thing I learned about him, it's that his actions were always deliberate. After all, the Kingswood family claimed Kader as a spiritual associate since the mid-1880s. It was through photographs like this one that the alchemists reached out and contacted the disembodied saint to seek his wisdom, protection, and support for their Great Work. For this reason, GK would consider any photograph of Kader to be precious and deeply meaningful.

Beneath Kader's photo was another envelope. This one was a standard, nondescript manila envelope, like one that could be found in any office. Lifting the end flap, I pulled out a line drawing of Ra and a black-and-white photo of me, both cropped to head and shoulders. I remembered GK taking the picture with a 35mm film camera as I sat in his parlor, preparing to begin the day's interview. This was the first time I'd seen the image. The light came in from a window to my right, illuminating one side of my face and illustrating a textbook example of Rembrandt lighting.

I presume GK created Ra's ink drawing. The paper was square and proportional to the frame surrounding the portrait. It was as if one were gazing at the profile of the avian god's face through a lens. The overall presentation of the artwork emphasized the power of the deity's piercing gaze. The piece appeared to have been crafted with care and devotion, perhaps with the support of an incantation that reached out to invoke Ra's inspiration. I believed it would be perfectly at home hanging on GK's wall, among the many sacred images in the Kingswood temple room. I sensed that Ra was present in the likeness. GK always said that each image of Ra was a divine light-form, inseparable from the manifestation of his god-form.

In the depths of the envelope was a small item wrapped in thin black paper. Sealed inside was a small, rectangular silver plate. It was thinner than a dime and about an inch and a half long. Engraved on its surface were the words "Ego Video Esse," the same Kingswood maxim that was etched into the bodies of GK's cameras. I intended to attach the plate to my DSLR as a reminder of my time with the alchemystical philosopher.

Finally, at the bottom of the box lay the manuscript. I flipped through the stack of papers, catching glimpses of handwritten notes and sketches in various margins. This was the product of our collaboration, a record of previously untold insights on GK's steep ascent toward self-transmutation. GK wrote on the cover page, "This text is replete with secrets. Selah." That word he placed at the end, "selah," is one that GK said was an old Hebrew term used in ancient Kabbalistic manuscripts. It's the instruction to pause and think carefully about what you read.

In a way, this mound of papers felt like my arrival at an apex. Holding the stack and feeling its weight gave me a sense of accomplishment.

There was also a feeling of finality, like death. It's the sensation of having been on an exciting adventure combined with the sadness of its ending. To think it all started when a stranger pointed me down a path toward an alchemist—what a thrill! Along the way, I listened, discovered, photographed, and learned as I wrote. Everything led up to this moment in time, a decisive instant when I realized this book was finished. Writing this conclusion marks a point of finality. The book's contents will go on to make new chapters in my own story. It will reveal unseen paths, bringing much more knowledge to light.

I can't help but wonder about all I haven't learned from GK regarding his magical, artful work and its ancient roots. After years of photo sessions and interviews, I still feel as if I know very little about alchemy or the alchemist. Perhaps it's because I'm an academic, not a practitioner. Even so, I believe that everything I gathered about this philosopher has been limited to precisely what he wanted me to know. I asked many questions because I'm naturally curious. Sometimes my queries were met with silence, which left me wanting to learn more. I imagine that if I had the ability to use this gifted photo of Kader, I would open a line of communication. I'd want to learn everything the Sufi master could tell me about GK, his enigmatic 21st-century associate.

GK provided us with a glimpse into his personal history, intimate life experiences, and philosophical legacy. My role was to share some of Kingswood's wealth of arcane knowledge. However, the scope of revelation in this text is relatively limited compared to the accumulated insights hidden within a collection of well over 100 Kingswood family journals. They remain tucked away on the shelves of GK's study, library, and laboratory. Their secrets are hermetically sealed between worn covers. It keeps me awake at night, pondering all the knowledge I haven't been able to uncover, all that Kingswood wisdom regarding photography and alchemy that I still don't grasp. To me, GK's teachings are a gold mine. He serves as the missing link between spiritual alchemy and the photographic arts. All I can do is hold on to the questions he hasn't answered and hope that someday he will.

I reflect on the conversations held in the quiet atmosphere of his library. I can almost hear him say,

> True knowledge is a form of perpetual energy and, as such, is never lost. It has always existed and will always be available to those who look with intentional, watchful eyes. If someone is enlightened by gnosis (the first emanation of light), their questions will not go unanswered. All will be known.

With those words, I must trust that the rest of the story isn't permanently hidden in the clandestine rooms of the Kingswood household. It's out there, all around us, all the time. And if we miss the opportunities

Picture 34.2 George Kingswood's Library. Photograph by Garin Horner, 2020.

presented in every moment to "see the light," there's still hope. We can take photographs that allow us to stop time and look within for those messages we failed to see in real time. GK has taught me that there is deeply meaningful knowledge in imagery. It's present within the subtle gradation of tonality, and where shadows and light press against one another. We need only evolve our perception enough to read the light between the lines.

Revlatur

Pictures & References

I. Introduction

References
Phillipson, Gerry. From an email to the author, July 16, 2023.

End Sign: Turn of the century cabinet card for Ira F. Collins, Huntsville, Atlanta.

PART 1: Secrets of the Arts of Fire AND Operations of the Sun
Picture: Garin Horner, based on Title page from *Basilica chymica*, Oswald Croll, Franckfurt: Bey Gottfried Tampachen, 1629. https://en.wikipedia.org/wiki/Oswald_Croll Accesssed June 1, 2025.

I. Portraits of Devotion

Pictures
1.1 Secrets of the Arts of Fire AND Operations of the Sun. Composite by Garin Horner & George Kingswood.

1.2 Our Ancestors Guide Us and Protect Us. Photograph by Garin Horner, 2016.

1.3 Solve et Coagula, Mylius, Johann Daniel. Anatomia auri. N.p., n.p, 1628. Part V, p. 15. https://archive.org/details/joannisdanielis00myligoog/page/n344/mode/2up. Accessed December 14, 2023.

1.4. George Kingswood's Laboratorium. Photograph by Garin Horner, 2022.

1.5 Alchemical and rosicrucian compendium, 1760. Beinecke Rare Book and Manuscript Library, Mellon MS 110. https://collections.library.yale.edu/catalog/32367749. Accessed 12 Dec. 2022.

References
Albertus, Frater. *The Alchemist's Handbook*, Samuel Wiser, Inc., New York, 1978, p. 103.

Atwood, Mary Anne. *Hermetic Philosophy and Alchemy: A Suggestive Inquiry into the Hermetic Mystery with a Dissertation on the More Celebrated of the Alchemical Philosophers,* Routledge, 2005, p. 103. *Abardoncompanion,* http://abardoncompanion.de/Alex/Atwood.pdf. Accessed December 14, 2022.

Blavatsky, Helena. *ISIS Unveiled: A Master-Key to the Mysteries of Ancient and Modern Science and Theology*, Theosophy Trust, 2006, p. 4. *Anthroweb.info,* https://www.anthroweb.info/fileadmin/pdfs/Isis_Unveiled.pdf. Accessed 15, Dec. 2022.

Carty, Donald G. *The Emerald Tablet: And the Alchemy of Spiritual Transformation*, Personal Development Institute, 2007, p. 10, www.alchemystudy.com/download/Emerald_Tablet-Carty(plagiarized_from_Hauck's%20book).pdf. Accessed December 14, 2022.

Corbin, Henry. *Creative Imagination in the Ṣūfism of Ibn ʿArabī*, Routledge & K. Paul, United Kingdom, 1969, p. 191.

Edson, Gary. *Mysticism and Alchemy Through the Ages: The Quest for Transformation,* McFarland & Company, London, 2012, p. 79.

Gross, Philippe L., and S. I. Shapiro. *The Tao of Photography: Seeing beyond Seeing*, Ten Speed Press, United Kingdom, 2001, p. 34.

Kernan, Sean. *Looking into the Light: Creativity and Photography*, 2014, p. 2.

Kingswood, George. *A Personal Journal of GK*, 2022.

Lévi, Éliphas. "Book 2." *Dogme Et Rituel De La Haute Magie*, Rider & Company, England, 1896, p. 42. *Academia.edu,* https://www.academia.edu/27051672/Dogme_et_Rituel_de_la_Haute_Magie?email_work_card=view-paper. Accessed 14 Dec. 2022.

Russell, B. *Mysticism and Logic*, W.W. Norton, New York, 1929, p. 9.

Underhill, Evelyn. *Mysticism: A Study in the Nature and Development of Spiritual Consciousness*, Dover Publications, 2002, p. 141, 81.

Zuber, Mike A. *Spiritual Alchemy: From Jacob Boehme to Mary Anne Atwood*, Oxford University Press, New York, NY, 2021, p. 38.

2. The Confessions of George Kingswood

Pictures
2.1 Modified (Garin Horner) engraving of a "portable" camera obscura in Athanasius Kircher's Ars Magna Lucis Et Umbrae (1645).

2.2 The Emerald Tablet, in Amphitheatrum sapientiae aeternae by Heinrich Khunrath, 1602. *Emerald Tablet*, Steele & Singer, 1928, p. 42. p. 42/486 (English), p. 48/492 (Latin)

End Sign: The Orphic Egg, "Ophis et ovum mundanum Tyriorum" by James Basire. 1774. Accessed December 14, 2023.

References
Aldersey-Willaim, Hugh. Conveyor Magazine, no. 6, 2014, p. 11.

Almenberg, Gustaf. *Notes on Participatory Art: Toward a Manifesto Differentiating It from Open Work, Interactive Art and Relational Art*, AuthorHouse UK, United Kingdom, 2010, p. 45.

Atwood, Mary Anne. *Hermetic Philosophy and Alchemy: A Suggestive Inquiry into the Hermetic Mystery with a Dissertation on the More Celebrated of the Alchemical Philosophers*, Routledge, 2005, p. 86. *Abardoncompanion*, http://abardoncompanion.de/Alex/Atwood.pdf. Accessed 15 Dec. 2022.

Blavatsky, Helena. *ISIS Unveiled: A Master-Key to the Mysteries of Ancient and Modern Science and Theology*, Theosophy Trust, 2006, p. 185. *Anthroweb.info*, https://www.anthroweb.info/fileadmin/pdfs/Isis_Unveiled.pdf. Accessed 15 Dec. 2022.

Budge, E. A. Wallis. *Egyptian Magic: A History of Ancient Egyptian Magical Practices Including Amulets, Names, Spells, Enchantments, Figures, Formulae, Supernatural Ceremonies, and Words of Power*. United Kingdom, Book Sales, 2016. p. 142.

Cheak, Aaron. *Alchemical Traditions: From Antiquity to the Avant-Garde*, Numen Books, 2013, p. 19. *Academia.edu*, https://www.academia.edu/379294/Alchemical_Traditions_From_Antiquity_to_the_Avant_Garde?email_work_card=view-paper. Accessed 15 Dec. 2022.

Christopher, Lyam Thomas. *Kabbalah, Magic, and the Great Work of Self-Transformation: A Complete Course*, Llewellyn Publications, Woodbury, MN, 2006, p. 59, p. 27.

Eliade, Mircea. *Forge and the Crucible*, University of Chicago Press, Chicago, 1978, p. 159. *Internet Archive*, https://archive.org/details/forgecrucible00eliarich/page/158/mode/2up. Accessed 15 Dec. 2022.

Fowden, Garth. *The Egyptian Hermes: A Historical Approach to the Late Pagan Mind*, Cambridge University Press, 1986, pp. 65–68.

Gencay, Kerem. *Dogme Et Rituel De La Haute Magie*, 1854, p. 25. *Academia.edu*, https://www.academia.edu/27051672/Dogme_et_Rituel_de_la_Haute_Magie?email_work_card=view-paper. Accessed 15 Dec. 2022.

Green, H.L. *The Free Thought Magazine*, 1901, p. 207.

Haik, Jeremy. *Conveyor Magazine*, no. 6, 2014, p. 10.

Lee-Niinioja, Hee Sook. *Creative Manipulation of Photography as a Religious Means for Sacred Gothic Buildings*, 2016. *Academia.edu*, https://www.academia.edu/30356419/Creative_Manipulation_of_Photography_as_a_Religious_Means_for_Sacred_Gothic_Buildings. Accessed 17 Dec. 2022.

Miele, Jean. https://www.jeanmiele.com/more-black-and-white-landscapes/. Accessed 14 Dec. 2022

Paracelsus, Theophrastus, and Kurt Friedrich Leidecker. *Volumen Medicinae Paramirum*, John Hopkins Press, Baltimore, 1949, p. 34. *Internet Archive*, https://archive.org/details/VolumenMedicinaeParamirum/mode/2up. Accessed 15 Dec. 2022.

Loori, John Daido. *The Zen of Creativity: Cultivating Your Artistic Life*, Random House Publishing Group, United Kingdom, 2007, p. 1.

Psychology and Alchemy, 5 Oct. 2022. *Wikipedia*, https://en.wikipedia.org/wiki/Psychology_and_Alchemy. Accessed 15 Dec. 2022.

Read, John. *From Alchemy to Chemistry*, Dover Publications, New York, New York, 1995, pp. 14-15, https://ia902806.us.archive.org/5/items/AlchemyToChemistry/Alchemy%20to%20Chemistry.pdfAccessed 15 Dec. 2022.

Regardie, Israel. *The Tree of Life: A Study of Magic*, Literary Licensing, LLC, 2013, p. 28.

Shun-liang Chao. "The Alchemy of Photography: 'Grotesque Realism' and Hybrid Nature in Jerry Uelsmann's Photomontages." *Criticism*, vol. 59, no. 2, 2017, p. 301. *JSTOR*, https://doi.org/10.13110/criticism.59.2.0301. Accessed 17 Dec. 2022.

Vredefort Impact Structure, 11 Dec. 2022. *Wikipedia*, https://en.wikipedia.org/wiki/Vredefort_impact_structure. Accessed 15 Dec. 2022.

Wamberg, Jacob. *Art & Alchemy*, Museum Tusculanum Press, Copenhagen, 2006, p. 85.

Williams, Alastair. "The Idea of Photography." *Medium*, Photo Dojo, 6 Dec. 2020, https://medium.com/photo-dojo/the-idea-of-photography-4f5d286c44b.

3. FOREWARNING AND VISUALIZATION

Pictures
3.1 Sun Temple at Heliopolis (after Borchardt 1905: Bl. 1, 6).
https://www.semanticscholar.org/paper/An-enigmatic-graffito-from-the-sun-temple-of-and-of-Nuzzolo/868e38f928fcba3f282c6ced23af159a3a273305/figure/1 Accessed 6 Dec. 2020.

References
Atwood, Mary Anne. *Hermetic Philosophy and Alchemy: A Suggestive Inquiry into the Hermetic Mystery with a Dissertation on the More Celebrated of the Alchemical Philosophers*, Jazzybee Verlag, 2012. (note: no page number available)

Hall, Manly Palmer. *The Secret Teachings of All Ages: An Encyclopedic Outline of Masonic, Hermetic, Qabbalistic, and Rosicrucian Symbolical Philosophy: Being an Interpretation of the Secret Teachings Concealed within the Rituals, Allegories, and Mysteries of All Ages*, Philosophical Research Society, Los Angeles, California, 1988, p. 37.

Harpur, Patrick. *Mercurius, or, the Marriage of Heaven & Earth*, Blue Angel Gallery, Glen Waverly, Vic., 2007, p. 17.

Hurd, Richard, and William Warburton. *The Divine Legation of Moses Demonstrated*, Thomas Tegg, United Kingdom, 1846, p. 278.

4. AN AUSPICIOUS CONJUNCTION OF ARTS

References
Atwood, Mary Anne. *Hermetic Philosophy and Alchemy: A Suggestive Inquiry into the Hermetic Mystery with a Dissertation on the More Celebrated of the Alchemical Philosophers*, Routledge, 2005, p. 76. *Abardoncompanion*, http://abardoncompanion.de/Alex/Atwood.pdf. Accessed 18 Dec. 2022.

Berger, John. *Ways of Seeing*, Penguin Books Limited, United Kingdom, 2008, p. 10.

Bunyan, Marcus. Art Blart, *Text / review: 'A Vocabulary of Printing and the Syntax of the Image' from the exhibition 'KHEM' at Strange Neighbour, Fitzroy, Melbourne*, https://artblart.com/tag/the-keepers-of-light-a-history-and-working-guide-to-early-photographic-processes/, 2014. Accessed 19 Dec. 2022.

Castaneda, Carlos. *The Teachings of Don Juan: A Yaqui Way of Knowledge*, Univ of California Press, 1968, p. 19. http://metaphysicspirit.com/books/The%20Teachings%20of%20Don%20Juan%20-%20A%20Yaqui%20Way%20of%20Knowledge.pdf. Accessed 18 Dec. 2022.

Chang, C.Y. *Creativity and Taoism: A Study of Chinese Philosophy, Art, and Poetry*, Harper & Row, New York, New York, 1970, p. 124.

Crawford, William. *The Keepers of Light—A History & Working Guide to Early Photographic Processes*, Morgan & Morgan, New York, New York, 1979, p. 2. *Archive.org*, https://archive.org/details/aa147-TheKeepersOfLight/page/n13/mode/2up?ref=ol. Accessed 18 Dec. 2022.

Davenport, Leslie. *Transformative Imagery : Cultivating the Imagination for Healing, Change, and Growth*, Jessica Kingsley Publishers, 2016, p. 60.

DeLillo, Don. *Underworld: A Novel*, Scribner, United Kingdom, 2007, p. 177.

Dowman, Keith. *The Sacred Life of Tibet*, Thorsons, United Kingdom, 1997, p. 90.

Edson, Gary. *Mysticism and Alchemy Through the Ages: The Quest for Transformation*, McFarland & Co., 2012, p. 235.

Gross, P. L., & Shapiro, S. I. (1996). Characteristics of the Taoist sage in the *Chuang-tzu* and the creative photographer. *Journal of Transpersonal Psychology, 28*(2), 176.

Grundberg, Andy. Photography View: Minor White's Quest for Symbolic Significance, NY Times, April 30, 1989, Section 2, p33.

Guiley, Rosemary. *The Encyclopedia of Magic and Alchemy*, 2006, p. 7. *Academia.edu*, https://www.academia.edu/5021522/Encyclopedia_of_Magic_and_Alchemy?email_work_card=view-paper. Accessed 19 Dec. 2022.

Hellenic Faith, *Theourgia*, 14 Apr. 2020, https://hellenicfaith.com/ritual/. Accessed 22 Jan. 2023.

Minor White Archive, p. 142.
CreativeGuide.com, www.creativeguide.com/Resources/pdf%20files/DP_Ch5.pdf. Accessed 18 Dec. 2022.

Nieberding, William. *Photography, Phenomenology and Sight: Toward an Understanding of Photography through the Discourse of Vision*, 2011, p. 77. *Academia.edu*, https://www.academia.edu/934609/Photography_Phenomenology_and_Sight_Toward_an_Understanding_of_Photography_through_the_Discourse_of_Vision?email_work_card=view-paper. Accessed 18 Dec. 2022.

Occult of personality. Facebook post, 15 March 2022. Accessed 22 Jan. 2023.

"Photography and Alchemy." *Art Blart*, https://artblart.com/tag/photography-and-alchemy/.

Regardie, Israel. *The Tree of Life: A Study of Magic*, Literary Licensing, LLC, 2013, p. 23, 28, 31.

Sontag, Susan. *On Photography.*, Picador, New York, New York, 2001, pp. 3–4.

Steiner, George. *Real Presences*. United States, Open Road Media, 2013. (no page number available) https://www.google.com/books/edition/Real_Presences/NsN7alUl2HcC?hl=en&gbpv=1&dq=the+tenebrous+spiral+staircase+of+the+self&pg=PT79&printsec=frontcover. Accessed 22 Jan. 2023.

Ulrich, David. Deep Perception: Cultivating the Art of Seeing, Chapter 5, The Creative Response, p. 142. unpublished ms.

Zakia, Richard. *Focal Encyclopedia of Photography*, edited by Michael R. Peres, 4th ed., Focal Press, Burlington, Massachusetts, 2007, p. 460.

5. A PHILOSOPHER'S LEXICON

References

12 Elements of a Merit Image: Professional Photographers of America." *12 Elements of a Merit Image | Professional Photographers of America*, https://www.ppa.com/events/photo-competitions/the-12-elements-of-a-merit-image.

Aldersey-William, Hugh. *Conveyor Magazine*, 2014, p. 21.

Beaumont, Sheona, and Madeleine Emerald Thiele. *Transforming Christian Thought in the Visual Arts: Theology, Aesthetics, and Practice*. Routledge, 2021.

Davenport, Leslie. *Transformative Imagery: Cultivating the Imagination for Healing, Change, and Growth*, Jessica Kingsley Publishers, 2016, p. 60.

Duggan, Bob. *Piercing the Surface: Thomas Merton's Zen Photography*, 2 Sept. 2015, https://bigthink.com/culture-religion/piercing-the-surface-thomas-mertons-zen-photography/.

Gray, William G. *Inner Traditions of Magic*, Samuel Weiser INC., New York, New York, p. 108, https://phoreverphoenix.tripod.com/webonmediacontents/Gray_%20-_Inner_Traditions_of_Magic.pdf. Accessed 22 Dec. 2022.

"Let Us Not Delude Ourselves by the Seemingly Scien: Photoquotes." *Photo Quotes*, https://photoquotes.com/quote/let-us-not-delude-ourselves-by-the-seemingly-scien. Uelsmann, Jerry. *Jerry Uelsmann: Other Realities*, Bulfinch Press, New York, New York, 2005, p. 54.

Loori, John Daido. *The Zen of Creativity: Cultivating Your Artistic Life*, Ballantine Books, United States, 2005, p. 192, https://www.spiritualityandpractice.com/book-reviews/excerpts/view/14398/the-zen-of-creativity. Accessed 22 Dec. 2022.

Lyons, Noah. *Remedios Varo: An Alchemical Artist*, p. 1. *Academia.edu*, 2012, https://www.academia.edu/8851411/Remedios_Varo_An_Alchemical_Artist?email_work_card=view-paper. Accessed 19 Dec. 2022.

"Man Ray Tribute." *Escape Into Life*, https://www.escapeintolife.com/art-videos/man-ray/. FlaglerLive. "Move over, Magritte: Alchemist-Photographer Jerry Uelsmann Documents States of Consciousness." *FlaglerLive*, 19 Jan. 2018, https://flaglerlive.com/116551/jerry-uelsmann/.

"Spell." *The Word Detective*, http://www.word-detective.com/2013/07/spell-2/.

Three Initiates, and William Walker Atkinson. *The Kybalion: A Study of The Hermetic Philosophy of Ancient Egypt and Greece*, YOGeBooks, 2010, p. 66. *Yogebooks.com*, http://www.yogebooks.com/english/atkinson/1908kybalion.pdf. Accessed 22 Dec. 2022.

Wamberg, Jacob. *The Material Ethereal: Photography and the Alchemical Ancestor*, edited by Laurie Dahlberg, Museum Tusculanum Press, University of Copenhagen, 2006, p. 93.

6. FOUR GENERATIONS OF KINGSWOOD ADEPTS

Pictures
6.1 Turn of the Century Developing Equipment, Dillaye, Frédéric. La Théorie, la pratique et l'art en photographie. Le Paysage artistique en photographie, avec le procédé au gélatino-bromure d'argent. France, J. Taillandier, 1907. p. 106.

6.2: Photographer, Dillaye, Frédéric. La Théorie, la pratique et l'art en photographie. Le Paysage artistique en photographie, avec le procédé au gélatino-bromure d'argent. France, J. Taillandier, 1907. p. 106.

6.3 An Alchemist in His Laboratory. Theatrum Chemicum Brittanicum by Elias Ashmole, 1652.

6.4 Painting of Ra. From George Kingswood's Temple Room. Reprinted with permission from George Kingswood, artist unknown..

References

Anonymous. "The Modern Priests and Temples of the Sun." *Chambers Journal*, no. 472, 17 Jan. 1863, pp. 33–36.

Barthes, Roland. *Camera Lucida: Reflections on Photography*, Macmillan, 1981, p. 161.

Behrend, Heike. "Photo Magic: Photographs in Practices of Healing and Harming in East Africa." *Journal of Religion in Africa*, vol. 33, no. 2, 2003, pp. 129–45. *JSTOR*, https://www.jstor.org/stable/1581652. Accessed 22 Dec. 2022.

Benjamin, Walter. On Photography. United Kingdom, Reaktion Books, 2015.

Coates, James. *Photographing the Invisible Practical Studies in Spirit Photography, Spirit Portraiture, and Other Rare but Allied Phenomena*, The Advanced Thought Publishing Co., Chicago, Illinois, 1911, p. 1. *Iapsop.com*, http://iapsop.com/ssoc/1911__coates___photographing_the_invisible.pdf. Accessed 22 Dec. 2022.

"Daguerreotype Process." *Camera*, http://camera-wiki.org/wiki/Daguerreotype_Process

Daniel, Malcolm. "Daguerre (1787–1851) and the Invention of Photography." *Metmuseum.org*, Oct. 2004, https://www.metmuseum.org/toah/hd/dagu/hd_dagu.htm.

Daniel, Malcolm. "William Henry Fox Talbot (1800–1877) and the Invention of Photography." *Metmuseum.org*, Oct. 2004, https://www.metmuseum.org/toah/hd/tlbt/hd_tlbt.htm.

Davenport, Leslie. *Transformative Imagery : Cultivating the Imagination for Healing, Change, and Growth*, Jessica Kingsley Publishers, 2016, pp. 32–33, 34.

"Define Fetish." *Google Search*, Google, https://www.google.com/search?q=define%2Bfetish&rlz=1C5CHFA_enUS875US877&oq=define%2Bfetish&aqs=chrome.0.69i59j0i512.6913j1j7&sourceid=chrome&ie=UTF-8.

Descartes, R., and P.J. Olscamp. *Discourse on Method, Optics, Geometry, and Meteorology*, Bobbs-Merrill, Indianapolis, Indiana, 1965, p. 65.

Downs, James. "Ministers of the Black Art': The Engagement of British Clergy with Photography, 1839-1914." 2018, pp. 13–14.

Eco, Umberto. *Les Limites De L'interprétation*, Grasset, Paris, 1992, p. 87.
Chevalier, Jean, and Alain Gheerbrant. *Dictionnaire Des Symboles*, Robert Laffont, Paris, 1982, p. 642.

Eliade, Mircea. *The Forge and the Crucible: The Origins and Structure of Alchemy*, University of Chicago Press, 1978, p. 156. *Archive.org*, https://archive.org/details/forgecrucible00eliarich/page/156/mode/2up. Accessed 26 Dec. 2022.

Freedberg, David. *The Power of Images*, University of Chicago Press, Chicago, Illinois, 1991, p. 1, http://eclass.asfa.gr/modules/document/file.php/AHT4108/Freedberg%20-%20Power%20of%20Images%20ch%201.pdf. Accessed 26 Dec. 2022.

Gunning, Tom. "'Phantom Images and Modern Manifestations: Magic Theatre, Trick Films and Photography's Uncanny.'" *Patrice Petro, Fugitive Images- from Photography to Video*, 1995, pp. 42–43.

Green, H.L. *The Free Thought Magazine*, 1901, p. 205.

Hall, Manly P. *The Secret Teachings of All Ages*, 1928, p. 53. *Cia.gov*, https://www.cia.gov/library/abbottabad-compound/E4/E4AAFF6DAF6863F459A8B4E52DFB9FF4_Manly.P.Hall_The.Secret.Teachings.of.All.Ages.pdf. Accessed 26 Dec. 2022.

"Heliopolis (Ancient Egypt)." *Wikipedia*, Wikimedia Foundation, 18 Dec. 2022, https://en.wikipedia.org/wiki/Heliopolis_(ancient_Egypt).

Kotansky, Roy. "Amulets." *Dictionary of Gnosis Western and Esotericism*, vol. 1, 2005, p. 47. *Academia.edu*, https://www.academia.edu/3147599/Amulets?email_work_card=reading-history. Accessed 26 Dec. 2022.

Nadar, et al. *When I Was a Photographer*, The MIT Press, Cambridge, MA, 2016, p. 2. *Eclass.uoa*, https://eclass.uoa.gr/modules/document/file.php/PSPA254/NADAR-WHEN%20I%20WAS%20A%20PHOTOGRAPHER.pdf. Accessed 26 Dec. 2022.

Lauzon, Jean. Vol. 11, 2000. *Docplayer.fr*, https://doi.org//802948ar. Accessed 22 Dec. 2022.

Millesima, Iulia. *"Loïc Tréhédel and Nicéphore Niépce's Photochemistry."* LabyrinthDesigners & the Art of Fire, 13 Oct. 2022, https://www.labyrinthdesigners.org/alchemy-science-history/loic-trehedel-and-nicephore-niepces-photochemistry/.

Oppenheim, Janet. *The Other World: Spiritualism and Psychical Research in Victorian Britain, 1850-1914*. Cambridge University Press, 1985, p. 28.

Scharf, Aaron. *Pioneer of Photography: An Album of Pictures and Words*, Harry N. Abrams, INC., Publishers, New York, New York, 1976, p. 11. *Monoskop.org*, https://monoskop.org/images/0/0c/Scharf_Aaron_Pioneers_of_Photography_1976.pdf. Accessed 22 Dec. 2022.

Smith, Graham. *Disciples of Light: Photographs in the Brewster Album*, J. Paul Getty Museum, 1990, p. 27, http://foxtalbot.dmu.ac.uk/ . Accessed 26 Dec. 2022.

Van Lennep, Jacques. *L'art Alchimique Et Le Surréel*, 1979, p. 295. *Erudit.org*, https://www.erudit.org/en/journals/hphi/#journal-info-about. Accessed 22 Dec. 2022. *Dictionnaire Le Petit Robert*, Paris, 1979, p. 1842.

Wamberg, Jacob. *Art & Alchemy*, Museum Tusculanum Press, University of Copenhagen, 2006, p. 84, https://www.google.com/books/edition/Art_Alchemy/LmlA9o8EFBYC?hl=en&gbpv=1&dq=alchemy+in+the+history+of+photography&pg=PA98&printsec=frontcover. Accessed 22 Dec. 2022.

7. Ra Sails Over the Blazing Dawn

Pictures
7.1: Thoth, the Egyptian God of magic, writing, sacred texts, the moon, deliverer of knowledge, and scribe of the gods.
https://upload.wikimedia.org/wikipedia/commons/archive/7/76/20141013053807%21Thoout%2C_Thoth_Deux_fois_Grand%2C_le_Second_Herm%C3%A9s%2C_N372.2A.jpg

7.2 Ra. Budge, E. A. Wallis. The Gods of the Egyptians, Volume 2. United States, Dover Publications, 1969. p 35. Originally published in 1904.

7.3 Picture 7.3 The Hierophant Ascending, Garin Horner, 2025.

7.4 Ra Writing Heka. General Research Division, The New York Public Library. "Thèbes, Karnac [Thebes, Karnak]. Temple de Khons. 1. Grande porte; 2. Porte du pylône; 3. Salle hypostyle; 4. Paroi du pronaos." *The New York Public Library Digital Collections*. 1845. https://digitalcollections.nypl.org/items/b9aaa5a0-c5f8-012f-390b-58d385a7bc34

References
Bunnell, Peter C., et al. *Minor White, the Eye That Shapes*, Art Museum, Princeton University, 1989, p. 19.

Hall, Manly P. *The Secret Teachings of All Ages*, 1928, p. 53. *Cia.gov*, https://www.cia.gov/library/abbottabad-compound/E4/E4AAFF6DAF6863F459A8B4E52DFB9FF4_Manly.P.Hall_The.Secret.Teachings.of.All.Ages.pdf. Accessed 26 Dec. 2022.

Lévi, Éliphas. *Dogme Et Rituel De La Haute Magie*, Rider & Company, England, 1896, p. 1. *Academia.edu*, https://www.academia.edu/27051672/Dogme_et_Rituel_de_la_Haute_Magie?email_work_card=view-paper. Accessed 14 Dec. 2022.

Lienhard, John H. *No. 76: About Alchemists*, https://uh.edu/engines/epi76.htm.

"RA: The Sun God of Egypt." *The Egyptian God Ra | Sun God of Egypt | Eye of Ra*, https://www.ancient-egypt-online.com/egyptian-god-ra.html. Accessed Dec. 2022.

Taylor, Thomas, translator. *Political Fragments of Archytas, Charondas, Zaleucus, and Other Ancient Pythagoreans Preserved by Stobæus; and Also, Ethical Fragments of Hierocles... Prserved by the Same Author,* C. Whittingham, United Kingdom, 1822, pp. 12–13.

Wilkinson, Richard H. *Reading Egyptian Art: A Hieroglyphic Guide to Ancient Egyptian Painting and Sculpture,* Thames & Hudson, 1992, p. 43.

8. CORRESPONDENCES: A NETWORK OF LUMINOUS FILAMENTS

Pictures
8.1 - *mdw ntr* (the words of the gods).
https://en.wiktionary.org/wiki/mdw_n%E1%B9%AFr. Accessed 27 Dec. 2022.

8.2 The Kemetic Kabbalah. Reproduction from Abraham Kingswood's
Egyptian Tree of Life drawing. By Garin Horner and George Kingswood.

References from within the artwork (all accessed June 1, 2020):
   Alchemical Characters: https://pixels.com/featured/kabbalistic-tree-of-life-zapista-ou.html
   Column Top: https://www-jstor-
org.adriancollege.idm.oclc.org/stable/23269886?seq=11#metadata_info_tab_contents
Egyptian Deity Illustrations: https://en.wikipedia.org/wiki/Ra
Egyptian Hieroglyphics: https://www.um.es/cepoat/egipcio/wp-content/uploads/egyptianhierogly.pdf

8.3 The Monas Glyph, https://arthistoryproject.com/artists/john-dee/monas-hieroglyphica/. Accessed 27 Dec. 2022.

8.4 The Monas Hieroglyphica of John Dee, Latin MS 82 from the John Rylands Library, Manchester, England. Accessed 27 Dec. 2022.
https://stephenrgordon.wordpress.com/2017/05/09/an-alchemical-miscellany-from-the-john-rylands-library/

8.5 *Obeliscus Pamphilius: hoc est, Interpretatio noua & Hucusque Intentata Obelisci Hieroglyphici* by Athanasius Kircher, 1650. Accessed 27 Dec. 2022.
https://digi.ub.uni-heidelberg.de/diglit/kircher1650/0437/image

References
Annus, Amar, editor. *Divination and Interpretation of Signs in the Ancient World,* Oriental Institute of the University of Chicago, Chicago, Illinois, 2010, p. 145,
https://faculty.washington.edu/snoegel/PDFs/articles/Noegel%2057%20-%20OI%202009.pdf. Accessed 29 Dec. 2022.

"Archaeo-Optics." *Wikipedia,* Wikimedia Foundation, 3 Mar. 2022,
https://en.wikipedia.org/wiki/Archaeo-optics.

Atwood, Mary Anne. *Hermetic Philosophy and Alchemy: A Suggestive Inquiry into the Hermetic Mystery with a Dissertation on the More Celebrated of the Alchemical Philosophers,* Routledge, 2005, p. 3. *Abardoncompanion,* http://abardoncompanion.de/Alex/Atwood.pdf. Accessed 14 Dec. 2022.

Budge, E. A. Wallis, translator. *The Egyptian Book of the Dead,* Kegan Paul, Trench, Trübner &Co., LTD, London, 1898, p. 165, http://www.public-
library.uk/dailyebook/The%20Egyptian%20Book%20of%20the%20Dead.pdf. Accessed 26 Dec. 2022.

Christopher, Lyam Thomas. *Kabbalah, Magic, and The Great Work of Self-Transformation: A Complete Course,* Llewellyn Publications, Woodbury, Minnesota, 2006, pp. 103–104.

Cirlot, J.E. *A Dictionary of Symbols,* translated by Jack Sage, 2nd ed., Routledge, London, 1962, p. 36, https://ia801306.us.archive.org/9/items/DictionaryOfSymbols/Dictionary%20of%20Symbols.pdf. Accessed 26 Dec. 2022.

"Define Connectionism." *Google Search,* Google,
https://www.google.com/search?q=define%2Bconnectionism&rlz=1C5CHFA_enUS875US877&oq=define
%2Bconnectionism&aqs=chrome..69i57j0i512j0i22i30l2j0i390.2073j1j4&sourceid=chrome&ie=UTF-8.
Accessed 29 Dec. 2022.

Eber, Mark. *The Everything Kabbalah Book: Explore This Mystical Tradition--From Ancient Rituals to Modern Day Practices*, Adam's Media, 2006, p. 137.

Gatton, M. "First Light: Inside the Palaeolithic Camera Obscura." *In Acts of Seeing: Artists, Scientists and the History of the Visual: a Volume Dedicated to Martin Kemp (Assimina Kaniari and Marina Wallace, Eds.)*, 2009, p. 153.

Hermetic Kabbalah, http://www.digital-brilliance.com/themes/tol.php.
"Tree of Life (Kabbalah)." *Wikipedia*, Wikimedia Foundation, 26 Dec. 2022,
https://en.wikipedia.org/wiki/Tree_of_life_(Kabbalah). Accessed 26 Dec. 2022

"Kabbalah: An Archetypal Interpretation." *Kabbalah*,
http://www.newkabbalah.com/Jung3.html. Accessed 26 Dec. 2022.

"Kabbalah." *Wikipedia*, Wikimedia Foundation, 21 Dec. 2022, https://en.wikipedia.org/wiki/Kabbalah.

Kerstein, Benjamin. "Kabbalah." *World History Encyclopedia*,
https://www.worldhistory.org#organization, 27 Dec. 2022, https://www.worldhistory.org/Kabbalah/.
Accessed 27 Dec. 2022.

Kotansky, Roy. "Amulets." *Dictionary of Gnosis Western and Esotericism*, vol. 1, 2005, p.
48. *Academia.edu*, https://www.academia.edu/3147599/Amulets?email_work_card=reading-history.
Accessed 26 Dec. 2022.

Landman, Isaac. *The Universal Jewish Encyclopedia ...: An Authoritative and Popular Presentation of Jews and Judaism Since the Earliest Times*, 1939.

Leigh, Oliver Herbrand Gordon. *Universal Classics Library*, Dunn, 1901, p. 161.

Levi, Eliphas. The Doctrine of Transcendental Magic. Germany, Jazzybee Verlag, 2013.

Mills, Robert. *Kabbalah - The Tree of Life*. Byzant Mystical. "Tree of Life: Explained." *Token Rock*, 29 July 2021, https://www.tokenrock.com/subjects/tree-of-life/. Accessed 26 Dec. 2022.

"Neural Networks." *A Brief Introduction to the Brain:Neural Nets*, (Universidad Nacional Autónoma de México/Instituto de Fisología Celular, 2022)
http://www.ifc.unam.mx/Brain/nenet.htm#:~:text=NEURAL%20NETWORKS,of%20fine%20structures%20
called%20dendrites.&text=When%20a%20neuron%20receives%20excitatory,action%20potential. Accessed 29 Dec. 2022.

Nieberding, William. *Photography, Phenomenology and Sight: Toward an Understanding of Photography through the Discourse of Vision*, 2011, p. 77. *Academia.edu*,
https://www.academia.edu/934609/Photography_Phenomenology_and_Sight_Toward_an_Understanding_of
_Photography_through_the_Discourse_of_Vision?email_work_card=view-paper. Accessed 29 Dec. 2022.

Nix, Elizabeth. "Where Did the RX Symbol Come from?" *History.com*, A&E Television Networks, 7 May 2014, https://www.history.com/news/where-did-the-rx-symbol-come-from. Accessed 26 Dec. 2022.

Paracelsus: Selected Writings. United Kingdom, Princeton University Press, 1988.
p. 133.

Peterson, Joseph H. "Monas Hieroglyphica." *Monas Hieroglyphica ('The Hieroglyphic Monad') of John Dee (1564)*, http://www.esotericarchives.com/dee/monad.htm. Accessed 27 Dec. 2022.

Pinch, Geraldine. *Magic in Ancient Egypt*, British Museum Press, 1994, p. 80,
https://pauladaunt.com/books/Magic%20in%20ancient%20Egypt.pdf. Accessed 29 Dec. 2022.

Rabinowitz, Isaac. *A Witness Forever: Ancient Israel's Perception of Literature and the Resultant Hebrew Bible*, CDL Press, Bethesa, Maryland, 1993, p. 16.

Scholem, Gershom. *Origins of the Kabbalah*, Princeton, NJ, 1990, pp. 24–29.

9. THE PHOTO-ALCHEMICAL EMBLEM

References

Bunnell, Peter C., et al. *Minor White, the Eye That Shapes,* Art Museum, Princeton University, 1989, p. 21.

Child, Heather. *Christian Symbols Ancient and Modern*, edited by Dorothy Colles, G. Bell and Sons, London, 1971, p. 1.

"Éliphas Lévi Quotes (Author of Transcendental Magic)." *Goodreads*, Goodreads, https://www.goodreads.com/author/quotes/142174._liphas_L_vi. Accessed 29 Dec. 2022.

Geoffroy, Éric. "Métaphysique Et Modernité Chez Abd El-Kader : La Photographie Comme Théophanie." *Abd El-Kader, Un Spirituel Dans La Modernité - Métaphysique Et Modernité Chez Abd El-Kader : La Photographie Comme Théophanie*, Presses De L'Ifpo, 1 Jan. 1970, https://books-openedition-org.translate.goog/ifpo/1837?_x_tr_sl=fr&_x_tr_tl=en&_x_tr_hl=en&_x_tr_pto=sc. Accessed 29 Dec. 2022.

Merton, Thomas. "Turning Toward the World: The Pivotal Years 1960-1963." *The Journals of Thomas Merton*, Edited by Victor A. Kramer, vol. 4, 1996, p. 123. *Merton.org*, http://www.merton.org/hiddenwholeness/Patnaik%20Photo%20Essay.pdf. Accessed 29 Dec. 2022.

Merton, Thomas. "The Conjectures of a Guilty Bystander." *The Journals of Thomas Merton*, Doubleday, New York, New York, 1989, p. 281. *Merton.org*, http://www.merton.org/hiddenwholeness/Patnaik%20Photo%20Essay.pdf. Accessed 29 Dec. 2022.

Merton, Thomas. "The Literary Essays of Thomas Merton." *The Journals of Thomas Merton*, 1985, p. 30. *Merton.org*, http://www.merton.org/hiddenwholeness/Patnaik%20Photo%20Essay.pdf. Accessed 29 Dec. 2022.

Merton, Thomas. "Notes on Art and Worship." *Unpublished Mimeograph*, p. 21. *Merton.org*, http://www.merton.org/hiddenwholeness/Patnaik%20Photo%20Essay.pdf. Accessed 29 Dec. 2022.

Merton, Thomas. "The Other Side of the Mountain: The End of the Journey." *The Journals of Thomas Merton*, edited by Patrick Hart, Harper Collins, San Francisco, California, 1998, p. 323. *Merton.org*, http://www.merton.org/hiddenwholeness/Patnaik%20Photo%20Essay.pdf. Accessed 29 Dec. 2022.

Merton, Thomas. "The Literary Essays of Thomas Merton." *The Journals of Thomas Merton*, 1985, p. 100. *Merton.org*, http://www.merton.org/hiddenwholeness/Patnaik%20Photo%20Essay.pdf. Accessed 29 Dec. 2022.

Oring, Stuart. *The Aesthetic Theories of Minor White*, 1 Jan. 2021, p. 48. *Academia.edu*, https://www.academia.edu/34503349/The_Aesthetic_Theories_Of_Minor_White_pdf. Accessed 29 Dec. 2022.

Patnaik, Deba P. *Through A Glass Purely. Merton.org*, http://www.merton.org/hiddenwholeness/Patnaik%20Photo%20Essay.pdf. Accessed 29 Dec. 2022.

Raina, Mariette. "In Spirit: Photography and Metaphysics, Reflection of the Self." *Never Apart*, https://www.neverapart.com/features/in-spirit-photography-and-metaphysics/. Accessed 29 Dec. 2022.

10. ALCHEMY & PHOTOGRAPHY: THE ARTS OF FIRE

Pictures

10.1: Vuur, Adriaen Collaert, after Maerten de Vos, 1580 - 1584
https://www.rijksmuseum.nl/en/collection/RP-P-BI-6064 Accessed 13 Nov. 2022.

10.2 *Ars magna lucis et umbrae* by Athanasius Kircher, 1646.
https://www.compendiumnaturalis.net/Wordpress/wp-content/uploads/Frontispice_Ars_magna_lucis_et_umbrae_Athanasius_Kircher.jpg. Accessed 12 Nov. 2022.

10.3 Spirit Photograph by William Hope (1863-1933)
https://publicdomainreview.org/collection/the-spirit-photographs-of-william-hope. Accessed 12 Nov. 2022.

10.4 Spirit Photograph by F.M. Parkes (ca. 1872).
https://www.eldritchoculum.com/inventory/p/spirit-photograph-by-parkes-carbon-print-carte-de-visite-c-1870. Accessed 12 Nov. 2022.

References

Ahmed, Syed Akheel. Islam and Scientific Enterprise, I. K. International Pvt Ltd, 2013, p. 75.

"Alchemy." Wikipedia, Wikimedia Foundation, 26 Dec. 2022,
https://en.wikipedia.org/wiki/Alchemy.

Aperture. Spirituality, Aperture Foundation, Inc. , 2019, pp. 39–40.

Aristotle. Translator Graham, Daniel W. Physics: Book VIII, p. 4-6. Kiribati, Clarendon Press, 1999.

Ars Magna Lucis Et Umbrae, 9 July 2012,
https://aquariumofvulcan.blogspot.com/2012/07/ars-magna-lucis-et-umbrae_9.html. Accessed 2 Jan. 2023.

"Ars Magna Lucis Et Umbrae." Wikipedia, Wikimedia Foundation, 14 June 2022,
https://en.wikipedia.org/wiki/Ars_Magna_Lucis_et_Umbrae. Accessed 2 Jan. 2023.

Atwood, Mary Anne. Hermetic Philosophy and Alchemy: A Suggestive Inquiry into the
Hermetic Mystery with a Dissertation on the More Celebrated of the Alchemical Philosophers, Routledge,
2005, p. 56. Abardoncompanion, http://abardoncompanion.de/Alex/Atwood.pdf. Accessed 29 Dec. 2022.

Bacon, Roger. The Opus Majus. 1897, p. CXLVII.

Barrett, Francis. The Lives of Alchemystical Philosophers, vol. 1815ccc. Academia.edu,
https://www.academia.edu/28090713/Barrett_F_The_Lives_of_Alchemystical_Philosophers_1815ccc.
Accessed 2 Jan. 2023.

Barrett, Francis, and Arthur Edward Waite. Lives of Alchemystical Philosophers Based on Materials
Collected in 1815: And Supplemented by Recent Researches with a Philosophical Demonstration of the True
Principles of the Magnum Opus, Or Great Work of Alchemical Re-Construction, and Some Account of the
Spiritual Chemistry, G. Redway, United Kingdom, 1888, p. 99-100.

Bierce, Ambrose. The Devil's Dictionary,
https://xroads.virginia.edu/~Hyper/Bierce/bierce.html#M. Accessed 25 Dec. 2022.

Brice, E., and Alipili. Centrum Naturae Concentratum, or, the Salt of Nature Regenerated: For the Most Part
Improperly Called the Philosopher's Stone ; Written in Arabick ... Published in Low Dutch, 1694, and Now
Done into English, United Kingdom, 1696, p. 78. For J. Harris.

Chéroux, Clément. Photographs of Fluids. An Alphabet of Invisible Rays, New Haven: Yale UP, 2005, 119.

Cintas, Pedro. "Francis Bacon: An Alchemical Odyssey Through the Novum Organum." Bull. Hist. Chem.,
vol. 28, no. 2, 2003. Illinois.edu, http://acshist.scs.illinois.edu/bulletin_open_access/v28-2/v28-2%20p65-
75.pdf. Accessed 2 Jan. 2023.

Coates, James. Photographing the Invisible: Practical Studies In Spirit Photography, Spirit Portraiture and
Other Rare but Allied Phenomena, The Advanced Thought Publishing Co., Chicago, Illinois, 1911, p. 2.
Iapsop.com, http://iapsop.com/ssoc/1911__coates___photographing_the_invisible.pdf. Accessed 2 Jan.
2023.

Ferre, Lux, and Valentin Bewick. "Gold." OCCULT WORLD, 6 Oct. 2017,
https://occult-world.com/gold/. Accessed 29 Dec. 2022.

Goldberg, V. The Power of Photography: How Photographs Changed Our Lives (Expanded and Updated).
Abbeville Publishing Group, 1993.

Gross, Phillipe L., and S. I. Shapiro. The Tao of Photography: Seeing Beyond Seeing, Ten Speed Press,
United Kingdom, 2001, p. 45.

Harvey, John. "The Perfect Medium: Photography and the Occult." Material Religion, vol. 2, no. 2, July
2006. Gale Academic,
https://go.gale.com/ps/i.do?p=AONE&u=googlescholar&id=GALE|A175874309&v=2.1&it=r&sid=googleS
cholar&asid=15045c9f. Accessed 2 Jan. 2023.

"Hermes Trismegistus." Wikipedia, Wikimedia Foundation, 10 Oct. 2022,
https://en.wikipedia.org/wiki/Hermes_Trismegistus.

Kircher, Athanasius. Oedipus Aegyptiacus, 1652. pp. 567–568.

Klossowski de Rola, Stanislas. The Golden Game: Alchemical Engravings of the Seventeenth Century,
Thames & Hudson, 1997, p. 19.

Kotansky, Roy. "Amulets." Dictionary of Gnosis Western and Esotericism, vol. 1, 2005, p.
37. Academia.edu, https://www.academia.edu/3147599/Amulets?email_work_card=reading-history.
Accessed 2 Jan. 2023.

Lemagny, Jean-Claude, and Andre Rouille. A History of Photography: Social and Cultural Perspectives,
Cambridge University Press, 1987, pp. 14–15.

Occult Influences in Photography, http://adelsouto.com/3.20.2013_lecture.html. Accessed 2 Jan. 2023.

"Opus Majus." Wikipedia, Wikimedia Foundation, 25 Sept. 2022,
https://en.wikipedia.org/wiki/Opus_Majus. Accessed 2 Jan. 2023.

Photography, The Journal of the Amateur, the Profession, and the Trade. Vol. 5, Iliffe and Son, London.
1893, p. 272.

Pope, Alexander. Epitaph on Sir Isaac Newton, https://www.bartleby.com/297/154.html. Accessed 2 Jan.
2023.

Principe, Lawerence M. "The End of Alchemy?: The Repudiation and Persistence of Chrysopoeia at the
Académie Royale Des Sciences in the Eighteenth Century." Chemical Knowledge in the Early Modern
World , vol. 29, no. 1, Jan. 2014, p. 97. JSTOR, https://www-jstor
org.adriancollege.idm.oclc.org/stable/10.1086/678099?seq=2#metadata_info_tab_contents. Accessed 2 Jan.
2023.

Silberer, Herbert. Hidden Symbolism of Alchemy and the Occult Arts, Dover Publications, 1971, p. 91.

"Sir Thomas Browne and the Kabbalah ." Sir Thomas Browne and the Kabbalah, 19 Oct. 2015,
https://aquariumofvulcan.blogspot.com/2015/10/sir-thomas-browne-and-kabbalah.html?m=1. Accessed 2
Jan. 2023.

Souto, Adel. Occult Influences in Photography, 2013. https://adelsouto.com/3.20.2013_lecture.html.
Accessed 2, April 2023.

"Spirit Photography." Spirit Photography - Dead Media Archive,
http://cultureandcommunication.org/deadmedia/index.php/Spirit_Photography. Accessed 2 Jan. 2023.

"Spirit Photography." Wikipedia, Wikimedia Foundation,
https://en.wikipedia.org/wiki/Spirit_photography. Accessed 31 Dec. 2022.

Sussman, Herbert. "The Perfect Medium: Photography and the Occult." Victorian Literature and Culture, 1st
ed., vol. 35, Cambridge University Press, 2007, p. 339. JSTOR, http://www.jstor.org/stable/40347140.
Accessed 2 Jan. 2023.

"The Great Art of Light and Shadow." Ars Magna Lucis Et Umbrae, 2 Sept. 2008,
http://bibliodyssey.blogspot.com/2008/09/ars-magna-lucis-et-umbrae.html. Accessed 2 Jan. 2023.

"The Public Domain Review", Theatrum Chemicum Britannicum (1652),
https://publicdomainreview.org/collection/theatrum-chemicum/. Accessed Nov. 10, 2022.

Underhill, Evelyn. Mysticism: A Study in the Nature and Development of Spiritual
Consciousness, 12th ed., Dover, Mineola, New York, 2002, p. 143.

Wilford, John Noble. "Transforming the Alchemists." The New York Times, The New York Times, 1 Aug.
2006, https://www.nytimes.com/2006/08/01/science/01alch.html. Accessed 2 Jan. 2023.

Windling, Terri. "'Into the Woods' Series, 45: Elemental Magic." Myth & Moor, 17 Mar. 2015,
https://www.terriwindling.com/blog/2015/03/elemental-magic.html. Accessed 29 Dec. 2022.

11. A Tradition of Secrecy

Pictures

11.1 Giulio Bonasone, *Study for Harpocrates (Silentio Deum Cole)*. 1500.
https://www.nga.gov/collection/art-object-page.55080.html. Accessed 2 Jan. 2023.
Courtesy National Gallery of Art, Washington.
Public Domain Policy: https://www.nga.gov/notices/open-access-policy.html

End Sign: The Absoute Key to the Occult Sciences, Tarot of the Bohemians by Papus. From the French by
A. P. Morton, London. 1896.
https://www.google.com/books/edition/The_Tarot_of_the_Bohemians/6g9H4lMd03QC?hl=en&gbpv=1&pg
=PA3&printsec=frontcover Accessed May 26, 2025.

References

Atwood, Mary Anne. *Hermetic Philosophy and Alchemy: A Suggestive Inquiry into the
Hermetic Mystery with a Dissertation on the More Celebrated of the Alchemical Philosophers*, Routledge,
2005, p. 20, 22, 26. *Abardoncompanion*, http://abardoncompanion.de/Alex/Atwood.pdf. Accessed 2 Jan.
2023.

Bardon, Franz. *Initiation Into Hermetics: A Course of Instruction of Magic Theory and
Practice*. Germany, p. 34, D. Rüggeberg, 1976.

Barth, Fredrik. *Ritual and Knowledge Among the Baktaman of New Guinea*, 1975, p. 220. *JSTOR*,
https://www-jstor-org.adriancollege.idm.oclc.org/stable/640319?seq=8#metadata_info_tab_contents.
Accessed 2 Jan. 2023.

Bolat, A. "Introduction to Photography." *Visual Arts and Visual Communication Design*,
https://abolat.wordpress.com/page/2/. Accessed 2 Jan. 2023.

Bradley, Marion Zimmer. *The Mists of Avalon*, Sphere, New York, 1983, pp. 190–191,
http://www.themiltondoddreaders.weebly.com/uploads/1/0/8/1/10819822/the_mists_of_avalon.pdf.
Accessed 2 Jan. 2023.

Guiley, Rosemary. *The Encyclopedia of Magic and Alchemy*, 2006, p. 7. *Academia.edu*,
https://www.academia.edu/5021522/Encyclopedia_of_Magic_and_Alchemy?email_work_card=view-paper.
Accessed 19 Dec. 2022.

Holy Crusader. "The Gnostic Science of Alchemy Chapter Ten." *San Graal*, 21 Nov.
2022, http://www.sangraal.com/library/gsa10.html. Accessed 2 Jan. 2023.

Kotansky, Roy. "Amulets." *Dictionary of Gnosis Western and Esotericism*, vol. 1, 2005, pp. 21–22.
Academia.edu, https://www.academia.edu/3147599/Amulets?email_work_card=reading-history. Accessed 2
Jan. 2023.

Luhrmann, T.M. "The Magic of Secrecy." *Ethos*, vol. 17, no. 2, June 1989, pp. 136–137, p. 142.
JSTOR, https://www.jstor.org
https://www-jstor-org.adriancollege.idm.oclc.org/stable/640319?seq=12#metadata_info_tab_contents.
Accessed 2 Jan. 2023.

National Geographic, Oct. 1989, p. 530., Accessed 2 Jan. 2023.

Philalethes, Eirenaens, and William Cooper. *Ripley Reviv'd, or, An Exposition upon Sir George Ripley's
Hermetico-Poetical Works Containing the Plainest and Most Excellent Discoveries of the Most Hidden
Secrets of the Ancient Philosophers, That Were Ever Yet Published*, p. 371, 357.
https://quod.lib.umich.edu/e/eebo/A61326.0001.001/1:13?rgn=div1;view=fulltext. Accessed 2 Jan. 2023.

"Royal Photographic Society." *Wikipedia*, Wikimedia Foundation, 1 Jan. 2023,
https://en.wikipedia.org/wiki/Royal_Photographic_Society. Accessed 2 Jan. 2023.

"RPS: History." *The Royal Photographic Society*, https://rps.org/about/history/. Accessed 2 Jan. 2023.

Scharf, Aaron. *Pioneer of Photography: An Album of Pictures and Words*, Harry N. Abrams, INC., Publishers, New York, New York, 1976, p. 11. *Monoskop.org*, https://monoskop.org/images/0/0c/Scharf_Aaron_Pioneers_of_Photography_1976.pdf. Accessed 22 Dec. 2022.

"The Secret Work of The Hermetic Philosophy." *The Hermetic Arcanum*, https://www.alchemywebsite.com/harcanum.html. Accessed 2 Jan. 2023.

The Eclectic Pythagorean. "In Search of Western Civilisation's Lost Classics." *The Eclectic Pythagorean*, 25 Oct. 2008, https://pythagoras10.wordpress.com/. Accessed 2 Jan. 2023.

12. Twin Flames: The Alchemist & Ra

Pictures
12.1 Abraham Kingswood's Divine Falcon Seal. Reprinted with permission from George Kingswood.

12.2 Fuchs, Cölestin A. Arcana Divina: Ms. d. Stiftes Ossegg. N.p., Seltmann, 1912.

12.3 Cartouche of Ra, the Egyptian God of Light by Garin Horner, 2022, based on a drawing by Abraham Kingswood Kingswood, ca. 1870.

12.4 Votive portraits for George Kingswood's Temple Room. Photographs by Garin Horner, 2022.

References
About Zenju Earthlyn Manuelis a Soto Zen priest, and Lion's Roar Staff. "Making Offerings to Our Ancestors." *Lions Roar*, 2 June 2022, https://www.lionsroar.com/making-offerings-to-our-ancestors/. Accessed 3 Jan. 2023.

"Analogy of the Sun." *Wikipedia*, Wikimedia Foundation, 26 Sept. 2022, https://en.wikipedia.org/wiki/Analogy_of_the_sun#:~:text=Plato%20uses%20the%20image%20of,see%20the%20world%20around%20us. Accessed 3 Jan. 2023.

Ancient Church, 1914, p. 54. *Higher Meaning*, http://highermeaning.org/Authors/CTOdhner/Egypt.shtml. Accessed 3 Jan. 2023.

Atwood, Mary Anne. *Hermetic Philosophy and Alchemy: A Suggestive Inquiry into the Hermetic Mystery with a Dissertation on the More Celebrated of the Alchemical Philosophers*, Routledge, 2005. *Abardoncompanion*, http://abardoncompanion.de/Alex/Atwood.pdf. Accessed 2 Jan. 2023.

Barthes, Roland. *Camera Lucida: Reflections on Photography*, Macmillan, 1981, p. 13.

Berger, John. *Ways of Seeing*, Penguin Books Limited, United Kingdom, 2008, p. 9.

Budge, E.A. Wallis. *The Gods of the Egyptians*, vol. 1, Dover Publications, Inc., New York, 1969, p. 222. "The Correspondences of Egypt." *A Study in the Theology of The Ancient Church*, 1914, p. 79.

Christopher, Lyam Thomas. *Kabbalah, Magic, and The Great Work of Self-Transformation: A Complete Course,* Llewellyn Publications, Woodbury, Minnesota, 2006, p. 201.

Festivals in the Ancient Egyptian Calendar, https://www.ucl.ac.uk/museums-static/digitalegypt/ideology/festivaldates.html. Accessed 3 Jan. 2023.

Fields, Kitty. "Ra Egyptian God of the Sun: 8 Ways to Work with Him in Your Practice." *Otherworldly Oracle*, 15 July 2021, https://otherworldlyoracle.com/ra-egyptian-god-of-the-sun/. Accessed 2 Jan. 2023.

Garstin, E.J. Langford. *The Secret Fire: An Alchemical Study*, The Search Publishing Company Ltd., London, 1932. *Hermetics.org*, http://www.hermetics.org/secretfire1.html. Accessed 3 Jan. 2023.

Geoffroy, Éric. "Métaphysique Et Modernité Chez Abd El-Kader : La Photographie Comme Théophanie." *Abd El-Kader, Un Spirituel Dans La Modernité - Métaphysique Et Modernité Chez Abd El-Kader : La Photographie Comme Théophanie, Presses De L'Ifpo*, 1 Jan. 1970, https://books-openedition-org.translate.goog/ifpo/1837?_x_tr_sl=fr&_x_tr_tl=en&_x_tr_hl=en&_x_tr_pto=sc. Accessed 3 Jan. 2023.

Godley, translator. *Herodotus, Histories*, vol. 2, p. 73. Greek Historian C5th B.C.

Goran, David. "The Mysterious Benben Stone: An Obelisk-like Stone That Was Symbolic of the Primeval Mound of Creation in Heliopolis." *Thevintagenews,* 14 Sept. 2016, https://www.thevintagenews.com/2016/09/15/mysterious-benben-stone-obelisk-like-stone-symbolic-primeval-mound-creation-heliopolis/?chrome=1. Accessed 3 Jan. 2023.

Hall, Manly P. *The Secret Teaching of All Ages*, 1928, p. 51. *Cia.gov,* https://www.cia.gov/library/abbottabad-compound/E4/E4AAFF6DAF6863F459A8B4E52DFB9FF4_Manly.P.Hall_The.Secret.Teachings.of.All.Ages.pdf. Accessed 3 Jan. 2023.

"Heliopolis (Ancient Egypt)." *Wikipedia,* Wikimedia Foundation, 31 Dec. 2022, https://en.wikipedia.org/wiki/Heliopolis_(ancient_Egypt). Accessed 3 Jan. 2023.

Higher Meaning, http://highermeaning.org/Authors/CTOdhner/Egypt.shtml. Accessed 3 Jan. 2023.

Hollenback, Jess. *Mysticism: Experience, Response, and Empowerment,* The Pennsylvania State University Press, University Park, Pennsylvania, 1996, p. 1, 6.

Klotz, David. *Adoration of the Ram: Five Hymns to Amun-Re from Hibis Temple*, Yale Egyptological Seminar, New Haven, Connecticut, 2006, p. 13.
Pap. Berlin 3550, XIII, 9–XIX, 3 (= Moret, Le Rituel de culte divin journalier, pp. 121–38); Blackman and Fairman, in Miscellanea Gregoriana, pp. 397–428; Alliot, Le Culte d'Horus à Edfou, pp. 133–58; Colin, in Hommages Daumas, I, p. 27; Zivie, Le Temple de Deir Chelouit III, No. 151.

La Grange, Ashley. *Basic Critical Theory for Photographers*, Elsevier Focal Press, Germany, 2005, p. 78.

Maspero, G. *History Of Egypt, Chaldæa, Syria, Babylonia, and Assyria*, edited by A.H. Sayce, translated by M.L. McClure, vol. 1, The Grolier Society Publishers, London, p. 229. *Gutenberg.org,* https://www.gutenberg.org/files/19400/19400-h/19400-h.htm. Accessed 3 Jan. 2023.

Odhner, C.TH. "The Correspondences of Egypt." *A Study in the Theology of The Ancient Church*, 1914, pp. 54, 75–76, 77. *Higher Meaning,* http://highermeaning.org/Authors/CTOdhner/Egypt.shtml#g. Accessed 3 Jan. 2023.

"RA Definition & Meaning." *Merriam-Webster,* Merriam-Webster, https://www.merriam-webster.com/dictionary/ra. Accessed 3 Jan. 2023.
"The Correspondences of Egypt." *A Study in the Theology of The Ancient Church,* 1914, p.79.

Raina, Mariette. "In Spirit: Photography and Metaphysics, Reflection of the Self." *Never Apart,* https://www.neverapart.com/features/in-spirit-photography-and-metaphysics/. Accessed 29 Dec. 2022.

"The Geological Society of London - Iron from the Sky." *The Geological Society,* https://www.geolsoc.org.uk/Geoscientist/Archive/April-2014/Iron-from-the-sky. Accessed 3 Jan. 2023.

Urarov, Graf Sergeï Semenovich. *Essay on the Mysteries of Eleusis*, Rodwell and Martin, 1817. *Archive.org,* https://archive.org/stream/essayonmysterie00chrigoog/essayonmysterie00chrigoog_djvu.txt. Accessed 3 Jan. 2023.

Wilkinson, John Gardner. *The Manners and Customs of the Ancient Egyptians: Including Their Private Life, Government, Laws, Arts, Manufactures, Religion, Agriculture and Early History,* vol. 4, John Murray, 1847, p. 295.

Wilkinson, John Gardner. *The Manners and Customs of the Ancient Egyptians,* vol. 5, John Murray, London, 1847, p. 205, 301.

13. Wisdom from the Solar King

Pictures
13.1 Iechmann, Gerd. Deir el-Medina, tomb of Inherkha, 1982. CC BY-SA 4.0.
This photo was edited to increase clarity, accentuate color, and remove spots.
https://commons.wikimedia.org/wiki/File:Deir_el-Medina-26-Grab_359-Inherkha-Barke_mit_Storch-1982-gje.jpg Accessed 6 June 2025.

13.2 Ra-Horakhty-Atum in the Tomb of Sennedjm, 19th-20th dynasty. Reprinted with permission from Shawn Milner, 2025.

End Sign: Emblem by Crispijn van de Passse. A collection of Emblems, Ancient and Modern; Wither's Emblemes by George Wither. 1635. https://digital.libraries.psu.edu/digital/collection/emblem/id/1010. Accessed 5, April 2023.

References

Aristotle. "Chapter 1." *Metaphysics: Book 1.*

Moore, Robert. *Self Observation: The Awakening of Conscience An Owner's Manual,* HOHM PRESS, Prescott, Arizona, 2009, pp. 1–2.

Atwood, Mary Anne. *Hermetic Philosophy and Alchemy: A Suggestive Inquiry into the Hermetic Mystery with a Dissertation on the More Celebrated of the Alchemical Philosophers,* Routledge, 2005, p. 61. *Abardoncompanion,* http://abardoncompanion.de/Alex/Atwood.pdf. Accessed 4 Jan. 2023.

Budge, E. A. Wallis, translator. *The Egyptian Book of the Dead,* Kegan Paul, Trench, Trübner & Co., LTD, London, 1898, p. 145, 199-202, http://www.public-library.uk/dailyebook/The%20Egyptian%20Book%20of%20the%20Dead.pdf. Accessed 4 Jan. 2023.

Bunnell, Peter C., et al. "Memorable Fancies." *Minor White, the Eye That Shapes,* Art Museum, Princeton University, Boston, 1989, p. 98.

Kaminsky, Greg. Received by Garin Horner, *Notes for the 2017 DPKA Presentation,* 2 Feb. 2022.

Mahoney, Michael J., and Donald K. Granvold. "Constructivism and Psychotherapy." *World Psychiatry,* June 2005, pp. 74–77., https://www.ncbi.nlm.nih.gov/pmc/articles/PMC1414735/. Accessed 4 Jan. 2023.

Maspero, G. *History Of Egypt, Chaldæa, Syria, Babylonia, and Assyria,* edited by A.H. Sayce, translated by M.L. McClure, vol. 1, The Grolier Society Publishers, London. *Gutenberg.org,* https://www.gutenberg.org/files/19400/19400-h/19400-h.htm. Accessed 3 Jan. 2023.

Murray, M.A. "The Name of Ra." *Ancient Egyptian Legends,* 1929, pp. 83–84. *Archive.org,* https://archive.org/details/ancientegyptianl00murr/page/n3/mode/2up?q=living+flame. Accessed 4 Jan. 2023.

"Proverbs 2: 4, 5." *Bible: King James Version,* 2008.

Smith, David Chaim. *Deep Principles of Kabbalistic Alchemy,* David Chaim Smith, 2017, pp. 2–3.

Triphook, R. *The Metamorphosis, Or, Golden Ass, and Philosophical Works, of Apuleius,* edited by T. Rodd, United Kingdom, 1822, pp. 263–264.

14. SPLENDOR SOLIS AND THE EMPYREAN LIGHT

Pictures

14.1 Mirror of Fire: Specvlvm Vrens. Twelve mirrors with which man tries to see God, 1610. https://commons.wikimedia.org/wiki/File:Duodecim_specula_deum_aliquando_videre_desideranti_concinna ta_(1610)_(14745042832).jpg

14.2 Ascension to the Aperture Gate. Composite made by Garin Horner (2020). Based on an illustration in the Anotomia Auri by Joannis Danielis Mylii. 1628. https://www.google.com/books/edition/Anatomia_auri/kNJQAAAAcAAJ?hl=en&gbpv=1&printsec=frontco ver Accessed 12 Jan. 2023.

References

Armstrong, Carol. "'The Perfect Medium: Photography and the Occult.'" *The Online Edition of Artforum International Magazine,* Artforum, 1 Dec. 2005, https://www.artforum.com/print/reviews/200510/the-perfect-medium-photography-and-the-occult-9862. Accessed 13 Jan. 2023.

Atwood, Mary Anne. *Hermetic Philosophy and Alchemy: A Suggestive Inquiry into the Hermetic Mystery with a Dissertation on the More Celebrated of the Alchemical Philosophers,* Routledge, 2005, p. 99. *Abardoncompanion,* http://abardoncompanion.de/Alex/Atwood.pdf. Accessed 13 Jan. 2023.

Babbitt, Edwin D. *The Principles of Light and Color*, Babbitt & Co, 1 Jan. 1878, https://library.si.edu/digital-library/book/principlesoflig00babb. Accessed 13 Jan. 2023.

Century Illustrated Monthly Magazine, 1913, p. 656, https://www.google.com/books/edition/Century_Illustrated_Monthly_Magazine/PIdHAQAAMAAJ?hl=en&gbpv=1&dq=Crookes,+It+is+not+improbable+that+other+sentient+beings&pg=PA656&printsec=frontcover. Accessed 13 Jan. 2023.

"Dynamis Definition & Meaning." *Merriam-Webster*, Merriam-Webster, https://www.merriam-webster.com/dictionary/dynamis. Accessed Dec. 1, 2022.

Flammarion, Camille. *Lumen*, Dodd, Mead, United Kingdom, 1897, pp. 131–132.

Freiherr von Bunsen, and Christian Karl Josias. *Outlines of the Philosophy of Universal History, Applied to Language and Religion*, Longman, Brown, Green, and Longmans, United Kingdom, 1854, p. 118.

Guiley, Rosemary Ellen. *The Encyclopedia of Magic and Alchemy*, 2006, p. 20. *Academia.edu*, https://www.academia.edu/5021522/Encyclopedia_of_Magic_and_Alchemy?email_work_card=view-paper. Accessed 13 Jan. 2023.

Harpur, Patrick. *The Secret Tradition of the Soul*, North Atlantic Books, 2011, p. 47.

Jung, Carl G. *Alchemical Studies*, vol. 13, pp. 160–161. *Academia.edu*, https://www.academia.edu/9234735/Carl_G_Jung_Vol_13_Alchemical_Studies. Accessed 13 Jan. 2023.

Miller, Andrew. *Darkrooms as Metaphors; Darkrooms as Origins: Michael S. Harper's Dark Room Poems*, Sept. 2013, p. 219., http://www.concentric-literature.url.tw/Temporarily/Concentric.files/files/12AndrewMiller.pdf. Accessed 13 Jan. 2023.

Paracelsus. *Astronomia Magna*, Sudhoff Ed., 8, p. 23, "De Podagricis", Huser ed., 1, p. 566, CW13, 1571, pp. 113-114n6.

Porphyry, Sententiae. *Auxiliaries to the Perception of Intelligible Natures*, Translated by Thomas Taylor, 1823, p. 169n9., https://www.tertullian.org/fathers/porphyry_sententiae_02_trans.htm. Accessed 13 Jan. 2023.

Scharf, Aaron. *Pioneer of Photography: An Album of Pictures and Words*, Harry N. Abrams, INC., Publishers, New York, New York, 1976, p. 10. *Monoskop.org*, https://monoskop.org/images/0/0c/Scharf_Aaron_Pioneers_of_Photography_1976.pdf. Accessed 13 Jan. 2023.

15. The Sacred Union of Alchemy and Photography

Pictures

15.1 De cavernis Metallorum occultus est, qui Lapis est venerabilis Hermes. De cavernis Metallorum occultus est, qui Lapis est venerabilis Hermes by
Alexandre-Toussaint Limojon de Saint-Didier, 1745. Limojon de Saint Disdier, Alexandre Toussaint de. Le triomphe hermétique, ou La pierre philosophale victorieuse. Traité plus complet et plus intelligible, qu'il y en ait eu jusques ici, touchant le magistre hermétique. Netherlands, chez Henry Wetstein, 1689. Frontispiece. https://archive.org/details/hermeticaltriump00limo/page/n5/mode/2up.

15.2 Michael Maier's emblem titled, *Sol et ejus umbra perficiunt opus*, or, *The sun and its shadow bring the work to perfection.* 1687.
https://commons.wikimedia.org/wiki/File:Fotothek_df_tg_0008204_Theosophie_%5E_Alchemie.jpg
Deutsche Fotothek, Public domain, via Wikimedia Commons.

15.3 The Alchemist by Thomas Wijck, late 17th century.
https://commons.wikimedia.org/wiki/File:Thomas_Wijck,_The_alchemist.jpeg
https://upload.wikimedia.org/wikipedia/commons/d/da/Thomas_Wijck%2C_The_alchemist.jpeg
Thomas Wijck, Public domain, via Wikimedia Commons. Accessed 22 Jan. 2023.

References

"Alchemy." *Art Blart*, https://artblart.com/tag/alchemy/. Accessed 13 Jan. 2023.

Amar, Pierre-Jean. *History of Photography*, 1997, p. 3.

Beigent, M. *The Elixir and the Stone: A History of Magic and Alchemy*, edited by R. Leigh, pp. 208–209.

Burland, C. A. *The Arts of the Alchemists*, Macmillan, New York, New York, 1968, p. 37. *Archive.org*, https://archive.org/details/artsofalchemists0000burl. Accessed 13 Jan. 2023.

Cartier-Bresson, H. Aperture, New York, 1976, p. 333.

Charuty, Giordana. "La " Boîte Aux Ancêtres "." *Terrain. Anthropologie & Sciences Humaines*, Association Terrain, 28 Apr. 2005, https://journals.openedition.org/terrain/2693#ftn16. Accessed 13 Jan. 2023.

Conrad, Joseph. *The Complete Novels of Joseph Conrad - All 20 Works in One Premium Edition: Including Unforgettable Titles like Heart of Darkness, Lord Jim, The Secret Agent, Nostromo, Under Western Eyes and Many More (With Author's Letters, Memoirs and Critical Essays)*, 2015, p. 4543.

"Doings of the Sunbeam" (Excerpts) Oliver Wendell Holmes Atlantic ... https://americainclass.org/wp-content/uploads/2012/05/7_Doings-of-the-Sunbeam.pdf.Accessed 13 Jan. 2023.

Drago, Elisabeth Berry. *Painted Alchemists: Early Modern Artistry and Experiment in the Work of Thomas Wijck*, Amsterdam University Press, 2019, pp. 97–98.

Edson, Gary. *Mysticism and Alchemy through the Ages*, McFarland & Company Inc., London, England, 2012, pp. 220–222.

Gizzarelli, Camille. "Mysticism in Art." *BellaOnline*, 2022, https://www.bellaonline.com/articles/art307765.asp. Accessed 13 Jan. 2023.

"Magnum Opus." *Appliedjung*, 9 Jan. 2023, https://appliedjung.com/the-magnum-opus/#:~:text=The%20four%20stages%20of%20the,%2C%20Illumination%2C%20Education%20and%20Transformation. Accessed 13 Jan. 2023.

Maier, Michael. "Discourse XLV." *Atalanta Fugiens: The Fleeing of Atalanta or New Chymical Emblems of the Secrets of Nature*, Hieronymus Gallerus, 1618, p. 134, http://93beast.fea.st.user.fm/files/section1/maier/Maier%20-%20Atalanta%20Fugiens.pdf. Accessed 13 Jan. 2023.

Millesima, Iulia. "Loïc Tréhédel and Nicéphore Niépce's Photochemistry." *LabyrinthDesigners & the Art of Fire*, 5 Jan. 2023, https://www.labyrinthdesigners.org/alchemy-science-history/loic-trehedel-and-nicephore-niepces-photochemistry/. Accessed 13 Jan. 2023.

Modiano, Raimonda, et al., editors. *Voice, Text, Hypertext Emerging Practices in Textual Studies*, University of Washington Press, 2017, p. 136.

Ramsay, Jay. *Alchemy: The Art of Transformation*, Thorsons, United Kingdom, 1997, pp. 32–33.

Scharf, Aaron. *Pioneer of Photography: An Album of Pictures and Words*, Harry N. Abrams, INC., Publishers, New York, New York, 1976, p. 10. *Monoskop.org*, https://monoskop.org/images/0/0c/Scharf_Aaron_Pioneers_of_Photography_1976.pdf. Accessed 13 Jan. 2023.

"The Mystical Modernism of Franz Marc, Whose Art Was a 'Bridge into the Spirit World': Christie's." *The Foxes by Franz Marc, a Masterpiece by One of the Key Figures of German Expressionism | Christie's*, Christies, 4 Feb. 2022, https://www.christies.com/features/the-mystical-modernism-of-franz-marc-12062-1.aspx?sc_lang=en. Accessed 13 Jan. 2023.

Tissandier, Gaston. *A History and Handbook of Photography*, Edited by J. Thomas, 1877, pp. 6–7. *Archive.org*, https://archive.org/details/historyhandbooko00tissuoft/page/n33/mode/2up. Accessed 13 Jan. 2023.

Webster, Chris. "Earlier Photography and the Esoteric Camera Obscura." *Atmostfear Entertainment*, 15 Oct. 2019, https://www.atmostfear-entertainment.com/culture/photography/earlier-photography-and-the-esoteric-camera-obscura/. Accessed 13 Jan. 2023.

PART 2: Useful Rites to Light the Eyes Afire & Ways to Stoke the Ignited Soul
Garin Horner, Picture modified from Tabula Aurea Salomonis et Hermetis, Leipzig, 1739.
https://play.google.com/books/reader?id=ToA9GMRtBjEC&pg=GBS.PA16-IA1&hl=es_419
Accessed July 1, 2025.

16. Divination: Catching Sparks of Future's Flame

Pictures
16.1 Composite image of "Tabula Aurea Sancti Thomæ Aquinatis
By Pietro da Bergamo, O.P., 1873. https://archive.org/details/TabulaAurea. Accessed 25 Dec. 2023.

16.2 Consulting the Oracle of Delphi by John Augustus Knapp 1853-1938. Reprinted with permission from The Philosophical Research Society, Inc., all rights reserved.
https://www.universalfreemasonry.org/en/gallery/secret-teachings/oracle-delphi. Accessed 25 Dec. 2023

16.3: Example of a Kingswood Oracle Card and its Back. The two sides represent the microcosm and macrocosm. Designs by Garin Horner, based on Abraham Kingwood's descriptions. 2023.

References
Botterweck, G. J., and H. Ringgren. Theological Dictionary of the Old Testament, vol. 4, 1977. Infobooks.org, https://www.infobooks.org/pdfview/6081-a-theological-ancient-hellenistic-and-psycho-logical-look-at-the-dreams-of-pharaohs-chief-cup-bearer-and-chief-baker-genesis-40-5-13-16-18-yong-lu/. Accessed 21 Jan. 2023.

Buchanan, Joseph Rodes. Manual of Psychometry: The Dawn of a New Civilization, Holman Brothers, Press of the Roxbury Advocate, 1885, pp. l-3.

Campbell, Joseph, and Richard Roberts. Tarot Revelations, Vernal Equinox, 1982, p. 41.

"Chapter 1 The Scientific Literature of Dream-Blems (UP TO 1900)." The Interpretation of Dreams Sigmund Freud, https://psychclassics.yorku.ca/Freud/Dreams/dreams.pdf. Paragraph 1. Accessed 21 Jan. 2023.

"Dream Sending." Occult World, https://occult-world.com/dream-sending/. Accessed 19 Dec. 2022.

Duell, Mark. "British Photographer William Hope Caught 'Ghost like' Images in the 1920's." Daily Mail Online, Associated Newspapers, 3 Jan. 2017, https://www.dailymail.co.uk/news/article-3871650/The-ghosts-caught-camera-spirit-photographs-world-captivated-1920s-wasn-t-seems.html. Accessed 21 Jan. 2023.

Epstein, Gerald, et al. The Encyclopedia of Mental Imagery: Colette Aboulker-Muscat's 2,100 Visualizations Exercises for Personal Development, Healing, and Self-Knowledge, ACMI Press, 2012, p. 9.

Flammarion, Camille. L'inconnu: The Unknown, 1900, p. 481. Archive.org, https://archive.org/details/linconnuunknown02flamgoog/page/480/mode/2up?q=without+eyes. Accessed 21 Jan. 2023.

Guiley, Rosemary. The Encyclopedia of Magic and Alchemy, 2006, p. 82. Academia.edu, https://www.academia.edu/5021522/Encyclopedia_of_Magic_and_Alchemy?email_work_card=view-paper. Accessed 19 Dec. 2022.

Hall, Adam C. Divination: The Power to Create a Multi-Dimensional Life Experience, 28 Dec. 2020, https://www.adamhall.solutions/blog/2019/5/15/divination-the-power-to-create-a-multi-dimensional-life-experience. Accessed 26 Dec. 2022.

Hall, Manly P. The Secret Teachings of All Ages, 1928, p. 63. Cia.gov, https://www.cia.gov/library/abbottabad-compound/E4/E4AAFF6DAF6863F459A8B4E52DFB9FF4_Manly.P.Hall_The.Secret.Teachings.of.All.Ages.pdf. Accessed 26 Dec. 2022.

Irwin, Lee. Supernal Dreaming: On Myth and Metaphysics, 26 Oct. 2020, p. 2. Infobooks.org, https://www.infobooks.org/pdfview/6077-supernal-dreaming-on-myth-and-metaphysics-lee-irwin/. Accessed 21 Jan. 2023.

Miller, Gustavus Hindman. The Wordsworth Dictionary of Dreams, Wordsworth, 1995, p. 9.

Morris, Theresa J. Ascension Lightworkers Guide, Lulu Enterprises, Raleigh, North Carolina, 2011, p. 18.

Newman, Barbara. "Hildegard of Bingen: Visions and Validation." Church History, vol. 54, no. 2, 1985, pp. 164–165. JSTOR, https://www-jstor-org.adriancollege.idm.oclc.org/stable/3167233?seq=3. Accessed 21 Jan. 2023.

Oppenheim, Janet. The Other World: Spiritualism and Psychical Research in England, 1850-1914, Cambridge University Press, 1985.

"Photochemical Alchemy in Sub-Arctic Finland." Art Journal Open, 24 July 2019, http://artjournal.collegeart.org/?page_id=11098. Accessed 21 Jan. 2023.

Photographic and Prophetic Truth: Daguerreotypes, the Holy Land, and the Bible According to Reverend Alexander Keith. Academia.edu, https://www.academia.edu/38589379/Photographic_and_Prophetic_Truth_Daguerreotypes_the_Holy_Land_and_the_Bible_According_to_Reverend_Alexander_Keith. Accessed 21 Jan. 2023.

"Prophetic Photography - What Is It?" Red Door Sentinel, http://kwinrc.blogspot.com/2011/11/prophetic-photography-what-is-it.html. Accessed 26 Dec. 2022.

"Psychic (Adj.)." Etymology, https://www.etymonline.com/word/psychic. Accessed 26 Dec. 2023

"Psychometry." Psychometry - Association of Independent Readers and Rootworkers, http://readersandrootworkers.org/wiki/Category:Psychometry. Accessed 21 Jan. 2023.

Regardie, Israel. The Tree of Life: A Study of Magic, Literary Licensing, LLC, 2013, p. 25, 26.

Scott, Clive. Spoken Image: Photography and Language, Reaktion Books, 1999, p. 19.

"Synesius, Dreams." Livius, https://www.livius.org/sources/content/synesius/synesius-dreams/. Accessed 21 Jan. 2023.

"Synesius, Dreams 3." Livius, https://www.livius.org/sources/content/synesius/synesius-dreams/synesius-dreams-3/. Accessed 21 Jan. 2023.

Taylor, Thomas. Select Works of Plotinus, edited by G.R.S. Mead, London, 1895, pp. 66–67.

Sontag, Susan. On Photography. United States, New Library Press LLC, 2001. p 96.

"Three Visions of Zosimus." 3AM Magazine, 8 June 2015, https://www.3ammagazine.com/3am/three-visions-of-zosimus/. Accessed 21 Jan. 2023.

"Vision Definition & Meaning." Merriam-Webster, Merriam-Webster, https://www.merriam-webster.com/dictionary/vision. Accessed 21 Jan. 2023.

Williams, Charles. The Greater Trumps, Pellegrini & Cudahy, 1950, p. 20.

17. THE GREAT PYRAMID: STAIRWAY TO THE EVERBURNING LIGHT

Pictures
17.1 Pyramid Mysteries by Daniel Martin Diaz. Reprinted with permission from the artist.

17.2 The Great Mer Pyramid of Light. Composite illustration by Garin Horner (2023) from from Joannis Danielis Mylii, Anatomia auri, 1628. https://archive.org/details/joannisdanielis00myligoog/page/n354/mode/2up p. 26. Accessed May 1, 2023.

17.3 Hall of Judgment - Unknown artist in Giza, Egypt. Papyrus from the collection of George Kingswood.

End Sign: Ignis, The Alchemical Manual of Ulrich Ruosch (1628-1698).
https://www.facebook.com/photo/?fbid=830543307009959&set=a.818352748229015 Accessed May 26, 2025.

References

Abt, T., and E. Hornung. *Knowledge for the Afterlife: The Egyptian Amduat—A Quest for Immortality*, Living Human Heritage Publications, Zurich, Switzerland, 2003, p. 144.

Adams, Hunter Havelin. "African and African-American Contributions to Science and Technology. In African-American Baseline Essays." *Portland, Oregon: Portland Public Schools*, 1990.

Adams, W. Marsham. *The House of the Hidden Places*, 1895, p. x, https://www.sacred-texts.com/earth/hhp/hhp02.htm. Accessed 27 Jan. 2023.

Allen, Thomas George, translator. "Spell 30." *The Book of the Dead or Going Forth by Day: Ideas of the Ancient Egyptians Concerning the Hereafter as Expressed in Their Own Terms*, University of Chicago Press, 1974, pp. 39–40. *Uchicago.edu*, https://oi.uchicago.edu/sites/oi.uchicago.edu/files/uploads/shared/docs/saoc37.pdf. Accessed 27 Jan. 2023.

Blavatsky, Helena. *ISIS Unveiled: A Master-Key to the Mysteries of Ancient and Modern Science and Theology*, Theosophy Trust, 2006, pp. 22–23. *Anthroweb.info*, https://www.anthroweb.info/fileadmin/pdfs/Isis_Unveiled.pdf. Accessed 27 Jan. 2023.

Carelli, Francesco. *The Book of Death: Weighing Your Heart*, July 2011, pp. 86–87., https://www.ncbi.nlm.nih.gov/pmc/articles/PMC3960665/. Accessed 27 Jan. 2023.

George, John Jack. *The Soul's Journey Through the Ancient Egyptian Afterlife*, 8 July 2022. *Owlcation.com*, https://owlcation.com/humanities/Journey-of-the-Soul-in-the-Ancient-Egyptian-Afterlife. Accessed 27 Jan. 2023.

Hall, Manly P. *The Secret Teachings of All Ages*, 1928, p. 41. *Cia.gov*, https://www.cia.gov/library/abbottabad-compound/E4/E4AAFF6DAF6863F459A8B4E52DFB9FF4_Manly.P.Hall_The.Secret.Teachings.of.All.Ages.pdf. Accessed 27 Jan. 2023.

Hall, Manly P. *The Secret Teachings of All Ages*, 1928, p. 44-45. *Cia.gov*, https://www.cia.gov/library/abbottabad-compound/E4/E4AAFF6DAF6863F459A8B4E52DFB9FF4_Manly.P.Hall_The.Secret.Teachings.of.All.Ages.pdf. Accessed 27 Jan. 2023.

Hall, Manly P. *The Secret Teachings of All Ages*, 1928, p. 45. *Cia.gov*, https://www.cia.gov/library/abbottabad-compound/E4/E4AAFF6DAF6863F459A8B4E52DFB9FF4_Manly.P.Hall_The.Secret.Teachings.of.All.Ages.pdf. Accessed 27 Jan. 2023.

Lévi, Éliphas. *Dogme Et Rituel De La Haute Magie*, Rider & Company, England, 1896, p. 3. *Academia.edu*, https://www.academia.edu/27051672/Dogme_et_Rituel_de_la_Haute_Magie?email_work_card=view-paper. Accessed 27 Jan. 2023.

NEWTON | Autograph Manuscript Notes on the Great Pyramid of Egypt, c. 1680s. https://www.sothebys.com/en/buy/auction/2020/english-literature-history-science-chidrens-books-and-illustrations. Accessed 27 Jan. 2023.

Otto, Rudolph. *THE IDEA OF THE HOLY: An Inquiry into the Non-Rational Factor in the Idea of the Divine and Its Relation to the Rational*, translated by John. W. Harvey, Oxford University Press, pp. 22–23. *Trinity.edu*, http://faculty.trinity.edu/mbrown/whatisreligion/PDF%20readings/Otto-Idea%20of%20the%20Holy.pdf. Accessed 27 Jan. 2023.

Porphyry, Sententiae. "Section 2." *Auxiliaries to the Perception of Intelligible Natures*, translated by Thomas Taylor, pp. 169n34, https://www.tertullian.org/fathers/porphyry_sententiae_02_trans.htm. Accessed 27 Jan. 2023.

"RA: The Sun God of Egypt." *The Egyptian God Ra | Sun God of Egypt | Eye of Ra*, https://www.ancient-egypt-online.com/egyptian-god-ra.html. Accessed 27 Jan. 2023.

Smyth, Charles Piazzi. *Our Inheritance in the Great Pyramid*, 5th ed., A. D. F. Randolph and Co., 1890, pp. 19–20, 41.

The Ancient Code, "Napoleon Bonaparte's Mystical Experience inside the Great Pyramid of Giza." 24 May 2022, https://www.ancient-code.com/napoleon-bonapartes-mystical-experience-inside-the-great-pyramid-of-giza/. Accessed 27 Jan. 2023.

THE CHALDÆAN ORACLES OF ZOROASTER., https://www.sacred-texts.com/cla/af/af08.htm. Accessed 27 Jan. 2023.

18. ALTAR OF THE SUN

Pictures
18.1 George Kingswood's Apothecary. Photograph by Garin Horner, 2021

18.2 George Kingswood's Temple Room. Photograph by Garin Horner, 2022

References
Bardon, Franz. *Initiation Into Hermetics- A Course of Instruction of Magic Theory & Practice*, translated by A. Radspieler, Dieter Ruggeberg, Wuppertal, West Germany, 1971, p. 57. *Themasonictrowel.com*, http://www.themasonictrowel.com/ebooks/hermetic/franz_bardon_initiation_into_hermetics.pdf. Accessed 27 Feb. 2023.

Budge, E.A. Wallis, translator. The Egyptian Book of the Dead, Keegan Paul, Trench,
Butler, Eliza Marian. Ritual Magic, Cambridge University Press, United Kingdom, 1979, p. 10.

Cerwinske, Laura. In a Spiritual Style: The Home as Sanctuary, Thames & Hudson, United States, 2000, p. 78.

"Define Focus." Google Search, Google, https://www.google.com/search?q=define%2Bfocus&rlz=1C5CHFA_enUS875US877&oq=define%2Bfocus&aqs=chrome..69i57j0i512l9.1922j1j7&sourceid=chrome&ie=UTF-8. Accessed 27 Feb. 2023.

Otto, Rudolf. THE IDEA OF THE HOLY: An Inquiry into the Non-Rational Factor in the Idea of the Divine and Its Relation to the Rational, translated by John W Harvey, Oxford University Press, 1957, pp. 12–13. Trinity.edu, http://faculty.trinity.edu/mbrown/whatisreligion/PDF%20readings/Otto-Idea%20of%20the%20Holy.pdf. Accessed 27 Feb. 2023.

Trübner & Co., LTD, London, 1898, p. 146, http://www.public-library.uk/dailyebook/The%20Egyptian%20Book%20of%20the%20Dead.pdf. Accessed 27 Feb. 2023.

Turner, Kay. Beautiful Necessity: The Art and Meaning of Women's Altars, Thames & Hudson, United Kingdom, 1999, p. 7, 27.

19. IMAGINATION'S WELLSPRING

Pictures
19.1 As if in a dream, Pharaoh receives divine life force and heka (magic) from the gods Thoth and Ra. Based on J.-F. Champollion, Monuments de l'Égypte et de la Nubie, vol. 1 (Paris, 1835), pl. 45. Accessed 5, April 2023. https://digitalcollections.nypl.org/items/510d47e2-5d41-a3d9-e040-e00a18064a99/book?parent=3e2a4be0-c5f8-012f-8126-58d385a7bc34#page/51/mode/2up

References
Atwood, Mary Anne. Hermetic Philosophy and Alchemy: A Suggestive Inquiry into the Hermetic Mystery with a Dissertation on the More Celebrated of the Alchemical Philosophers, 245. Routledge, 2005. http://abardoncompanion.de/Alex/Atwood.pdf. Accessed 16 Mar. 2023.

Brill, E J. "Amulets." Essay. In Dictionary of Gnosis and Western Esotericism 1, 25, 2005. https://www.academia.edu/3147599/Amulets?email_work_card=reading-history. Accessed 1, April 2023.

Carty, Donald Gordon. Essay. In The Emerald Tablet: And the Alchemy of Spiritual Transformation, 53. Personal Development Institute, 2007. https://www.alchemystudy.com/download/Emerald_Tablet-Carty (plagiarized_from_Hauck's%20book).pdf. Accessed 5, April 2023.

Corbin, Henry. Essay. In Creative Imagination in the Sufism of Ibn Arabi, 189, 193. Princeton, New Jersey: Princeton University Press, 1969.

Dahlberg, Laurie. Edited by Jacob Wamberg. Art & Alchemy, 2006, 96.

Davenport, Leslie, and Martin L. Rossman. Essay. In Transformative Imagery: Cultivating the Imagination for Healing, Change and Growth, 61. London: Jessica Kingsley Publishers, 2016.

Gray, William G. Essay. In Inner Traditions of Magic, 13. Samuel Weiser Inc., 1978. Accessed March 17, 2023. https://phoreverphoenix.tripod.com/webonmediacontents/Gray_%20-_Inner_Traditions_of_Magic.pdf. Accessed 1, April, 2023.

Haskell, Ellen Davina. Essay. In Mystical Resistance Uncovering the Zohar's Conversations with Christianity. New York, NY: Oxford University Press, 2016. No page numbers.

Herdt, Gilbert, and Michele Stephen. "Self, the Sacred Other, and Autonomous Imagination." Essay. In The Religious Imagination in New Guinea, 45. New Brunswick, New Jersey: Rutgers University Press, 1989. (Herdt et al., 1989, 41-61).

Keith, Alexander. "Evidence of the Truth of the Christian Religion, Derived from the Literal Fulfilment of Prophecy with a Refutation of A.P. Stanley's Poetical Interpretations," 1859, 3.

Koyré, Alexandre. Essay. In Mystiques, Spirituels, Alchimistes Du XVIeme Siecle Allemand, 59-60, 1955.

Lévi, Éliphas. Dogme Et Rituel De La Haute Magie, Rider & Company, England, 1896, p. 6. Academia.edu, https://www.academia.edu/27051672/Dogme_et_Rituel_de_la_Haute_Magie?email_work_card=view-paper. Accessed 14 Dec. 2022.

Manu, Alexander. The Imagination Challenge: Strategic Foresight and Innovation in the Global Economy. United Kingdom, New Riders, 2007.

Morgan, David. The Sacred Gaze: Religious Visual Culture in Theory and Practice. United Kingdom, University of California Press, 2005. p. 76.

Ostrow, Saul. Essay. In Focal Encyclopedia of Photography, edited by Michael R. Peres, 4th ed., 180. Burlington, MA: Focal Press, 2013.

Raff, Jeffrey. (2019) The Alchemy of Imagination, Psychological Perspectives, 62:2-3, 278, DOI: 10.1080/00332925.2019.1626669

Stiegler, Bernard, Jacques Derrida, and Jennifer Bajorek. Essay. In Echographies of Television: Filmed Interviews, 145. Cambridge: Polity Press, 2002. (Stiegler et al., 2002, 145).

"Synesius, On Dreams 3." Livius. 400 AD, Accessed March 16, 2023. https://www.livius.org/sources/content/synesius/synesius-dreams/synesius-dreams-3/. (Synesius).

Thomas, Nigel J. T. "Imagination, Mental Imagery, Consciousness, and Cognition: Scientific, Philosophical and Historical Approaches." Imagination, Mental Imagery, Consciousness, Cognition: Science, Philosophy & History.

Thomas, Nigel J.T. The Multidimensional Spectrum of Imagination: Images, Dreams, Hallucinations, and Active, Imaginative Perception, February 3, 2010, 1. https://citeseerx.ist.psu.edu/viewdoc/download?doi=10.1.1.1052.1517&rep=rep1&type=pdf.. Accessed 1, April 2023.

Three Initiates, and William Walker Atkinson. Essay. In The Kybalion: A Study of The Hermetic Philosophy of Ancient Egypt and Greece, 21–29. Chicago, Illinois, 2017. Accessed March 16, 2023. http://www.yogebooks.com/english/atkinson/1908kybalion.pdf. Accessed 1, April 2023.

Tucker, S. D. Forgotten Science: Strange Ideas from the Scrapheap of History. Amberley Publishing, 2016. (No page numbers).

Wood, Christopher S. Review of Bild-Anthropologie: Entwiirfe fur eine Bildwissenschaf Munich: Wilhelm Fink, 2001, . *Art Bulletin* 8, no. 2, (June 2004): 371. https://www.collegeart.org/pdf/artbulletin/Art%20Bulletin%20Vol%2086%20No%202%20Wood.pdf. Accessed 1, April 2023.

20. Telesmic Projection from The Lantern of Wisdom

Pictures
End Sign: Ouroboros, *Allgemeine Betrachtungen über das Weltgebäude*, 1808.
https://en.wikipedia.org/wiki/Johann_Elert_Bode#/media/File:Bode,_Johann_Ehlert_%E2%80%93_Allgeme ine_Betrachtungen_%C3%BCber_das_Weltgeb%C3%A4ude,_1808_%E2%80%93_BEIC_766161.jpg Accessed May 27, 2025.

References

A Perfumed Skull: Anthropology, Esotericism, and notes on the Numious. "To See Is to Call: Tantric Visualization, Summoning Spirits and the Mind as Petting Zoo." May 9, 2017. https://perfumedskull.com/2017/05/07/to-see-is-to-call-tantric-visualization-summoning-spirits-and-the-mind-as-a-petting-zoo/. Accessed 1, April 2023.

Barkley, Christine. Essay. In Stephen R. Donaldson and the Modern Epic Vision: A Critical Study of the "Chronicles of Thomas Covenant" Novels, 29. McFarland & Co., 2014.

Beyer, Stephan. Essay. In The Cult of Tara: Magic and Ritual in Tibet, 87-88. University of California Press, 1978.

Beyer, Stephan. Essay. In The Cult of Tara: Magic and Ritual in Tibet, 89. University of California Press, 1978.

Dan. September 20, 2016, 11:07am, "Comment on," Hine, Phil, "Bringing the Gods to Mind: On Visualisation – I", Bringing the gods to mind: on visualisation – I", 2016. http://enfolding.org/bringing-the-gods-to-mind-on-visualisation-i/. Accessed 1, April 2023.

Feder, Sandra. "Stanford Researchers Identify Two Factors in Experience of Otherworldly Phenomena." Stanford News, January 25, 2021. https://news.stanford.edu/2021/01/25/two-key-factors-facilitate-experience-spirits-gods/. Accessed 1, April 2023.

Hine, Phil. "Bringing the Gods to Mind: On Visualisation – I." Bringing the gods to mind: on visualisation – I " enfolding.org, 2016. http://enfolding.org/bringing-the-gods-to-mind-on-visualisation-i/. Accessed 1, April 2023.

Lévi, Éliphas. Essay. In Transcendental Magic: Its Doctrine and Ritual, 34. G. Redway, 1896.

Sontag, Susan. Essay. In On Photography, 116. New York: Picador, 2001.

Tarabout, Gilles. "Visualizing the Gods." Essay. In A Magazine of the Arts, 2. Maarg, 2011. https://hal.science/hal-00869882/document. Accessed 1, April 2023.

21. Ritual: Acts of Power

Pictures
End Sign: Vol. II. Les Clavicules de R. Salomon, 1796. Translated from Hebrew into French by M. Pierre Morissoneau. https://wellcomecollection.org/works/zpvhnbcs Accessed May 27 2025.

References

Arcana Mundi: Magic and the Occult in the Greek and Roman Worlds: A Collection of Ancient Texts. United Kingdom, Johns Hopkins University Press, 2006. pg. 51 from (*Procl. Theol. Plat.* [63 Dodds]).

Atwood, Mary Anne. *Hermetic Philosophy and Alchemy: A Suggestive Inquiry into the Hermetic Mystery with a Dissertation on the More Celebrated of the Alchemical Philosophers,* 108-109. Routledge, 2005. Accessed 18 Mar. 2023. http://abardoncompanion.de/Alex/Atwood.pdf. Accessed 1, April 2023.

Bardon, Franz. Essay. In Initiation Into Hermetics A Course of Instruction of Magic Theory & Practice, 36. Dieter Ruggeberg, 1987. http://www.themasonictrowel.com/ebooks/hermetic/franz_bardon_-_initiation_into_hermetics.pdf. Accessed 1, April 2023.

Berger, John. Essay. In Ways of Seeing, 32. Penguin Books Limited, 2008.

Hall, Manly P. The Secret Teachings of All Ages, 1928, p. 57. Cia.gov, https://www.cia.gov/library/abbottabad-compound/E4/E4AAFF6DAF6863F459A8B4E52DFB9FF4_Manly.P.Hall_The.Secret.Teachings.of.All.Ages.pdf. Accessed 18 March 2022.

Heidegger, Martin. "The Age of the World Picture." Essay. In In The Question Concerning Technology, and Other Essays, translated by W. Lovitt, 115. Harper & Row, 1938.

Helmond, Johannes. Essay. In Alchemy Unveiled, edited by Deborah Brumlich, translated by Gerard Hanswille, 32. Merker Publishing Co. Ltd, 1996. http://www.alchemypottery.com/articles/Alchemy_Unveiled-Helmond.pdf. Accessed 1, April 2023. ibid, p. 32.

Mathers, Samel Liddell Macgregor. Essay. In The Sacred Magic of Abramelin the Mage: As Delivered by Abraham the Jew unto His Son Lamech, A.D. 1458. Woodbury, MN: Troy Books Inc., 2016. (No page numbers).

Patnaik, Deba P. Essay. In Through A Glass Purely, 10–15, 1980. http://www.merton.org/hiddenwholeness/Patnaik%20Photo%20Essay.pdf. Accessed 1, April 2023.

Pinch, Geraldine. Magic in Ancient Egypt. United Kingdom, British Museum Press, 2006. p. 77.

Plato. "Socrates." 389-387 BCE. Essay. In Republic VII.

22 The Grand Circle of Evocations

Pictures
22.1 George Kingswood's Studio of Invocations. Photograph by Garin Horner, 2021.

22.2 The Kingswood family's collection of five hermetic scepters. Drawing by artist Sage Billups, 2023. Copyright owned by Garin Horner.

22.3 Scepter emblem from George Kingswood's description. Drawing by Garin Horner, 2020.

22.4 The Magic Circle. From Crystal Gazing and The Wonders of Clairvoyance. W. Foulsham & Company, LTD. London, 1910, pg. 21. https://www.ehbritten.org/docs/melville_crystal_gazing_and_clairvoyance.pdf. Accessed 28 Dec. 2023.

References
Bell, Catherine M. Essay. In Ritual: Perspectives and Dimensions, 11. Oxford: Oxford University Press, 2009.

Bunyan, Marcus. "Alchemy." Art Blart.2014. Accessed March 18, 2023. https://artblart.com/tag/alchemy/. Accessed 1, April 2023.

"Event Horizon: Black Hole." Encyclopaedia Britannica. www.britannica.com/topic/event-horizon-black-hole. Accessed March 18, 2023.

Laska, Brynne. Magical Materialism: The Role of Costume in the Rituals of The Hermetic Order of The Golden Dawn and E. Nesbit's The Enchanted Castle, 2015, 73.

Mjaaland, Thera. "Imagining the Real: The Photographic Image and Imagination in Knowledge Production." Visual Anthropology 30, no. 1 (2017): 2.

Stavish, Mark. Essay. In Path of Alchemy, 4. Llewellyn, 2006.

23. The Elements: Silvery Water & Starry Earth

Pictures

23.1 Viridarium Chymicum by Daniel Stolz von Stolzenberg, 1624.
https://commons.wikimedia.org/wiki/File:Four_elements_in_Viridarium_chymicum.jpg

23.2 Elemental Pentagram with pyramidion. Composite by Garin Horner, from George Kingswood, 2021.

23.3 Ignis Seal. Composite by Garin Horner, from description by George Kingswood, 2023.

23.4 Aeris Seal. Composite by Garin Horner, from description by George Kingswood, 2023.

23.5 Aqua Seal. Composite by Garin Horner, from description by George Kingswood, 2023.

End Sign: Alessandro Cagliostro, 1600, p. 229. Manly Palmer Hall collection of alchemical manuscripts, 1500-1825. https://archive.org/details/manlypalmerhabox11hall/page228/mode/2up
Accessed May 27, 2025.

References

Agrippa, Henry Cornelius. "Book 1, Chapter 2." Essay. In Three Books of Occult Philosophy, 1898, 3. Accessed March 19, 2023. https://quod.lib.umich.edu/e/eebo/A26565.0001.001/1:13.2?rgn=div2;view=fulltext. Accessed 1, April 2023.

Anonymous. The Hymn to the Nile, 1350.
https://college.cengage.com/history/primary_sources/west/the_hymn_to_the_nile.htm. Accessed 1, April 2023.

Atwood, Mary Anne. Hermetic Philosophy and Alchemy: A Suggestive Inquiry into the Hermetic Mystery with a Dissertation on the More Celebrated of the Alchemical Philosophers, 41, 68, 73, 113. Routledge, 2005. Accessed 19 Mar. 2023. http://abardoncompanion.de/Alex/Atwood.pdf. Accessed 1, April 2023.

Aubert, Marcel. Essay. In Gothic Cathedral of France and Their Treasure, 52. Kaye, 1959.

Bové, Laia. Kemetic Yoga Explained & 12 Ancient Poses For Ancestral Connection, December 4, 2022. Accessed 19 Mar. 2023. https://yogajala.com/kemetic-yoga/. Accessed 1, April 2023.

Burch, Beth. "Cauldron and Brew." Cauldron and Brew, March 13, 2023.
https://cauldronandbrew.com/. Accessed 1, April 2023.

Caldwell, R. R., An introduction to quintessence, Brazilian Journal of Physics, 2000.
https://doi.org/10.1590/S0103-97332000000200002. Accessed 1, April 2023.

Campbell, Gordon. "Empedocles (c. 492—432 B.C.E.)." Internet Encyclopedia of Philosophy.
https://iep.utm.edu/empedocles/#H2. Accessed 1, April 2023.

Choppara, Sriya. "The Evolution of Light in Art," January 28, 2021.
https://t-artmagazine.com/the-evolution-of-light-in-art/.

Coelho, Paulo.
https://www.goodreads.com/search?q=%22I+came+to+set+fire+to+the+earth.+And+I+am+watchful+that+the+fire+grow%22&search%5Bsource%5D=goodreads&search_type=quotes&tab=quotes. Accessed 2, April 2023.

Collinson, Brian. "Jungian Therapy and the Meaning of Dreams, 5: Water." Journeying Toward Wholeness, June 14, 2021. https://www.briancollinson.ca/index.php/2012/11/jungian-therapy-the-meaning-of-dreams-5-water.html. Accessed 1, April 2023.

Corbin, Henry. Essay. In Creative Imagination in the Sufism of Ibn Arabi, 170, 184. Princeton, New Jersey: Princeton University Press, 1969.

Corbin, Henry. Essay. In Creative Imagination in the Sufism of Ibn Arabi, 186. Princeton, New Jersey: Princeton University Press, 1969.

Gumm, Alexander. "Secrets Of Alchemy The Emerald Tablet Decoded." Full text of "secrets of alchemy the Emerald Tablet decoded" No date or page numbers. Accessed March 19, 2023. https://archive.org/stream/SecretsOfAlchemy_201609/Secrets_Of_Alchemy_djvu.txt. Accessed 1, April 2023.

Hall, Manly P. The Secret Teachings of All Ages, 1928, p. 106. Cia.gov, https://www.cia.gov/library/abbottabad-compound/E4/E4AAFF6DAF6863F459A8B4E52DFB9FF4_Manly.P.Hall_The.Secret.Teachings.of.All.Ages.pdf. Accessed 26 Dec. 2022.

Hartmann, Franz. In the Pronaos of the Temple of Wisdom: Containing the History of the True and the False Rosicrucians: with an Introduction Into the Mysteries of the Hermetic Philosophy. United Kingdom, Theosophical Pub. Society, 1890. p. 86, 91.

Hermes, and Mead, G R S. Essay. In Thrice Greatest Hermes: Studies in Hellenistic Theosophy and Gnosis, Being a Translation of the Extant Sermons and Fragments of the Trismegistic Literature, with Prolegomena, Commentaries, and Notes, 310–11. Samuel Weiser, 2001.

Helmenstine, Anne Marie, Ph.D. "Aether Definition in Alchemy and Science." ThoughtCo, Feb. 16, 2021, thoughtco.com/aether-in-alchemy-and-science-604750. Accessed 1, April 2023.

Helmond, Johannes. Essay. In Alchemy Unveiled, edited by Deborah Brumlich, translated by Gerard Hanswille, 23, 49-50, 186. Merker Publishing Co. Ltd, 1996. http://www.alchemypottery.com/articles/Alchemy_Unveiled-Helmond.pdf. Accessed 1, April 2023.

Hotep, Yirser Ra. The 7 Core Values of the Original Kemetic Yoga Practice, The Ficklin Media Group, LLC. 2014. https://tomficklin.blogspot.com/2014/07/the-7-core-values-of-original-kemetic.html

Kingsley, K. Scarlett, and Richard Parry. "Empedocles." Stanford Encyclopedia of Philosophy. Stanford University, April 7, 2020. https://plato.stanford.edu/entries/empedocles/#:~:text=In%20the%20middle%20of%20the,later%20philosophy%2C%20medicine%2C%20mysticism%2C. Accessed 1, April 2023.

Kingsley, K. Scarlett, and Richard Parry. Sec. 2.1 Roots and Forces.

Kotansky, Roy. "Amulets." Dictionary of Gnosis Western and Esotericism, vol. 1, 2005, 19. Academia.edu, https://www.academia.edu/3147599/Amulets?email_work_card=reading-history. Accessed 19 Mar. 2023.

Levinson, Leonard Louis. Bartlett's Unfamiliar Quotations. Cowles Book Company, Inc., Chicago, 1971. p 185. Jung, Carl. "'The Structure of the Psyche.'" Essay, 1927.

Longfellow's, Henry Wadsworth. "Excerpt from 'Haunted Houses,'" 1858. https://poets.org/poem/haunted-houses. Accessed 1, April 2023.

Lydus, Johannes Laurentius, and Richard Wuensch. Essay. In De Mensibus, 41, 1967.

Mark, Joshua J. The Soul in Ancient Egypt, 2017. https://www.worldhistory.org/article/1023/the-soul-in-ancient-egypt/. Accessed 1, April 2023.

Philalethes, Eirenaeus. "The Marrow of Alchemy", 11. KUPDF, 1993. https://kupdf.net/download/the-marrow-of-alchemy-1654-eirenaeus-philalethespdf_59aec929dc0d60f724568edd_pdf. Accessed 1, April 2023.

Preisendanz, Karl, and Albert Henrichs. Essay. In Papyri Graecae Magicae 1, 1st ed., 1:111. Die Griechischen Zauberpapyri, 2001. No page numbers.

Pseudo-Llull. "Liber De Secretis Naturae Seu De Quinta Essentia The Book of the Secrets of Nature or of the Quintessence." Science History Institute, 1498. https://digital.sciencehistory.org/works/82ul4ik. Accessed 1, April 2023.

Rankine, David, and D'Este, Sorita. Practical Elemental Magick: Working the Magick of the Four Elements in the Western Mystery Tradition, 22-23. United Kingdom, Avalonia, 2008.

Roszak, Theodore. Where the Wasteland Ends: Politics and Transcendence in Postindustrial Society, 296, Berkeley: Celestial Arts, 1989.

Schuler, Robert M. Essay. In Alchemical Poetry, 1575-1700: From Previously Unpublished Manuscripts, 61. London: Routledge, 2013.

"The Alchemy of the Four Elements – Solutio – the Alchemy of Water." Kimchee and Catnip, September 20, 2018. https://kimcheeandcatnip.wordpress.com/2018/09/23/solutio-the-alchemy-of-water/. Accessed 1, April 2023.

"The poem of the philosopher Theophrastos upon the sacred art". https://www.alchemywebsite.com/Text_Poem_of_Theophrastus.html. Accessed 1, April 2023.

"The Story behind Apollo 8's Famous Earthrise Photo." NASA. 2018. https://solarsystem.nasa.gov/resources/2234/the-story-behind-apollo-8s-famous-earthrise-photo/. Accessed 1, April 2023.

Vaughan, Thomas. "Aula Lucis, or, The House of Light." Accessed March 18, 2023. http://www.levity.com/alchemy/aula_lucis.html. Accessed 1, April 2023. (No page numbers).

Wilkinson, Richard H. "Brazier." Essay. In Reading Egyptian Art: A Hieroglyphic Guide to Ancient Egyptian Painting and Sculpture, 161. London: Thames & Hudson, 1992.

Wisdom of Solomon 7:17 KJV. Accessed March 19, 2023. https://www.kingjamesbibleonline.org/Wisdom-of-Solomon-7-17/. Accessed 1, April 2023.

Yarker, John and Hermes. "Section I." Essay. In "Aureus": The Golden Tractate of Hermes Trismegistus. Concerning the Physical Secret of the Philosopher's Stone ... Bath, 1886. http://www.levity.com/alchemy/goldtrac.html. Accessed 5, April 2023.

Yonker, Tori, and Iseult Iseult Gillespie. "The Alchemy of Early Photography." Edge Effects, October 12, 2019. https://edgeeffects.net/historical-photographic-techniques/. Accessed 1, April 2023.

24. ALLIES: A GATHERING OF SPIRITS

Pictures
24.1 Saul and the Witch of Endor by Washington Allston, 1779-1843 (Artist), J. Andrews, J. (Engraver), and Charles Edward, 1808-1850 (Engraver). 1851. https://www.historicnewengland.org/explore/collections-access/gusn/199069. Accessed 1, April 2023.

End Sign: Emblem 75 by Crispijn van de Passse. A collection of Emblems, Ancient and Modern; Wither's Emblemes by George Wither. 1635. https://digital.libraries.psu.edu/digital/collection/emblem/id/1010. Accessed 5, April 2023.

References
Atwood, Mary Anne. Hermetic Philosophy and Alchemy: A Suggestive Inquiry into the Hermetic Mystery with a Dissertation on the More Celebrated of the Alchemical Philosophers, 94. Routledge, 2005. Accessed 20 Mar. 2023. http://abardoncompanion.de/Alex/Atwood.pdf. Accessed 1, April 2023.

Coleman, Alan D. "Harry Callahan: An Interview." Essay. In Creative Camera International Yearbook, 76, 1976.

Contenau, Georges. Essay. In Everyday Life in Babylon and Assyria, 164. London: Edward Arnold, 1955.

Green, H. L. The Free Thought Magazine 19, 1901. p 205, 208.

Massey, Gerald. Essay. In Ancient Egypt: The Light of the World, 121. New York: Cosimo Classics, 2007.

Minor White. Letter to Gerald Robinson. "Letter To," September 4, 1964.
Minor White. Memorable Fancies, 1942. https://archive.org/details/minor-white-some-excerpts-from-minor-whites-memorable-fancies. Accessed 5, April 2023.

Modiano, Raimonda, Leroy F. Searle, and Peter L. Shillingsburg. Essay. In Voice, Text, Hypertext Emerging Practices in Textual Studies, 137. Seattle: University of Washington Press, 2017.

"Oxford Languages and Google - English." Oxford Languages. Accessed March 20, 2023. https://languages.oup.com/google-dictionary-en/. Accessed 1, April 2023.

Porphyry, Sententiae, and Thomas Taylor. Essay. In Auxiliaries to the Perception of Intelligible Natures, 32, 1823. https://www.tertullian.org/fathers/porphyry_sententiae_02_trans.htm. Accessed 1, April 2023.

Taylor, Thomas. Essay. In Iamblichus on the Mysteries of the Egyptians, Chaldeans, and Assyrians, 271–272. Bertram Dobell, 2018. http://www.platonic-philosophy.org/files/Iamblichus%20-%20On%20the%20Mysteries.pdf. Accessed 1, April 2023.

Valentinus, Basilius, and Theodor Kerchring. Essay. In Basil Valentine His Triumphant Chariot of Antimony, with Annotations of Theodore Kirkringius, M.D. with The True Book of the Learned Synesius ... Concerning the Philosopher's Stone, 5. London: Dorman Newman, 1678.

25. Motivation as Fuel for the Fire

References
"Define Artist." Webster, Noah. Webster's [eight] New Collegiate Dictionary: Marriam-Webster. Based on Webster's Third New Intl. Dictionary. 63, United States, Merriam, 1973.

Sontag, Susan. Essay. In On Photography, 3-4. New York: Picador, 2001.

Turner, Luke. "Photography as Metamodern Alchemy." Notes on Metamodernism, September 18, 2012. http://www.metamodernism.com/2012/05/09/photography-a-metamodern-alchemy-the-work-of-stuart-bailes/. Accessed 1, April 2023.

26. The Alchemistical Photographer-Magician

Pictures
26.1 The Magician, from the Rider-Waite Coleman Smith Tarot Deck, 1910. Source: https://en.wikipedia.org/wiki/The_Magician_%28tarot_card%29#/media/File:RWS_Tarot_01_Magician.jpg

26.2 The Magus of Power from the Hermetic Tarot Deck by Godfrey Dowson, U.S. Games, 1980. https://www.usgamesinc.com/hermetic-tarot-deck.html

Picture 26.3 Kingswood's Caduceus, Garin Horner (2020) from Abraham Kingswood's notes.

End Sign: Gainsboro Portrait and Photography Studio, photographer unknown. 1890-1910.

References
Edson, Gary. Essay. In Mysticism and Alchemy through the Ages, 223. London: McFarland & Company Inc., 2012.

Kim, Eric. "How to Photograph with Your Soul. March 1, 2017. https://erickimphotography.com/blog/how-to-photograph-with-your-soul/. Accessed 1, April 2023.

Regardie, Israel. Essay. In Complete Golden Dawn System of Magic, 132. New Falcon Publications, 1995.

27. The Alchemist's Camera — The Dark Room Temple

Pictures
27.1 Turn of the century view camera. Picture by Dillaye, Frédéric. La Théorie, la pratique et l'art en photographie. Le Paysage artistique en photographie, avec le procédé au gélatino-bromure d'argent. France, J. Taillandier, 1907. p. 14 https://books.google.com.cu/books?id=WIQ_iJ_bNyEC&printsec=frontcover&source=gbs_ge_summary_r&cad=0#v=onepage&q&f=false. Accessed 1, April 2022.

27.2 The Pyramids of El-Geezeh, from the Southwest by Francis Firth, 1857.

https://commons.wikimedia.org/wiki/File:Francis_Frith_-_Pyramids_Of_El-Geezeh_%28From_The_Southwest%29_-_Google_Art_Project.jpg

27.3 The Egyptian Camera Obscura Temple by Artist Enes Gücük, 2023. Copyright owned by Garin Horner.

27.4 The Camera Temple by Artist Lee Cushard, 2024. Copyright owned by Garin Horner.

End Sign: Ego Video Esse, composite by Garin Horner. Reference: https://www.lookandlearn.com/history-images/YR0477175/Study-sheet-with-drawing-examples-eyes-heads-and-animals?t=1&q=human+eye&n=44 Accessed May 31, 2025.

References
"40 Inspirational Minor White Quotes on Intuition and Found Photography." Photogpedia, June 5, 2021. https://photogpedia.com/minor-white-quotes/. Accessed 1, April 2023.

Adams, Ansel. "The Key to a Photograph from Ansel Adams." The Ansel Adams Gallery, February 20, 2020. https://www.anseladams.com/the-key-to-a-photograph-from-ansel-adams/. Accessed 1, April 2023.

Cheetam, Tom. Essay. In For Henry Corbin the Bridge between Creature and Creator Is hTa'Wil, the Transformation of the Sensory World into Symbols, into Open-Ended Mysteries That Shatter, Engage, and Transform the Entire Being of the Creature. 2012. http://thedepartinglandscape.blogspot.com/2010/11/tawil-unveiling-hidden-treasure.html. Accessed March 20, 2023.

Cheetam, Tom, and Henry Corbin. "The Angels Part IV." 2014. http://thedepartinglandscape.blogspot.com/2010/11/the-angels-part-iv-text-excerpts-corbin.html. Accessed 1, April 2023.

"Define Focus (n.)." Etymology. https://www.etymonline.com/word/focus. Accessed 1, April 2023.

"Define Optic (Adj.)." Etymology. https://www.etymonline.com/word/optic. Accessed 1, April 2023.

Foster, Steven D. - https://thedepartinglandscape.blogspot.com/2010/11/tawil-unveiling-hidden-treasure.html. Accessed 2, April 2023.

Scharf, Aaron. Essay. In Pioneers of Photography An Album of Pictures and Words Written and Compiled, 11. Harry N. Abrams, INC., Publishers, 1975. https://monoskop.org/images/0/0c/Scharf_Aaron_Pioneers_of_Photography_1976.pdf. Accessed 1, April 2023.

28. AN ANCIENT & EVERLASTING MAGIC

Pictures
28.1 A Zoroastrian priest reads from a book while performing a sacrifice, Bernard Picart (1673–1733). Accessed 1 April, 2023. https://commons.wikimedia.org/wiki/File:ZoroastrianPriest_Banier1741a.png

28.2 Turn of the Century Darkroom, Dillaye, Frédéric. La Théorie, la pratique et l'art en photographie. Le Paysage artistique en photographie, avec le procédé au gélatino-bromure d'argent. France, J. Taillandier, 1907. p. 176.

28.3 Schluckbildchen, 1780. Accessed 1 April 2023. https://en.wikipedia.org/wiki/Devotional_pictures_for_swallowing

References
Atwood, Mary Anne. Hermetic Philosophy and Alchemy: A Suggestive Inquiry into the Hermetic Mystery with a Dissertation on the More Celebrated of the Alchemical Philosophers, 215. Routledge, 2005. http://abardoncompanion.de/Alex/Atwood.pdf. Accessed 24 Mar. 2023.

Berger, John. Essay. In Ways of Seeing, 10. Penguin Books Limited, 2008.

Cavalli, Thom F. "The Alchemical Osiris: From Ra to Radium." Psychological Perspectives 59, no. 1, 2016.

Cheak, Aaron (ed.). Essay. In Alchemical Traditions: From Antiquity to the Avant-Garde from Antiquity to the Avant-Garde, 82. Melbourne, Australia: Numen Books, 2013.

Douglass, John S., and Glenn P. Harnden. The Art of Technique: An Aesthetic Approach to Film and Video Production, 119. Boston: Allyn & Bacon, 1996.

Edson, Gary. Essay. In Mysticism and Alchemy through the Ages: The Quest for Transformation, 159. Jefferson, North Carolina: McFarland & Company, 2012.
Pinch, Geraldine. Magic in Ancient Egypt. United Kingdom, British Museum Press, 2006. p. 47.

Holmes, Oliver Wendell. "Doings of the Sunbeam." Essay. In Soundings from the Atlantic, 4–5. Boston, Massachusetts: Ticknor and Fields, 1864. https://www.unz.com/print/AtlanticMonthly-1863jul-00001/. Accessed 1, April 2023.

Kaminsky, Greg. Occultofpersonality.com interview with Rubaphilos Salfluĕre, MS17 Rubaphilos on Rejuvenation, 2013.

Lévi, Éliphas. Essay. In Dogme Ed Ritual De La Haute Magic, x–xi. England: Rider & Company, 1896. https://www.academia.edu/27051672/Dogme_et_Rituel_de_la_Haute_Magie?email_work_card=view-paper. Accessed 1, April, 2023.

Lin, Kemy. "Photography as Mummification." Hyperallergic, December 21, 2015. https://hyperallergic.com/260566/photography-as-mummification/. Accessed 1, April 2023.

Mann, John. Rudi: 14 Years with My Teacher. Cambridge, Massachusetts: Rudra Press, 1987.

Norbert Guterman. Princeton University Press, 1988. (No page numbers).

Paracelsus. Essay. In Paracelsus: Selected Writings, edited by Jolande Jacobi, translated by Norbert Gutterman, Bollinger Series, XXVIII, Princeton University Press, 1951.

Pinch, Geraldine. Essay. In Magic in Ancient Egypt, 47. Austin, Texas: University of Texas Press, 1994.

Radin, Dean. Real Magic: Ancient Wisdom, Modern Science, and a Guide to The Secret Power of the Universe, 1. New York: Harmony Books, 2018.

Ritner, Robert Kriech. Essay. In The Mechanics of Ancient Egyptian Magical Practice, 192. Chicago, Illinois: Oriental Institute of the University of Chicago, 1993.

Wilkins, Katharina. "Drinking the Quran, Swallowing the Madonna." Essay. In Alternative Voices: A Plurality Approach for Religious Studies, 244–46. Göttingen, Germany: Vandenhoeck & Ruprecht, 2013.

Zinn, Katharina. "Magic, Pharaonic Egypt." Essay. In The Encyclopedia of Ancient History, 1st ed., 4227–31. Blackwell Publishing Ltd, 2012.

29. Protection from Friends and Enemies

Pictures
29.1 The Witches of Warboyse. A Complete History of Magik, 1715. Wikimedia: https://commons.wikimedia.org/wiki/File:A_compleat_history_of_magik,_sorcery,_and_wi_Welcome_L0026620.jpg. Accessed 26 Dec. 2022.
(https://creativecommons.org/licenses/by/4.0/)

End Sign: Illuminor by Daniel Cramer, Emblematum Sacrorum, 1624, pg. 37. https://archive.org/details/emblematasacraho00cram/page/n39/mode/2up Accessed July 1, 2025.

References
Harpur, Patrick. Essay. In Mercurius: The Marriage of Heaven and Earth, 17. Butleigh: Squeeze, 2008.

30. Keys to the Principles of Magic

Pictures

30.1 Spell Diagram, by Garin Horner (2023), as described in writings by Abraham Kingswood.

30.2 Ra's Life Bestowing Rays, by Garin Horner (2019), based on Akhenaten Worshipping the Sun. https://commons.wikimedia.org/wiki/File:C%2BB-Egypt-Fig12-AkhnatenWorshippingSun.PNG Accessed June 20, 2023.

References
Carty, Donald G. The Emerald Tablet: And the Alchemy of Spiritual Transformation, Personal Development Institute, 2007, p. 6, https://www.alchemystudy.com/download/Emerald_Tablet-Carty(plagiarized_from_Hauck's%20book).pdf. Accessed 24 Mar. 2023.
Collier, Graham. "Sympathetic Magic." Psychology Today. Sussex Publishers, March 11, 2014. https://www.psychologytoday.com/us/blog/the-consciousness-question/201403/sympathetic-magic. Accessed 1, April 2023.

Frazer, James George. The Golden Bough: A Study in Magic and Religion. The Macmillan Company, 1925, p. 11.
https://www.google.com/books/edition/The_Golden_Bough/S8wnAAAAYAAJ?hl=en&gbpv=1&dq=the+golden+bough+by+frazer&printsec=frontcover. Accessed 22 Dec. 2022.

Smith, Julius O. III, "Newton's Three Laws of Motion." W3K Publishing, CCRMA, 2022. https://ccrma.stanford.edu/~jos/pasp/Newton_s_Three_Laws_Motion.html. Accessed 1, April 2023.

Sullivan, J.W.N. "Chapter III: The Web of Reason." Essay. In Limitations of Science. Read Books Limited, 2018. (No page numbers).

31. A Brief Note on the Laws of Time

References
Duggan, Bob. "Piercing the Surface: Thomas Merton's Zen Photography." Big Think, April 19, 2022. https://bigthink.com/culture-religion/piercing-the-surface-thomas-mertons-zen-photography/. Accessed 1, April 2023.

Edson, Gary. Essay. In Mysticism and Alchemy through the Ages, 27–28. McFarland & Company Inc., 2012.

Foster, Hal. Postmodernism in Parallax 63 (October 1993): 5–6. http://www.jstor.org/stable/778862. Accessed 1, April 2023.

Gross, Phillipe L., and S. I. Shapiro. The Tao of Photography: Seeing Beyond Seeing, Ten Speed Press, United Kingdom, 2001, p. 183.

Hägglund, Martin. Aperture. Essay. In Spirituality: Aperture 237, 34. Aperture Foundation, Incorporated, 2019.

"SACRED TIME AND SPACE - CEMETERY." Encyclopedia Britannica, 1995. https://www.cultus.hk/cemetery_studies/sacred_space.html. Accessed 1, April 2023.

Soth, Amelia. "Elixirs of Immortal Life Were a Deadly Obsession." JSTOR daily, December 28, 2018. https://daily.jstor.org/elixir-immortal-life-deadly-obsessions/. Accessed 2 April 2023.

Zakia, Richard. Focal Encyclopedia of Photography, edited by John Kaplan and Michael R. Peres, 4th ed., Focal Press, Burlington, Massachusetts, 2007, p. 29, 452.

32. A Separate Reality

Pictures
32.1 Allegorical representation with Heaven and Earth (cropped) by Joseph Mulder, 1685. https://www.lookandlearn.com/history-images/YR0419917/Allegorical-representation-with-Heaven-and-Earth Accessed May 27, 2025.

References

Atwood, Mary Anne. Hermetic Philosophy and Alchemy: A Suggestive Inquiry into the Hermetic Mystery with a Dissertation on the More Celebrated of the Alchemical Philosophers, 79, 101, 107, 248. Routledge, 2005. http://abardoncompanion.de/Alex/Atwood.pdf. Accessed 1, April 2023.

Christopher, Lyam Thomas. Kabbalah, Magic, and The Great Work of Self-Transformation: A Complete Course, 7. Llewellyn Publications, Woodbury, Minnesota, 2006.

Clark, Graham. Essay. In The Photograph, 11. Oxford University Press, 1997.

Copenhaver, Brian P., and Hermes. Essay. In Hermetica: The Greek Corpus Hermeticum and the Latin Asclepius in a New English Translation, with Notes and Introduction, 50. Cambridge; New York: Cambridge University Press, 1995.

Edson, Gary. Essay. In Mysticism and Alchemy through the Ages, 10. McFarland & Company Inc., 2012.

Green, Marian. Essay. In Magic for the Aquarian Age, 79. Wellingborough, Northamptonshire: Aquarian, 1983.

Haustein, Katja. Essay. In Regarding Lost Time: Photography, Identity, and the Affect in Proust, Benjamin, and Barthes, 6. Routledge, Taylor and Francis Group, 2012.

Kenney, John Peter. Essay. In The Mysticism of Saint Augustine: Re-Reading the Confessions, 130–31. Routledge, 2005.

Kingsolver, Barbara. Animal Dreams: A Novel. United States, HarperCollins, 1990. p. 48

Kotansky, Roy. "Amulets." Dictionary of Gnosis Western and Esotericism, vol. 1, 2005, p. 17-18. Academia.edu, https://www.academia.edu/3147599/Amulets?email_work_card=reading-history. Accessed 24 Mar. 2023.

Neuroskeptic. "A New Theory of Dreaming." Discover Magazine. Discover Magazine, July 27, 2020. https://www.discovermagazine.com/mind/a-new-theory-of-dreaming. Accessed 1, April 2023.

Panchadasi. Essay. In Clairvoyance and Occult Powers: Including Clairvoyance, 15, 33. Chicago: Yogi Publication Society, 1916. https://archive.org/details/clairvoyanceoccu00panciala/page/16/mode/2up?view=theater&q=delusions. Accessed 1, April 2023.

Patterson, Freeman. Essay. In Photography and the Art of Seeing, 10. Van Nostrand Reinhold, 1979.

Raff, Jeffrey. Psychological Perspectives. Apr-Sep 2019, Vol. 62 Issue 2/3, p. 276-284.

Sontag, Susan. Essay. In On Photography, 6, 18. New York: Picador, 2001.

Taylor, Thomas. "Porphyry's Life." Essay. In Select Works of Plotinus, 66–67, 1895. https://www.scribd.com/doc/143807500/Select-Works-of-Plotinus-Porphyry-s-Life-Thomas-Taylor-1895. Accessed 1, April 2023.

University of Glasgow. "What Our Eyes Can't See, the Brain Fills In." Medical Xpress - medical research advances and health news. Medical Xpress, April 4, 2011. https://medicalxpress.com/news/2011-04-eyes-brain.html. Accessed 1, April 2023.

Zakia, Richard. Focal Encyclopedia of Photography, edited by Michael R. Peres, 4th ed., Focal Press, Burlington, Massachusetts, 2007, p. 460, 468.

33. Seal of the Four Gates

Pictures
33.1 Emblem-Diagram of the Arche Chamber of High Choice, courtesy of George Kingswood.

33.2 Athanasius Kircher, Public domain, via Wikimedia Commons. Turris Babel by Athanasius Kircher, 1679. https://commons.wikimedia.org/wiki/File:Athanasius_Kircher_-_Turris_Babel_-_1679_(page_105_crop).jpg

References

Chandler, John, F.M. Van Helmont, and H. Blunden. Essay. In Oriatrike, or, Physick Refined. The Common Errors Therein Refuted, and the Whole Art Reformed & Rectified: Being a New Rise and Progress of Philosophy and Medicine for the Destruction of Diseases and Prolongation of Life., 462. Lodowick Loyd, 1662.

Hugo, Kristin. "Ancient Egyptians May Have Used the Sun to Align Pyramids." Newsweek, February 20, 2018. https://www.newsweek.com/ancient-egypt-giza-pyramids-cardinal-points-equinox-812045. Accessed 1, April 2023.

Regardie, Israel. The Tree of Life: A Study of Magic, 32. Literary Licensing, LLC, 2013.

Rumi and Mary Foundation, https://rumiandmaryfoundation.org/, Accessed 10 Jan 2023.

Smith, David Chaim, Black Aether. Essay. In *The Lightning Flash of Alef* Series, Vol. 6. David Chaim Smith Publishers, 2022. https://www.facebook.com/lightningflashofalef/posts/4641256289220447/. Accessed 4 April 2023.

CONCLUSION

Pictures

34.1 Photo of Abd el-Kader Carte de Visite by Mayer & Pierson "Photographers of His Majesty the Emperor" Carte de Visite - front and back, 1855.

34.2 George Kingswood's Library. Photograph by Garin Horner, 2020.

34.3 "kmt": The conclusion, it is complete.

References End Sign: Emblem of the Sun, Mundus symbolicus by Filippo Picinelli. Coloniae Agrippinae: Sumptibus Hermanni Demen, 1687, p. 15.
https://archive.org/details/mundussymbolicus00pici/page/n69/mode/2up Accessed May 26, 2025.

Introducing the Hardbound Colllector's Edition

A Feather on the Breathof Ra

BY
Garin Horner

Signed & Numbered Copies

{

- ◎ 382 PAGES (52 FULL COLOR PAGES)
- ◎ PREMIUM 7 X 10 INCH FORMAT
- ◎ HARD COVER WITH SEWN THROUGH BINDING
- ◎ BLACK BUCKGRAM BOOK CLOTH
- ◎ HAND MARBLED END SHEETS
- ◎ GOLD FOIL IMPRINT ON COVERS & SPINE
- ◎ FULL COVERAGE HIEROGLYPHIC DEBOSS

*NOTE: PHOTO ABOVE IS FOR VISUALIZATION PURPOSES ONLY   GO TO HELIOGRAPHISPRESS.COM FOR INFO ON AVAILABILITY

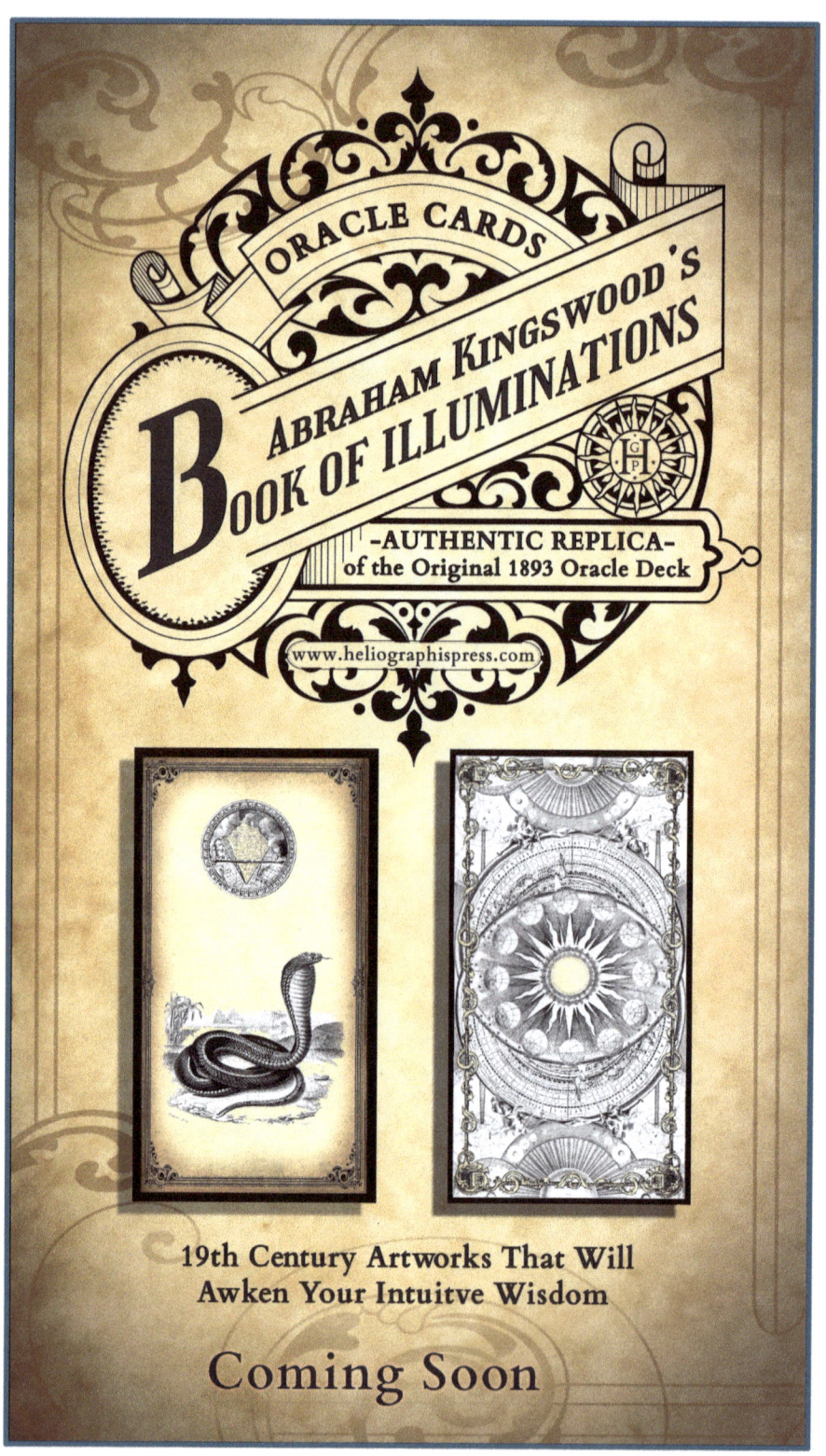

ORACLE CARDS

ABRAHAM KINGSWOOD'S

BOOK OF ILLUMINATIONS

-AUTHENTIC REPLICA-
of the Original 1893 Oracle Deck

www.heliographispress.com

19th Century Artworks That Will
Awken Your Intuitve Wisdom

Coming Soon